Creating Links and Innovative Overviews for a New History Research Agenda
for the Citizens of a Growing Europe

THEMATIC WORK GROUP 6

Europe and the World

I

The Consortium

Karl-Franzens-Universität Graz (Austria)
Universiteit Gent (Belgium)
Sofiyski Universitet „Sveti Kliment Ohridski" (Bulgaria)
Univerzita Karlova v Praze (Czech Republic)
Panepistimio Kyprou (Cyprus)
Roskilde Universitetscenter (Denmark)
Tartu Ülikool (Estonia)
Turun Yliopisto (Finland)
Université Pierre Mendès-France, Grenoble II (France)
Université de Toulouse II - Le Mirail (France)
Universität Hannover (Germany)
Forschungszentrum Europäische Aufklärung (Germany)
University of Aberdeen (Great Britain)
Cardiff University (Great Britain)
University of Sussex (Great Britain)
Ethniko kai Kapodistriako Panepistimio Athinon (Greece)
Aristotelio Panepistimio Thessalonikis (Greece)
Debreceni Egyetem (Hungary)
Miskolci Egyetem (Hungary)
Háskóli Íslands (Iceland)
National University of Ireland, Galway/ Ollscoil na hÉireann, Gaillimh (Ireland)
Università di Bologna (Italy)
Università degli Studi di Milano (Italy)
Università degli Studi di Padova (Italy)
Università di Pisa (Italy)
Latvijas Universitāte, Riga (Latvia)
L-Università Ta' Malta (Malta)
Universiteit Utrecht (The Netherlands)
Universitetet i Oslo (Norway)
Uniwersytet Jagiellonski, Krakow (Poland)
Universidade de Coimbra (Portugal)
Universidade Aberta (Portugal)
Universitatea Babeş Bolyai din Cluj-Napoca (Romania)
Universitatea 'Stefan cel Mare', Suceava (Romania)
Moskowskij Gosudarstvennyj Oblastnoj Universitet (Russian Federation)
Slovenskej Akademie Vied (Slovakia)
Univerza v Mariboru (Slovenia)
University of KwaZulu-Natal (South Africa)
Universidad de Alcalá de Henares (Spain)
Universidad de Deusto (Spain)
Universidad Autónoma de Madrid (Spain)
Universitat de Valencia (Spain)
Universität Basel (Switzerland)
Orta Dogu Teknik Üniversitesi (Turkey)

Europe and the World in European Historiography

edited by

Csaba Lévai

EDIZIONI
plus
pisa university press

Europe and the world in European historiography / edited by Csaba Lévai
(Thematic work group)

940.072 (21.)
1. Europa - Storiografia I. Lévai, Csaba

CIP a cura del Sistema bibliotecario dell'Università di Pisa

This volume is published, thanks to the support of the Directorate General for Research of the European Commission, by the Sixth Framework Network of Excellence CLIOHRES.net under the contract CIT3-CT-2005-006164.
The volume is solely the responsibility of the Network and the authors; the European Community cannot be held responsible for its contents or for any use which may be made of it.

Volumes published (2006)

I. *Thematic Work Groups*

I. Public Power in Europe: Studies in Historical Transformations
II. Power and Culture: Hegemony, Interaction and Dissent
III. Religion, Ritual and Mythology. Aspects of Identity Formation in Europe
IV. Professions and Social Identity. New European Historical Research on Work, Gender and Society
V. Frontiers and Identities: Exploring the Research Area
VI. Europe and the World in European Historiography

II. *Transversal Theme*

I. Citizenship in Historical Perspective

III. *Doctoral Dissertations*

I. F. Peyrou, La Comunidad de Ciudadanos. El Discurso Democrático-Republicano en España, 1840-1868

Cover: *World Map* (Amsterdam 1662), Spencer Collection, New York Public Library. © 2006. Photo: The New York Public Library/Art Resource/Scala, Florence.

© Copyright 2006 by Edizioni Plus – Pisa University Press
Lungarno Pacinotti, 43
56126 Pisa
Tel. 050 2212056 – Fax 050 2212945
info-plus@edizioniplus.it
www.edizioniplus.it - Section "Biblioteca"

ISBN 88-8492-403-0

Manager
Claudia Napolitano

Editing
Francesca Petrucci

Informatic assistance
Michele Gasparello

Contents

Preface

Europe and the World in European Historiography seems to bear a paradoxical title. The paradox, or the complexity, lies in the subject matter. Europe, as Csaba Lévai reminds us in his *Introduction*, is continuously changing and being redefined. Many definitions and realities coexist in today's many-faceted Europe, relating to both the geographical and the political space we refer to as Europe. Correspondingly, the reality and the definition of what is 'not Europe' changes continually, in a specular and connected way. Historiography is affected by this process and affects it profoundly.

It is with pleasure that we present this stimulating and provocative volume to the academic and research community as well as to the general reader. The volume explores some of the many perspectives in which various historiographies – mostly European but not exclusively, given a contribution from South Africa – look, or do not look, at non-European histories. It is one of seven volumes in the first publication cycle of our pan-European Network of Excellence, CLIOHRES.net (www.cliohres.net). With this book, the Network's Thematic Work Group 6, on "Europe and the World", initiates its five year research plan.

The aim of the work group is to examine how various historiographies treat areas outside of Europe, with what methodologies, with what selection of problems and with what explicit and implicit agendas. The volume shows in a particularly clear way how national policies and changes in the cultural and political environment in which professional historians work strongly influences their work, largely determining the directions they will take, both as teachers and as researchers. This is true of the historian's craft in general, but since 'non-Europe' is much larger and more varied than Europe itself, the selective nature of historiography results even more sharply.

The group has chosen to begin its investigation by examining how, over a period of time, a relevant problem has been approached, or not approached, in a particular national historiography. Taken together, the examples chosen allow us to glimpse a paradigmatic model based on a variety of coordinates. It is not surprising that historians tend to choose to study places, persons, processes and events perceived as having a particular relevance for the national context in which they operate. It is that generalised perception that moulds the organisation and financing of university teaching and hence gives an imprint to staff and doctoral students' scholarly interests. Such themes may be positive or negative: e. g. the heritage of colonialism may be seen to contribute to national glory or to national guilt. We can observe how a theme over decades or even centuries has come into or gone out of fashion in correspondence with the changes occurring in each country. In many cases explicit censorship has discouraged or excluded certain subjects of research or certain conclusions. Perhaps even more striking is how even in the absence of openly repressive measures, academic historians, even if they are aware of certain uncomfortable truths, may not be willing or able to communicate their findings to the public or to influence the way matters are presented to school children. Thus, a stratified, dialogic and highly selective interest for a small number of issues may continue to hold sway, not only in the interests of researchers and research bodies, but also in the national self representation and representation of the past.

Each contribution is interesting in its own right. Overall, the volume's interest lies in its potential for generating insight about how historiography works, for us and against us. This goal is part of the overall CLIOHRES.net agenda of rethinking current research practices and strategies in European history, by placing them in a broad analytical and comparative context, and using this juxtaposition to achieve a new level of critical understanding, necessary for an informed citizenship.

Strangely, for something so pervasive, history is often thought of as remote and unconnected with daily life. It is usually absorbed in the form of general 'knowledge', and often assumes the form of generally shared convictions, orientations and prejudices which have their roots in national narratives. These narratives took form everywhere in specific political and cultural contexts, but very few are aware of how and why they have taken the shapes they have. Our Network of Excellence is based on observations made over a number of years on the power of history in forming social and political attitudes, and in moulding our perceptions of ourselves and of others. Received ideas about the past influence each of us in our interaction with society and with other individuals, and in our decisions regarding actions to be taken and values to be observed or enforced. Such ideas form the foundation for the division of the world into ethnic or social groups, whose historical construction and maintenance serve as the basis for virtually all claims of national and other collective identities.

CLIOHRES.net began its work in June 2005, thanks to a five year research contract with the European Commission through the Sixth Framework Programme of its Directorate General for Research, under Priority 7, dealing with "Citizenship". As a matter of fact, CLIOHRES.net is an important result of the long term cooperation among a large number of European universities. Collaboration originally began with the ECTS History Network, which grew out of a pilot project launched at the end of the 1980s. Then the History Subject Area Group of the pilot project assumed the task of testing and developing methods of credit transfer and transparent rules for assessing performance in order to facilitate student mobility and recognition throughout Europe. At the outset, the ECTS History Network counted fifteen universities in eleven member states of the European Union; when the project ended in 1995, the Network had expanded to include 26 institutions in 16 EU and EFTA countries. In the following years, the partners developed two Socrates Curriculum development projects, the second of which, CLIOH ("Refounding Europe: Creating Links, Insights and Overviews for a new History agenda") was privileged to be able to include members from central and eastern Europe for the first time. CLIOH grew into CLIOHnet, the Erasmus Thematic Network for History (www.clioh.net), which at present has 80 partner institutions in 35 European countries, as well as a large number of associate partners. CLIOHnet has promoted inclusion and reciprocal knowledge and has extended its membership as fast as possible to partners from newly eligible countries and from various kinds of institutions. It is a sister Network, specialising in issues of higher education, and an essential complement to our research Network of Excellence.

CLIOHnet and CLIOHRES.net are intertwined with the remarkable social and political transformations which have taken place in Europe during the last twenty years, with the integration, consolidation and expansion of the European Union and the formation of a unique polity. The Networks correspond to a vision of what Europe is and should be. In this context, "excellence" does not mean a closed club of a few institutions of recognised prestige. "Excellence" means taking advantage of unique opportunities of cooperating across and beyond the European Union. It means finding ways for motivated and open-minded academics and researchers from many of the excellent universities and centres in Europe to collaborate, creating new knowledge and insights thanks to their very different points of view. Doing so means developing innovative teaching and research programmes, and requires that the two be tightly linked.

The CLIOHRES Network of Excellence builds on the experience gained to develop the field of historical and related research in an innovative way. Its name stands for "Creating Links and Innovative Overviews for a New History Research Agenda for the Citizens of a Growing Europe". The Network is a consortium of 45 universities and research institutions in 31 countries. Each institution is represented by two senior researchers and two doctoral students, coming from various academic fields – primarily from history, but also from art history, sociology, archaeology, architecture, philology, political science, literary studies and geography. Thus the network serves as a platform for dialogue and debate, comparisons and cooperation across national, generational and disciplinary boundaries. The 180 researchers in the network are divided into six thematic work groups, each of which deals with a broadly designated research area – 'states, institutions and legislation', 'power and culture', 'religious and philosophical concepts', 'work, gender and society'; 'frontiers and identities' and, finally, 'Europe and the world'. Furthermore, the Network as a whole addresses 'transversal themes' of which one is emphasised each year. These are 'citizenship', 'identity', 'migration', 'gender', 'discrimination' and 'tolerance'. Each of the thematic work groups addresses these transversal themes from its specific point of view. During the first year, the theme addressed was 'citizenship', which is the topic of another volume included in the same publication cycle.

As a network of excellence, CLIOHRES is not an ordinary research project. It does not focus on a narrowly defined research question or on a set of specific questions. Rather it is conceived as a forum where researchers representing various national and regional traditions can meet and elaborate their work in new ways thanks to structured interaction with their colleagues. The objective is not only to transcend the national boundaries that still largely define historical research agendas, opening new avenues for research, but also to use those very national differences to become critically aware of how current research agendas have evolved.

In order to create a meaningful context for dialogue, the people engaged in it need to recognize both the similarities and marked differences between the various historical traditions in Europe. For this reason, the first phase of the project has been devoted to 'mapping', to exploring how the questions perceived as important for each thematic area appear in different national historiographies. In future years, further mapping will take place, while the groups proceed through the further stages of identifying research themes that can be of interest for all historiographies, comparing methodologies and sources, demonstrating how problems defined in one historiographical tradition can be developed in new contexts. In this way, in its five years of activity, the Network intends to create novel paradigms for European historical research.

In order to present the discussions and debates that take place in to Network to the wider public, CLIOHRES.net plans five publication cycles. Every year, the work groups will present at least one volume each, and the Network as a whole will treat one of the 'transversal' themes. This year's volumes vary in nature, but may be considered collections of working papers, documenting progress, rather than claiming to be the last word on the subject they deal with. They bring together scholars from very different stages in their professional careers. Some of the authors are doctoral students, while others are established professors with long experience of academic work. They also represent various discursive traditions, which is only appropriate, as history is perhaps the most heterogeneous scientific field that exists. CLIOHRES aims to facilitate dialogue between traditions and to open paths towards new critical understanding, but not to homogenize historical research in Europe. Diversity is intended and desired. History can be and is studied and narrated in many different ways – these ways in themselves being products of history, and worthy of investigation.

As the first year of this project comes to a close, we express our gratitude to the European Commission and its Directorate General for Research which has supported our Network generously through the Priority 7 of the Sixth Framework Programme. The grant awarded has given the Network the financial means to carry out its ambitious programme. Even more importantly, it is a recognition of the important role that history can play in shaping a better future for European citizens. We thank our project officers, Giulia Amaducci and Ioannis Kampolis. Their careful and knowledgeable support and advice has been of great importance.

Our thanks also go to the University of Pisa and to its Rector, Marco Pasquali. The University of Pisa supports the Network very generously in addition to giving great moral support. Without the understanding and backing of the coordinating institution, it would be impossible to carry out a programme of this kind. We thank the director of the central administration of the University, Dr Riccardo Grasso, for accepting the responsibilities connected with the management of the Network; Miriana Donati and Elisa Cascio for their special help; the Pisa team, Laura Burgisano, Adrian Marinescu and Pasquale Cuomo for their total immersion; and our student helpers Ileana Buzic, Lorenzo Gatti, Andreas Verdigi, Nicoletta Scapparone and Marina Cappelli, for their assistance in various different phases of the project.

Above all we are grateful to all members of the Network for a stimulating, challenging and productive year. We express our appreciation to the members of Thematic Work Group 6. The group has given an important contribution by writing the chapters in the present volume and participating in the debates and dialogues which have shaped it. We thank the institutions that co-organised the group meetings.

Many members of TWG 6, on "Europe and the World" have contributed not only to this book but also to the research carried out by the entire Network on the theme of "Citizenship", whose results are published in a separate volume. These are Geert Castryck, María Jesús Cava Mesa, Matjaž Klemenčič, Donal McCracken and István Kornél Vida.

For the success of both endeavours our special thanks go to the group's leaders. Csaba Lévai of the University of Debrecen is the Thematic Work Group leader and editor of the present volume. Luc François of Ghent University is the reference person for the TWG in the CLIOHRES.net Management Group. Alongside the leaders, the members of the University of Debrecen and the Ghent University teams (Attila Barány, Gábor Demeter, István Kornél Vida, Geert Castryck and Rein Reynebeau) gave an important contribution to the success of the enterprise, and we are grateful to them.

We express particular gratitude to Mary Harris of the National University of Ireland, Galway, for being willing to take on the responsibility of co-leadership, joining the CLIOHRES.net Management Group. Her help in editing the volume has been indispensable.

Ann Katherine Isaacs
Guðmundur Hálfdanarson

Coordinators, CLIOHRES.net

Pisa - Reykjavik, May 2006

Introduction

This volume contains a number of short chapters about the historical connections between Europe and the World. But what is Europe, and what is the World? And what characterized the relationship between Europe and the rest of the World from the beginnings of human history to the present day? It is very difficult to answer these questions for several reasons. First of all, it is not easy to define the concepts of Europe and the World. The debates about the geographical, cultural, spiritual or political boundaries of Europe are very well known. Does Russia belong to Europe, or not? And what about Turkey? As a result of the emergence of the European Union as a new political and economic entity, the political leaders and the representatives of different professions were forced to define the boundaries and the concept of Europe. This was also true for the historical profession, the representatives of which had to realize that it is an extraordinarily difficult task. It is not easy to determine the boundaries of Europe in a given moment of time, but it is even more difficult to describe the historical changes of the concept of "Europeanness" during long periods of human history. In ancient times for example, the "civilized world" also contained territories which belonged to other continents than Europe in the geographical sense of the word. And *vice versa*, some regions we consider the integral part of Europe in every sense of the word belonged to the *barbaricum* for the inhabitants of ancient Greece or the Roman Empire. The territories of present day Syria or Tunisia were much more familiar for an educated Roman citizen than the wild forests of Germania, not to mention Scandinavia, or the territory of the present day Baltic states or Ireland. The concept of Europe as we know it, was absolutely absent, and this was also true for the medieval ages when the concept of "Christianity" substituted it.

It is not the task of this introduction to formulate the final verdict about the historical definition of Europe. I would simply like to call the attention to the fact that the definition of Europe determines what is not Europe at the same time. Historically, Europe is a fluid category and, as a result, this is also true for the "world outside Europe". The boundaries of Europe have been changing in history and there are frontier regions, which were considered the part of Europe in a given period of history, and belonged to the "world outside Europe" in another. But in one way or another, the definition of the boundaries and the concept of Europe always contain the elements of inclusion and exclusion. We might classify a country, a region, a culture, a nation or a religion as un-European because we deem it different from the concept of Europe we have in mind at a given moment of time. It means that the definition of "Europeanness" automatically determines the concept of Europeans about "otherness". The two concepts could not exist without each other. In this sense, the historical relationship between Europe and the "world outside Europe" is the history of the constant definition of the concepts of "Europeanness" and "otherness", but in several ways. That is, not only Europeans conceptualized the characteristics of "Europeanness", but so did the representatives of the "world outside Europe", who encountered Europeans in one way or another. For them, Europeans represented "the others", and when they struggled with the characterization of "Europeanness", they invented the definition of "otherness" in reference to themselves. When Europeans and the representatives of the "world outside Europe" encountered each other both parties started to formulate the concepts of "otherness", and it was not easy for either of them to decipher the formulations of their counterpart.

The case of Cabeza de Vaca (c. 1490-1557), the 16th century Spanish soldier is a good example. De Vaca was the treasurer and the second-in-command of the expedition of Panfilo de Narváez (c. 1478-1528) to discover and conquer Florida and the lands beyond in 1528. But the fierce resistance of the Apalachee Indians of Northern Florida forced the conquistadors to retreat to the coast where the Spanish constructed five barges to coast around the Gulf of Mexico. They were shipwrecked on the coast of present day Texas, and most of the conquerors soon died of disease, exposure, and malnutrition. The surviving few became the slaves of the Karankawa Indians. This was the total reversal of the original roles, and interestingly enough eventually the four surviving conquistadors became the magical healers of the natives, who assumed that only they possessed the power to cure the deadly new illnesses associated with the arrival of the Spaniards. One band of Indians passed the healers on to the next group, and in this way they moved westward across Texas and New Mexico into northwestern Mexico, where they were "liberated" by Spanish slavers. As a result of his experiences among the Indians de Vaca internalized many of the values of the natives and started to view his former role as conquistador from a different angle. He saw his "liberators" with the eyes of the natives when he noted in one of his writings that "We healed the sick, they killed the sound; we came naked and barefoot, they clothed, horsed, and lanced; we coveted nothing but gave whatever we were given, while they robbed whomever they found". As Alan Taylor noted, in the narrative of de Vaca "the *they* described his own past as well as the immediate slavers, for in them he saw what he had been eight years before in Florida with a sword in hand, destroying Apalachee villages"[1].

But only a few Europeans went through the same experiences and most of the Europeans encountering "the others" did not realize the other side of the coin. In most cases, mutual understanding of the perception of "otherness" proved to be very difficult between Europeans and the representatives of the "world outside Europe" for most of the five centuries after the "great explorations". The sixth thematic workgroup of CLIOHRES.net project is dedicated to the study of the historical connections between Europe and the rest of the World, and one of the fundamental aims of this co-operation is the promotion of mutual understanding of "otherness" among Europeans and the representatives of the "world outside Europe", through the study of history. Fifteen eminent staff members and eleven doctoral students represent ten European and one African university in the thematic workgroup. We have members from northwestern (University of Iceland, Ghent University, National University of Ireland, Galway, University of Sussex), southern (University of Deusto, Bilbao, University of Valencia, Portuguese Open University,

Lisbon), and eastern Europe (University of Debrecen, University of Maribor, Moscow State Regional University), while Africa is represented by the University of KwaZulu Natal (Durban, South Africa). The staff members and the doctoral students have very different backgrounds and fields of interest. But it is a common characteristic of all of them that, in one way or another, they are dedicated to the research and understanding of the extremely complex historical relationship of Europe and the "world outside Europe". CLIOHRES.net is a five-year project and we hope that by the end of this period our group will develop a sophisticated and well-organized co-operation dedicated to the research of certain aspects of the historical relations of Europe and the rest of the World. We are still at the beginning of this process, but we have made the first steps towards the above-mentioned goal. We have finished the first year of the project, the fundamental task of which was the mapping and exploration of current definitions, problems and approaches regarding "Europe and the World" in national historiographies. This volume is the result of this "mapping and exploration".

Very different countries with very different historical and historiographical traditions are represented in this thematic workgroup. One can find real great powers in it with long-standing imperial and maritime traditions (Great Britain, Spain, Russia), smaller countries, which once were the cores of their own imperial structures (Portugal, Belgium), Atlantic and African countries, which were the parts of larger empires for significant periods of their history (Iceland, Ireland, South Africa), and East Central European regions, which belonged to European continental empires for centuries (Hungary, Slovenia). Due to their different geographical positions and historical past the intensity and the characteristics of their relationship with the "world outside Europe" was also very different. The Vikings departing from Iceland were playing a leading role in the early European discovery of Greenland and North America in the 10th century. Spain, Great Britain and Russia were the cores of large empires including extensive non-European territories. Portugal and Belgium were much smaller countries, but they could establish their own extensive empires outside Europe. Ireland and South Africa became part of the British Empire and as a result both of them had intense relations with the "world outside Europe" on the one hand, and with the Old Continent on the other. In the case of these countries the relevance of the study of the historical contacts between Europe and the "world outside Europe" is clear and well established from the point of view of their historiography. But this is not unequivocal in the case of such countries as Hungary and Slovenia, the geographical position of which prevented them from playing any significant role in the expansion of Europe after the 15th century. But this does not mean at the same time that the history of the relationship of Europe and the rest of the world is totally irrelevant for the historians of these countries. For centuries, both of them constituted parts of the Habsburg Empire which was one of the major players in European great power politics. In the 16th and 17th centuries the Habsburgs also ruled the Spanish Empire and as a result, the conflicts of the European maritime empires such as Britain, France or Spain also inevitably affected the Eastern or Danubian Habsburg Empire, including the historical Hungarian Kingdom and the regions inhabited by the

Slovenes. And in some periods of their history more direct connections were also established between Eastern Europe and the "world outside Europe". The peoples of this European region constituted the most important element among the immigrants to the United States of America between 1903 and 1913, for example. All the nations of the Austro-Hungarian Monarchy took part in the migratory phenomenon, including the Hungarians and the Slovenes.

The chapters of this volume mirror the differences of these distinct traditions of historiography. All contributions discuss the historiography of a special topic relating to the history of Europe and the "world outside Europe". Since the interests of the staff members and the doctoral students contributing to this volume are very different, we decided to arrange the chapters according to the continents involved in the historical relations with Europe which they study. The first part contains three chapters, which were not classifiable in this way, since they relate to the historical relationship of Europe with more than one continent, or in a more general manner. Anna Agnarsdóttir (staff member, University of Iceland) provides a summary of Iceland's interesting and not very well known relations with the "world outside Europe", which in the case of this relatively isolated island practically meant everything outside itself. Matjaz Klemenčič and Danijel Grafenauer (staff member and doctoral student, University of Maribor) show us how the history of the world outside Europe has been taught in a small East Central European country with relatively weak traditions in this field. Victor N. Zakharov (staff member, Moscow State Regional University) discusses the development of historiography on Western European merchants in Russia in the 18th century, a very relevant topic from the point of view of Europe and the world, since this was the period of the emergence of Russia as a multi-continental empire. And the last chapter of part one was composed by Emilio Saenz-Francés San Baldomero (doctoral student, University of Deusto Bilbao) who explores the complicated foreign relations of Spain towards the world outside Europe during World War II on the basis of some new documentation.

Part two contains three studies on the historical contacts between Europe and Africa. Two Belgian scholars struggle with the inheritance of their country's colonial past. Guy Vanthemsche summarizes the different trends of Belgian historiography regarding the country's colonizing activities in Congo, while Geert Castryck (doctoral student, Ghent University) focuses on the "home front" and studies the manifestations of the colonial past in Belgium's public sphere. The author of the third study about Africa is Donal McCracken (staff member, University Kwa-Zulu Natal), who discusses the complex interdependence of South Africa's African and European historical inheritance in the historiographical tradition of the country.

Part three is about the relationship of Europe and Asia and contains four studies. Attila Bárány (staff member, University of Debrecen) calls the attention of the historical profession to the not very well-known role that Hungary and some Hungarian kings played in the history of Crusades. Vinita Damodaran (University of Sussex) explores how the British perceived and constructed at the same time the different races and tribes in India during the 19th century. Ana Paula Avelar (staff member, Aberta University) reveals how the newly explored Asian territories were depicted and interpreted in 16th century Portuguese historiography. And in the last study of part three Gábor Demeter (doctoral student, University of Debrecen) summarizes the debates about domestic and foreign politics in the Ottoman Empire at the beginning of the 20th century from a historiographical point of view.

The concluding section is about the relationship of Europe and the American continent and comprised four studies, two about Europe and Latin America, and two about Europe and North America. In respect of Latin America, Mary N. Harris (Staff member National University of Ireland, Galway) surveys the perception of Irish-Latin American contacts in Irish historiography, while Maria Alexandra Gago da Câmara (staff member, Aberta University) explores the mutual impact of baroque art in Portugal and Brazil. Regarding the historical contacts of Europe and North America István Kornél Vida (doctoral student, University of Debrecen) provides an overview of the historiography of Hungarian emigration to the United States of America after the Hungarian Revolution and War for Independence in 1848-1849, and Csaba Lévai (staff member, University of Debrecen) summarizes the evaluation of the American Revolution in Hungarian historiography during the decades after World War II.

Due to the very different special fields of the members of our workgroup this volume provides only a first approach to the extremely complex historical interdependence of Europe and the "world outside Europe" and the ways that historiography in different contexts has approached the issue. Nevertheless, we hope that our volume genuinely represents some recent trends of historiography concerning the relationship of Europe and the rest of the world, and serves the fundamental aim of our workgroup: the promotion of the mutual understanding of "otherness" from a historical perspective.

Csaba Lévai
University of Debrecen

Note

1 Cabeza De Vaca is quoted by A. Taylor, *American Colonies,* New York 2001, p. 70.

Iceland and the World: From the Discovery of America to U.S. Defence

Anna Agnarsdóttir
University of Iceland, Reykjavík

Greinin fjallar um rannsóknir sem íslenskir sagnfræðingar hafa birt og varða sögu heimsins utan Evrópu. Þar er ekki um auðugan garð að gresja. Flestir íslenskir sagnfræðingar rannsaka sögu Íslands. Reyndar hafa þessar rannsóknir oft verið settar í evrópskt samhengi og margir hafa rannsakað tengsl Íslands við Evrópu. En í þessu verkefni er heimurinn skilgreindur sem allar heimsálfur nema Evrópa. Þarafleiðandi er mér ansi þröngur stakkur skorinn. Spurningin sem ég hef þurft að glíma við í þessari grein er hvað hafa íslenskir sagnfræðingar rannsakað í sögu annarra álfa utan Evrópu?

Tvær fyrstu greinarnar fjalla um Ameríku á miðöldum. Inga Huld Hákonardóttir hefur skrifað grein um hina víðförlu Guðríði Þorbjarnardóttur, sem talin er hafa fætt fyrsta "hvíta" barnið í Ameríku og Þórunn Valdimarsdóttir hefur komið með þá athyglisverðu kenningu hvort hugsanlegt sé að Björn Breiðfirðingakappi hafi verið skeggjaði höfðinginn Quetzalcoatl, sem varð að guði Mexíkana? Í splunkunýrri doktorsritgerð skrifaði Sverrir Jakobsson um heimsmynd Íslendinga á tímabilinu 1100-1400, þar sem heimsmyndin nær óumdeilanlega út fyrir Evrópu, til Afríku og Asíu. Samkvæmt þeirri heimsmynd var t.d. Vínland Leifs heppna staðsett í Afríku.

Ég stóðst ekki freistinguna að kynna fyrir erlendum lesendum Reisubók Jóns Indíafara enda fór hann víða um Austurlönd í byrjun 17. aldar og lýsir reynslu sinni á afar athyglisverðan hátt. Rannsóknir Þorsteins Helgasonar á Tyrkjaráninu eru kynntar og lesendum bent á að þar voru ekki "Tyrkir" á ferð, þótt áfangastaður hinna 400 íslensku fanga var Norður-Afríka.

Vesturfarar og -ferðir hafa verið mikið rannsakaðar en ég fjalla eingöngu um fræðilegar rannsóknir þeirra Helga Skúla Kjartanssonar og Júníusar H. Kristinssonar. Vesturfaraskránni er lýst og sagt frá greiningu Helga Skúla á t.d. fjölda Vesturfara, aldri þeirra og kyni. Einnig er minnst á skýringar hans á orsökum og afleiðingum landflóttans til Ameríku fyrir íslenskt samfélag.

Loks er kafli um samskipti Íslands við Bandaríkin á 20. öld. Þar hafa prófessorarnir Þór Whitehead og Valur Ingmundarson unnið ötullega að margvíslegum rannsóknum í tengslum við síðari heimsstyrjöldina, lýðveldisstofnunina, Keflavíkursamninginn og herstöðina, inngöngu Íslands í NATO og samskipti Íslands og Bandaríkjanna meðan á Kalda stríðinu stóð svo dæmi séu nefnd.

Að síðustu er bent á þá staðreynd að Valur Ingimundarson (sem er yngsti kennarinn við Sagnfræðiskor) og Ellen Gunnarsdóttir, sem skrifaði doktorsritgerð um heilagar konur í

Mexíkó við Cambridge-háskóla, rituðu bæði doktorsritgerðir sem tengjast ekki á nokkurn hátt sögu Íslands. Er þetta merki um breyttar áherslur, einkum þegar haft er í huga að Sagnfræðiskor ætlar frá og með haustinu 2006 að leggja meiri áherslu á heimssögu og draga úr kennslu í Evrópusögu?

Introduction: Research in World History

Being asked to write about the historiography of research in world history in Iceland, I feel very much like the author of a book on Iceland who famously entitled a chapter of the book "Snakes in Iceland". This was a short chapter, indeed only one sentence: "There are no snakes in Iceland". In the same manner I can write: "There is no research into world history in the Department of History of the University of Iceland". The academic staff, almost without exception, focuses on Icelandic history and if research is placed in a wider perspective it will most likely be in a European context. Indeed, relations between Iceland and other European countries have been extensively studied by members of the department.

When discussing this lack of research into world – that is to say non-European – history, it must be understood that the University of Iceland was not founded until 1911. The three existing schools of Theology, Medicine, and Law were combined, each becoming a separate faculty and only one new faculty was added, the Faculty of Arts, which to begin with taught only philosophy and Icelandic studies (i.e. Icelandic literature, language and history).

There are now eleven faculties at the University of Iceland covering most academic subjects. It is a national university and the only research university in Iceland. The Department of History is the only one in Iceland. It is one of the seven departments of the Faculty of Humanities – formerly the Faculty of Arts – which now boasts 34 disciplines. In the History Department there are at present eleven tenured professors and one adjunct. It was not until 1965 that history, comprising both Icelandic and world history, became an independent discipline, severing all links with Icelandic literature and language (now in the Department of Icelandic Studies). The academic staff in 1965 understood their main function as preparing their students for a teaching career in secondary schools. In the 1960s and 70s students were permitted to write dissertations, at both the BA and MA levels, on aspects of World or European history, e.g. the Korean War or Peter the Great. This is no longer the case. Though many of our graduates choose to go into teaching on the secondary level, the current staff considers it imperative that the students have a good grounding in historical research. Thus the B.A. dissertation now stipulates the use of primary sources and the only ones readily available in Iceland are obviously Icelandic. Students are, however, encouraged to place the subjects of their dissertations in a European perspective or attempt a subject in comparative history. Considering the fact that we are a nation of only 300.000 people with 1100 years of history, there is no shortage of topics in Icelandic history inviting research.

Writing history has been a popular pastime in Iceland. It was commonly believed that no special training was necessary. Since the introduction of history as a specific academic discipline in 1965 this attitude has changed somewhat. In this paper only research undertaken by trained Icelandic historians will be discussed. Both the former Soviet Union to the east and Greenland[1] to the west will be considered European countries and thus research by Icelandic historians concerning these countries are outside the scope of this chapter. The research subjects are arranged chronologically.

The Middle Ages: America

It is traditionally believed that Iceland's relations with the world began in the year 1000 when Leifur Eiríksson, or Leif the Lucky as he is popularly known, discovered, by accident, the North American continent, almost 500 years before Columbus[2]. He called it *Vínland* [Land of the Vines] as he and his crew purportedly found grapes growing there. Historians, however, have not shown much interest in this. The sources are the Icelandic sagas[3], written in the 12th and 13th centuries, and the discovery of America has been the province of scholars of medieval Icelandic literature rather than historians. Where actually Vínland was situated has been a source of great debate, but archaeologists have proved irrefutably at least that there were Nordic settlers in L'Anse aux Meadows in Newfoundland in the 11th century[4].

One of the women settlers aroused the interest of historian Inga Huld Hákonardóttir. She wrote an article on Guðríður Þorbjarnardóttir, wife of the explorer Þorfinnur Karlsefni who led the largest expedition to America in the wake of Leifur's discovery (1000-1005). In America Guðríður gave birth to Snorri, believed to be the first Caucasian baby born there. Later she returned with her husband and three-year old son to Iceland and eventually went on a pilgrimage to Rome, making her perhaps the most widely-travelled western woman in the Middle Ages[5].

Þórunn Valdimarsdóttir, a well-known and prolific historian, studied history for a time in Mexico. She was struck by the similarities between the descriptions of an Icelander in the ancient saga literature and of the Aztec god Quetzalcoatl. She has written an interesting article on the possibility that the Icelander Björn Breiðvíkingur Ásbrandsson or Björn Breiðvíkingakappi [Björn the champion from Breiðafjörður], was in fact the bearded stranger from the east, namely the legendary god Quetzelcoatl[6]. She describes how Montezuma, king of the Aztecs, welcomed Hernando Cortés, in the belief that he was the incarnation of Quetzalcoatl. The attributes were a pale skin and a beard in a beardless continent.

According to the Icelandic saga *Eyrbyggja*[7], written in the first half of the 13th century, Björn sailed off course to a great land in the south-west ocean where he became the leader of the people there, ca. 1030. Quetzalcoatl and Björn were apparently contemporaries. This is a tantalizing theory, which Þórunn rightly stresses needs further research and scholarly co-operation between Icelandic and Mexican historians.

1100-1400: The World-view of The Icelanders

Sverrir Jakobsson is a young Icelandic historian who defended his doctoral thesis last year in 2005[8]. It is an analysis of the dominant world-view in Icelandic society during the medieval period 1100-1400, its general mentality and how the world-view relates to the question of the identity of the medieval Icelanders. This is a fascinating study. The Icelandic world-view was centred on the Roman-Catholic one, Asia being in the middle of their world. The Icelanders, however, appear to have had little understanding of the Great Schism, the emperor in Constantinople being described in the saga literature as the head of all Christendom.

Africa, Asia and Jerusalem are examples of places frequently mentioned in this thesis. The Icelanders found new locations for newly discovered lands, though always within the known framework of their world. These were widely off the mark: Greenland was located close to Bjarmaland (the area around the White Sea) and Vínland (the land discovered by Leifur Eiríksson in North America) was located in Africa.

For Icelandic chieftains a way to gain honour was to travel southwards, most commonly to Rome, although trips to Jerusalem were naturally enough more prestigious. Interestingly, Icelandic chieftains traced their ancestry back to Asia, primarily to Turkey. Ari the Learned (1068-1148), traditionally regarded as the first Icelandic historian[9], for example traced his own family back to the king of Turks.

Hauksbók, written by Haukur Erlendsson (d. 1334) a secular official, is of especial interest as it contains both a survey of world geography and important narratives on world history. Haukur mentioned many foreign countries, but none beyond the recognized world history of the time. He also chose to trace his family back to Asia.

Snorri Sturluson (1178-1241), politician and historian and perhaps the most famous medieval Icelander, was Ari's successor. His *Heimskringla* [History of the Kings of Norway] begins with a description of the world in which the story of the Turkish origins of both the leading Icelandic and Norwegian leaders are emphasized.

The 16th-17th centuries. A Primary Source: Jón the World Traveller

I cannot refrain from mentioning a primary source which perfectly fits the topic under discussion, namely Iceland and the world. An Icelander, Jón Ólafsson (1593-1679), set off from Iceland on an English ship as a seaman in 1615 – naturally enough he first went to Europe: to England, Denmark, the Faroes and Norway, and even to Spitzbergen and the White Sea. But then he went further to extremely exotic destinations: India, Ceylon, the Danish colony Tranquebar in India, Table Island, the Cape of Good Hope, to Africa and Madagascar, the Comoro Island and Coromandel Coast, Ascension Island and Saint Helena. He returned to Iceland in 1626 and was called Jón the India Traveller (*Jón Indíafari*). He began writing his autobiography in 1661, a superb account of his travels and the lands he visited. Its value was recognised early and has been published at intervals in Iceland, most recently in 1992.[10] It was first translated into English by Dame Bertha S. Philpotts, Mistress of Girton College Cambridge, and a renowned scholar. The first volume was published for the Hakluyt Society in 1923, the second in 1932[11]. It is a fascinating read, full of adventure and the descriptions of an exotic world as experienced by an Icelander brought up in a turf cottage at the turn of the 17th century.

1627: The 'Turkish Raid'

In 1627 Barbary corsairs from Algiers and Salé (Morocco) descended on Iceland, taking around 400 prisoners, the population of Iceland being reasonably estimated to have been then about 60,000. This dramatic event is popularly known as *Tyrkjaránið* – the Turkish Raid – as the two cities were then part of the Ottoman Empire. Four ships attacked the eastern and southern coast as well as the Westmann Islands, off the south coast of Iceland. About thirty people were killed in addition to the 400 taken prisoner. Ten years later 27 made it back to Iceland. The pirates never came again, probably because the Icelanders were too poor to pay ransom for their loved ones. The fear of the 'Turks' (Janissary Turks, Moors of various kinds and European renegades who were the leaders of the assault), however, lived on well into the 19th century[12].

In 1902 The Historical Association (*Sögufélag)* was founded in Reykjavík. Its aim was to publish primary sources in Icelandic history. One of its first projects was to gather all available contemporary documents dealing with the raid. This 500 page volume[13] included chronicles, annals, prayers against the Turks, letters and a travel account of one of the victims, the Reverend Ólafur Egilsson[14], who was one of the few who made it back to Iceland.

Despite the relative abundance of primary sources, no one has yet written a serious study of this blood-curdling event. This is about to change. An associate professor at the Iceland University of Education, Þorsteinn Helgason, is working on a doctoral dissertation and has already published a couple of articles on the subject. He has surveyed the foreign sources, identified the origin and nationality of the corsairs themselves as well as placing this Barbary raid in its European and African/Asian perspective[15].

Late 19th and Early 20th Centuries: Emigration to America

The first Icelanders to immigrate to America were Icelandic Mormons who moved to Utah in 1855-1856. A few people, not more than forty at the most, emigrated from Northern Iceland to Brazil in 1861. But it was not until the early 1870s that mass emigration began. In 1875 *New Iceland* was established on the shores of Lake Winnipeg with its own government and constitution. This republic was short-lived, New Iceland joining the province of Manitoba in 1887. Winnipeg has remained the Western-Icelandic centre (frequently visited by Icelandic politicians) though many people of Icelandic descent eventually migrated to the west, all the way to British Columbia[16], while others settled in Minnesota, Nebraska and North Dakota. In general the Icelandic settlements tended to be both north and south of the US-Canadian border[17].

Considerable research has been done on these so-called 'Western-Icelanders', though here only academic studies will be discussed. In 1976 Helgi Skúli Kjartansson, now professor at the Iceland University of Education, wrote a dissertation for his master's degree on the subject of the Icelandic emigration to North America. Besides being a general survey, his thesis was primarily a statistical study of data on Icelandic emigrants which had been compiled by the Institute of History of the University of Iceland in connection with a Nordic research project on transatlantic emigration.

Subsequently the late historian Júníus H. Kristinsson turned to this field of research[18]. Funded by the government, he undertook an immense task, listing all the Icelanders that had definitely emigrated to America. Only those emigrants were included where reliable documentary information was available. The total is 14,268 to be exact. It goes without saying that this is a valuable record of all known Icelandic emigrants to America and the book was published by the Institute of History in 1983. The major sources used were parish registers and passenger lists, but when these two sources were compared only 6000 emigrants proved to be listed in both sources. Obviously, other sources had to be used and contracts between the emigrants and the agents of the shipping lines regarding fares and emigrant lists compiled by the sheriffs of each district in Iceland proved particularly useful. It is estimated that thousands emigrated without documentary trace. Perhaps the total was somewhere around 15-20,000 from 1870-1914[19]. Kristinsson gave the following information on each emigrant: the year of emigration, the last place of residence in Iceland, occupation, age[20], the port of embarkation, the name of the ship travelled on and finally the destination.

Recently in 2003 Professor Kjartansson decided to publish his master's thesis, in a thoroughly revised form with the statistics calculated anew[21]. His study analyses the reasons for the emigration, placing the emphasis on economic development and business cycles, on both sides of the Atlantic, as principal contributing factors. Nevertheless, he does not reject the traditional causes of land-hunger and the harsh climatic conditions in Iceland in the late 19th century. A subsidised passage and 200 acres of land was an attractive proposition for an impoverished Icelander. Kjartansson considers the initiative of the Canadian Allan line and its agent, supported by Canadian authorities, as being instrumental in initiating the mass emigration from Iceland and in establishing Canada as the preferred destination. His analysis of the data shows that there was a population loss of about 20%, most emigrants coming from Northern and Eastern Iceland. The average age was 20-34 years old, more than half were female, a high proportion were married couples with a correspondingly high number of children. Finally, he assesses the consequences of this mass exodus on Icelandic society.

The sudden termination of mass emigration in 1906 is a peculiarity of Iceland, standing as it does in contrast to Scandinavia and Britain. Kjartansson explains this by the general optimism following the introduction of Home Rule from Denmark in 1904. Indeed, much was accomplished in the next decade: motor boats and steam trawlers were introduced into the Icelandic fisheries, rivers were bridged, a new bank was established with foreign capital and the University of Iceland was founded, to give a few examples.

Finally, it might be mentioned that case studies have been made; for example Bergsteinn Jónsson, professor emeritus of the University of Iceland, wrote an article on the Icelandic settlers in Wisconsin[22].

The 20th century: Relations with the United States

Before a discussion can begin of this thorny and controversial subject it is necessary to sketch in the historical background[23]. In 1918 Iceland, a dependency of Denmark since 1380, gained its sovereignty and entered into a personal union with Denmark. It proudly asserted its status as being one of 'perpetual neutrality'. In 1944, while Denmark was occupied by the Germans, Iceland proclaimed its independence as a republic, after ensuring the support of Britain and the United States. It is necessary to stress that Iceland has never had an army. During the Second World War Iceland was first occupied by the British in 1940. When British forces were needed elsewhere in Europe the Icelandic government, in June 1941, agreed to invite the Americans, at the instigation of the British, to take on Iceland's defence and eventually a military base was built at Keflavík. In this manner the United States first became an active participant in the Second World War. In 1949 Iceland became a founding member of NATO. These two issues: the U.S. military base at Keflavík and Iceland's membership of NATO have been the most hotly contested post-Second World War political issues in Iceland, particularly in the 1940s and 50s and again in the early 1970s.

Since the opening of the archives abroad and in Iceland two professors at the University of Iceland, Þór Whitehead and Valur Ingimundarson, have done a great deal of research into Icelandic-U.S. relations. Professor Whitehead completed his doctorate at Oxford University on the subject of Iceland in the Second World War in 1978 and subsequently became the first scholar to engage in research on Icelandic foreign policy during the Cold War period 1946-1956, publishing his first article in 1973[24]. The reasons for Iceland's abandonment of its policy of perpetual neutrality and the decision to become a founding member of NATO have been the major subjects of debate. Whitehead has always stressed the geopolitical and economic reasons for Iceland joining the Western bloc. His interpretation regarding the abandonment of Iceland's avowed policy of neutrality was that it was a reflection of the realities of the Cold War and the vital importance of Iceland's strategic geographic position in the North Atlantic.

In the 1990s Professor Whitehead returned to the subject outlining his argument in detail in his book *The Ally Who Came in from the Cold*[25]. There he discusses the U.S. request for bases during 1945-46, the Icelandic-U.S. defence agreement of 1951, the U.S. attempts at expanding its military facilities during 1952-54, the Icelandic parliament's demands for

U.S. withdrawal and the search for a compromise, ending with the final settlement, the status quo at Keflavík, which he regarded primarily as a result of the international crisis in 1956, with the Soviet intervention in Hungary. The leaders of the pro-Western parties in Iceland's coalition government were faced with three major factors: the problem of Iceland's security in the light of Soviet expansionist policy, a problem compounded by Iceland's strategic position; the necessity of maintaining foreign trade with the United States and Britain (which had become of extreme importance during the Second World War) to avert economic depression and "the need to expand markets for a vastly increased fish production thereby obtaining foreign capital to modernize Iceland's backward economy"[26]. He concluded that concern for national security was "the paramount determinant" of Icelandic foreign policy[27]. This is the so-called orthodox view.

The revisionists of course disagreed. Elfar Loftsson, a political scientist, argued that the abandonment of the policy of Icelandic neutrality was due to direct intervention by the United States into Icelandic affairs hand-in-hand with pro-Western Icelandic politicians more interested in economic interests than security issues[28].

In 1995 Valur Ingimundarson wrote about the reasons for the 1956 decision of the left-wing government of the time to abandon its stated policy of repealing the U.S. – Icelandic Defence Agreement of 1951 and the withdrawal of U.S. soldiers. The major reason was U.S. economic assistance. He argued that the right-wing of the Social Democratic Party (one of the coalition) had decided to make a deal with the United States and that this decision was taken before the Soviet suppression of the Hungarian Revolution. He demonstrated clearly that the Eisenhower administration had offered much-needed economic aid on the condition that the U.S. military base remain[29].

In 1996 Ingimundarson published a book on Cold War Icelandic-U.S. relations during 1945-60[30]. The book, with an orthodox bias, sought to demonstrate that economic considerations were always a factor in Icelandic foreign policy and in the calculations of Icelandic politicians. It also dismissed the idea that security was a secondary – or non-existent – factor when Iceland joined NATO and agreed to sign the Defence Agreement with the United States. Ingimundarson uses a theoretical approach, mainly applying the theories of Melvyn Leffler and Geir Lundestad.

Another controversy in Iceland has been the question whether nuclear weapons have ever been stationed at the U.S. military base in Keflavík. This has been examined by Ingimundarson in the above-mentioned book. No evidence has been found of nuclear weapons at the Keflavík base in Iceland in the 1950s but he presents new findings that the Americans planned to put up anti-aircraft missile systems with nuclear warheads, only deciding against it because their systems were needed elsewhere.

In yet another book published in 2001[31] Professor Ingimundarson focuses on Iceland's relationship with the United States and NATO. He discusses why the Icelandic republic's second left-wing coalition government of 1971-1974, which, as the first did, promised to revise or abrogate the U.S.-Icelandic defence treaty, failed to do so. He argues that the key factor was political differences over economic policies – the government could not reach a consensus on how far it should go in slackening the military ties with the West. An interesting factor which influenced the outcome was the fishing dispute with Britain. In 1972 Iceland unilaterally extended its fishery limits from 12 to 50 miles. A 'Cod War' broke out and British frigates moved into Icelandic waters. This nearly destroyed Iceland's relationship with both NATO and the United States. The crisis was dispelled in 1973 with the result that the pro-Western proponents gained control. Ingimundurson again uses a theoretical approach, using the theories of Pierre Bourdieu and theories of nationalism with even some postmodernist aspects.

A right-wing coalition government was duly elected in August 1974 and since then the question of a U.S. military base on Icelandic soil has ceased to be a major issue in Icelandic politics. As Professor Ingimundarson writes: "Iceland is firmly anchored in the Western alliance"[32].

The 20th Century: Iceland and the United Nations

Valdimar Unnar Valdimarsson (1958-1988) graduated from the University of Iceland with a master's degree and went on to the London School of Economics to write a doctoral thesis on Iceland's role in the United Nations from 1946-1980. He had published one article on this subject before his untimely death. This was a discussion of Iceland's position regarding China's membership to the United Nations[33]. His thesis was eventually edited and co-authored by Gunnar Á. Gunnarsson and Guðmundur R. Árnason and published in 1993[34]. It is a general survey of Iceland's policy and decision-making in the United Nations from the date when Iceland became a member in 1946 (as Iceland was not a belligerent it could not be a founding member) to 1980. As far as global politics go Valdimarsson discussed Iceland's foreign policy and position in the UN regarding not only China but South Africa and the Middle East.

From the above it will be seen that only two professors of the Department of History of the University of Iceland have ventured into what might be called world history – relations with the United States. At the same time they are of course writing important chapters in the history of Iceland.

Perhaps though an interesting development is taking place. Professor Valur Ingimundarson, the youngest member of the Department of History, received his doctorate from Columbia University. Its subject, on American political history, had nothing to do with Iceland, though, as will be quite clear to the reader, he has subsequently turned to researching Icelandic history in an international framework. Recently, in 1998, a young historian, Ellen Gunnarsdóttir, was granted her doctorate from Cambridge University. Her thesis was, indeed, very far removed from Icelandic history. It dealt with Mexican beatas in the Baroque period and has been published in the U.S.A.[35]. It is certainly non-European. It is perhaps a sign of the times that the Department of History of the University of Iceland will introduce for the next academic year (2006-2007) a new curriculum emphasizing global history at the expense of European history. This will hopefully lead to more interest in doing research into world history.

Notes

1 Greenland is a dependency of Denmark, albeit with Home Rule. I have always considered it as being part of Europe, though it is of course geographically closer to the North American continent. Icelandic historians, and historians of other nationalities, continue to study the mystery of the disappearance of the Nordic settlement in Greenland in the late Middle Ages. No consensus has yet been reached

2 And sensibly lost it again. This is a popular joke in Iceland.

3 *Erik the Red's Saga* (Eiríks saga rauða) and *The Saga of the Greenlanders* (Grænlendingasaga). They are both published in English in the first volume of *The Complete Sagas of Icelanders*, general editor V. Hreinsson, Reykjavík 1997.

4 See e.g. H. Ingstad, *Westward to Vinland*, London 1965. The most recent book on the Vinland debate is by P. Bergþórsson, a meteorologist, *Vínlandsgátan* [The Vínland Mystery], Reykjavík 1997.

5 I.H. Hákonardóttir, *Guðríður Þorbjarnardóttir. Frá New York til Rómar?* [Guðríður Þorbjarnardóttir. From New York to Rome], in A. Agnarsdóttir et al. (eds.), *Kvennaslóðir. Rit til heiðurs Sigríði Th. Erlendsdóttur*, Reykjavík 2001, pp. 60-74.

6 Þ. Valdimarsdóttir, *Var Björn Breiðvíkingakappi skeggjaði höfðinginn Quetzalcoatl sem kom úr austri*? [Was Björn Breiðfirðingakappi the bearded chieftain Quetzalcoatl who came from the east?]; A. Agnarsdóttir et al. (eds.), *Kvennaslóðir. Rit til heiðurs Sigríði Th. Erlendsdóttur*, Reykjavík 2001, pp. 99-107.

7 Translated into English as *The Saga of the People of Eyri* in vol. V of *The Complete Sagas of Icelanders*.

8 S. Jakobsson, *Við og veröldin. Heimsmynd Íslendinga 1100-1400*, [Us and the World. The World-View of the Icelanders 1100-1400], Reykjavík 2005. This chapter is abstracted from the English summary, pp. 363-68.

9 See the *Book of Icelanders* [Íslendingabók], written between 1122 and 1133.

10 V. Óskarsson (ed.), *Reisubók Jóns Ólafssonar Indíafara*, Reykjavík 1992.

11 *The Life of the Icelander Jón Ólafsson Traveller to India...*, London 1923-1932, 2 vols . The second volume was edited by R. Temple and L.M. Anstey. Incidentally, there is a copy of the manuscript, unexamined as far as is known, in the British Library Add. MS. 11227, dating from the end of the 17th century. There are about 20 handwritten copies in Iceland – it was a popular book – and it has also been translated into German and Danish. In 1998 Inger Barnes edited and translated part of the book as *Memoirs of Jón Ólafsson Icelander and Traveller to India...*, published in Cambridge.

12 For example when Sir Joseph Banks led the first foreign scientific expedition to Iceland in 1772 his arrival caused great alarm until he managed to convince the people that the members of the party were Christians.

13 J. Þorkelsson (ed.), *Tyrkjaránið á Íslandi 1627*, Reykjavík 1906-1909.

14 Later published separately: S. Kristjánsson (ed.), *Reisubók Séra Ólafs Egilssonar*, Reykjavík 1969.

15 Þ. Helgason, *Hverjir voru Tyrkjaránsmenn?* [Who were the Turkish raiders?], "Saga", 33, 1995, pp. 110-134, with an English summary; Þ. Helgason, *Íslendingar keyptir heim í kjölfar Tyrkjaráns* [Icelanders ransomed after the Turkish raid], "Íslenska söguþingið", 28.-31. maí 1997, Reykjavík 1998, I, pp. 331-342; Þ. Helgason, *Historical narrative as collective therapy: the case of the Turkish raid in Iceland*, "Scandinavian Journal of History", 22, 1997, pp. 275 H.S. Kjartansson - S. Hreiðarsson, *Framtíð handan hafs. Vesturfarir frá Íslandi 1870-1914*, [A Future across the Ocean. Western Emigration from Iceland 1870-1914], Reykjavík 2003. There is a summary in English, pp. 157-162-289.

16 Kjartansson - Hreiðarsson, *Framtíð handan hafs* cit., pp. 157-162.

17 For example there is still an old people's home for people of Icelandic descent in Blaine, Washington.

18 *Vesturfararskrá 1870-1914*, Reykjavík 1983.

19 E. Laxness, *Íslandssaga a til ö*, Reykjavík 1995, I, p. 37.

20 The age of children was often unreliable as a lower age meant a lower fare.

21 He was helped by a graduate student, Steinþór Hreiðarsson, who became his co-author.

22 B. Jónsson, *Frá sauðfjárbúskap í Bárðardal til akuryrkju í Wisconsin. Þættir úr dagbókum Jóns Jónssonar frá Mjóadal,* [From sheep-farming in Bárðardal to agriculture in Wisconsin. Excerpts from the journals of Jón Jónsson from Mjóidalur], "Saga", 15, 1985, pp. 59-96.

23 V. Ingimundarson, *Post-Cold War Historiography in Iceland*, in T.B. Olesen (ed.), *The Cold War and the Nordic Countries. Historiography at a Crossroads*, Odense 2004. The author is much indebted to this useful historiographical article which includes a comprehensive list of Cold War writings by Icelanders.

24 Þ. Whitehead, *Stórveldin og lýðveldið 1941-1944* [The Big Powers and the Republic], "Skírnir", 1947; Þ. Whitehead, *Lýðveldi og herstöðvar 1941-1946* [The Republic and Military Bases 1941-1946], "Skírnir", 1950.

25 Published in Reykjavík in 1998. See also *Leiðin frá hlutleysi 1945-1949*, [The Road from Neutrality 1945-1949], "Saga", 1991, pp. 63-121 with an English summary.

26 Whitehead, *The Ally Who Came in from the Cold* cit., p. 85.

27 *Ibid.*, p. 82.

28 E. Loftsson, *Island i NATO-partierna og försvarsfrågan.* Disseratation at the University of Gothenburg; Id., *The Disguised Threat. Iceland during the Cold war*, "Scandinavian Journal of History, 10, 3, 1985.

29 V. Ingimundarson, *Áhrif bandarísks fjármagns á stefnubreytingu vinstri stjórnarinnar í varnarmálum árið 1956* [American Money and the Policy Change of the Left-Wing Government in Defence Affairs in 1956], "Saga", 33, 1995, pp. 9-53 with an English summary.

30 V. Ingimundarson, *Í eldlínu kalda stríðsins. Samskipti Íslands og Bandaríkjanna 1945-60*, Reykjavík 1996.

31 Id., *Uppgjör við umheiminn. Samskpti Íslands, Bandaríkjanna og NATO 1960-1974* [A Time of Reckoning: Iceland's Relations with the United States and NATO, 1964-1974], Reykjavík 2001. See also the same author's *The Struggle for Western Integration. Iceland, the United States and NATO during the First Cold War*, Oslo 1999.

32 Ingimundarson, *Post-Cold War Historiography* cit., p. 90.

33 V.U. Valdimarsson, *Alþyðulýðveldið og Ísland. Ísland og aðild Kína að Sameinuðu þjóðunum*, "Ný saga", 1988, pp. 110-119 with an English summary.

34 *Ísland í eldlínu alþjóðamála. Stefnumótun og samvinna innan Sameinuðu þjóðanna 1946-1980.*

35 E. Gunnarsdóttir, *Mexican karismata. The baroque vocation of Francisca de los Ángeles, 1674-1744*, published by the University of Nebraska Press, Lincoln 2004. See also: E. Gunnarsdóttir, *Trúarheimur kvenna í barokk Mexíkó* [The Woman's World of Faith in Baroque Mexico], in A. Agnarsdóttir et al. (eds.), *Kvennaslóðir. Rit til heiðurs Sigríði Th. Erlendsdóttur*, Reykjavík 2001, pp. 152-161.

Bibliography

Barnes I. (ed.), *Memoirs of Jón Ólafsson Icelander and Traveller to India...*, Cambridge 1998.

Bergþórsson P., *Vínlandsgátan* [The Vínland Mystery], Reykjavík 1997.

Gunnarsdóttir E., *Mexican karismata. The baroque vocation of Francisca de los Ángeles, 1674-1744*, Lincoln, Nebraska 2004.

Id., *Trúarheimur kvenna í barokk Mexíkó* [The Woman's World of Faith in Baroque Mexico], in A. Agnarsdóttir et al. (eds.), *Kvennaslóðir. Rit til heiðurs Sigríði Th. Erlendsdóttur*, Reykjavík 2001, pp.152-161.

Hákonardóttir I.H., *Guðríður Þorbjarnardóttir. Frá New York til Rómar?* [Guðríður Þorbjarnardóttir. From New York to Rome?], in Agnarsdóttir A. et al. (eds), *Kvennaslóðir. Rit til heiðurs Sigríði Th. Erlendsdóttur*, Reykjavík 2001, pp. 60-74.

Helgason Þ., *Hverjir voru Tyrkjaránsmenn?*[Who were the Turkish Raiders?], "Saga", 33, 1995, pp. 110-134 .

Id., *Íslendingar keyptir heim í kjölfar Tyrkjaráns* [Icelanders Ransomed after the Turkish Raid], in Guðmundsson G.J. - Björnsson E.K. (eds.), *Íslenska söguþingið 28.-31. maí 1997*, Reykjavík 1998, I, pp. 331-342 .

Id., *Historical narrative as collective therapy: the case of the Turkish raid in Iceland,* "Scandinavian Journal of History", 1997, 22, pp. 275-289.

Hreinsson V. (general ed.), *The Complete Sagas of Icelanders*, Reykjavík 1997.

Ingimundarson V., *Áhrif bandarísks fjármagns á stefnubreytingu vinstri stjórnarinnar í varnarmálum árið 1956* [American Money and the Policy Change of the Left-Wing Government in Defence Affairs in 1956], "Saga", 33, 1995, XXXIII, pp. 9-53.

Id., *Í eldlínu kalda stríðsins. Samskipti Íslands og Bandaríkjanna 1945-60* [In the Throes of the Cold War. Relations Between Iceland and the United States 1945-60], Reykjavík 1996.

Id., *The Struggle for Western Integration. Iceland, the United States and NATO during the First Cold War*, Oslo 1999.

Id., *Uppgjör við umheiminn. Samskipti Íslands, Bandaríkjanna og NATO 1960-1974* [A Time of Reckoning: Iceland's Relations with the United States and NATO, 1964-1974], Reykjavík 2001.

Id., *Post-Cold War Historiography in Iceland* , in Olesen T.B. (ed.), *The Cold War and the Nordic Countries. Historiography at a Crossroads*, Odense 2004.

Ingstad H., *Westward to Vinland*, London 1965.

Jakobsson S., *Við og veröldin. Heimsmynd Íslendinga 1100-1400* [We and the World. The World-View of the Icelanders 1100-1400], Reykjavík 2005 .

Jónsson B., *Frá sauðfjárbúskap í Bárðardal til akuryrkju í Wisconsin. Þættir úr dagbókum Jóns Jónssonar frá Mjóadal* [From Sheep-farming in Bárðardal to Agriculture in Wisconsin. Excerpts from the Journals of Jón Jónsson from Mjóidalur], "Saga", 15, 1985, pp. 59-96.

Kjartansson H.S. - Hreiðarsson S., *Framtíð handan hafs. Vesturfarir frá Íslandi 1870-1914* [A Future across the Ocean.Western Emigration from Iceland 1870-1914], Reykjavík 2003.

Kristinsson J.H., *Vesturfararskrá 1870-1914* [List of the Emigrants from Iceland to North America 1870-1914], Reykjavík 1983.

Kristjánsson S. (ed.), *Reisubók Séra Ólafs Egilssonar*, Reykjavík 1969.

Laxness E., *Íslandssaga a til ö*, Reykjavík 1995, I.

Loftsson E., *Island i NATO-partierna og försvarsfrågan.* Dissertation at the University of Gothenburg 1980.

Id., *The Disguised Threat. Iceland during the Cold War* in *Scandinavian Journal of History*, 1985, 10, 3.

Óskarsson V. (ed.), *Reisubók Jóns Ólafssonar Indíafara*, Reykjavík 1992.

Philpotts B. - Temple R. - Anstey M. (eds.), *The Life of the Icelander Jón Ólafsson Traveller to India...*, London 1923 and 1932, II vols.

Valdimarsdóttir Þ., *Var Björn Breiðvíkingakappi skeggjaði höfðinginn Quetzalcoatl sem kom úr austri?* [Was Björn the Champion from Breiðafjörður the Bearded Chieftain Quetzalcoatl who Came from the East?], in Agnarsdóttir A. et al (eds.), *Kvennaslóðir. Rit til heiðurs Sigríði Th. Erlendsdóttur*, Reykjavík 2001, pp. 99-107.

Valdimarsson V.U., *Alþyðulýðveldið og Ísland. Ísland og aðild Kína að Sameinuðu þjóðunum* [The People's Republic of China and Iceland. Iceland's Position Regarding Membership of China to the United Nations], "Ný saga", 1988, pp. 110-119.

Valdimarsson V.U. - Gunnarsson G.A. - Árnason G.R., *Ísland í eldlínu alþjóðamála. Stefnumótun og samvinna innan Sameinuðu þjóðanna 1946-1980* [Iceland and International Affairs. Policy-making and Co-operation in the United Nations 1946-1980], Reykjavík 1993.

Whitehead Þ., *Stórveldin og lýðveldið 1941-1944* [The Big Powers and the Republic], "Skírnir", 1973.

Id., *Lýðveldi og herstöðvar 1941-1946* [The Republic and Military Bases 1941-1946], "Skírnir", 1976.

Id., *Leiðin frá hlutleysi 1945-1949* [The Road from Neutrality 1945-1949], "Saga", 1991, pp. 63-121.

Id., *The Ally Who Came in from the Cold*, Reykjavík 1998.

Þorkelsson J. (ed.), *Tyrkjaránið á Íslandi 1627*, Reykjavík 1906-1909.

How the History of the World Outside Europe is Taught and Researched in Slovenia

MATJAŽ KLEMENČIČ, DANIJEL GRAFENAUER
University of Maribor

Z vprašanji izvenevropske zgodovine in etnografije so se med Slovenci prvi ukvarjali misijonarji. Med temi velja omeniti Friderika Barago, ki je deloval med severnoameriškimi Indijanci. Prvi resnejši poskus zgodovine izvenevropskih držav pa predstavlja knjiga Amerika in Amerikanci duhovnika Jurija Trunka, ki je še danes eno izmed temeljnih del za raziskovalce, ki se ukvarjajo s slovenskimi izseljenci v ZDA.

Raziskovanje in poučevanje izvenevropske zgodovine v Sloveniji se danes vrši v večji ali manjši meri na vseh treh slovenskih univerzah (Univerza v Ljubljani, Univerza v Mariboru, Univerza na Primorskem) ter še na nekaterih inštitutih (Inštitut za slovensko izseljenstvo v okviru ZRC SAZU, Inštitut za novejšo zgodovino, Inštitut za narodnostna vprašanja). Omembe vreden je tudi prispevek pripadnikov slovenske manjšine v Italiji k našemu vedenju o teh vprašanjih. Slovensko zgodovinopisje, ki se je do nedavnega ukvarjalo pretežno z "narodno zgodovino", v zadnjem času kaže velik napredek pri preučevanju zgodovine izvenevropskih dežel, predvsem v povezavi z raziskovanjem problematike slovenskega izseljenstva. Poleg zgodovinarjev se ukvarjajo z raziskovanjem te tematike v Sloveniji tudi nekateri literarni zgodovinarji, antropologi in geografi. Večino knjig in člankov iz področja izvenevropskega zgodovinopisja predstavljajo dela avtorjev, ki se ukvarjajo z vprašanji slovenskega izseljenstva v ZDA, Kanadi, Avstraliji in Južni Ameriki.

INTRODUCTION

Today history is taught and researched at all three universities in Slovenia. In addition to the University of Maribor, which is the younger sister of the University of Ljubljana, the new University of Primorska (Coastland University) in Koper/Capodistria has been opened, accepting its first students of history in the academic year 2004/05. The three departments of history are not the only places for historical research in Slovenia, however. Additionally there are research institutes like, for example, those within the framework of the Scientific Research Center of the Slovene Academy of Arts and Sciences in Ljubljana (Institute for World and National History and Institute for Slovene Emigration Studies). Independent institutes for history include the Institute for Contemporary History, which developed from the Institute of the History of the Workers' Movement (established by the Central Committee of the Communist Party of Slovenia soon after World War II), and the Institute for Ethnic Studies in Ljubljana, which deals primarily with themes connected with the history and contemporary realities of Slovenes who live as autochthonous minorities or emigrants outside the Republic of Slovenia. This institute also does research on the history of immigrant groups to Slovenia and autochthonous Italians and Hungarians in Slovenia.

As Slovenia is a relatively small country and the research capacities are dispersed, history departments are relatively small. The chairs are divided so that there is one professor for the history of antiquity, and two professors each for the history of the Middle Ages, the history of the period from the 16th to the 18th centuries, the history of the period from the French Revolution until World War I, and the period from post-World War II to the present. Anything more represents "luxury" and means that places for that "more" are usually not available. Even those nine chairs are usually not filled.

Due to the fact that Slovenia is a new, young state that which has had to explain its existence before the world, historical science in Slovenia has dealt primarily with the national history of Slovenia and Slovenes, problems of Slovene identity, history of the development of the Slovene people, borders and frontiers, and the modern history of Slovenes, who, after World War I (after the establishment of the Yugoslav state), were minorities in neighboring countries (Austria, Italy, and Hungary), encompassing the history of "the Yugoslav question" and the history of the Yugoslav state, which to a great extent represents the history of the solving of national questions.

Therefore, it is not surprising that most of the research works published in Slovenia that deal with the history of non-European states or continents do so in the context of the history of Slovene emigration.

Researching History of Non-European Continents and Countries in the Past

Some notes on the history of non-European countries were written in Slovene ethnic territories as early as the Middle Ages in conjunction with travel diaries. Thus these writings were not systematic histories of individual countries or continents. The first to show more interest in the history of overseas countries or continents were Slovene missionaries, among them Marcus Antonius Kappus (*1657, Kamna Gorica in today's Slovenia – †1717, somewhere in Mexico). This Jesuit missionary went to America in 1687 and labored among the Opata Indians in the Mexican region of Sonora, on today's Mexican-U.S. border.

He sent to the homeland (then Austria-Hungary) news on discoveries made by his friend Eusebius Franciscus Kino from South Tyrol, including that Lower California is a giant peninsula connected to the continental mainland and not an island, as was thought until then. He also sent the news that the Gulf of California is not a giant strait, encircling the whole American continent in the North, which was the previous belief. Kappus also sent a map of Sonora and the Gulf of California made by Kino to

Vienna in 1701. On this map Kino's dedication was written: "Reverendo P. Marco Antonio Kappus, S. I., Colegii Matapensis Rectori Harum Novarum Regionum, et Missionum, Fautori et Benefactori se enixè commendat Eusebius Franciscus Kinus S. I." [To the Rev. Father Marcus Antonius Kappus, S. J., Rector of the College in Matape, promotor and benefactor of these new regions and missions, with the warm wishes of Eusebius Franciscus Kinus, S. J.].

In addition Kappus wrote numerous letters in which he described the circumstances of life, climate, and food in Sonora. About thirty of these letters are preserved; and they are still today an important source for the history of Sonora at the turn of the 1700s, especially since news from colonial America before the War of Independence of 1776 was very scarce[1].

Some other Slovene missionaries also deserve mentioning as writers of histories of the non-European continents. They worked as missionaries among American Indians in the Midwest in the first half of the 19th century. Among them we have to mention in the first place Friderik Irenej Baraga (*1797, Mala vas pri Dobrniču – †1868, Marquette), who worked as a missionary among the American Indians around the Great Lakes from 1831 until the 1860s[2]. Baraga himself learned Indian languages and wrote a dictionary and a grammar book on the language of the Chippewa. He studied the Chippewa language for twenty years and published many religious books in the Ottawa and Otchipwe languages[3]. He also published *A Theoretical and Practical Grammar of the Otchipwe Language – For the Use of Missionaries* in Detroit in 1850[4], and three years later, in Cincinnati, *A Dictionary of the Otchipwe Language – For the Use of Missionaries*[5].

Baraga published his knowledge on North American Indians in the book *Popis navad in zaderžanja Indijanov Polnočne Amerike*[6] [On the Manners and Customs of the Indians], which he also published in German[7] and in French[8] in 1837. In this book Baraga described Indians from the anthropological point of view, their material culture (what they wore, their housing, food, artisanal products, hunting, fishing), their social life (family life, rearing of the children, forms of government) and the other aspects of their life (religion, magicians, diseases, and medicines)[9].

Franc Pirc (*1785, Kamnik – †1880, Ljubljana), who usually spelled his name Francis Pierz in the United States, also wrote about the North American Indians in the Midwest. Pirc worked as a missionary among the Ottawa, Ojibwe, Otchipwe, and Winnebago Indian tribes from 1835 to 1873. The Ottawa lived in different centers of the Michigan Peninsula. The Ojibwe and Otchipwe tribes lived on the northern shores of Lake Huron and Lake Superior and in northern Minnesota. The Winnebago tribe lived in central Minnesota and southern Wisconsin. The Ojibwe tribe was engaged in ongoing wars with the Sioux (Dakota), who lived in northwestern Minnesota. Therefore Pirc did not have many contacts with the Sioux tribe[10]. Pirc published his views in a book in the German language, *Die Indianer in Nord – Amerika, ihre Lebensweise, Sitten, Gebräuche u.s.w*[11]. There is considerable difference between Baraga's books on

American Indians and Pirc's books on the same topics. Pirc wrote on the American Indians almost exclusively on the basis of his own experience[12].

Slovene historians, literary historians, and theologians devoted many books to the life and work of Bishop Baraga[13] and Rev. Pirc[14]. In connection with their lives and works the writers also dealt with history, language, and everyday life of Indian tribes in the American Midwest.

An important contribution towards enrichment of the knowledge of Slovenians about non-European continents is provided also by the works of Andrej Bernard Smolnikar (*1795, Kamnik – †1869, Philadelphia). He went to the United States as a priest in autumn 1837 and resigned as priest in spring 1838. Then he established contact with Harvard University, especially with its library. He was the first Slovene in the United States who alone, without connection with any church organization, received quite considerable attention among important representatives of American cultural life. Of interest for Slovene historiography is especially his fourth book, *Eines ist Noth* (Philadelphia 1841), which was also published in English translation as *The One Thing Needful* (Philadelphia 1841). In the most interesting part of this book, Smolnikar's journey through the American Midwest is described. During this journey he visited Michigan and Ohio too.

We also have to mention another group of three books that Smolnikar published in the United States: *Denkwürdige Ereignisse I* (Cambridge near Boston 1838); *Denkwürdige Ereignisse II* (Philadelphia 1839); *Denkwürdige Ereignisse III* (New York 1840). These books on the one hand show an interesting picture of Smolnikar's life in the United States; on the other hand they provide some interesting data on cultural life in Slovenia that he witnessed before he left for the United States and that he could not publish in Austria at that time as it was under the Metternich regime[15]. Smolnikar was the first Slovene who, in 1841, published his own newspaper, *Friedenbotschaft an alle Völker*, also published in English as *Message of Peace to All Nations*[16].

The views of political émigré Anton Fister (*1808, Radovljica – †1881, Vienna), are also of interest. He had to flee Austria due to his active engagement in the March Revolution of 1848. He participated actively in the Revolution of 1848 as professor of theology of the University of Vienna. He spent twenty-eight years as an émigré in the United States, during which time he lectured on religion, society, and education[17]. He thought that the time had come to change societal institutions and that schools had to develop freethinking, independent, and creative people. Fister also fought for the abolition of slavery in the United States and was a great admirer of Abraham Lincoln[18].

The works in which authors from Slovene ethnic territories later dealt with overseas countries (mostly the U.S.A.) were published in the period of Slovenians mass emigration. Most of the authors also dealt with Slovene emigration. On occasion of the 400th anniversary of the discovery of America by Christopher Columbus, Rev. Frančišek Saleški Sušteršič published an article in the 1894 *Mohorjev koledar* [Almanac of St. Hermagoras] *Slovenci v Ameriki* [Slovenes in America][19]. His intention was to get Slovenians acquainted with America and American Slovenes. In the article he wrote on geographic particularities of North and South America, and he described the emigration of Europeans and especially Slovenians to the United States. He also wrote a survey of the history of the United States, including a U.S. map on which places of Slovene settlements were marked. Šušteršič's article was the first attempt to write a history of Slovenians in the United States[20].

The geography and history of the United States and the history of Slovene immigration to North America as well are much better described in Rev. Jurij Trunk's book *Amerika in Amerikanci* [America and the Americans], published in 1913. Trunk decided to write his book after his third trip to the United States, and he gathered materials for it on the fourth trip too. The book *Amerika in Amerikanci* is the first work on America and American Slovenes written in a Slovene ethnic territory, and it remains still today the basic work for research on Slovene immigration to America. At the time the book was published it could serve as a textbook for students of American studies, especially because the first six parts present America on an interdisciplinary basis. If footnotes had been included it could have been considered a scholarly book[21]. When it was published, *Amerika in Amerikanci* had an impact on Slovene ethnic territory as well as among Slovene immigrants to the United States[22]. Trunk also published a German version of the book, *Quer durch Amerika* [Across America], which was published in 1915[23].

Trunk also dealt with the history of countries outside Europe in the book *Na Jutrovem* [In the Orient][24], which he wrote after his journey in the Orient from February to June 1906 (published by St. Hermagoras' Society in 1911)[25]. During his visit to Egypt and the Near East he visited Alexandria, Cairo, Jerusalem, and some other holy places (Nazareth, Lake Tiberias, Bethlehem, Mt. Tabor, Tripoli, Beirut, Haifa). This book showed Slovene readers the history of the Holy Land until World War I. Trunk lived the first fifty years of his life (until 1921) in southern Carinthia, which was then predominantly Slovene. After a majority of the inhabitants decided in a 1920 plebiscite that southern Carinthia should belong to Austria, Trunk, who was a Slovene political activist before and during World War I and who served as a member of the plebiscite commission, decided to emigrate to the United States, where he lived until 1973.

From the last period of Trunk's life, his manuscript *Amerika* [America][26] is worth mentioning. He wrote it in San Francisco when he was already almost eighty years old. Thise unpublished book, entitled simply "America", represents a continuation of his book *Amerika in Amerikanci*. He not only provides additional facts, but he also analyszes the reasons that America rose to the level of a superpower. He got the idea for this book when Europe was divided into two political, military, and economic blocks and from other events that made up the history of Europe and Yugoslavia during the years that followed World War II. With this book he wanted to make his countrymen aware of the processes through which American society had to go before it became free and democratic. At the same time, the reader of his manuscript will be made aware of his philosophical views on relations between America and Russia and of what was then

Yugoslavia's status and the status of Slavs in the world after World War II[27]. It is interesting to note Trunk's viewpoints on history:

> ... History is a teacher. This is valid for America and America has quite a few years of history behind it. Pure mentioning of years and events is not real history. Why did this or that event occur? It is a pragmatic and real history ...[28]

As we can ascertain from the above-mentioned books and articles that deal with the history of non-European countries by Slovene authors, most of them are about U.S. history and in parallel with the history of Slovenians in the United States. This is not surprising because most of the emigrants from Slovene ethnic territories before 1924 emigrated to this country. Later Slovenians emigrated to some other overseas countries also (Canada, South American countries, Australia); and newspapers that were printed in Slovene ethnic territories published many articles on these countries too.

Non-European History in Slovene Universities Today

Among Slovenian Universities today, it is perhaps the Department of History of the University of Maribor that gives the most attention to the history of the continents outside Europe. In accordance with the history curriculum offered there since the mid-1990s, the history of so-called "outside Europe" has become a special subject. European history is also taught as a special subject. Therefore, university teachers are required to teach non-European history as well.

One must admit, however, that due to specific university laws and the process of systematization of chairs, it was not possible to undertake a "normal" process of transition towards teaching of "non-European" history; i.e. to educate specialists for this history at good universities outside Slovenia and after that start teaching it. In spite of this, the fact that these subjects are taught separately constitutes a first step towards achieving distinguished research and teaching in the new areas. It is a fact of life that even in ideal circumstances, due to the lack of teachers, we shall never be able to cover with research all the continents in all the historical periods. It should be possible, however, to cover one of the continents outside Europe with research and teaching, while teaching the history of the other continents. Professors of history at the University of Maribor in part also do research on the particular problems of history of non-European continents.

At our university (Maribor), ancient history is taught by Janez Marolt, assistant professor, with excellent knowledge and also knowledge of languages, since he first studied theology and later history.

Although he primarily deals with the history of former Yugoslav lands in the ancient period in his research, he wrote a long article comparing Hamurabi's Laws and the Laws of the XII Tables[29]. He also wrote on the history of the Jews and the history of the period of Alexander the Great. He was a mentor for an M.A. on Arabia as the connecting link between the East and the Mediterranean in antiquity, and for the 45 B.A. final papers, in which his students dealt with ancient history in India, China, Tibet, Egypt, Mesopotamia, and Persia, with history of high cultures in America before Columbus (Maya, Inca, Aztecs, Zapotecs), with history of Jews, and history of Phoenicians, Hittites, Etruscans, Aborigines, Sasanides, etc.

Matjaž Klemenčič teaches history of Western Europe and outside-European history 1750-1918. He specializes in history of American immigration and in history of nationalism. His doctoral dissertation is devoted to history of Slovene Americans during World War II. In 1988/89 he was a Fulbright Scholar at Yale University. He is author of numerous published works in which he deals with U.S. history, especially local history of those regions and cities that were settled by Slovene immigrants. He addresses those questions in his published doctoral dissertation, *Ameriški Slovenci in NOB v Jugoslaviji: naseljevanje, zemljepisna razprostranjenost in odnos ameriških Slovencev do stare domovine od sredine 19. stoletja do konca druge svetovne vojne* [American Slovenes and the National Liberation Movement in Yugoslavia: Settlement, Geographical Dispersion, and the Attitude of American Slovenes toward the Old Country from the Mid-19thnineteenth Century to World War II]. In the second part of this book he deals with activities of Slovene Americans during the two world wars, with special emphasis on their reactions to the events in the old homeland[30].

In the book *Slovenes of Cleveland: The Creation of a New Nation and a New World Community: Slovenia and the Slovenes of Cleveland, Ohio*, Klemenčič looks at the history of Cleveland, which has the greatest concentration of Slovene population outside Slovene ethnic territories. He describes the process of settlement of Slovenians in Cleveland, the establishment of their settlements, and their organizations, i.e. Catholic parishes, fraternal organizations, and Slovene national homes. He also deals with the political process and integration of the Slovene community into the American mainstream. Slovenes of Cleveland contributed city councilmen, mayors, and members of the Ohio legislature, Ohio governors, and members of the U.S. House of Representatives and Senate[31].

The book *Jurij Trunk med Koroško in Združenimi državami Amerike ter zgodovina slovenskih naselbin v Leadvillu, Kolorado in San Franciscu, Kalifornija* [Jurij Trunk Between Carinthia and the United States and the History of the Slovene Settlements in Leadville, Colorado, and San Francisco, California] is about the life and work of the Slovene Catholic priest, writer, and politician George Trunk in Carinthia and in the USA. In this book the author wrote about the history of Leadville, Colorado, and its Slovenes from the mid-1880s to the 1990s[32].

Klemenčič also wrote a number of articles on Slovene immigrants to North America, in which he described the history of Slovene settlements in California and the history of Rock Springs, Wyoming, and also of Slovenes and other ethnic groups in the United States. His sources included censuses by mother tongue and/or ancestry. Among them the article on development of Slovene immigrants in Rock Springs, Wyoming, deserves comment. Rock Springs was a typical mining town in the American West whose coalmines, in the second half of the 19thth century, attracted numerous immigrants – members of 28 different nations, or on the basis of the political divisions of the world at that time, comimg coming from 24 states[33]. In Klemenčič's contribution on Croatian and Slovene missionaries, written with Ivan Čizmić, he introduces Bishop Baraga and Rev. Pirc not only as missionaries who brought Christianity to certain American Indian tribes, but also as inventors, writers, and historians of the American Midwest[34].

Slovene historians from Slovenia had written quite a few works on the workers' movement even before 1986, focusing especially on the reactions of leftist Slovenes in America to the events in the old homeland, particularly during the world wars[35]. Klemenčič also co-organized with Ivan Čizmić a conference sponsored by the University of Maribor and the Zagreb Center for Migration Research on the workers' movement. The results were published in *Migracijske teme* in Zagreb[36]. Klemenčič touched on this topic when he wrote about the workers' movement in Cleveland in his book on the Slovenes in Cleveland[37].

Klemenčič organized a conference at the University of Maribor in 1991 on the ethnic immigrant press. Many colleagues from both sides of the Atlantic Ocean attended. The result was an edited volume of articles that deals not only with the Slovene but also with the German and East and Southeast European ethnic press in the United States and some of the other immigrant countries. It was published by the University of Maribor and the Institute for Slovene Emigration at the Scientific Research Center of the Slovene Academy of Arts and Sciences[38]. In 1999 this Institute organized a round table on the significance of the ethnic press for researchers on immigration[39].

Klemenčič also edited a volume from the international symposium "Razvoj in pomen fraternalističnega gibanja in fraternalističnih organizacij med priseljenci v priseljenskih državah/The Development and Significance of the Fraternal Movement and Fraternal Organizations among Immigrants in Immigrant Countries", which he organized in May 1994 at the University of Maribor. The contributions deal with the history of ethnic fraternalism in immigrant countries, with special emphasis on Slovenes. They also address ethnic fraternalism within Polish, German, Slovak, Hungarian, and Croatian ethnic communities in the United States[40]. The rest of the symposium papers were published in a special issue of *Dve domovini/Two Homelands*[41].

With Milica Trebše-Štolfa, Klemenčič also edited a volume of articles, *Slovensko izseljenstvo* [Slovene Emigrants], which was published on the occasion of the 50th anniversary of the Slovene Emigrant Society. In addition to the activities of the Slovene Emigrant Society, this volume describes different aspects of the history of Slovenians outside the Slovene ethnic territories in all continents of the world[42].

Also worth mentioning is a sourcebook, *Viri o demokratizaciji in osamosvojitvi Slovenije. IV. del: Slovenci v zamejstvu in po svetu ter mednarodno priznanje Slovenije* [Sources on Democratization and the Independence Movement of Slovenia. Part 4: Slovenians in Neighboring Countries and in the World and International Recognition of Slovenia], which was edited by Klemenčič and Trebše-Štolfa[43].

Klemenčič was also a mentor/principal adviser to a doctoral student, Mihael Kuzmič, who wrote a dissertation on the Slovene ethnic community in Bethlehem, PA. Rev. Kuzmič later published it as a book[44]. He was also mentor to five graduate students who finished their M.A. theses on the history of Slovene and Croatian fraternal organizations in the USA, on the Slovene Catholic Church in the United States, and on biographies of important Slovene Americans. He was also mentor to 25 undergraduate students who wrote their final B.A. papers on the history of Slovene immigrant communities in the USA, history of American Indians, Latin America, the Middle East, Africa, India, and China. Currently one of his doctoral students is researching the life and work of an important Slovene American, Ivan Molek, the editor of *Prosveta*, an organ of the fraternal organization Slovene National Benefit Society.

Darko Friš deals with the history of Slovenes in the USA, with special emphasis on the history of the role that the Catholic Church played among Slovene Americans. He studied especially the history of Slovene ethnic parishes in the USA. He authored a book on the Slovene Catholic Church and Slovene Americans[45] and co-authored a book on the history of the fraternal organization American Slovene Catholic Union[46]. He also published letters of Slovene American Catholic priests [47] and some articles in both the Slovene and English languages. The majority of them deal with Slovene American history. He also tutored eight final B.A papers in which students dealt with the history of Slovene immigrants to the USA, including histories of Slovene fraternal organizations, of Slovene Franciscans in the USA, the role of American Slovenes in the fight of Slovenia for independence in the 1990s, and visits of Bishop of Ljubljana Gregorij Rožman among Slovene Americans after World War I.

In addition to his contribution to the work on KSKJ[48], Andrej Vovko has written quite a few articles on different aspects of Slovene–U.S. history[49].Dragan Potočnik has published a book on the history of Asian continent and contempory life of Asian peoples.

There are also studies on the reasons for immigration of Slovenes to America as well as images of America among potential migrants. Marjan Drnovšek has studied the reasons for emigration in his unpublished doctoral dissertation[50]. Klemenčič has published an article on the images of America among the potential migrants[51]. Later this became a topic of Marjan Drnovšek's book[52] and numerous articles. Also the process of transportation from the Slovene ethnic territory to America was the topic of a book by Drnovšek[53].

At the Department of History at the University of Ljubljana the theme of history of the non-European world is formally part of the subjects of general history; in reality – in accord with the specialties of their teachers – particular stress is placed on the history of Central Europe or the Habsburg Monarchy.

There are, however, works by literary historians that deal with Slovene immigrants and their life and work, and those works touch also on the general history of the countries of immigration. Historians of literature wrote a survey of the history of literary works of Slovene immigrants and their descendants. In this three-volume book edited by Janja

Žitnik, from the Scientific Research Center of the Slovene Academy of Arts and Sciences, and Helga Glušič, from the Faculty of Arts at the University of Ljubljana, histories of Slovene movement to the major countries of immigration are described[54].

In an edited volume on the cultural works of Slovenians of South America, Mirko Jurak and Irene Mislej have also described the histories of those immigrants[55]. Mirko Jurak was also the adviser of Andrej Podbrežnik, who wrote a dissertation on cultural connections between Slovenia and New Zealand from 1923 to 2000[56].

Jerneja Petrič wrote from the point of view of a literary historian on the life and work of Louis Adamic[57] and later on Slovene immigrant autobiographies[58]. Of course, she touched upon political histories of those writers, especially since they were also politicians within Slovene-American communities and nationally. Furthermore, she was the mentor of Irena Milanič, who wrote on the history of a Slovene-American paper, *Mladinski list-Juvenile*[59].

Janez Stanonik, now professor emeritus of literary history, wrote about the correspondence of Slovene priest Marcus Antonius Kappus from colonial North America[60], about Bishop Baraga[61], about Ojibwe and Ottawa Indians[62], and about Father Pirc[63].

Zmago Šmitek, a Slovene ethnologist, likewise covers the history of non-European countries, especially during his research on encounters with far-away cultures[64]. The results are two books in which he discusses Slovenians encounters with non-European cultures. He is also author of quite a few treatises in which he describes the histories of Slovene missionaries[65], histories of some overseas countries[66], and contacts of Slovenians with the Holy Land in the Middle Ages[67].

The University of Primorska in Koper/Capodistria is formally at the beginning of its development, and the administration should give emphasis to the history of the Mediterranean, which ought to mean history of North Africa and the Near East. In reality, they are not able to offer those these subjects, even as alternative subjects, due to lack of teachers.

History of Non-European Countries at the Institute for Studies of Slovene Emigration at the Scientific Research Center of the Slovene Academy of Arts and Sciences

The researchers at the Institute for Studies of Slovene Emigration at the Scientific Research Center of the Slovene Academy of Arts and Sciences examine Slovene emigration and in connection with it, the history of non-European countries as well.

Marjan Drnovšek has written on the experiences of the so-called "common man" in Slovene American history. The sources he used were primarily letters from the immigrants to their relatives and friends at home and articles in contemporary Slovene newspapers[68]. Among his works, books on images of America among Slovenes in the homeland[69] and a book on the travels of Slovene immigrants to the United States[70] deserve mention.

Janja Žitnik authored three books on Louis Adamic in which she approaches his work from the standpoint of a literary historian as well as from the historian's point of view[71]. She also edited three volumes of books on Slovene literature among Slovene emigrants all over the world[72] for which she wrote quite a few contributions. In those books, histories of lands in which Slovenians settled are described. Žitnik authored some articles as well[73].

Zvone Žigon, an anthropologist, wrote two books in which he deals with Slovene émigrés in Argentina and in other South American countries (*Otroci dveh domovin: slovenstvo v Južni Ameriki*) [74] and a book on Slovenians in Africa (*Izzivi drugačnosti: Slovenci v Afriki in na Arabskem polotoku*) in which he provides the reader with detailed descriptions of Slovene emigrants in Egypt, the South African Republic, and Kenya. He also mentions Slovenians in Jordan, Israel, Ghana, and Kuwait[75].

Other Researchers on the History of Non-European Countries

Researchers from other disciplines also deal with the history of lands outside Europe. For example, Rado Genorijo, a Slovene geographer, wrote books and articles on Slovene immigrant communities in Canada[76]and Argentina[77]; but he also wrote about Slovene emigration in general[78].

A Slovene historian from Trieste authored some articles on Slovene immigrants to the U.S.A., especially the history of Slovene missionaries[79]. We should mention Rev. Bogdan Kolar, too, a professor of theology at the University of Ljubljana, who wrote on the role of the Catholic Church among Slovene immigrants all over the world[80] and on missionary Franc Pirc. Finally, Marjan Britovšek, emeritus professor of history at the University of Ljubljana, wrote a book on Anton Fister[81], in which he includes Fister's American period[82].

Conclusion

Brief surveys of the universities, institutes, and researchers who dealt and deal with the history of non-European countries shows us that the research capacities in Slovenia are dispersed. This is normal for a relatively small country. In Slovenia we have three universities. The oldest is the University of Ljubljana, her younger sister is the University of Maribor, and the youngest in this family of universities is the University of Primorska. In the Republic of Slovenia, it is the University of Maribor's Department of History that greatest attention is given to continents outside Europe. The most fruitful author here is Prof. Matjaž Klemenčič. In the mid-1990s, history of the so-called "outside Europe" at the University of Maribor became a special subject. Other professors of history at the University of Maribor also do research on the particular problems of history of the continents outside European.

At the Department of History of the University of Ljubljana, history of the non-European world is formally one of the subjects of general history, but in accord with the specialties of its teachers, particular stress is given to the history of Central Europe or the Habsburg Monarchy. There are, however, works by literary historians and ethnologists that deal with Slovene immigrants and their life and work, and these works also touch on the general history of countries of immigration and in this way cover the history of non-European countries.

The University of Primorska is just starting to develop its curriculum because it only enrolled its first students of history in the academic year 2004/05.

The three departments of history are not the only places for research of history in Slovenia. There are also research institutes, for example, institutes within the framework of the Scientific Research Center of the Slovene Academy of Arts and Sciences in Ljubljana (Institute for World and National History and Institute for Slovene Emigration Studies). Independent institutes for history include the Institute for Contemporary History and Institute for Ethnic Studies in Ljubljana, which deals primarily with themes connected with history and contemporary realities of Slovenes who live as autochthonous minorities or emigrants outside the Republic of Slovenia. Members of this institute are also researching the history of immigrant groups to Slovenia and autochthonous Italians and Hungarians in Slovenia.

The bibliography about the history of non-European continents and countries shows that the first Slovene authors on non-Europeans were Slovene missionaries who labored above all among the Indians in North America. Besides missionaries, noteworthy is Rev. Jurij Trunk, whose book *Amerika in Amerikanci* [America and the Americans], published in 1913, is still today the basic reference for researchers on the Slovene immigration to America and also the first book in the Slovene language in which the author treats the history of the United States of America and Slovene immigrants.

Most books and articles that cover the history of non-European countries by Slovene authors deal with U.S.A. history in the context of the history of Slovenians in the United States. This is not surprising because most of the emigrants from Slovene ethnic territories went to that country.

Slovenian researchers deal with other continents only in accordance to the specialties of their research topics.

In general we can conclude that research in Slovenia on topics concerning the history of non-European countries is quite well organized and productive, especially if we take into consideration that Slovenia is a very small country with limited resources.

Notes

1 J. Stanonik, *Marcus Antonius Kappus*, in J. Žitnik - H. Glišič (eds.), *Slovenska izseljenska književnost 2: Severna Amerika* [Slovene Immigrant Literature 2; North America], Ljubljana 1999, p. 22.

2 J. Stanonik, *Friderik Baraga*, in Žitnik - Glišič (eds.), *Slovenska izseljenska književnost 2* cit., p. 391; J. Trunk, *Amerika in Amerikanci* [America and Americans], Celovec 1912, pp. 544-547.

3 F. Baraga, *Otawa Anamie Misinaigan* [Ottawa Prayer Book], Wawiyatanong 1932; Id., *Otchipwe An-*

amie Misinaigan [Ojibwe Prayer Book], Paris 1837; Id., *Katolik Anamie Misinaigan* [Catholic Prayer Book], Detroit 1846 – in Ottawa language; Id., *Katolik Anamie Misinaigan* [Catholic Prayer Book], Detroit 1846 – in Ojibwe Language; Id., *Jesus obimadisiwin ajonda aking* [Life of Jesus], Paris 1837 – in Ottawa language; Id., *Jesus obimadisiwin ona aking* [Life of Jesus], Paris 1837 – in Ojibwe language; Id., *Katolik Enamiad a nanagatawendamowinan* [Ojibwe: Catholic Christian Thoughts], Detroit 1850; Id., *Kagige debwewinan kaginig Ge-Takwendang Katolik Enamiad* [Ojibwe: Eternal Truths], Cincinnati 1855.

4 Id., *A Theoretical and Practical Grammar of the Otchipwe Language – For the use of Missionaries*, Detroit 1850.

5 Id., *Popis navad in zaderžanja Indijanov Polnočne Amerike* [Description of Indians of North America], Ljubljana 1837.

6 *Ibid.*

7 F. Baraga, *Geschichte, Charakter, Sitten und Gebräuche der nord-amerikanischer Indier*, Laibach 1837.

8 Id., *Abrégé de l'histoire des Indiens de l'Amérique septentrionale*, Paris 1837.

9 M. Klemenčič, *Frederic Irenej Baraga (1797-1868): Catholic Bishop, Missionary, and Scholar – Slovene*, in E.R. Barkan (ed.), *Making It in America: A Sourcebook on Eminent Ethnic Americans*, Santa Barbara 2001, p. 28; I. Čizmić - M. Klemenčič, *Croatian and Slovene Missionaries as Inventors and Explorers of the American West and Midwest*, "Društvena istraživanja", vol. 11., n. 4-5, 2002, pp. 767-773.

10 *Ibid.*, pp. 773-778.

11 F. Pierz, *Die Indianer in Nord-Amerika, ihre Lebensweise, Sitten, Gebräuche u.s.w, nach zehnjährigen Aufenhalte und gesammelten Erfahrungen unter den verschiedenen Stämmen*, St. Louis 1855.

12 Stanonik, *Franc Pirc* cit., p. 61..

13 B. Požar, *Friderick Baraga and His Book on the Manners of American Indians*, "Acta Neophilologica", 6, 1973, pp. 29-71; Stanonik, *Friderik Baraga: ob dvestoletnici rojstva* [Friderick Baraga: On the Occasion of the 200th Anniversary of His Birth], "Dve domovini/Two Homelands", 7, 1996, pp. 15-32; A. Vovko, *Baragova podoba v delih slovenskih zgodovinarjev*, [Baraga's Image in the Works of Slovene Historians], in S. Granda - M. Zupančič - P. Rot (eds.), *Baraga in Trebnje: predavanja na Baragovem simpoziju v Trebnjem, 9. januarja 1998*, Trebnje 1998, pp. 97-111; E. Škulj (ed.), *Baragov simpozij v Rimu*, Celje 2000, pp. 157-170; Klemenčič, *Frederic Irenej Baraga (1797–1868)* cit., p. 28; Čizmić - Klemenčič, *Croatian and Slovene Missionaries* cit., pp. 767-773.

14 J. Stanonik, *Franc Pirc v Ameriki*, in F. Adamič et al. (eds.), *V spomin Francu Pircu* [In Memory of Franc Pirc] *(1785-1880)*, Ljubljana 1982, pp. 27-32; M. Kodrič, *Franc Pirc in nastanek prvih slovenskih naselbin v Združenih državah Amerike* [Franc Pirc and the Establishment of the First Slovene Settlements in the U.S.A.], "Dve domovini/Two Homelands" 18, 2003, pp. 53-62; A. Vovko, *Pomembnejši slovenski biografski prispevki o misijonarju in izseljenskem duhovniku Francu Pircu* [Important Slovene Contributions to the Biography of Missionary and Emigrant Priest Franc Pirc], "Dve domovini/Two Homelands", 18, 2003, pp. 8-24; Čizmić - Klemenčič, *Croatian and Slovene Missionaries* cit, pp. 773-778.

15 J. Stanonik, *Andrej Bernard Smolnikar*, "Zgodovinski časopis", vol. 49, n. 2, 1995, pp. 183-191; Id., *Andrej Bernard Smolnikar*, in Žitnik - Glišič (eds.), *Slovenska izseljenska književnost 2* cit., pp. 63-68; Id., *Longfellow and Smolnikar*, "Acta Neophilologica", 1, 1968, pp. 3-40.

16 Id., *Andrej Bernard Smolnikar* cit., pp. 63-68; Id., *Andrej Bernard Smolnikar in prvi slovenski poskus izdaje periodičnega glasila v Združenih državah* [Andrej Bernard Smolnikar and the First Slovene Attempt to Publish a Periodical in the USA], – manuscript, Ljubljana 1980 (A copy of the manuscript is stored by the Institute for Studies of Slovene Emigration at the Scientific Research Center of the Slovene Academy of Arts and Sciences.

17 Those lectures were published by the Archive of the Republic of Slovenia and the Scientific Institute of the Faculty of Arts, University of Ljubljana, in 1991 in a book by A. Fister, *Izbrani spisi. Knjiga III:*

Govori o religiji [A. Fister: Selected Writings, Book III: Speeches on Religion], trans. by F. Jerman, Ljubljana 1992.

18 M. Britovšek, *Anton Füster in revolucija 1848 v Avstriji*, Maribor 1980; J. Stanonik, *Anton Füster – A Slovene Forty-Eighter*, "Acta Neophilologica", 31, 1998, pp. 81-93.

19 F.S. Šusteršič, *Slovenci v Ameriki* [Slovenes in America], "Mohorjev koledar 1894", pp. 15-27.

20 M. Klemenčič, *Jurij Trunk med Koroško in Združenimi državami Amerike ter zgodovina slovenskih naslebin v Laevillu, Kolorado, in v San Franciscu, Kalifornija* [Jurij Trunk Between Carinthia and the United States and the History of the Slovene Settlements in Leadville, Colorado, and San Francisco, California], Celovec-Ljubljana-Dunaj 1999, pp. 130-131.

21 *Ibid.*, pp. 127-130.

22 More on impact of Trunk's book *Amerika in Amerikanci* see in M. Drnovšek, *Odmevnost Trunkove knjige Amerika in Amerikanci v letih 1912–1913*, [Impact of Trunk's Book *Amerika in Amerikanci* during the Years 1912–1913], vol. 43, n. 4, "Zgodovinski časopis", 1989, pp. 606-609; Klemenčič, *Jurij Trunk med Koroško in Združenimi državami Amerike* cit., pp. 131-135.

23 J. Trunk, *Quer durch Amerika. Reisse Skizzen von Georg Trunk* [Across America. Travel Sketches by George Trunk], Klagenfurt 1915.

24 Id., *Na Jutrovem: Potopisne črtice iz Svete dežele* [At the Orient: Travel Stories from the Holy Land], Celovec 1911.

25 Klemenčič, *Jurij Trunk med Koroško in Združenimi državami Amerike* cit., pp. 34-37.

26 J. Trunk, *Amerika* [America], unpublished paper, San Francisco 1948.

27 Klemenčič, *Jurij Trunk med Koroško in Združenimi državami Amerike* cit., pp. 397-404.

28 Trunk, *Amerika* cit., pp. 6-7; Klemenčič, *Jurij Trunk med Koroško in Združenimi državami Amerike* cit., p. 399.

29 J. Marolt, *Primerjava med Hamurabijevim zakonikom, Pentatevhom/Peteroknjižjem in zakonikom XII plošč* [Hamurabi's Laws and the Laws of XII Tables], "Čaopis za zgodovino in narodopisje", vol. 69 (34), n. 2, 1998, pp. 209-245.

30 M. Klemenčič, *Ameriški Slovenci in NOB v Jugoslaviji: naseljevanje, zemljepisna razprostranjenost in odnos ameriških Slovencev do stare domovine od sredine 19. stoletja do konca druge svetovne vojne* [American Slovenes and the National Liberation Movement in Yugoslavia: Settlement, Geographical Dispersion, and the Attitude of American Slovenes toward the Old Country from the Mid-nineteenth Century to World War II], Maribor 1987.

31 Id., *Slovenes of Cleveland: The Creation of a New Nation and a New World Community: Slovenia and the Slovenes of Cleveland, Ohio*, Novo mesto 1995.

32 Id., *Jurij Trunk med Koroško in Združenimi državami Amerike* cit..

33 Id., *Nacionalna struktura mesta Rock Springs in okraja Sweetwater (Wyoming) s posebnim ozirom na Slovence* [Ethnic Structure of the City of Rock Springs and Sweetwater County (WY) with special Emphasis on the Slovenes], in I. Štrukelj (ed.), *Kultura, identiteta in jezik v procesih evropske integracije*, Ljubljana 2000, pp. 214–233; M. Klemenčič, *Razvoj slovenske izseljenske skupnosti v Rock Springsu, Wyoming, od naselitve do začetka 30-let 20. stoletja* [Development of the Slovene Immigrant Community in Rock Springs, WY, from the First Slovene Settlers until the Beginning of the 1930s], "Dve domovini/Two Homelands", 13, 2001, pp. 73-99.

34 Čizmić - Klemenčič, *Croatian and Slovene Missionaries* cit., pp. 761-783.

35 M. Drnovšek, *O staliŠčih slovenskih socialistov v ZDA do vojne in jugoslovanskega vprašanja med prvo svetovno vojno* [On the Standpoints of Slovene Socialists in the USA towards the War and the Yugoslav Question during World War I], "Prispevki za. zgodovino delavskega gibanja", vol. 25/26, n. 1/2, 1975/76, pp. 75-96; M. Klemenčič, *Proletarec and the Acculturation of Slovene Workers in the United*

States, in C. Harzig (ed.), *Labor Migration Project. Labor Newspaper Preservation Project: The Press of Labor Migrants in Europe and North America from 1880's to 1930's*, Bremen 1985, pp. 475-486.

36 M. Kodrič, *Class consciousness among the second generation: expectations and responses within the Slovene National Benefit Society in the 1920s*, "Migracijske teme", vol. 4, n. 1-2, 1988, pp. 111-128.

37 Klemenčič, *Slovenes of Cleveland* cit., p. 414.

38 M. Klemenčič (ed.), *Slovenski izseljenski tisk*, "Znanstvena revija: humanistika", vol. 3, n. 2, 1991, pp. 291-558; published also in "Dve domovini/Two Homelands", 2-3, 1992.

39 A. Giordano - J. Žitnik - K. Djupedal - U. Beijbom - H. Bender - D. Tolfsby - O. Koivukangas - M. Klemenčič - J. Wurl - B. Lambkin - A. Walaszek, *Press and Emigration*. Roundtable discussion, 1 October 1999, [within] AEMI - The Association of European Migration Institutions Annual Meeting, Portorož, Slovenia, 29 September – 2 October 1999, "Dve domovini/Two Homelands", 10, 1999, pp. 151-167

40 M. Klemenčič (ed.), *Etnični fraternalizem v priseljenskih deželah / Ethnic Fraternalism in Immigrant Countries*, Maribor 1996.

41 "Dve domovini/Two Homelands", 2-3, 1992, pp. 7-424.

42 M. Trebše-Štolfa - M. Klemenčič (eds.), *Slovensko izseljenstvo: zbornik ob 50-letnici Slovenske izseljenske matice*, [Slovene Emigration; Almanac on the Occasion of the 50th Anniversary of the Slovene Emigrant Society], Ljubljana 2001.

43 M. Klemenčič - J. Stergar - S. Kristen - K. Munda-Hirnök - M. Trebše-Štolfa, *Viri o demokratizaciji in osamosvojitvi Slovenije. (Del 4: Slovenci v zamejstvu in po svetu ter mednarodno priznanje Slovenije)* [Sources on Democratization and the Independence Movement of Slovenia. (Part 4: Slovenes in Neighboring Countries and in the World and International Recognition of Slovenia] (=Viri, 20), Ljubljana 2005.

44 M. Kuzmič, *Slovenski izseljenci iz Prekmurja v Bethlehemu v ZDA, 1893-1924: naselitev in njihove zgodovinske, socialne, politične, literarne in verske dejavnosti* [Slovene Emigrants from Prekmurje in Bethlehem, PA, in the USA, 1893–1924: Settlement and their Historic, Socio-Political, Literary and Religious Activities] (=Migracije, 2), Ljubljana 2001.

45 D. Friš, *Ameriški Slovenci in Katoliška cerkev: 1871-1924* [American Slovenes and the Catholic Church: 1871–1924], Celovec-Ljubljana-Dunaj 1995.

46 D. Friš - B. Kolar - A. Vovko, *Prvih sto let Kranjsko slovenske katoliške jednote: pregled zgodovine KSKJ, 1894–1994* [The First One Hundred Years of the Carnolian Slovene Catholic Union 1894–1994], Ljubljana 1997.

47 D. Friš, *Korespondenca Kazimirja Zakrajška, O.F.M. (1907-1928)* [Correspondence of Kazimir Zakrajšek, O.F.M. (1907-1928)], Ljubljana 1993; D. Friš, *Korespondenca Kazimirja Zakrajška, O.F.M. (1928-1958)* [Correspondence of Kazimir Zakrajšek, O.F.M. (1928-1958)], Ljubljana 1995; D. Friš, *Korespondenca slovenskih katoličanov v ZDA med leti 1882-1924* [Correspondence of Slovene Catholics in the USA 1882-1924], Ljubljana 1999.

48 A. Vovko, *The Foundation of the Yugoslav Emergency Council in New York*, "Slovene Studies", vol. 10, n. 2, 1988, pp. 191-197.

49 A. Vovko, *Udje družbe sv. Mohorja v ZDA do leta 1900* [The U.S. Members of St. Hermagoras Society until 1900], "Dve domovini/Two Homelands", 1, 1990, pp. 121-135; A. Vovko, *The Myth of America and the Society of St. Raphael*, "Slovene Studies", vol. 13, n. 1, 1991, pp.107-110; A. Vovko, *Odmev mita o Ameriki v Družbi sv. Rafaela* [The Echo of the Myth of America in the Society of St. Raphael], "Zgodovinski časopis vol. 47, n. 4, 1993, pp. 563-568; A. Vovko, *Življenje in delo Friderika Baraga v luči znanstvenih objav in bibliografskih podatkov* [Life and Work of Friderick Baraga As Reflected by Scholarly Publications and Bibliographic Data], in Škulj (ed.), *Baragov simpozij v Rimu* cit., pp. 207-225.

50 M. Drnovšek, *Izseljevanje iz širše ljubljanske okolice 1890-1914* [Emigration from the Broader Vicinity of Ljubljana 1890-1914], Ph.D. Dissertation, Ljubljana 1993.

51 M. Klemenčič, *Images of America among Slovene and Other Yugoslav Migrants*, in *Distant Magnets: Expectations and Realities in the Immigrant Experience, 1840-1930*, New York 1993, pp. 199-221.

52 M. Drnovšek, *Usodna privlačnost Amerike* [The Fatal Attraction of America], Ljubljana 1998.

53 M. Drnovšek, *Pot slovenskih izseljencev na tuje: od Ljubljane do Ellis Islanda – Otoka solza v New Yorku, 1880-1924* [The Road of Slovene Emigrants to Foreign Lands; From Ljubljana to Ellis Island – Island of Tears in New York City, 1880-1924], Ljubljana 1991.

54 J. Žitnik - H. Glušič (eds.), *Slovenska izseljenska književnost* [Slovene Emigrant Literature], 3 vols., Ljubljana 1999.

55 M. Jurak - I. Mislej, *Kulturno ustvarjanje Slovencev v Južni Ameriki:* zbornik [Cultural Creativity of Slovenes in South America], Ljubljana 1995.

56 A. Podbrežnik, *Kulturni stiki med Slovenijo in Novo Zelandijo (1923-2000)* [Cultural Connections between Slovenia and New Zealand], Ph.D. Dissertation, Ljubljana 2003.

57 J. Petrič, *Svetovi Louisa Adamiča: ob tridesetletnici smrti* [The Worlds of Louis Adamic: On the Occasion of the 30th Anniversary of His Death], Ljubljana 1981.

58 Id., *Avtobiografije slovenskih izseljencev v Združenih državah Amerike* – [Autobiographies of Slovene Immigrants to the United States of America], Ph.D. Dissertation, Ljubljana 1987.

59 I. Milanič, *Tematski sklopi v reviji Mladinski list-Juvenile (1922-1944)* [The Themes in the Review *Mladinski list-Juvenile (1922-1944*], Ph.D. Dissertation, Ljubljana 2003.

60 J. Stanonik, *Letters of Marcus Antonius Kappus from Colonial America*. Part I, "Acta Neophilologica", 19, 1986, pp. 33-57; Part II, "Acta Neophilologica", 20, 1987, pp. 25-38; Part III, "Acta Neophilologica", 21, 1988, pp. 3-9; Part IV, "Acta Neophilologica", 22, 1989, pp. 39-50; Part V, "Acta Neophilologica", 23, 1990, pp. 27-37; Part VI, "Acta Neophilologica", 30, 1997, pp. 43-57.

61 Stanonik, *Friderik Baraga: ob dvestoletnici rojstva* cit., pp. 15-32.

62 Id., *Očipve in Ottawa* [Otchibwe and Ottawa], "Zgodovinski časopis", vol. 50, n. 1, 1996, pp. 65-69.

63 Id., *Franc Pirc v Ameriki* cit., pp. 27-32.

64 Z. Šmitek, *Srečevanja z drugačnostjo: slovenska izkustva eksotike* [Meetings with the Other, Slovenes Encounter with the Exotics], Radovljica 1995; Id., *Klic daljnih svetov: Slovenci in neevropske kulture*, [The Call from Very Far Away; Slovenes and Non-European Culture], Ljubljana 1986.

65 Id., *Janez Krstnik Mesar - portret tonkinškega misijonarja iz 18. stoletja* [Janez Krstnik Mesar A Portrait of a Tonking Missionary from the 18th Century] , "Dve domovini/Two Homelands", 5, 1994, pp. 7-17.

66 Id., *Egipt - dežela slovenske fascinacije* [Egypt - The Land of Slovene Fascination], "Časopis za kritiko znanosti", vol. 29, n. 204-206, pp. 30-51; Id., *Po Nilu v osrčje Afrike* [Via Nile into the Midst of Africa], in J. Žontar - M. Benedik (eds.), *Dokumenti slovenstva*, Ljubljana 1994, pp. 239-243.

67 Id., *Crusaders, Pilgrims, Penitents: Slovenian Medieval Contacts with the Holy Land*, in W. Moskovich - O. Luthar - S. Schwarzband (eds.), *Jerusalem in Slavic Culture*, (=Jews and Slavs, 6), Ljubljana and Jerusalem 1999, pp. 203-214; Id., *Križarji, romarji, spokorniki: naši srednjeveški stiki s Sveto deželo*, "Časopis za zgodovino in narodopisje", vol. 71=36, n. 1-2, 2000, pp. 119-132.

68 Drnovšek: *Pot slovenskih izseljencev na tuje* cit., p. 244; Id., *Usodna privlačnost Amerike* cit., p. 39.

69 *Ibid.*

70 Id., *Pot slovenskih izseljencev na tuje* cit., p. 244.

71 J. Žitnik, *Louis Adamič in sodobniki: 1948-1951* [Louis Adamic and Contemporaries: 1948-1951], Ljubljana 1992; Id., *Pero in politika: zadnja leta Louisa Adamiča* [The Pen and Politics: Adamic's Last Years of Life], Ljubljana 1993; Id., *Orel in korenine med 'brušenjem' in cenzuro* [The Eagle and The Roots between Grinding and Censorship], Ljubljana 1995.

72 Žitnik - Glušič (eds.), *Slovenska izseljenska književnost* cit

73 J. Žitnik, *The Return of Slovene Emigrant Literature*, "AEMI journal", 1, 2003, pp. 106-111; Id., *Globalization and the Prospects of Multicultural Coexistence and World Peace*, "Journal of National Development", vol. 16, n. 1/2, 2003, pp. 49-66.

74 Z. Žigon, *Otroci dveh domovin: slovenstvo v Južni Ameriki* [The Children of Two Homelands; Slovenes in South America], Ljubljana 1998.

75 Id., *Izzivi drugačnosti: Slovenci v Afriki in na Arabskem polotoku* [Provocation of Differentiation: Slovenians in Africa and in the Arab Peninsula], Ljubljana 2003.

76 R. Genorio, *Slovenci v Kanadi / Slovenes in Canada* (=Geographica Slovenica, 17), Ljubljana 1989.

77 Id., *Slovenci v Argentini: geografske razsežnosti priseljevanja in razvoj njihovih naselbin v Buenos Airesu in Cordobi* [Slovenians in Argentina: Geographic Dimensions of Slovene Immigration and Development of their Settlements in Buenos Aires and Cordoba], Ph.D. Dissertation

78 Id., *Geographical Dimensions of Slovene Emigration around the World*, "GeoJournal", vol. 30, n. 3, 1993, pp. 225-229.

79 M. Kodrič, *The Press as a Link between the Leaders and the Rank and File of an Ethnic Fraternal Organization: Handling the Situation of Second Generation Membership in the KSKJ'S Organs*, "Dve domovini/Two Homelands", 2/3, 1992, pp. 195-207; Id., *Nekateri pristopi k problematiki druge generacije v okviru raziskovanja priseljenstva v ZDA*, [The Issues of the Second Generation in U.S Immigration Research], "Dve domovini/Two Homelands", 1, 1990, pp. 161-177; Id., *Franc Pirc in nastanek prvih slovenskih naselbin* cit., pp. 53-62; Id., *Zanimanje slovenskih misijonarjev v Severni Ameriki za izseljevanje rojakov, kot se odraža v dopisih v Zgodnji danici* [The Interest of Slovene Missionaries in North America in Slovene Immigration as Seen in Their Letters to Zgodnja Danica], "Dve domovini/Two Homelands", 6, 1995, pp. 9-20.

80 B. Kolar, *St. Joseph KSKJ local lodge, Bridgeport, Connecticut*, "Dve domovini/Two Homelands", 10, 1999, pp. 61-78; Id., *Družba svetega Rafaela do ustanovitve ljubljanske podružnice* [St. Raphael Society until the Establishment of Its Ljubljana Branch], "Dve domovini/Two Homelands

81 Britovšek, *Anton Füster in revolucija 1848 v Avstriji* cit.

82 B. Kolar, *Izvirne poteze delovanja misijonarja Franca Pirca* [Original Features in the Activities of Missionary Franc Pirc] "Dve domovini/Two Homelands", n.18, 2003, pp. 35-52.

83 N. Canny, *Why the reformation failed in Irland*, "Journal of Ecclesiastic History", XX, 1979, pp. 12-25. For obvious reasons I cannot deal here wit, problems of political thought and the fundamental relationship that exists between ancient states and the elaboration of modern political thought. It suffices to think of Machiavelli or the role of politics in Plato, Aristotle or Polybius in the development of political thought.

Bibliography

Adamič F. et al. (eds.), *V spomin Francu Pircu (1785-1880)* [In Memory of Franc Pirc], Ljubljana 1982.

Baraga F., *Abrégé de l'histoire des Indiens de l'Amérique septentrionale*, Paris 1837.

Id., *A Dictionary of the Otchipwe Language Explained in English - For the Use of Missionaries*: Part I (pp. 3-420) Otchipwe-English; Part II (pp. 427-659) English-Otchipwe, Cincinnati 1853.

Id., *A Theoretical and Practical Grammar of the Otchipwe Language – For the use of Missionaries*, Detroit 1850.

Id., *Geschichte, Charakter, Sitten und Gebräuche der nord-amerikanischer Indier*, Laibach 1837.

Id., *Jesus obimadisiwin ajonda aking* [Life of Jesus], Paris 1837 – in Ojibwe language.

Id., *Jesus obimadisiwin ona aking* [Life of Jesus], Paris 1837 – in Ottawa language.

Id., *Kagige debwewinan kaginig Ge-Takwendang Katolik Enamiad* [Ojibwe: Eternal Truths], Cincinnati 1855.

Id., *Katolik Anamie Misinaigan* [Catholic Prayer Book], Detroit 1846 – in Ojibwe language.

Id., *Katolik Anamie Misinaigan* [Catholic Prayer Book], Detroit 1846 – in Ottawa language.

Id., *Katolik Enamiad a nanagatawendamowinan* [Ojibwe: Catholic Christian Thoughts], Detroit 1850.

Id., *Otawa Anamie Misinaigan* [Ottawa Prayer Book], Wawiyatanong 1932.

Id., *Otchipwe Anamie Misinaigan* [Ojibwe Prayer Book], Paris 1837.

Id., *Popis navad in zaderžanja Indijanov Polnočne Amerike* [On the Manners and Customs of the Indians], Ljubljana 1837.

Britovšek M., *Anton Füster in revolucija 1848 v Avstriji*, Maribor 1980.

Čizmić I. - Klemenčič M., *Croatian and Slovene Missionaries as Inventors and Explorers of the American West and Midwest*, "Društvena istraživanja", vol. 11, n. 4-5, 2002, pp. 767-773.

Drnovšek M., *Izseljevanje iz širše ljubljanske okolice 1890-1914* [Emigration from the Broader Vicinity of Ljubljana 1890-1914], Ph.D. Dissertation, Ljubljana 1993.

Id., *O stališčih slovenskih socialistov v ZDA do vojne in jugoslovanskega vprašanja med prvo svetovno vojno* [On the Standpoints of Slovene Socialists in the USA towards the War and the Yugoslav Question during World War I], "Prispevki za. zgodovino delavskega gibanja", vol. 25/26, n. 1/2, 1975/76, pp. 75-96.

Id., *Odmevnost Trunkove knjige Amerika in Amerikanci v letih 1912-1913* [Echoes of Trunk's Book *Amerika in Amerikanci* during the Years 1912-1913], "Zgodovinski časopis", vol. 43, n. 4, 1989, pp. 606-609.

Id., *Pot slovenskih izseljencev na tuje: od Ljubljane do Ellis Islanda – Otoka solza v New Yorku, 1880-1924* [The Road of Slovene Emigrants to the Foreign Lands; From Ljubljana to Ellis Island – Island of Tears in New York City], Ljubljana 1991.

Id., *Usodna privlačnost Amerike: pričevanja izseljencev o prvih stikih z novim svetom* [The Fatal Attraction of America], Ljubljana 1998.

Fister A., *Izbrani spisi. Knjiga III: Govori o religiji* [Selected Writings, Book III: Speeches on Religion], translated by F. Jerman, Ljubljana 1992.

Friš D., *Ameriški Slovenci in Katoliška cerkev: 1871-1924* [American Slovenes and Catholic Church: 1871-1924], Celovec-Ljubljana-Dunaj 1995.

Id., *Korespondenca Kazimirja Zakrajška, O.F.M. (1907-1928)* [Correspondence of Kazimir Zakrajšek, O.F.M. (1907-1928)], Ljubljana 1993.

Id., *Korespondenca Kazimirja Zakrajška, O.F.M. (1928-1958)* [Correspondence of Kazimir Zakrajšek, O.F.M. (1928-1958)], Ljubljana 1995.

Id., *Korespondenca slovenskih katoličanov v ZDA med leti 1882-1924* [Correspondence of Slovene Catholics in the USA 1882-1924], Ljubljana 1999.

Friš D. - Kolar B.- Vovko A., *Prvih sto let Kranjsko slovenske katoliške jednote: pregled zgodovine KSKJ, 1894-1994* [The First One Hundred Years of the Carnolian Slovene Catholic Union 1894-1994], Ljubljana 1997.

Genorio R., *Geographical dimensions of Slovene emigration around the world*, "GeoJournal", vol. 30, n. 3, 1993, pp. 225-229.

Id., *Slovenci v Argentini: geografske razsežnosti priseljevanja in razvoj njihovih naselbin v Buenos Airesu in Cordobi* [Slovenians in Argentina: Geographic Dimensions of Slovene Immigration and Development of their Settlements in Buenos Aires and Cordoba] – Ph.D. Dissertation, Ljubljana 1991.

Id., *Slovenci v Kanadi / Slovenes in Canada* (=Geographica Slovenica, 17), Ljubljana 1989.

Giordano A. - Žitnik J. - Djupedal K. - Beijbom U. - Bender H. - Tolfsby D. - Koivukangas O. - Klemenčič M. - Wurl J. - Lambkin B. - Walaszek A., *Press and emigration*. Roundtable discussion, 1 October 1999, [within] AEMI - The Association of European Migration Institutions Annual Meeting, Portorož, Slovenia, 29 September - 2 October 1999, "Dve domovini/Two Homelands", 10, 1999, pp. 151-167.

Granda S. - Zupančič M. - Rot P. (eds.), *Baraga in Trebnje: predavanja na Baragovem simpoziju v Trebnjem,*

9. januarja 1998 [Baraga and Trebnje: lectures at Baraga Symposium in Trebnje], Trebnje 1998.

Harzig C. (ed.), *Labor migration Project. Labor Newspaper Presevation Project: The Press of Labor Migrants in Europe and North America from 1880's to 1930's*, Bremen 1985.

Jezernik M., *Frederik Baraga. Zbirka rimskih dokumentov*, Ljubljana 1980.

Jurak M. - Mislej I., *Kulturno ustvarjanje Slovencev v Južni Ameriki: zbornik* [Cultural Creativity of Slovenes in South America], Ljubljana 1995.

Klemenčič M., *Ameriški Slovenci in NOB v Jugoslaviji: naseljevanje, zemljepisna razprostranjenost in odnos ameriških Slovencev do stare domovine od sredine 19. stoletja do konca druge svetovne vojne* [American Slovenes and the National Liberation Movement in Yugoslavia: Settlement, geographical dispersion, and the attitude of American Slovenes toward the Old Country from the mid-nineteenth century to World War II], Maribor 1987.

Id. (ed), *Etnični fraternalizem v priseljenskih deželah / Ethnic Fraternalism in Immigrant Countries*, Maribor 1996.

Id., *Frederic Irenej Baraga (1797-1868): Catholic Bishop, Missionary, and Scholar – Slovene*, in Barkan E.R. (ed.), *Making it in America: a sourcebook on eminent ethnic Americans*, Santa Barbara 2001, p. 28.

Id., *Images of America among Slovene and Other Yugoslav Migrants*, in *Distant Magnets: expectations and realities in the immigrant experience, 1840-1930*, New York 1993, pp. 199-221.

Id., *Jurij Trunk med Koroško in Združenimi državami Amerike ter zgodovina slovenskih naslebin v Laevillu, Kolorado, in v San Franciscu, Kalifornija* [Jurij Trunk Between Carinthia and the United States and the History of the Slovene Settlements in Leadville, Colorado, and San Francisco, California], Celovec-Ljubljana-Dunaj 1999.

Id., *Nacionalna struktura mesta Rock Springs in okraja Sweetwater (Wyoming) s posebnim ozirom na Slovence* [Ethnic Structure of the City of Rock Springs and Sweetwater County (WY) with special Emphasis on the Slovenes], in Štrukelj I. (ed.), *Kultura, identiteta in jezik v procesih evropske integracije* [Culture, Identity and language in the Processes of European integration], Ljubljana 2000, pp. 214-233;

Id., *Politično delo Etbina Kristana*, "Migracijske teme", vol. 4, n. 1-2, 1987, pp. 103-109.

Id., *Prihod slovenskih beguncev v ZDA po drugi svetovni vojni* [Slovene refugees coming into the US after World War 2], "Celovški zvon", vol. 13, n. 47, 1995, pp. 71-85.

Id., *Razvoj slovenske izseljenske skupnosti v Rock Springsu, Wyoming, od naselitve do začetka 30-let 20. stoletja* [Development of the Slovene Immigrant Community in Rock Springs, WY, from the First Slovene Settlers until the Beginning of the 1930s], "Dve domovini/Two Homelands", 13, 2001, pp. 73-99.

Id., *Slovenes of Cleveland: The Creation of a New Nation and a New World Community: Slovenia and the Slovenes of Cleveland, Ohio*, Novo mesto 1995.

Id., *Slovenski izseljenski tisk* [Slovene Immigrant Press], "Znanstvena revija: humanistika", vol. 3, n. 2, 1991, pp. 291-558.

Klemenčič M. - Stergar J. - Kristen S. - Munda-Hirnök K. - Trenše-Štolfa M., *Viri o demokratizaciji in osamosvojitvi Slovenije. (Del 4: Slovenci v zamejstvu in po svetu ter mednarodno priznanje Slovenije)* [Sources on Democratization and the Independence Movement of Slovenia. (Part 4: Slovenes in Neighboring Countries and in the World and the International Recognition of Slovenia] (=Viri, 20)], Ljubljana 2005.

Kodrič M., *Etbin Kristan in socialistično gibanje jugoslovanskih izseljencev v ZDA v letih 1914-1920* [Etbin Kristan and the Socialist Movement of Yugoslav Immigrants in the USA during the 1914-1920 period], "Prispevki za zgodovino delavskega gibanja", vol. 23, n. 1/2, 1983, pp. 63-87.

Id., *Franc Pirc in nastanek prvih slovenskih naselbin v Združenih državah Amerike* [Franc Pirc and the establishing of the first Slovene settlements in U.S.A.], "Dve domovini/Two Homelands" 18, 2003, pp. 53-62.

Id., *Nekateri pristopi k problematiki druge generacije v okviru raziskovanja priseljenstva v ZDA* [The Issues of the Second Generation in U.S. Immigration Research], "Dve domovini/Two Homelands", 1, 1990, pp. 161-177

Id., *The press as a link between the leaders and the rank and file of an ethnic fraternal organization: handling the situation of second generation membership in the KSKJ'S organs*, "Dve domovini/Two Homelands", 2/3, 1992, pp. 195-207.

Id., *Zanimanje slovenskih misijonarjev v Severni Ameriki za izseljevanje rojakov, kot se odraža v dopisih v Zgodnji danici* [The Interest of Slovene Missionaries in North America in Slovene Immigration as Seen in Their Letters to Zgodnja Danica], "Dve domovini/Two Homelands", 6, 1995, pp. 9-20.

Id., *Class consciousness among the second generation: expectations and responses within the Slovene National Benefit Society in the 1920s*, "Migracijske teme", vol. 4, n. 1-2, 1988, pp. 111-128.

Kolar B., *Družba svetega Rafaela do ustanovitve ljubljanske podružnice* [St. Raphael Society until the Establishment of Its Ljubljana Branch], "Dve domovini/Two Homelands", 1, 1990, pp. 107-119.

Id., *Izvirne poteze delovanja misijonarja Franca Pirca* [Original Features in the Activities of Missionary Franc Pirc], "Dve domovini/Two Homelands", 2003, n.18, pp. 35-52.

Id., *St. Joseph KSKJ local lodge, Bridgeport, Connecticut*, "Dve domovini/Two Homelands", 10, 1999, pp. 61-78.

Kuzmič M., *Slovenski izseljenci iz Prekmurja v Bethlehemu v ZDA, 1893-1924: naselitev in njihove zgodovinske, socialne, politične, literarne in verske dejavnosti* [Slovene Emigrants from Prekmurje in Bethlehem, PA, in the USA, 1893-1924: Settlement and their Historic, Socio-Political, Literary and Religious Activities], Ljubljana 2001.

Milanič I., *Tematski sklopi v reviji Mladinski list-Juvenile (1922-1944)* [The Themes in the Review *Mladinski list-Juvenile (1922-1944)*] – Ph.D. Dissertation, Ljubljana 2003.

Petrič J., *Avtobiografije slovenskih izseljencev v Združenih državah Amerike* [Autobiographies of Slovene Immigrants to the United States of America] – Ph.D. Disseration, Ljubljana 1987.

Id., *Svetovi Louisa Adamiča: ob tridesetletnici smrti* [The Worlds of Louis Adamic: On the Occasion of the 30th Anniversary of His Death], Ljubljana 1981.

Pirz F., *Die Indianer in Nord-Amerika, ihre Lebensweise, Sitten, Gebräuche u.s.w, nach zehnjährigen Aufenhalte und gesammelten Erfahrungen unter den verschiedenen Stämmen*, St. Louis 1855.

Podbrežnik A., *Kulturni stiki med Slovenijo in Novo Zelandijo (1923-2000)* [Cultural Connections between Slovenia and New Zealand] – Ph.D. Dissertation, Ljubljana 2003.

Potočnik D., *Azija med preteklostjo in sedanjostjo* [Asia between past and present], Maribor 2006.

Požar B., *Friderick Baraga and His Book on the Manners of American Indians*, "Acta Neophilologica", 6, 1973, pp. 29-71.

Stanonik J., *Andrej Bernard Smolnikar*, "Zgodovinski časopis", vol. 49, n. 2, 1995, pp. 183-191.

Id., *Anton Füster - a Slovene forty-eighter*, "Acta Neophilologica", 31, 1998, pp. 81-93.

Id., *Friderik Baraga: ob dvestoletnici rojstva* [Friderick Baraga on the Occasion of 200th Anniversary of his Birth], "Dve domovini/Two Homelands", 7, 1996, pp. 15-32.

Id., *Letters of Marcus Antonius Kappus from Colonial America*. Part I, "Acta Neophilologica", 19, 1986, pp. 33-57; Part II, "Acta Neophilologica", 20, 1987, pp. 25-38; Part III, "Acta Neophilologica", 21, 1988, pp. 3-9; Part IV, "Acta Neophilologica", 22, 1989, pp. 39-50; Part V, "Acta Neophilologica", 23, 1990, pp. 27-37; Part VI, "Acta Neophilologica", 30, 1997, pp. 43-57.

Id., *Longfellow and Smolnikar*, "Acta Neophilologica", 1, 1968, pp. 3-40.

Id., *Očipve in Ottawa* [Ojibwe and Ottawa], "Zgodovinski časopis", vol. 50, n. 1, 1996, pp. 65-69.

Škulj E. (ed.), *Baragov simpozij v Rimu* [Baraga's Symposium in Rome], Celje 2000.

Šmitek Z., *Crusaders, pilgrims, penitents: Slovenian medieval contacts with the Holy Land*, in Moskovich W - Luthar O. - Schwarzband S. (eds.), *Jerusalem in Slavic culture*, (=Jews and Slavs, 6), Ljubljana-Jerusalem 1999, pp. 203-214

Id.., *Egipt - dežela slovenske fascinacije* [Egypt - The Land of Slovene Fascination], "Časopis za kritiko znanosti", vol. 29, n. 204-206, 2001, pp. 30-51.

Id., *Janez Krstnik Mesar - portret tonkinškega misijonarja iz 18. stoletja* [Janez Krstnik Mesar - A Portrait of a Tonking Missionary from the 18th Century], "Dve domovini/Two Homelands", 5, 1994, pp. 7-17.

Id., *Klic daljnih svetov: Slovenci in neevropske kulture* [The Call from Very Far Away; Slovenes and Non-European Culture], Ljubljana 1986.

Id., *Križarji, romarji, spokorniki: naši srednjeveški stiki s Sveto deželo* [Crusaders, Pilgrims, Penitents: Slovenian Medieval Contacts with the Holy Land], "Časopis za zgodovino in narodopisje", vol. 71=36, n. 1-2, 2000, pp. 119-132.

Id., *Po Nilu v osrčje Afrike* [Via Nile Into the Midst of Africa], in Žontar J. - Benedik M. (eds.), *Dokumenti slovenstva* [Documents of Slovene existence], Ljubljana 1994, pp. 239-243.

Id., *Srečevanja z drugačnostjo: slovenska izkustva eksotike* [Meetings with the Other, Slovenes Encounter with the Exotics], Radovljica 1995.

Šusteršič F.S., *Slovenci v Ameriki* [Slovenians in America], "Mohorjev koledar 1894", pp. 15-27.

Trebše-Štolfa M. - Klemenčič M. (eds.), *Slovensko izseljenstvo: zbornik ob 50-letnici Slovenske izseljenske matice*, Ljubljana 2001.

Trunk J., *Amerika* [America], unpublished paper, San Francisco 1948.

Id., *Amerika in Amerikanci* [America and Americans], Celovec 1912.

Id., *Na Jutrovem: Potopisne črtice iz Svete dežele* [At the Orient: Travel Stories from the Holy Land], Celovec 1911.

Id., *Quer durch Amerika. Reisse Skizzen von Georg Trunk* [Across America. Travel Sketches by George Trunk], Klagenfurt 1915.

Vovko A., *Pomembnejši slovenski biografski prispevki o misijonarju in izseljenskem duhovniku Francu Pircu* [Important Slovene Contributions to the Biography of Missionary and Emigrant Priest Franc Pirc], "Dve domovini/Two Homelands", 18, 2003, pp. 8-24.

Id., *The foundation of the Yugoslav Emergency Council in New York*, "Slovene Studies", vol. 10, n. 2, 1988, pp. 191-197.

Id., *The myth of America and the society of St. Raphael*, "Slovene Studies", vol. 13, n. 1, 1991, pp. 107-110.

Id., *Udje družbe sv. Mohorja v ZDA do leta 1900* [The U.S. Members of St. Hermagoras Society until 1900], "Dve domovini/Two Homelands", 1, 1990, pp. 121-135.

Žigon Z., *Izzivi drugačnosti: Slovenci v Afriki in na Arabskem polotoku* [Slovenes in Africa and in Arab Peninsula], Ljubljana 2003.

Id., *Otroci dveh domovin: slovenstvo v Južni Ameriki* [The Children of Two Homelands; Slovenes in South America], Ljubljana 1998.

Žitnik J., *Globalization and the prospects of multicultural coexistence and world peace*, "Journal of National Development", vol. 16, n. 1/2 2003, pp. 49-66.

Id., *Louis Adamič in sodobniki: 1948-1951* [Louis Adamic and Contemporaries: 1948-1951], Ljubljana 1992.

Id., *Orel in korenine med 'brušenjem' in cenzuro* [The Eagle and The Roots between Grinding and Censorship], Ljubljana 1995.

Id., *Pero in politika: zadnja leta Louisa Adamiča* [The Pen and Politics: Adamic's Last Years of Life], Ljubljana 1993.

Id., *The return of Slovene emigrant literature*, "AEMI journal", 1, 2003, pp. 106-111.

Žitnik J. - Glišič H. (eds.), *Slovenska izseljenska književnost* [Slovene Immigrant Literature], 3 vols., Ljubljana 1999.

SOURCE

Kadar govorimo o Ameriki in Amerikancih razumemo pod tem imenom skupino držav, ki nosijo ime "Zedinjene amerikanske države" – United states of America, in njih prebivalce. Skoraj tri stoletja se že izseljujejo iz Evrope v te neizmerne pokrajine. V zadnjem času je postal naval podoben pravemu preseljevanju narodov, ki so se mu pridružile tudi neštevilne čete Slovanov. Med temi četami je tudi Slovencev prav znatno število. Različni narodi so se sčasoma spojili v novo ljudstvo, ki je na novih tleh, pod ugodnim podnebjem, s čudovito duševno močjo ustvarilo novo omiko, na katero gleda ves svet z opravičenim občudovanjem. Tudi Slovenci so se udeleževali in se udeležujejo tega titanskega dela in zato je obilo vzrokov, da pogledamo tja, kjer stoji veliko naših bratov v vrstah delavcev za novo omiko.

When we talk about America and Americans we understand under this name a group of states bearing the name United States of America and their people.
For almost three centuries peoples from Europe immigrate to this vast land. In recent period this immigration became similar to real movement of peoples. Also many Slavic peoples are included. Among them there are quite a few Slovenes. Different nations participated in creation of one new nation, which under good environmental conditions with marvelous spiritual strength created a new state which created a new culture in broader sense and became an object of admiration of the world. Slovenes also participated and are still participating in this titanic work and therefore there are many reasons for our research on this phenomenon.

From: Trunk Jurij, *Amerika in Amerikanci* [America and Americans], Celovec [Klagenfurt], 1912, pp. 3-4.

On the History of West-European Merchants' Activity in Russia in the 18th Century

Victor N. Zakharov
State Regional University of Moscow

Деятельность западноевропейских купцов в России в XVIII в. представляет часть экспансии европейского торгового капитала во внешнем мире в эпоху новой истории. Россия, несомненно, европейская страна, может рассматриваться в данном контексте как часть внешнего мира по отношению к основным центрам деловой жизни и предпринимательства Западной Европы. В связи с этим история деятельности западноевропейских купцов в России может рассматриваться в рамках актуальной научной проблемы «Европа и мир».

В связи с этим изучение деятельности западноевропейских купцов на русском рынке в XVIII в. представляет особый интерес. Этот интерес возник уже в XVIII в., когда появились первые книги по истории российской торговли, где содержалась информация и о деятельности в России иностранных купцов.

С тех пор и до наших дней историю изучения деятельности западноевропейских купцов в России можно разделить на несколько периодов: период эмпирической историографии (до середины 19 в.), период национально-ориентированной историографии (вторая половина 19 – первая треть 20 в.), период идеологически-детерминированной историографии (середина 20 в.), период объективного изучения коммерческой деятельности (последняя треть 20 в.). Это в равной мере касается как российской историографии, так и зарубежной историографии. Можно говорить даже об определенной конвергенции в исследовании данной темы в российской и западной историографии, которая имела место уже во второй половине XX в.

В настоящее время уже в достаточной степени изучены особенности торговой деятельности иностранных купцов в России в XVIII в., выявлена их роль в экономической жизни страны, исследованы родственные связи. (См. работы Э.Амбургера, Д.Прайса, Э.Кросса, Я.В.Велувенкампа, В.А.Ковригиной, Н.Н.Репина, А.В.Демкина, В.Н.Захарова и др.). На данном этапе представляется актуальным проведение интегративных и компаративных исследований жизни и деятельности иноземцев в различных странах Европы, изучение проблем миграции, ассимиляции, идентичности, толерантности.

The activity of Western European merchants in Russia in the 18th century presents one of the aspects of European trading capital's expansion in the rest of the world in Modern period. Although Russia is undoubtedly a European country, it can be regarded in this context as a part of the rest of the world, considering its relation to the major centres of business undertakings that historically emerged in the most developed regions of Western, South-Western and Central Europe. In this sense the penetration of Western European merchants into the outlying markets of the continent, including Russia, is a part of their struggle to create and dominate the world market. In this connection, the history of the activity of Western European merchants in Russia can be regarded as lying within the framework of our present scientific problem "Europe and the world".

In the beginning of the 18th century Russia entered the epoch of modern history. The processes of modernization accelerated. Contacts with Western European countries increased rapidly and their influence spread. At the same time the activity of Western European trading companies in all regions of the world was lively. Western Europe became to a greater extent a consumer of raw materials and semi-finished products delivered from peripheral markets. Under these circumstances Russia became more and more involved in the system of world transcontinental contacts and the world division of labour. Western European merchants played a decisive role in the development of Russia. In this connection the study of their activity in the Russian market of the 18th century presents a special interest.

This interest was already manifest in the 18th century. It was at that time that the first books on history of the Russian trade as a whole appeared. Besides they contained information about contacts with Western European countries and the participation of foreign merchants in them. A multi-volume *Historical description of Russian commerce,* written by M.D. Chulkov, presents a vast, systematized collection of ukases and other governmental instructions on trade issues, various combined registers, materials of cases examined in the Senate, Commerce College, Commission on Commerce and other institutions[1]. But all this factual material was left without any comments as the author had determined only to collect a vast wealth of data on the history of trade. V.V. Krestinin, the first historian of Arkhangelsk, could not help but touch upon the activity of foreign merchants in the North. In his works he gave a list of foreigner traders who were staying in Arkhangelsk during Peter I's first visit there in 1693[2].

Some substantial works devoted to the Russian economy appeared at the end of the 18th and the beginning of the 19th centuries. Most of them were written by scholars of German origin who worked in Russia. Thus, H. Storch compiled a multi-volume description of Russia of the end of the 18th century. Five of eight volumes of this work were devoted to trade[3]. The statistics on foreign trade circulation in Russia during the 1740s-1790s collected by Storch are still used by historians. In the description of St. Petersburg he brings to light the activity of foreign merchants in the Russian capital and makes interesting observations on commission trading, which many of them conducted following the instructions of foreign firms, and on the use of credit[4]. Similar statistics and references on Russian trade at the end of the 18th century are collected in the works of Johann Gottlieb Georgi and Willhelm Christian Friebe[5].

Among the English authors William Tooke should be mentioned. He wrote a three-volume description of Russia during the reign of Catherine II supplying detailed information on foreign trade and commodity circulation of all the merchants trading in St. Petersburg during 1797-1799[6]. The fact that the author was very well informed seems easy to explain: he was the chaplain of an English trading station in St. Petersburg from 1774 onwards[7].

Some years later there appeared the first work on the history of the bilateral contacts between Russia and another European country, namely the Netherlands. It was a four-volume research work by a Dutch historian, Jacob Scheltema[8]. The appearance of the book at that time is quite explicable. After the victory over Napoleon, Russia's influence in Europe increased. The kingdom of the Netherlands was created due to the participation of Russian diplomacy. The sister of the tzar Alexander I, Anna Pavlovna, married a Dutch prince. Jacob Scheltema pays a great deal of attention to the reign of Peter I, as it was the period when Russian-Dutch relations were at their zenith. At the same time the author supplies a lot of data on the activity in Russia of Dutch merchants, who cooperated closely with the government and the treasury.

On the whole historians and economists of the 18th and the beginning of the 19th centuries provided systematized materials on foreign trade legislation, statistics on foreign trade circulation and on the scale of activity of single merchants and foreign merchants' staff in St. Petersburg and Arkhangelsk. The authors of the works mentioned mainly stressed the positive value of trade for the development of the Russian economy without making any concrete assessments of the activity of foreign traders. Hence the historiography of this period concerning foreign trade and foreigners' activity can be called empirical.

A new stage in the study of history of 18th century foreign trade begins at the end of the 19th century. It was determined by the formation of new scientific schools aiming at studying economic and social phenomena, daily life and routine. Along with this the researchers tried to investigate the interconnection between governmental and social institutions, and to consider the moods and demands of different social strata. All this awoke interest in the activity of native merchants and the role of foreign ones as well. This interest was heated by the debates which took place at the end of the 19th and at the beginning of the 20th century over the question of whether it was harmful or useful to attract foreign capital to the country. In connection with this debate, we may speak about a growing influence of the national factor in Russian historical science.

N.N. Firsov in his book on industrial policy of Catherine the Great noticed that in the Russian market foreigners acted together in order to coordinate prices of export and import goods to their mutual benefit, whereas Russian merchants competed with each other separately to the detriment of their common interests; moreover they lacked the necessary training. Overseas trade was completely dominated by foreigners, most of whom were English[9].

S.F. Ogorodnikov in a volume devoted to the history of Arkhangelsk gives approximately the same assessment as Firsov with regard to the activities of foreign and Russian merchants. Speaking about governmental policy towards foreign merchants, Ogorodnikov stresses the fact that the decisive role in moulding it was played by fiscal interests. Foreigners were given vast monopoly privileges at the expense of the interests of Russian merchants. S.F. Ogorodnikov makes an extremely negative assessment of the activity of the English merchant William Gomm, who obtained a right to harvest timber on the Onega river and as a result ruined vast regions in the North of Russia[10]. Because of the competition with each other Russian merchants could not resist against the foreigners who collaborated with each other; the Russian merchants either became entirely dependent on the foreigners or simply went bankrupt. Thus at that time the assessment of foreign merchants as strong and dangerous competitors for Russians was dominant.

P.A. Ostroukhov studied the policy of the Russian government on foreign tradesmen. As a student, under the supervision of P.B. Strouve, he was the first to investigate the Russian-English trade treaty of 1734 by using archival materials to illuminate the circumstances of its conclusion. But he was far from focussing on disadvantages of this treaty for Russian merchants[11]. This fact shows that the negative attitude towards foreigners had become less strong.

At the end of the 19th and the beginning of the 20th centuries in many other European countries the interest for the national past was also particularly lively. British, French and German historiographies witnessed active research on the countries' recent history in the fields of foreign trade, exploration of European and world markets, and the development of colonial trade in the Early Modern period. Some works by western researchers covered the activity of their compatriots in Russia. It was important for the authors of the time to study the historical experience of entrepreneurs of their countries in exploring new markets, and they evaluated the successes and the advantages and miscalculations in their own governments' policies in this field.

In this respect the historiography of the Netherlands occupies a special place. The Netherlands was a country that no longer belonged to the leading European powers, but the memory of the "Golden Age" of Dutch history (from the end of the 16th up to the beginning of the 18th centuries), when Dutch merchants dominated in many regions of the world market, acquired a special significance. Using navigation sources from the archives of Dutch merchants' guilds that had contacts with Russia in the 18th century, Simon van Brakel initiated the study of the foreign trade contacts of Russia with Western European countries[12].

German historiography also showed a considerable interest in Russia. Gustaw Schmoller published a long article on a Prussian company which delivered cloth to Russia in 1720-30s, and pointed out that it had been a tough competitor with Englishmen[13]. Ernst Baasch, who wrote a series of classical works on the commercial history of the city of Hamburg, also paid particular attention to the contacts of the "Elbemetropolie" with

Russia. He published addresses to the Senate of Hamburg from the local Society of Merchants who traded with Arkhangelsk[14].

The theme of Russia and Britain was investigated in a book by the German author Dieter Gerhard. He tried to prove that England played a great role in the process that led to Russia's becoming a European power in the middle and especially in the second half of the 18th century[15]. He noted the great significance of English-Russian trade ties and was among the first to explore the activity of British merchants in the Russian market. On the whole, this historian is quite positive in his assessment of English merchants' activity for the advancement of the Russian economy as, in his view, it promoted a constant flow of foreign capital to the country. The latter stimulated the growth of Russian trade to such a degree that by the end of the 18th century Russian merchants were able to get rid of the foreigners' supremacy[16].

In the case of historians of Great Britain and the United States of America, Russia became the focus of their attention a bit later. It was only in the 1930s that the first considerable work on Russian-English trade ties written in English was published. This was a book by Douglas Reading on the trade treaty of 1734[17]. Reading, like Gerhard, saw a mutual interest of Russia and England in developing trade contacts with one another. Reading, however, considered more carefully the conditions favouring the activity of the leading English merchants in Russia in 1730s, and highlighted their close ties with state monopolies. He also ascertained that by that time Englishmen had already ousted the Germans and the Dutch from the intermediary trade between Russia and South European countries.

Thus, at the end of the 19th and in the first quarter of the 20th centuries the activity of foreign merchants in Russia and the development of the world market as a whole was mainly researched within the framework of national schools of historiography. Historians, first of all, paid attention to the study of the interests of businessmen of the different countries and to the Russian government's policies.

In the middle of the 20th century the study of the ties between Russia and Western European countries was under the influence of ideological conceptions and politics. Thus, the Marxist concept became rooted in Soviet science in 1930s. Historians regarded the state policy on foreigners in the 18th century from the point of view of its relation to the interests of the ruling class and the nobility. The thesis of 'semi-colonial' dependence of Russia on western capital suggested by one of the first Marxist historians, M.N. Pokrovsky, at the beginning of the 20th century, preserved its significance in the 1930s.

In post-World War I years a negative attitude towards the role of foreigners in Russia increased against the background of the so-called 'struggle with cosmopolitanism'. In connection with this, there was either no mention of foreign merchants in Russia or an extremely negative assessment of the effects of their activities on the Russian economy. V.N. Yakovtsevsky wrote a significant work on the history of merchant capital in Russia[18]. He was one of the few who dedicated sufficient space (a whole chapter) to the activities of foreign merchants. The author noted the dominance of foreigners in Russian trade and accused Russian autocracy of making a policy in favour of the nobility who were interested in competition between native and foreign merchants in the Russian market. The book also mentions huge profits of foreign merchants (though without any substantial investigation in this respect) and states that many of them were adventurers and embezzlers of public funds. A book by L.A. Nikiforov devoted to Russian-English relations was published in the first post-war year. The author brought to light some historical problems of trade between both countries at the beginning of the 18th century judging English policy towards Russia to be hostile[19].

The 1930s also witnessed a decline of interest towards the study of Russian-Western European trade contacts in foreign historiography. The research that all the same touched upon this theme expressed a rather negative attitude towards the conditions under which foreign traders had to work in Russia. Thus, according to Walter Kirchner, in the 17th and 18th centuries foreign merchants in Russia dealt, first of all, with the state and monopolies connected with it. There were no banking institutions in the country and crediting was not reliable. It was very risky to deal with Russian merchants, as they knew a lot about trade and nothing about commerce. As a result, the profit of Russian tradesmen remained low. That is why few ordinary businessmen took the plunge to go to Russia. In the author's opinion one had to be at least an adventurer to do it[20]. Undoubtedly, Walter Kirchner is right in outlining many of the difficulties that foreign tradesmen faced in Russia, but he obviously exaggerated them as well as underestimating the level of development of independent business activity of Russian merchants.

During the war years, however, in US historiography one can observe the revival of an interest towards the history of trade between Russia and Western European countries[21], but with the beginning of the so-called "cold war" it ceased to exist.

In the 1940-1950s, in the difficult political conditions of World War II and the first post-war years, a certain sketchiness and narrow mindedness characterized the attempts of historiography at evaluating the activity of foreign tradesmen in Russia. Nevertheless, the existing methodological conceptions contained important prerequisites for an objective study of the problem when the ideological and political dictatorship was attenuated. Thus, a very important thesis of historical materialism concerned the predominant significance of socio-economic development and it led researchers to use mass data on the history of trade. In the mid-20th century Soviet researchers began to investigate archives widely and procure evidence on 17th- and 18th-century trade from customs records and from other documentary sources and they introduced the new methodologies and data into academia. On this basis, trade ties between different regions of the country were studied as were foreign trade contacts and foreign tradesmen.

A similar process can be observed in the West. While studying the Early Modern period much attention is paid to world trade, and a great deal of data on circulation of goods, on the changes in economic and social life resulting from foreign trade activity of the western countries was discovered and utilised. Significant results were obtained thanks to the methodological principles which had been developed since the 1920s by the school of the "Annales".

Fernand Braudel's three-volume work on the history of "material civilization" in the Early Modern period was of fundamental significance[22]. The author researched thoroughly the role of trade and Western European capital in the development of the world community, showing the formation and development of different forms of commerce (trade companies, commercial banks, circulation of bills of exchange, etc.). Many of the ideas suggested by Braudel were used and developed by historians specializing in studies on foreign trade. As far as the activity of foreign merchants in the Russian market in the 18th century is concerned, Braudel's conclusions – that in this period Russia experienced "a European intrusion" – are very important. Europe tried to conquer and arrange the Russian market for its own profit. Although Braudel pointed out the difficulty and dialectical character of this process, the Russian economy was not devoured by Western European capital but, on the contrary, it was able to defend its home market.

Thus, in spite of the differences in methodology and ideology, similar processes took place in the USSR as well as in the West. Scholars began to pay a great deal of attention to the investigation of a large number of materials on social and economic history. The weakening of the rigid ideological and political dictates over historiography at the end of the 1950s also contributed to the success of the process. All this stimulated a more objective investigation of the activity of foreign traders in Russia.

In this period there also appeared books and articles devoted to the activity of foreign traders in Russia in particular. The appearance of such works was primarily determined by the abundance of existing information on the foreign trade contacts of Russia with the western market. Secondly, Russian and foreign historiography of recent decades witnessed an obvious interest in the history of enterprise, i.e. the activity of single firms, companies and factors of commercial success. Thirdly, historians became more interested in personality and personalities as subjects of historical process. This especially is a characteristic of the Soviet historiography of the end of the 20th century which to a greater or less extent began to overcome the notorious sketchiness or abstraction of historical materialism with its inattention to the personal factor. Fourthly, in the Soviet science the nihilistic attitude to the study of the role of foreigners was eliminated and the interest in this theme increased abroad, particularly in the 1980s and 1990s.

Only with the 1970s, not earlier, after a long-term period of oblivion in Soviet science, did the necessity of an objective study of the activity of foreigners appear. V.A. Kovrigina was one of the first to address this theme. Her recently published book was a result of a long-standing research project and investigation of vast archival material about foreigners in Moscow in the second half of the 17th and at the beginning of the 18th centuries[23]. In this book she gives an objective assessment of the activity of merchants, their business and family relations, and their social status.

In the 1970s specialists studying the history of trade and economy of the country as a whole also posed questions connected with the professional activity of foreigners. First they addressed the problems, already familiar to scholars, connected with the activity of foreign traders (their hegemony in foreign trade, their relationships with the government and the treasury), but they treated them anew, on the basis of an analysis of extensive material. N.L. Rubinshtein doubted the thesis that foreigners had a hegemonic position in Russian foreign trade[24]. He showed that during the 18th century Russian merchants were able to achieve complete control over the transportation of goods to the ports. Besides, by the end of the century Russian citizens superseded foreigners in the scale of the circulation of goods in St. Petersburg and Arkhangelsk. However, other researchers did not accept this thesis as the transportation of goods to the ports is not a foreign trade proper, the main contents of which is delivery of goods from one country to another.

At the beginning of the 1970s B.N. Mironov objected to N.L. Rubinstein's views[25]. He noted that among the Russian citizens who were trading in the ports there were many merchants who were of foreign origin. The fact that foreigners had acquired Russian citizenship did not increase the share in foreign trade of Russian merchants proper. In the 1970s and 1980s, N.N. Repin gave grounds to the important view that by the beginning of the 18th century Russian merchants had already ousted foreigners completely from the home market and initiated their independent activity in foreign trade[26].

In the middle of the 18th century the field was investigated by A.V. Demkin. He is the author of a series of works on foreign merchants in Russia in the 17th century as well as on British traders in the 18th century[27]. Demkin's undoubted merit is that he introduced a vast complex of archival sources. Basing his work on this material, Demkin determined the range of goods exported and imported by merchants from different countries (in the 18th century mainly British), their business contacts with the treasury, and their activities in the industrial sphere. Demkin's view that governmental policy towards foreigners was benevolent seems well grounded. However, in some works Demkin's an 'illustrative' method prevails: most of the materials are supplied as mere examples rather than as the basis for quantitative studies.

The author of the present chapter also contributed several publications to the study of foreigners' trade in Russia and their credit operations[28].

Among foreign sources, the first investigation especially devoted to the activity of foreigners in the Russian market is a work of an American author, Jacob Price. It is about an English tobacco company that transported tobacco from Virginia at the beginning of the 18th century[29]. The author supplies statistics on the activity of the company and draws an objective conclusion about the reasons for its failure. He showed that many of the shareholders of the company did not use it to sell tobacco but rather to have an opportunity to buy valuable raw materials in Russia on preferential terms.

British literature on Russia published in recent decades would be incomplete without Anthony Cross' works. He produced some books on the history of Russian-English contacts in the 18th century and Englishmen in St. Petersburg in which he paid much attention to merchants in particular. Without expanding on their commercial activity he gave a detailed coverage of the organization of the activity of the English "Russian company", showing the role which its agents and consuls, who were the most significant British businessmen, played in the capital of Russia[30].

Erik Amburger occupies the first place among German researchers who studied the life and the activity of foreigners in Russia. Born in St. Petersburg, he was a descendant of German merchants who came to Russia at the end of the 18th century. Amburger collected and organised much biographical data on foreigners in Russia in the 17th and at the beginning of the 20th centuries concerning not only Germans but also Dutch, English, Swiss and many others as well. The author used traditional family history sources: church books with registrations of baptism, wedding and burial services. Among his numerous books and articles there are works devoted to lives of single merchant families in Russia such as Van Brienen, Brandt, Marselis, Amburger[31]. He tried to demonstrate the contribution of foreigners to the economic and cultural development of Russia. In reference to merchants he was not very successful, as he practically did not use the massive source material on the history of trade, credit, etc. Amburger left a vast archive with a card index for thousands of persons of foreign origin who lived in Russia before 1917. Now the archive and card index are kept in the Institute of Eastern Europe in Munich.

Among Dutch authors, Jan Willem Veluwenkamp made a great contribution to the study of contacts with Russia. His in practice was the first work on the life and activity of Dutch merchants in Russia at the end of the 16th and in the mid-18th century[32]. The author focussed on their trade, family ties, and structure of colonies (or "faktoria") in other countries (including Russia). He also explored the contacts of personnel in firms located in Amsterdam with their compatriots, relatives and partners in Russia. Moreover he brought to light the causes of their success and failures, which depended on the state of local and European markets.

As far as merchants from other countries are concerned, their activity has not been the object of particular study yet. Although there were numerous French merchants in Russia in the 18th century, there is only a small article written about them. This article written by an American author, Samuel Baron, and it treats Lavie's company which was active in Russia during the reign of Peter I[33]. In some works by Swiss authors devoted to their compatriots in pre-revolutionary Russia nothing is said about merchants of the 18th century[34]. There are also no special works on Scandinavian merchants in Russia.

Thus, the history of study of the activity of foreign tradesmen in Russia dates back to the 18th century, beginning with the stage of the so-called "empirical" historiography. Then it developed under the influence of nationally-oriented concepts (the end of the 19th and beginning of the 20th centuries). In the mid- 20th century it was under the influence of ideological methodology and politics. In the second half of the 20th century when those extremes were attenuated, the activity of foreigners in Russia began to receive rather objective assessments, with a large number of historical documents being widely used. These processes took place both in Russian (Soviet) historical science and abroad. So one may speak about a certain 'convergence' of historical research in the USSR (Russia) and the West. In the last decades of the 20th century in Russia, Germany, Great Britain and the Netherlands substantial investigations were made on Western European merchants in Russia in the 18th century. Most of them were devoted primarily to the trade activity of foreigners and their role in the development of Russian economy.

At present the issues of hegemony of foreigners in Russian foreign trade, conditions, directions and forms of their business activity and the policy of Russian authorities may be considered to be substantially clarified. The family ties of foreign traders and merchants have also been studied, more or less thoroughly, and biographical data of many of them have been collected.

Nowadays there seems that we have the task and the opportunity of creating large integrated research projects on the basis of existing works. These might be aimed at a comparative and generalizing study of the status of Western European businessmen in different countries, in various economic and cultural environments. Such research may raise the problems of identity preservation, assimilation, tolerance and gender studies.

Notes

1 M.D. *Chulkov, Istoricheskoe opisanie rossiyskoj kommercii pri vsekh portakh i granitsakh ot drevnikh vremen do nyne nastoyashchego...*, vols. 1-7, Saint Petersburg 1781-1787.

2 V.V. Krestinin, *Kratkaya istoriya o gorode Arkhangelskom*, Saint Petersburg 1792; Id., *Istoricheskiy opyt o vneshney torgovle Gosudarya imperatora Petra Velikogo, ot 1693 po 1795 god*, in *Mesyaceslov istoricheskiy i geograficheskiy na 1795 god*, Saint Petersburg 1795.

3 H. Storch, *Istorisch-Statistisches Gemälde des Russischen Reichs am Ende des achtzehnden Jahrhunderts*, vols. 1-8, Riga-Leipzig 1797-1803.

4 Id., *Gemälde von St. Petersburg*, vols. 1-2, Riga 1793-1794.

5 I.G. Georgi, *Opisanie rossiysko-imperatorskogo stolichnogo goroda S.-Peterburga*, Saint Petersburg 1996 (Reprint); W.Ch. Friebe, *Über Russlands Handel, landwirtschaftliche Kultur, Industrie und Producte*, vols. 1-2, Gotha-Saint Petersburg 1796-1797.

6 W. Tooke, *View of the Russian Empire during the Reign of Catherine the Second and the Close of the Present Century*, vols. 1-3, London 1799.

7 A.G. Cross, *British Residents and Visitors in Russia during the Reign of Catherine the Great: Tapped and Untapped Sources from British Archives*, in J.M. Hartley (ed.), *The Study of Russian History from British Archival Sources*, London-New York 1986, p. 90.

8 J. Scheltema, *Rusland en de Nederlanden beschouwd in derzelver wederkeerige betrekkingen*, vols. 1-4, Amsterdam 1817-1819.

9 N.N. Firsov, *Pravitelstvo i obshchestvo v ikh otnosheniyakh k vneshney torgovle Rossii v tsarstvovanie imperatritsy Ekateriny II*, Kazan 1902.

10 S.F. Ogorodnikov, *Ocherk istoriiu goroda Arkhangelska v torgovo-promyshlennom otnoshenii*, Saint Petersburg 1890.

11 P.A. Ostroukhov, *Anglo-russky torgovy dogovor 1734 g.*, Saint Petersburg 1914.

12 S. van Brakel, *Statistische en andere gegevens betreffende onzen handel en scheepvaart op Rusland gedurende de 18de eeuw*, "Bijdragen en mededelingen betreffende de geschiedenis der Nederlanden", 34, 1913, pp. 350-404.

13 G. Schmoller, *Die russische Kompagnie in Berlin. 1724-1738,* "Zeitschrift für preussische Geschichte und Landeskunde", 20, 1883.

14 E. Baasch, *Quellen zur Geschichte von Hamburgs Handel und Schiffahrt im 17.18. und 19. Jahrhundert*, Hamburg 1910, pp. 323-406.

15 D. Gerhard, *England und der Aufstieg Russlands*, Munich-Berlin 1933.

16 *Ibid.*, p. 75.

17 D. Reading, *The Anglo-Russian Commercial Treaty of 1734*, New Haven 1938.

18 V.N. Yakovtsevsky, *Kupechesky kapital v feodalno-krepostnicheskoy Rossii*, Moscow 1953.

19 L.A. Nikiforov, *Russko-angliyskie otnosheniya pri Petre I*, Moscow 1953.

20 W. Kirchner, *Commercial Relations between Russia and Europe 1400 to 1800*, Bloomington 1966, pp. 243-245.

21 I.D. Phillips, *Salem opens American Trade with Russia,* "The New England Quarterly", 4, 1941; O. Frederiksen, *Virginia Tobacco in Russia under Peter the Great,* "Slavonic and East European Review", 21, 1943.

22 F. Braudel, *Civilisation matérielle, économie et capitalisme, XVe-XVIIIe siècle*, vols. 1-3, Paris 1979.

23 V.A. Kovrigina, *Nemetskaya sloboda Moskvy i ee zhiteli v kontse XVII – pervoy chetverti XVIII vv.*, Moscow 1998.

24 N.L. Rubinstein, *Vneshnyaya torgovlya Rossii i russkoe kupechestvo vo vtoroy polovine XVIII v.*, "Istoricheskie zapiski, 54, 1955, pp. 343-361.

25 B.N. Mironov, *K voprosu o roli russkogo kupechestva vo vneshney torgovle Peterburga i Arkhangelska vo vtoroy polovine XVIII – nachale XIX v.*, "Istoriya SSSR", 6, 1973, pp. 129-140.

26 N.N. Repin, *Russkie i zapadnoevropeyskie kuptsy v Rossii XVII-XVIII vv. (K voprosu o periodizatsii borby za rynok)*, in *Torgovlya, promyshlennost i gorod v Rossii XVII – nachala XIX v.*, Moscow 1987, pp. 51-67.

27 A.V. Demkin, *Zapadnoevropeyskoe kupechestvo v Rossii v XVII v.*, vols. 1-2, Moscow 1994; Id., *Britanskoe kupechestvo v Rossii XVIII veka*, Moscow 1998.

28 V.N. Zakharov, *Zapadnoevropeyskie kuptsy v Rossii: Epokha Petra I*, Moscow 1996; Id., *Zapadnoevropeyskie kuptsy v rossiyskoy torgovle XVIII veka*, Moscow 2005.

29 J. Price - N. Zakharov, *Zapadnoevropeyskie kuptsy v Rossii: Epokha Petra I*, Moscow 1996; Id., *Zapadnoevropeyskie kuptsy v rossiyskoy torgovle XVIII veka*, Moscow 2005.

30 A.G. Cross, *By the Banks of the Neva*, Cambridge 1997; Id., *The Sutherland Affair and its Aftermath,* "The Slavonic and East European Review", 50, 1972, pp. 257-275.

31 See the bibliography of works by E. Amburger (before 1982): E. Amburger, *Fremde und einheimische im Wirtshafts- und Kulturleben des neuzeitlichen Russlands. Ausgewählte Aufsätze*, Wiesbaden 1982.

32 J.W. Veluwenkamp, *Archangel. Nederlandse ondernemers in Rusland. 1550-1785*, [s.l.] 2000.

33 S.H. Baron, *Henry Lavie and the Failed Campaign to Expand Franco-Russian Commercial Relations (1712-1723)*, "Forschungen zur osteuropäischen Geschichte", 38, Berlin 1995, pp. 29-50.

34 U. Rauber, *Schweizer Industrie in Rußland*, Zürich 1985.

Bibliography

Amburger E., *Fremde und einheimische im Wirtshafts- und Kulturleben des neuzeitlichen Russlands. Ausgewählte Aufsätze*, Wiesbaden 1982.

Baasch E., *Quellen zur Geschichte von Hamburgs Handel und Schiffahrt im 17. 18. und 19. Jahrhundert*, Hamburg 1910, pp. 323-406.

Baron S.H., *Henry Lavie and the Failed Campaign to Expand Franco-Russian Commercial Relations (1712-1723)*, "Forschungen zur osteuropäischen Geschichte", 38, Berlin 1995, pp. 29-50.

Brakel S. van, *Statistische en andere gegevens betreffende onzen handel en scheepvaart op Rusland gedurende de 18de eeuw*, "Bijdragen en mededelingen betreffende de geschiedenis der Nederlanden", 34, 1913, pp. 350-404.

Braudel F., *Civilisation matérielle, économie et capitalisme, XVe-XVIIIe siècle*, vols. 1-3, Paris 1979.

Chulkov M.D., *Istoricheskoe opisanie rossiyskoj kommercii pri vsekh portakh i granitsakh ot drevnikh vremen do nyne nastoyashchego...*, vols. 1-7, Saint Petersburg 1781-1787.

Cross A.G., *British Residents and Visitors in Russia during the Reign of Catherine the Great: Tapped and Untapped Sources from British Archives*, in Hartley J.M. (ed.), *The Study of Russian History from British Archival Sources*, London-New York 1986, p. 90.

Hartley J.M., *By the Banks of the Neva*, Cambridge 1997.

Id., *The Sutherland Affair and its Aftermath*, "The Slavonic and East European Review", 50, 1972.

Demkin A.V., *Zapadnoevropeyskoe kupechestvo v Rossii v XVII v.*, vols. 1-2, Moscow 1994.

Id., *Britanskoe kupechestvo v Rossii XVIII veka*, Moscow 1998.

Firsov N.N., *Pravitelstvo i obshchestvo v ikh otnosheniyakh k vneshney torgovle Rossii v tsarstvovanie imperatritsy Ekateriny II*, Kazan 1902.

Frederiksen O., *Virginia Tobacco in Russia under Peter the Great*, "Slavonic and East European Review", 21, 1943.

Friebe W.Ch., *Über Russlands Handel, landwirtschaftliche Kultur, Industrie und Producte*, vols. 1-2, Gotha-Saint Petersburg 1796-1797.

Georgi I.G., *Opisanie rossiysko-imperatorskogo stolichnogo goroda S.-Peterburga*, Saint Petersburg 1996 (Reprint).

Gerhard D., *England und der Aufstieg Russlands*, Munich-Berlin 1933.

Kirchner W., *Commercial Relations between Russia and Europe 1400 to 1800*, Bloomington 1966, pp. 243-245.

Kovrigina V.A., *Nemetskaya sloboda Moskvy i ee zhiteli v kontse XVII – pervoy chetverti XVIII vv.*, Moscow 1998.

Krestinin V.V., *Kratkaya istoriya o gorode Arkhangelskom*, Saint Petersburg 1792.

Id.., *Istoricheskiy opyt o vneshney torgovle Gosudarya imperatora Petra Velikogo, ot 1693 po 1795 god*, in *Mesyaceslov istoricheskiy i geograficheskiy na 1795 god*, Saint Petersburg 1795.

Mironov B.N., *K voprosu o roli russkogo kupechestva vo vneshney torgovle Peterburga i Arkhangelska vo vtoroy polovine XVIII – nachale XIX v.*, "Istoriya SSSR", 6, 1973, pp. 129-140.

Nikiforov L.A., *Russko-angliyskie otnosheniya pri Petre I*, Moscow 1953.

Ogorodnikov S.F., *Ocherk istoriiu goroda Arkhangelska v torgovo-promyshlennom otnoshenii*, Saint Petersburg 1890.

Ostroukhov P.A., *Anglo-russky torgovy dogovor 1734 g.*, Saint Petersburg 1914.

Phillips I.D., *Salem opens American Trade with Russia*, "The New England Quarterly", 4, 1941.

Rauber U., *Schweizer Industrie in Rußland*, Zürich 1985.

Reading D., *The Anglo-Russian Commercial Treaty of 1734*, New Haven 1938.

Repin N.N., *Russkie i zapadnoevropeyskie kuptsy v Rossii XVII-XVIII vv. (K voprosu o periodizatsii borby za rynok)*, in *Torgovlya, promyshlennost i gorod v Rossii XVII – nachala XIX v.*, Moscow 1987, pp. 51-67.

Rubinstein N.L., *Vneshnyaya torgovlya Rossii i russkoe kupechestvo vo vtoroy polovine XVIII v.*, "Istoricheskie zapiski, 54, 1955, pp. 343-361.

Scheltema J., *Rusland en de Nederlanden beschouwd in derzelver wederkeerige betrekkingen*, vols. 1-4, Amsterdam 1817-1819.

Schmoller G., *Die russische Kompagnie in Berlin. 1724-1738*, "Zeitschrift für preussische Geschichte und Landeskunde", 20, 1883.

Storch H., *Istorisch-Statistisches Gemälde des Russischen Reichs am Ende des achtzehnden Jahrhunderts*, vols. 1-8, Riga-Leipzig 1797-1803.

Id., *Gemälde von St. Petersburg*, vols. 1-2, Riga 1793-1794.

Tooke W., *View of the Russian Empire during the Reign of Catherine the Second and the Close of the Present Century*, vols.1-3, London 1799.

Veluwenkamp J.W., *Archangel. Nederlandse ondernemers in Rusland. 1550-1785*, [s.l.] 2000.

Yakovtsevsky V.N., *Kupechesky kapital v feodalno-krepostnicheskoy Rossii*, Moscow 1953.

Veluwenkamp J.W., *Archangel. Nederlandse ondernemers in Rusland. 1550-1785*, [s.l.] 2000.

Zacharov V., *Der Aussenhandel St. Petersburgs zu Beginn der 20er Jahre des 18. Jahrhunderts im Spiegel der Registrierung von Handelsschiffen*, in *Zwischen Lübeck und Nowgorod*, Lüneburg 1996.

Id., *Zapadnoevropejskie kupcy v Rossii. Epokha Petra I*, Moskow 1996.

Id., *Jan Lups - Der Handelsagent Peters I*, in *Around Peter the Great. Three Centuries of Russian-Dutch Relations*, Groningen 1997, pp. 78-85.

Id., *Der Anteil west- und mitteleuropäischer Kaufleute am Außenhandel Rußlands im 18.Jahrhundert*, in *Berliner Jahrbuch für osteuropäische Geschichte. 1997. (Unternehmertum in Rußland)*, Berlin 1998, pp. 29-48.

Id., *Inostarnnye kupcy v Arkhangelske vo vtoroj polovine XVIII v.*, in **R***usskij Sever i Zapadnaja Evropa, Sankt-Petersburg 1999*, pp. 360-387.

Id., *Inostrannye kupcy i ikh dvory v Vologde v XVII – pervoj chetverti XVIII veka*, "Vologda 2000", Vypusk 3, pp. 97-132. (with M.S. Cherkasova).

Id., *Die Herkunft und die familiären Verbindungen deutscher Kaufleute in Rußland im 18. Jahrhundert*, in Brüggemann K. - Bohn T.M. - Maier K. (eds.), *Kollektivität und Individualität. Der Mensch im östlichen Europa*, Hamburg 2001, pp. 172-182.

Id., *Russian trade policy in the 18th century*, in de Goey F. - Veluwenkamp J.W. (eds.), *Entrepreneurs and institutions in Europe and Asia. 1500-2000*, Amsterdam 2002, pp. 55-70.

Id., *Rostokskie kupcy v Peterburge*, in A.V. Jurasov (ed.), *Ot drevnej Rusi k Rossii novogo vremeni*, Moscow 2003, pp. 359-365.

Id., Die *Außenhandelstätigkeit der Kaufmannschaft Narvas im 18. Jahrhundert*, in Brüggemann K. (ed.), *Narva und die Ostseeregion*, Narva 2004, pp. 47-59.

Id., *Die Kreditgeschäfte ausländischer Kaufleute in St.Petersburg in der zweiten Hälfte des 18. Jahrhunderts*, in Dahlmann D. - Heller K. - Petrov J.A., *Eisenbahnen und Motoren – Zucker und Schokolade. Deutsche im russischen Wirtschaftsleben vom 18. bis zum 20. Jahrhundert*, Berlin 2005, pp. 15-31.

Id., *Zapadnoevropejskie kupcy v rossijskoj torgovle XVIII veka*, Moscow 2005.

Spanish Foreign Policy during the Second World War. A Historiographical Overview

Emilio Sáenz-Francés San Baldomero
University of Deusto, Bilbao

El artículo estudia los principales trabajos, líneas de investigación y escuelas de interpretación centrados en la política española durante la Segunda Guerra Mundial, con dos objetivos principales: En primer lugar, analizar las perspectivas desde las que la cuestión ha sido abordada, prestando atención a los logros y deficiencias persistentes de la historiografía sobre el periodo, a la luz de las más recientes investigaciones y, en segundo lugar, ponderar cómo y en qué extensión contextos no europeos (principalmente Iberoamérica y Asia) han merecido la atención de los historiadores de la política exterior del primer franquismo.

Así, el artículo se divide en tres apartados principales. En el primero de ellos, Memorias y Primeros Análisis, se abordan las interpretaciones iniciales sobre la cuestión, en gran medida las más complacientes con el régimen franquista, surgidas desde la inmediata posguerra. Por otro lado, el apartado analiza las memorias escritas en estos años por muchos de los más importantes protagonistas de la peripecia política y diplomática de los años de la Guerra.

En el segundo apartado, Corrientes Historiográficas Actuales, la atención se centra en los análisis realizados desde la instauración de la democracia en España, en 1978, y la apertura de los principales archivos sobre el periodo, fundamentalmente el del Ministerio de Asuntos Exteriores, hasta nuestros días. El artículo aborda la efervescencia historiográfica de las décadas de los ochenta y de los noventa, cerrándose con una reflexión sobre la relativa esterilidad que define el momento actual en lo referente a estudios o líneas de investigación novedosas sobre la cuestión analizada.

Finalmente, en el último apartado ¿Entornos Olvidados?. Iberoamérica y Asía, el artículo aborda las obras y los autores que se han centrado en el estudio de la importancia no sólo de Iberoamérica, cuyo peso específico en cualquier cuestión relativa a la política exterior española es insoslayable, sino también de Asia (principalmente de Japón y de las Filipinas), en el conjunto de la política exterior del régimen franquista durante la II Guerra Mundial. Por ejemplo, se presenta el debate sobre la naturaleza y alcance del concepto de Hispanidad (que se desarrolló, en este momento, con una clara voluntad expansiva) o el de la importancia real del Consejo de la Hispanidad o de la Falange Exterior como instrumentos de esa dialéctica beligerante, voluntariosa pero incapaz, cuyo planteamiento y posterior repliegue define la política sobre el periodo, en lo referido a estos ámbitos.

> A wonderful fact to reflect upon, that every human creature is constituted to be that profound secret and mystery to every other. A solemn consideration, when I enter a great city by night, that every one of those darkly clustered houses encloses its own secret; that every room in every one of them encloses its own secret; that every beating heart in the hundreds of thousands of breasts there, is, in some of its imaginings, a secret to the heart nearest it.
>
> Charles Dickens
> *A Tale of Two Cities.*

Introduction

Few historiographical debates generate as much controversy, not only in academia, but in Spanish society as a whole, as the development of Spanish policy during World War II. Nonetheless, publications on Franco's early regime that, to a greater or lesser extent, touch on the core question that this article approaches, are only relatively abundant, and have not developed into a general and regional body of studies[1]. Thus, the image projected by the historiography on this topic is that of a framework lacking articulation, and burdened not only by dispersal, but by what appear to be a more-than-surprising inability of the research community to generate, from the more important foci of scientific production, authentic schools of interpretation and identifiable lines of investigation, which would allow the principal contributions to the topic to be systematized in a coherent way. Thus, it is still an uncompleted task to promote the formation of varied work groups, committed to specific lines of investigation; which, probably, would avoid the reiterative character of many publications – and probably their excessive indebtedness to their predecessors.

Spanish foreign policy between 1939 and 1945 was determined by a series of phases that, broadly, are defined as the stages of neutrality, non-belligerency, and neutrality through which the Spanish State passed during the War. Each of these phases, with their own characteristics and circumstances, were formed against the background of the development of long-term relationships not only with the principal belligerents, but also with other nations which, thanks to their political, religious or historical affinity, form a complex system that very much transcends the core European area. Be that as it may, it was the relations with the belligerents that determined the pace of Spanish policy and, in this respect, the War implies a process, with its singular effects on Spanish policy, which would enshrine the United States as the country with most influence on Spain.

Historiography until 1975. Memoirs and Initial Analyses

It is almost unnecessary to indicate that it was not until the death of General Franco and the promulgation of the democratic Constitution of 1978 that, aside from it becoming possible to write with absolute freedom on history or any other topic, the opening of historical archives and the declassification of documents relating to the topic that we are analysing began. In the fundamental case of the archive of the Ministry of

Foreign Affairs, this was not to happen until 1984. Thus, the wealth of research carried out from that moment exceeded everything previously published, both in quality and quantity, although the dynamics of the first studies to which we refer in this section have marked, for varied reasons, the present-day historiographical debate beyond their concrete contribution.

We must emphasize that the question of Spanish policy during World War II generated an interest that led to the emergence of works on the subject not only after the War, but during it[2]. Thus, in 1941 was published *Reivindicaciones de España*, by José Maria de Areilza and Fernando Maria Castiella[3]. The book, a great success in its time, is a decalogue of the imperial aspirations of the new regime. It is necessary to understand the political volatility of post-war Spain and it is surprising, knowing the radical ideological evolution of the authors after the World War, to observe how outré some of their claims were[4]. In another order of things, in 1943, Allan Chase, who clearly identified with those defeated in the Civil War, published *Falange. The Axis Secret Army in the Americas*[5]: a work in which, with first hand information and a perspective that was understandably completely alarmist, the author analysed the influence of the Foreign Falange in the American continent (including the USA) and the Philippines. Chase's work, which is helpful in order to place oneself in the context of the moment, presented the Foreign Falange as a possible seed of a post-war fascism, a perception that was shared in the years after 1945 by the Allies when approaching the so-called 'Spanish Question'. In the same deprecatory tone, with respect to the Spanish position, we find a key work for any research on the topic. Sir Samuel Hoare published, in 1946, *Ambassador on Special Mission*[6], the memoirs of his embassy in Spain between 1940 and 1944, which, with a very valuable documentary contribution, carries out an eminently critical and even disdainful analysis of the digressive attitude of the Franco regime with regard to the conflict, with the fundamental exception of Francisco Gómez-Jordana's work as minister of Foreign Affairs, from 1942[7].

In this respect, it is paradoxical that it was from the transatlantic ally of the English that there came, since 1945, a new and, in a sense, surprising interpretation of Franco and his regime in the period we wish to analyse. In 1945, Carlton J.H. Hayes, US ambassador in Spain from spring of 1942 until 1945, published the memoirs of his *Wartime Mission in Spain*[8]. A work far more ingenuous than that of Hoare; it is sufficient in order to situate the reader with respect to the ambassador's perspective – not of identification, but rather of complaisance with the Franco regime – to mention that one year after its publication in the United States a Spanish edition appeared, printed in Madrid. This approach, inaugurated by Hayes's work, initiated, so to speak, a tradition and, in a sense, a fascination with the Franco regime, buoyed up by the trend in international political reality after the War. As we have indicated, this approach does not go to the length of fundamentally identifying with the Spanish dictatorial regime, but it does express praise, more or less veiled, for the small and defenceless country which was able to sail in turbulent waters without ever yielding to Hitler's pressures. This perspective is clearly exposed by Hayes himself:

> While the victory of the Axis seemed to him inevitable, with nearly the whole of the European continent under the control of Germany, with the Teutonic armies massed close to the Pyrenees and the seas around Spain infested with German submarines, he made Hitler and the whole world believe that he leant towards the Axis. (...) The fact is that, at least since he removed Serrano-Suñer from the Ministry of Foreign Affairs and the leadership of the Falange, general Franco directed or supported the members of his Government in the effort to bring the official position of Spain closer to the attitude of sympathy with the Allies of the great majority of the Spanish People[9].

In the same line, though from a less innocent position with regard to a reality that often imposes itself, and undoubtedly better depicted as a whole by Hoare, we may situate other works such as those of H. Feis, *The Spanish History, Franco and the Nations War*[10] or the memoirs of the counsellor of the American embassy in Madrid, Willard L. Beaulac, with the revealing title of *Franco, Secret Ally in the Second World War*[11]. From the Spanish perspective, it is possible that this unexpectedly favourable context was the fuse for the works of justification for Spanish actions published during the same period. Fundamentally these are the memoirs of Serrano-Suñer, principally *Entre Hendaya y Gibraltar*, which, in the context of the remarkable ideological development of the former minister in the post-war period, presents the non-entry of Spain in the War as the direct result of his policy and that of his brother-in-law, Franco[12]. Finally, another work eminently devoted to justification Spanish policy is *España Tenía Razón*, by Jose Maria Doussinague, General Director of Foreign Policy (equivalent to being second-in-command in the Palace of Santa Cruz), during the ministry of Gómez-Jordana[13].

The first scientific and academic work on the topic was a doctoral thesis written in 1956, *The Relations of General Franco and the Spanish Nationalists with the Axis Powers*[14], by Elizabeth Parr. The author does not work with unpublished materials, but with the existing bibliography and with the then insufficient published sources. These first studies, coming, for obvious reasons, from beyond Spanish borders, continue, already in the full flush of the Cold War, and to a great extent influenced by it, to present a more-or-less benign image of Franco's regime during the War years. Such is the case of the first scientific study on the Blue Division, Raymond Proctor's *Agony of a Neutral: Spanish-German Wartime Relations and the "Blue Division"*[15]. For Proctor, as late as 1974, the most notable facts of foreign Spanish policy during the War could be codified in the fact that, "Spain emerged from the Second World War with her government and her territorial integrity intact (...)"[16]. For this author, the presence of a voluntary Division fighting on the German side on the Eastern front does not change the nature of this balance. In the same line as Proctor's are the works of Halstead, Cortada or Detwiler[17].

Within Spanish historiography itself, because of the aforementioned imponderables, this thesis, necessarily with the title of an essay, sweetened and laudatory, with regard to the Spanish attitude and the role of Franco himself, was also presented. Ricardo de la Cierva's works correspond paradigmatically to this tendency; probably the most brilliant of historians connected to the regime, he has, until the present day, maintained the thesis of a Franco fundamentally resistant to the pressures of the Axis[18]. If in the case of de la Cierva his political commitment to the Franco regime is clear, it is also necessary to indicate that, with nuances, this thesis has also been maintained by the majority of conservative Spanish historians, not only before, but also after 1978.

Current Historiographical Trends

We must repeat that current historiography on the Spanish attitude during World War II is inevitably burdened by a necessarily limited temporal context and that, as we have indicated, although it begins, *strictu senso*, in 1978, with the restoration of the democratic regime, it could not reach its complete potential until the opening of the archives of the Ministry of Foreign Affairs, in 1984. On the other hand, logically, the primary interest of the investigators at this time was in the thorny question of the Civil War, which, as one of the most dramatic episodes in Spanish history, leading to the genesis of the Franco regime itself and as unavoidable reference point for any interpretation of the subsequent period, necessarily represented a land of promise for a whole generation of young researchers. Be that as it may, the question of the first years after the Civil War and the initial stages of Franco's diplomacy also quickly became objects of study. Nonetheless the balance that can be made of the state of the question is, in general lines, the same that professor Francisco Quintana outlined, considering the progress of the history of international relations in Spain, as late as 1996. For Quintana the situation could only be defined as a *chiaroscuro* determined by evident progress and persistent backwardness with regard to the wealth of approaches and methods utilised in other European contexts[19].

In this respect, the first catalyst for research activity in the Spanish environment was Klaus-Jörg Ruhl's work, *Franco Falange and Third Reich*[20], published in Germany in 1975, but not translated into Spanish until 1986. This study implied the first exhaustive investigation of the resources relating to Spain in German and English archives which, for its methodological value, continues today to be an essential reference point, acknowledged or not, for many of the investigations undertaken on the period undertaken. When analysing the rhythms of Spanish policy, Ruhl, fleeing from simplistic or propaganda-based explanations, analyses the development of the relations between the two countries, studying the policy of the different German ambassadors in Spain. On the other hand, the author also pays attention to the role that, for Hitler, Spain played in his European system; he considers for the first time General Muñoz Grandes[21] temptation to carry out a coup d'état, and approaches the tensions in the bosom of the different groups supporting the Franco regime, as well as the importance to Germany of Spanish exports of tungsten and the Allied pressures to halt this traffic. For Ruhl:

> During World War II, the question of the entry of Spain into the war on the Axis side, constituted the greatest test for Franco's regime. This question was closely linked to that of the reconstruction and organization of the Franco system and of its foreign policy orientation, such that during the years 1941-1942 and '43 Spain was on the verge of political destruction. Defenders and detractors recruited their followers from all the social estates (...)[22].

Returning to the Spanish context, we must emphasize that, although, as Quintana affirms, the development and modernization of the history of the international relations in the country took place in the university centres of the Spanish capital (Alcalá de Henares, the Autonomous University of Madrid, the CSIC [Higher Council of Scientific Research] and UNED [the National University of Distance Learning]), it was in the research environment of UNED that, from the start, the greatest impulse was given to tackling a necessary review of the approaches to Spanish foreign policy during World War II[23]. Javier Tussell, who died in 2005, is enshrined as an indisputable historiographical referent in Spanish historiography on the topic, not only as the author of key works from a certain perspective, which from the 1980s and 1990s was predominant, but also for his work as the director of many Doctoral Theses of the second generation of experts on the period. What we might call the historiographical school of the UNED, despite its character now being slightly clouded, is really the only definite referent for studies on the period.

The process of revision, almost the start of the archival investigation in the Spanish environment, led largely by the UNED school, was inaugurated by Víctor Morales-Lezcano in his work *Historia de la No-beligerancia Española Durante la Segunda Guerra Mundial (VI, 1940-X, 1943)*[24]. Morales-Lezcano's work meant the first approach of post-Franco Spanish historiography to the question of Spanish foreign policy during World War II, with new perspectives for a more correct understanding of the question, such as a new definition of the scope and intentions of the declaration of non-neutrality of 1940, defined as a (...) "gradual step of the new State towards belligerency"[25]. Regarding the debate on Spanish neutrality and its non-belligerent nuances, Morales-Lezcano gives a very critical interpretation of the Spanish attitude, which would later be taken up by Javier Tusell, fundamentally from 1995. In this respect, Morales-Lezcano affirms that:

> The whole polemic inspired by the Spanish "vigilant neutrality" is, to a great extent, the result of a few unilateral approaches, influenced by a historiography that should no longer have needed to be limited by the proximity of the event, and therefore for the passionate conditioning that – to a greater or lesser degree – we imagine would perturb the spirit of the historian of contemporary times[26].

In 1985, Javier Tusell, together with Genoveva García Queipo de Llano, published *Franco y Mussolini: la Política Española Durante la Segunda Guerra Mundial*[27]. In the context of the disproportionate exaltation of the Caudillo and his regime, for his skill in keeping Spain out of the war, without yielding to the pressures and excesses of either side, which had impregnated most of the previous historiographical trends, and in view of the documentary evidence, a review of concepts and periodisation was more than necessary. The work, fundamentally based on consultation of Italian, but also Spanish, archives, was much more balanced in its results, as we will see, than later studies on the topic by Tusell. The conclusions are necessarily placed at a middle point between opposing trends, later abandoned by the author who, in the next ten years, would experience a marked ideological drift from the political centre to more extreme positions. For Tusell:

> (...) There were certain constants in the Spanish position: undoubted sympathy for the Axis, caution and nationalism (...) This sympathy explains the misdiagnosis of the result of the conflict, very common in all the sectors of the Franco regime (...) On many occasions, during the conflict, Franco was neither skilful nor prudent. (...) Nevertheless, he was cautious and that means, especially, that he wanted to see clearly exposed the advantages that he would obtain from participating in the conflict. (...) While this was unclear, he was not going to take the risk[28].

On the lines opened by Tusell and García Queipo de Llano, in 1993 the UNED organized an *International Congress on Franco's Regime*, in which, almost for the first time, a scientific and, especially, global effort was made to approach the Franco political system from new perspectives[29]. An important number of the communications to the congress centred on the regime's foreign policy and among them we find contributions of interest. Jean François Berdah analysed British cultural propaganda in Spain during the first years of the regime[30]; Rafael García Perez, the imperialistic ambitions of Franco's early regime[31], Susana Sueiro centred on the territorial pretensions of Spain in Morocco, through the perspective of British diplomacy[32]; Francisco Torres García analysed the process of return to neutrality, via the negotiations for the retreat of the Blue Division[33]. Though here we do not consider some communications that, due to their specific nature, will be covered in the following section, the general balance of the conference, as regards our topic of study, was not entirely satisfactory. Franco's early regime had not yet been outlined and characterised methodologically as a definite period and the contributions on a question as relevant as that of foreign policy during World War II, were not sufficiently strong in relation to other topics, probably less important, in the whole context of the foreign action of the regime until 1975; even more so when the latter, after the War, was defined by its low profile and will to survival.

The historiographical thrust in the question, shown by the UNED, also materialized in the journal *Espacio Tiempo y Forma* (Contemporary History series) that acted, especially in the 1990s, as the principal collector of research on the period. Most of the 1994 issue was dedicated to analysing monographically the question of Spain and the Second World War. Besides the perspectives presented at the Congress of the previous year, which are repeated in the approach to the topic of the journal (articles by Susana Sueiro and Rafael García Perez[34]) the issue meant the first contact with relevant topics such as that of German propaganda in Spain during the War, approached by Carlos Velasco and Ingrid Schulze[35]; combined Anglo-American diplomacy between 1942 and 1945, analysed by Carlos Collado[36]; or Spanish relations with France or Portugal in the War years, a question approached by Maria Soledad Gómez de las Heras[37]. Other new and suggestive perspectives relating to Spanish policy with other more distant horizons, will be commented on in the following section[38].

The same year, 1994, Rafael García Perez, trained in the University of Alcalá de Henares (Madrid), published *Franquismo y III Reich*[39]: a work centred on the analysis of economic relations between Spain and Nazi Germany after the conclusion of the Civil War. Comparable to Ruhl's work for the extent of the German documentation covered and for its perspective, the work was a milestone that wove the economic factor together with the analysis of the political and diplomatic dynamics. For García Perez:

> (...) The Spanish attitude to the German Reich and implicitly, the position of Franco's regime in the Second World War, was determined by the heterogeneity of political forces supporting the Regime and by the lack of consensus to construct a State model. The period of greatest involvement of the Franco regime with Hitler's New Order, which chronologically corresponds with the ministry of Ramon Serrano-Suñer, became a chronicle of misunderstandings marked by mutual frustration (...)[40].

In 1995, Javier Tusell published *Franco, España y la Segunda Guerra Mundial, entre el Eje y la Neutralidad*[41]. The work is still considered today as the principal monographic study on Spanish foreign policy of the period and implies the consecration of the author's drift towards more extreme political positions, from his collaboration with the centrist governments of the UCD during the first years of the democracy. Tusell's central thesis, canonical for the majority of specialists until today – more in line with Morales-Lezcano than with his previous work on the topic, which we have analysed – now presents Franco as anxious, until 1941, to enter the War on Germany's side, as the inventor of Serrano-Suñer's vast pro-Axis policy, and convinced of the Reich's inevitable victory up to a very late date[42]. If Spain did not take part in the war it was, in the words of the author, "(...) a pure miracle (...)"[43], always derived from the actions of third countries or of politicians who were in no case Spanish. For Tusell, Spain only deserved the epithet of neutral at the beginning and end of the War, "(...) but only joined with another epithet, benevolent, and taking into account that in 1939 it was towards Germany and in 1945, towards the United States"[44]. The periodization presented by Tusell supports the rhythms he proposed in 1985, and can be discussed in the light of the analysis of the documentation of the Ministry of Foreign Affairs. He highlights a tendency, which has continued up to the present, which defines the critical moment for the entry of Spain in the conflict as the period framing the Hendaye meeting of 1940, giving less importance to the initial months of 1943, when Germany, in the face of a Spain that was beginning to distance itself from the Axis, intensely pressed Franco's regime to join the conflict. Drawing his conclusions, Tusell, at times, forces his sources too much in order to propose, from the first moment, his principal thesis, which he has defended, on occasions, in an excessively dogmatic way, in clear contrast with his previous monograph on the topic. Be that as it may, the importance of the study, which was born in a fertile area for aggressive approaches, means that the work continues to be the principal referent of Spanish historiography on the period[45].

It is natural that Tusell's work, which marked an increasing belligerent drift in the historiography on the period, did not please the academic community with links, to a greater or lesser extent, with Franco's regime[46]. It was a modernist of the old school, Luis Suárez, who articulated, through the study of documentation, then unpublished, of the *Francisco Franco Foundation*, the conservative response to Tusell's work. The revindicative value of the work is clear when we consider that, as part of a series of volumes on the history of Franco's regime, then being prepared by Suárez (*Franco, Crónica de un*

Tiempo), the publication of the second volume (corresponding to World War II) was brought forward to the same date as the first, focussed on the Civil War, to respond with maximum rapidity to Tusell's work. Thus, in 1997, *España, Franco y la Segunda Guerra Mundial*[47] appeared. In an extensive text with prolific data, with the pretensions of a manual, Suárez presents the other side of the coin of a debate that is still open today. A core point of the divergence with Tusell centres on the different interpretation of the role of Serrano-Suñer as Minister of Foreign Affairs. Though Suárez also affirms Suñer's Germanophilia, the work presents him, especially when referring to his meetings with Hitler and von Ribbentrop in November 1940, as resistant to the strong pressures of both to take new steps in favour of the Axis, thus giving credit to the memoirs and personal references of Serrano, refuted by Tusell. On the other hand, Suárez, necessarily, places more emphasis in his work to chapters such as the Spanish peace offer of 1943 and interprets and evaluates the Blue Division in a radically different way.

The state of the question, based on the references described above, has not suffered substantial modifications up to the present moment. The certain impulse shown by Spanish historiography up the mid-1990s has not had, probably, all the necessary development in later years, until 2002. In this year, besides the re-edition of Paul Preston's biography of Franco, published in 1993, appeared *La Guerra Secreta de Franco*, by Manuel Ros Agudo; a work that, due to its approach, documentary contribution and perspective, is the most relevant contribution to the question since 1995[48]. The book makes clear, in the historiographical line defined by Tusell, the Spanish military pacification to join the Axis until 1941, the German activities of espionage and sabotage carried out with the knowledge of the Spanish government until 1944,[49] as well as the Spanish collaboration with the Gestapo. For Ros Agudo, who emphasizes the importance of the (fantasy-prone) Spanish military planning – with a view to taking part in the conflict looming over Europe – prior even to the conclusion of the Civil War (which contradicts the supposed opportunist or transitory nature of Franco's policy), the field in which the Germans gained most benefit was that of information, an aspect that he analyzes thoroughly.

In the same line, though probably less novel for the documentary evidence produced, the year 2005 saw the publication of two works similar in their aims and titles, though not in their results. These are Enrique Moradiellos's study, *Franco frente a Churchill*, and *Churchill and Franco* by Richard Wigg[50]. This second work, due to the limitation of the archives consulted, is merely an approach, journalistic in tone, to Anglo-Spanish relations during the conflict. Moradiellos's work, though not novel as regards its approach or methodology, brings, thanks to the range of archives consulted, a significant documentary contribution.

Though at the end of this chapter we will dedicate a few lines to gathering some main conclusions, we may say, as a provisional evaluation, that beyond the publication of monographs and articles in the 1980s and 1990s, and the concern for research of which they are evidence, the recent past, aside from some exceptions, has been characterized as a tunnel of a certain sterility. Beside a lack of novel methodological approaches, perspectives or periodizations that would allow us to go forward in the historiographical debate on the question considered, we glimpse a new period in which, buoyed up by a brand new conservative historiography, challenging and probably less subtle than those preceding it (that of Suárez or de la Cierva as outstanding examples), we see not a new historiographical advance, but rather unbearable concentration on a sterile and repetitive contest between left- and right-wing tendencies, increasingly radicalized and, therefore, less scientific[51].

Forgotten environments? Latin America and Asia[52]

As has become clear in the above pages, the bibliographical corpus on Spanish foreign policy during World War II centres fundamentally on the analysis of Spanish relations with other countries in the European environment. Beyond the logical explanation that, with the exception of the United States and Japan, the core combatants were nations from this context, we have to consider, in order to evaluate correctly this eurocentrism, the logistic difficulties inherent in accomplishing a documentary search in more distant areas, such as the American continent or the region of the Pacific. Since the CLIOHRES work group, for which this study has been made, deals with Europe's relations with the world, we have left for this last section a very interesting group of works and authors, pioneers in a series of lines of research that have centred first and foremost on the role of relations with Spanish America, but also on more distant environments such as the Japanese empire, China, the Philippines and, to a lesser extent, Thailand (in these cases we can almost speak of a single individual). As these researchers belong to the second generation of historians of the democracy, who defended their theses during the 1980s and 1990s, we must emphasize that, very possibly due to the circumstances described at the close of the previous section, their works have not yet benefited by being continued by new generations of young researchers.

In 1988, Lorenzo Delgado, a CSIC researcher, published *Diplomacia Franquista y Política Cultural Hacia Iberoamérica, 1939-1953*[53]. The work meant a great advance in knowledge of the political articulation of the cultural diplomacy of Franco's regime with regard to an environment that is considered a canonical promised land for Spanish foreign policy. For the author, the policy of *Hispanidad* [Spanishness] materialized in the creation of the *Consejo de la Hispanidad* (2 November, 1940), under the Ministry of Foreign Affairs, then occupied by Ramon Serrano-Suñer, and implied an attempt to exploit the American heritage as a way to gain ground in the international theatre, with respect to the real relevance prefigured by the general characteristics of the Franco regime. It was a question, in the end, of boosting Spain's stock, first with Germany and later on, from a lower dialectical profile, with the victors of the War. For Delgado:

> Serrano-Suñer aspired to exploit the secular links with Latin America to allow a lasting closeness between the countries of that continent and Franco's Spain; in such a process the desire was perceptible –sometimes barely concealed– to practice a sort of patronage over the region. This tendency received the not-so-discreet support of the Nazi leaders, who saw in it a means of clandestinely meddling in American affairs...[54].

Though the aims of this over-ambitious policy meant concentrating on very specific measures, the reality is that: "...The Spanish regime did not have the mobilizing capacity nor sufficient resources to carry out plans that were as ambitious as they were Utopian at that historical moment..."[55].Thus, for Delgado, this was a policy frustrated from the beginning. From the end of 1941, several Latin-American governments prohibited subsidiaries of the Nazi Party and of the Falange in their countries, so that the work of the *Consejo de la Hispanidad* soon became limited to the cultural sphere. In any case, Delgado emphasizes that the American link was an essential axis of Spanish policy – one of few that they were able to put into action – up to the end of international isolation, in 1953.

In the aforementioned work, Delgado affirmed that his conclusions were at the level of hypotheses; the CSIC researcher would present his thesis in a more complete form in 1992. The work takes as its graphic title *Imperio de papel. Acción Cultural y Política Exterior Durante el Primer Franquismo*[56]. In the study, Delgado refines his references to the reorientation in diplomatic relations with Latin America, and in the strategic conception of this, after the arrival of Gómez Jordana at the Ministry of Foreign Affairs, carrying out, likewise, a study of the positions of several intellectuals on both sides of the Atlantic on the question, such as Ortega or Salvador de Madariaga. To define this process of mutation in Spanish foreign policy, Delgado coins the term "chamaeleonic coupling"[57], that well serves to define the spirit of Spanish foreign relations during much of Franco's regime[58].

Two years later, in 1994, Rosa Pardo Sanz, linked with the UNED, published *¡Con Franco hacia el Imperio! La política Exterior Española en América Latina 1939-1945*[59]. In a line that, inevitably, assumes Lorenzo Delgado's principal conclusions and perspectives and is indebted to Tusell's approaches, the work seeks to develop the analysis, not merely of cultural policy, but also of Spanish policy as a whole towards Latin America, in the period that we are analysing. The author presents as a great mistake of interpretation by Franco's diplomats and the Falange the belief that South America was fertile ground for a policy that was, even dialectically, expansionist and over-ambitious. Thus they perceived as encouraging signs the friendly attitude of Catholic and conservative groups towards the regime, as well as the conciliatory mien of the authorities of different countries towards Franco's Spain after the Civil War. For the author, the dictatorship underestimated the depth of antipathy towards the new regime generated during the Civil War, as well as the permanent reminder that Republican exiles constituted (in the case of Mexico especially), and the overwhelming influence of the United States, with which it was futile to compete. On the other hand, for Pardo: "(...) The attempt to bring the Spanish colonies under the Falangist yoke caused more problems than it resolved, provoking clashes and creating a power structure parallel to diplomacy with a program of action that was as radical as it was unviable (...)"[60]. Thus, for Pardo, the Foreign Falange in America entered a crisis from the beginning of the World War.

> In the political failure described, from the grand plans of 1939 up to the defensive strategy of Spring 1945, the factor that stands out is the blindness of the Spanish leaders to judge with equa-

> nimity the reality of the Latin American situation and their inability to internalise the fact that the American response had been clear since 1936. The paternalism and, at times, disdain that appear in the judgments of the diplomats conceal their resistance to recognizing the adulthood of the Latin American states and, therefore, the independence of their actions. (...) The naming of the section in charge of American affairs as "Utramar" ("Overseas [Dependencies]") until 1944 can not be considered as happenstance. Such a word had certain imperialistic connotations that spoke much of the more or less unconscious aspirations which they had never renounced (...)[61].

Besides these monographic references, there are some articles centred on the relations between Franco's regime and certain Latin American countries. Thus, Encarnación Ortega has analysed the Chilean case, which is located in the interpretative line previously exposed[62]. On the other hand, Mónica Quijada's article about the relations between Spain and Argentina during the War is of great interest. Quijada affirms the existence of a *Madrid-Buenos Aires Axis*, which appears as an exception to the trends pointed to by Delgado and Pardo. For the author it is conceivable that the favoured relationship between the two countries offered the German secret services a 'triangular field of action'[63] that could be used for such ends as propaganda and espionage. In any case, the author minimizes, in contrast with the exaggeration of these realities after the War, any real damage towards the Allies, finding negative effects rather for the axis countries. Finally, we must return to Rosa Pardo who has analysed the relations of the Ministry of Foreign Affairs with the colonies of pro-Republican exiles in America[64]. Pardo emphasizes the absence of a conciliatory policy (unsurprisingly) on the part of the Franco administration, once the Civil War was over, and which continued, in a more radical way, until 1945. The article brings us close to the rise and fall of the Foreign Falange as the agency responsible for the organization and vigilance of Spanish communities in Latin America, giving special attention to the case of Mexico and analysing the repressive measures that were proposed for the Republicans in America[65].

While, as we have seen, the American environment has deserved (marginally) the attention of the investigators in the context that we are analysing, we cannot say the same of Pacific region, that is, fundamentally, Japan, China, Thailand and the Philippines. Practically only a single researcher, Florentino Rodao, has recently given attention to an area that, in the light of the documentation of the Ministry of Foreign Affairs and of the fundamental importance of the country in question in the War, is far from secondary. In *Franco y el Imperio Japonés*[66], a work supported with an astounding wealth of documentary evidence, not only of Spanish and Japanese but also Italian, American, English and even Canadian files, Rodao exposes the perceptions that the two countries had of one another in 1939 and their evolution, emphasizing the superiority of Japan, where a definite academic concern developed for knowledge with regard to Spain[67]. Rodao analyses how Japan's membership in a common alliance with Spain (the Antikomintern agreement) allowed an image of the former country in the Franco regime to be created that was quite distinct from the general perception of the Asian world as a threat[68]. "This ideal image of Japan was brief. It had grown from 1937 and was intensified with the fall of France in the summer of 1940, but began to decline in the middle of 1941, with Japan's refusal to support the German attack on the Soviet Union (...) This idealization was comparable to that of the Soviet Union by the Spanish left wing (...)"[69]. On the other hand, Rodao studies the Spanish carrying out of Japanese interests in the United States after the assault on Pearl Harbour, the moment at which the increasing Japanese presence in the Pacific Ocean began to cause division and alarm among the Spanish leaders, which would materialize in the claim of independence (based on Christianity) for the Philippines by Spain[70]. Be that as it may, for Rodao, Spain had a key role in establishing the Japanese secret service, the *To network*, in the United States, at that moment, thanks to Serrano-Suñer: "The Falange and the Spanish Embassy in Washington were among the initial supports to put the network in action, the first for ideological reasons and the second for infrastructure reasons (...)"[71]. The arrival at the Ministry of Foreign Affairs of Gómez-Jordana meant the materialization of the slow cooling off of relations between the two countries, which he framed in the theory of Franco's three wars. This was a cynical diplomatic formulation used by Franco and his minister from 1943 which differentiated between the war of the Allies with Germany, of the latter with the Soviet Union and of the Pacific region with Japan. With this division Franco and the regime affirmed their increasing antipathy towards the Japanese cause.

> (...) Franco's critique of the Japanese as imperialists (this in 1943) showed his envy for their having obtained what his Spain so desired. His affirmation of the superficiality of the Japanese occidentalisation was a reflection of the mistrust that Japan was stimulating in very disparate political areas in the West and can be found both in British propaganda and in Hitler's *Mein Kampf* (...)[72].

In this change of attitude of the Spanish policy towards Japan, Franco's regime even considered the possibility of declaring war on the Japanese Empire in 1945. Rodao tells how the really astonishing idea of sending a new version of the Blue Division to fight alongside General MacArthur arose among the Falangist ranks [73].

Rodao's reflections also include the relations of Franco's regime with the turbulent China of the 1940s. First, the author analyses the relations of Spain with the puppet state of Machukuo, which demonstrate the limitations of Spanish foreign action, inherent in the diplomatic and economic weakness generated by the Civil War. Thus, though these relations were established in 1939, with Machukuo opening a delegation in Madrid, it would not be until 1942 that Spain designated an ambassador in return, having to resort to an uncontrollable diplomat located in Peking. Be that as it may, once the ambassador was named, he never remained in a permanent way in the precarious legation, a building whose temperature ranged between 7 and 10 degrees. The absence of a Spanish colony or of missions with Spanish priests in the area created the perception that, with grave limitations, the representation in Machukuo was merely trying to present a good image to the Axis[74].

More interesting, in this respect, are the manoeuvres of Franco's regime to chisel out a niche in the diplomatic sphere of convulsed central China. Rodao revisits the origins of the Chinese crisis and its derivation in the clash between the communists and the nationalists of the Guomingdang, complicated by the war with Japan (from 1937). In this respect, he analyzes how the Japanese prevalence, from 1939, tended to favour, more than the political fragmentation of the country, the implantation of a central government, coinciding with the moment when Franco's Spain turned its eyes towards Asia, after the Civil War[75]. The effort to re-establish relations with China, on this convulsed stage, was led by the diplomat Pedro de Igual, but Spain did not start out from a position of even vaguely accurate knowledge of the general situation of the country, which would have allowed it to act appropriately. This situation was aggravated by the absence of the right of *extraterritoriality* (the legal authority to exercise consular jurisdiction over citizens). This last factor made senseless any desire to design an independent diplomatic or consular work that, on the other hand, proved to be doubtful when recognizing either Wang's pro-Japanese or Jiang's nationalist government. The fortune of both sides in their struggle, together with the compulsory Spanish commitment to the diplomatic action of the countries of the Axis, especially Italy (that pressed Spain to return to the line favourable to Wang, facing with any lukewarm Spanish attempt to develop its own policy), led to the formal recognition of the latter by Spain in July 1941. In any case, this does not imply a significant advance in the solution of the principal concerns of Spain in China, principally extraterritoriality[76]. For Rodao: "The relationship with China had a single path, passing through Tokyo, Rome and Berlin"[77].

Relations with pro-Japanese Thailand are also touched on in Rodao's work. Spain had not renounced the unequal agreements of the western powers with the Asian country, since this renunciation took place in 1937, in the midst of the Civil War. The regime showed an interest in the Thai case after a letter from the *Gabrielist Brothers* addressed personally to General Franco invited him, based on Thai-Japanese friendship, to designate the Spanish minister in Tokyo as permanent representative in Bangkok. Optimism about the perspectives of the diplomatic relations with Thailand in the Ministry of Foreign Affairs ended when Bangkok requested prior renunciation of the unequal agreements. From 1943, the march of the War definitively paralysed the Thai project. Finally, we must emphasize that, beyond the time-frame we are analyzing, the Korean War gave Spain a chance to boost its stock with the United States. Then, Spain signed, in haste, a treaty, opening an embassy in 1953, with the mission to promote friendship with the American ally. After the war and the removal of North American interests from the region, Thailand returned, for Franco's regime, to where it had always been: the souvenir chest[78].

Finally, the Philippine question. This case took on a special relevance, since even at the time of the Second World War, the memory of the loss of the archipelago, together with that of Cuba in 1898, was still very present in Spain. Rodao analyses, with the same methodology used in the Japanese case, the evolution of the mentalities of the Spanish community in the Philippines and in the former colonizing power, and the desire to strengthen the bonds of union between the two, after the Civil War tinged this with an inevitable and increasing anti-Americanism, that grew with the march of the German victories. In this context, though soon this perception changed from seeing Japan as the liberating power from the Chinese threat to seeing it, as we have mentioned, with increasing distrust, its role was accepted as a lever to provoke the exit of the United States from the islands. The Falange, from this perspective, was an instrument in the service of the interests of the Axis and of the future role of imperial Spain, still vague, in what came to be considered the possibility of a new wave of Hispanicization of the region, thanks to the Japanese advance[79]. This positive perception ended, as we have seen, around 1941, the change being sharpened following the acceleration of the Japanese advance through the Pacific. In this context, Rodao's analysis of the Laurel incident is prominent. This was the letter of congratulation for the 'independence' of the Philippines – celebrated by the Axis – sent by the Ministry of Foreign Affairs to the Philippine puppet president, José Laurel, on 18 October, 1943. The letter generated great tension in the relations between Spain and the United States, which instrumentalized the crisis to increase pressure on Spain, demanding the cessation of German activities in Tangier and the suspension of tungsten shipments to the Reich, just after the Spanish return to neutrality. Only the firm attitude of Jordana (who threatened the allied ambassadors with his resignation) managed to smooth over the initial grave moments of tension[80].

> (...) Washington wheeled out this incident to use as a springboard. The scorn of Franco and other Spaniards towards Japan was no secret, as we have already seen, but Washington was not benefiting especially from it (...). Therefore it was normal that Washington should seek to shift this distaste of Madrid for Tokyo to a matter of much greater magnitude, relations with Berlin. (...) The collaboration with Germany was most affected by it, while that already existing with Japan suffered very little because it was already at a very low point. (...) The attitude of Washington had been the correct one, though it would then be delayed by the brave attitude of Jordana. (...)[81].

On October 23rd, the chief of intelligence of Foreign Affairs, the Marquess of Rialp, in a conversation with the Japanese ambassador, Suma, admitted that the exchange of telegrams implied formal recognition of Laurel, though he requested prudence by the Japanese in dealing with the matter, implicitly recognizing the fragile position of the Spanish government. The communication of this information by Suma to his government was intercepted by the United States who thus obtained, according to Rodao, benefit from its increasing technological superiority, by being able to judge accurately the effect of its pressure on Spain[82]. From this moment, as we have seen, Spain's Japanese policy would be an element designed to earn credibility with the Allies, whereas the United States enjoyed new sources of information to modulate its Spain policy[83].

Conclusions

Returning to Francisco Quintana's article, to which we referred in the second paragraph, it reviewed some of the principal weaknesses of the history of international relations in Spain ten years ago, such as the absence of a deep interdisciplinary debate, the survival of a descriptive historical discourse and a clear imbalance in the perspectives adopted and the approaches on which these were based. Many of these critical points still constitute today the elements on which, in the future, it will be necessary to act in order to advance knowledge of the period on which this chapter is focussed. Though we cannot ignore the important historiographical advances that have taken place concerning the question of Spanish foreign policy during the Second World War, which have permitted, in conditions that are not always suitable, an acceptable body of publications to be constructed practically from the foundations, nonetheless it is true that there are many points on which it is imperative to redouble the investigative work. The circumstances with whose description we closed the second section of this analysis mean that we are now at a crossroads for the historiography on the period. The great mass of documentation, some unpublished, preserved in the Spanish archives; the methodological innovations that new generations must define; the possibilities generated by interdisciplinary contact; as well as the perception that the increasing perspective with regard to the subject considered must encourage a diversification of approaches beyond a completely sterilizing over-simplification, and must urge the investigators to advance in the resolution of remaining uncertainties on the period, paying attention to the multitude of new perspectives and regional studies from whose results we can and should expect a great deal[84]. I hope that this chapter helps, at least, to identify some of them.

Notes

1 That is, focused on a specific area of foreign policy.

2 For more information about Spanish literature during the War and on the War, see J.C. Mainer, *La Segunda Guerra Mundial y la Literatura Española. Algunos Libros de 1940-1955,* in J.L. García Delgado (ed.), *El Primer Franquismo, España Durante la II Guerra Mundial,* V Coloquio de Historia Contemporánea de España, Madrid 1989, pp. 245-268.

3 J.M. de Areilza - F.M. Castiella, *Reivindicaciones de España*, Madrid 1941.

4 Large areas of north Africa, equatorial Africa, parts of Vietnam, ports in the entrance of the Red Sea and, evidently, Gibraltar.

5 A. Chase, *Falange. The Axis Secret Army in the Americas*, New York 1943.

6 S. Hoare, *Ambassador on Special Mission*, London 1946.

7 Jordana replaced Ramon Serrano-Suñer, of whom Hoare affirms that: "(...) for two years the Minister and I had been at almost open war with each other". Hoare, *Ambassador* cit., p. 166.

8 C.J.H. Hayes, *Wartime Mission in Spain: 1942-1945*, New York 1946. By the same author: *The United States and Spain, an Interpretation*, New York 1951. Hayes was an academic specialized in the history of Spain, without any previous diplomatic experience, and who connected, probably, more with the country than the always 'very British' Hoare. For an interpretation of Hayes's work, C.R. Halstead, *Historians in Politics: Carlton J.H. Hayes as an American Ambassador in Spain, 1942-45,* "Journal of Contemporary History", 10-13, 1975, pp. 383-405.

9 Hayes, *Mission of War* cit., p. 378.

10 H. Feis, *The Spanish History, Franco and The Nation's War,* New York 1948. Feis was Adviser of International Affairs of the U.S. State Department (1931-1944), First Chairman of The Iberian Peninsula Operating Committee, Special Adviser to the Secretary of The Army and Head of the Interdepartmental Committee of Strategic and Critical Raw Materials.

11 W.L. Beaulac, *Franco, Secret Ally in Second World War*, Carbondale 1986.

12 R. Serrano-Suñer, *Entre Hendaya y Gibraltar*, Madrid 1947. Also of the same author, *Memorias: Entre el Silencio y la Propaganda, la Historia como Fue*, Barcelona 1978.

[13] J.M. Doussinague, *España Tenía Razón*, Madrid 1949.

[14] E. Parr, *The Relations of General Franco and the Spanish Nationalists with the Axis Powers*, Aberystwyth, Wales 1956.

[15] R. Proctor, *Agony of a Neutral: Spanish-German Wartime Relations and the "Blue Division"*, Moscow, Idaho, 1974.

[16] Proctor, *Agony of a Neutral* cit., p. 273.

[17] C.R. Halstead, *Spain, the Powers and the Second World War*, Virginia 1962; J.W. Cortada, *United States-Spanish Relations, Wolfram and World War II*, Barcelona 1971; D.S. Detwiler, *Hitler, Franco und Gibraltar*, Wiesbaden 1962.

[18] R. de la Cierva, *Francisco Franco, Un Siglo de España*, Madrid 1973 (2 vols); Id., *Historia del Franquismo I, Orígenes y Configuración*, Barcelona 1975. It is understandable that the renovation of the practice of history in Spain, in the second half of the century, fundamentally by the School of the Annales, did not affect the period that we are analyzing.

[19] F. Quintana, L*a Historia de las Relaciones Internacionales en España, Apuntes para un Balance Historiográfico*, in *La Historia de las Relaciones Internacionales: Una visión desde España*, Madrid 1996, pp. 11-12.

[20] K.J. Ruhl, *Franco, Falange y III Reich. España durante la Segunda Guerra Mundial*, Madrid 1986.

[21] The first Commander in Chief of the Blue Division. He was sounded out by Hitler in 1942, presenting the idea of his substituting the Caudillo, or becoming president of a new Government in which Franco would be a figurehead, as step towards the participation of Spain in the War.

[22] Ruhl, *Franco, Falange* cit., p. 257.

[23] In this respect, it is necessary to mention a whole generation of historians who, in parallel to the efforts of the UNED, have led advances in the knowledge of our topic since the 1980s. In this respect we must mention Ángel Viñas, Manuel Espadas Burgos and Antonio Maquina. If this is the dominant trend it is necessary to state that, as an outstanding example, in 1984 Maria Jesus Cava published a biographical study on Jose Félix de Lequerica, ambassador in Vichy during the War, later minister of Foreign Affairs and ambassador to the United States. M.J. Cava, *Los Diplomáticos de Franco, José Félix de Lequerica, Temple y Tenacidad*, Bilbao 1984. The study was pioneering in a line of investigation, that of the labor – at times essential – of Franco's ambassadors during the war. We must emphasize that surely the methodological complexity of this type of investigations has left until now the work of diplomats such as Gines Vidal in Berlin, Juan Francisco de Cárdenas in the United States or the Duke of Alba in London, without a monographic study.

[24] V. Morales-Lezcano, *Historia de la No-beligerancia Española Durante la Segunda Guerra Mundial (VI, 1940-X, 1943)*, Valencia 1980.

[25] Morales Lezcano, *Historia de la No-Beligerancia* cit., p. 270.

[26] *Ibid.*, p. 103.

[27] J. Tusell - G. García, *Franco y Mussolini. La Política Española Durante la Segunda Guerra Mundial*, Barcelona 1985.

[28] *Ibid.*, p. 283.

[29] In 1992 the First Meeting of Historians on Franco's Regime took place.

[30] J.F. Berdah, *La Propaganda Cultural Británica en España durante la Segunda Guerra Mundial a través de la Acción del "British Council": Un aspecto de las relaciones Hispano-Británicas, 1939-1946*, in *El Régimen de Franco 1936-1975: Política y Relaciones Exteriores*, Madrid 1993, vol. II, pp. 273-287.

[31] R. García Pérez, *El Sueño Irrealizable, la Ambición Imperialista del Franquismo*, in *El Régimen de Franco 1936-1975* cit., pp. 287-299.

[32] S. Sueiro, *Sueños de Imperio. Las Pretensiones Territoriales Españolas en Marruecos y la Diplomacia Británica Durante la II Guerra Mundial*, in *El Régimen de Franco 1936-1975* cit., pp. 299-321.

33 F. Torres García, *El largo Camino hacia la Neutralidad: Las Difíciles Negociaciones para la Retirada de la División Azul, 1942-1943*, in *El Régimen de Franco 1936-1975* cit., pp. 329-343.

34 R. García Pérez, *España en la Europa Hitleriana*, "Espacio Tiempo y Forma (Serie Historia Contemporánea)", 7, 1994, pp. 35-51; S. Sueiro, *España en Tánger Durante la Segunda Guerra Mundial: La Consumación de un Viejo Anhelo*, "Espacio Tiempo y Forma (Serie Historia Contemporánea)", 7, 1994, pp. 135-165.

35 C. Velasco, *Propaganda y Publicidad Nazis en España durante la II Guerra Mundial: Algunas Características*, "Espacio Tiempo y Forma (Serie Historia Contemporánea)", 1994, 7, pp. 85-109; I. Schulze, *La propaganda Alemana en España, 1942-1944*, "Espacio Tiempo y Forma (Serie Historia Contemporánea)", 7, 1994, pp. 371-387.

36 C. Collado, *¿De España a San Francisco? Londres y Washington contra Franco y la Falange (1942-1945)*, "Espacio Tiempo y Forma (Serie Historia Contemporánea)", 7, 1994, pp. 51-85.

37 M.S. Gómez de las Heras, *España y Portugal ante la II Guerra Mundial desde 1939 hasta 1942*, "Espacio Tiempo y Forma (Serie Historia Contemporánea)", 7, 1994, pp. 165-181.

38 On the other hand we must note that the journal of the Association of Contemporary History, "Ayer", dedicated an issue in 1998 to the perception of Spain abroad, entitled *España, la Mirada del Otro*, with contributions of interest on Franco's regime, through the prism of the different European historiographies. Thus, Alfonso Botti and Ismael Saz Campos analyzed the Italian perspective, A. Botti, *El Franquismo en la Historiografía Italiana y la Mirada del Otro Sobre los Relatos de Otras Miradas*, "Ayer", 31, 1998, pp. 127-148; I. Saz, *El Objeto Cercano: La Dictadura Franquista en la Historiografía Italiana*, pp. 149-162; Patricia Digón and Enrique Moradiellos studied British Hispanicist approach, P. Digón, *El Hispanismo Británico y la Historiografía Contemporánea en España*, pp. 163-182; E. Moradiellos, *Más allá de la Leyenda Negra y del Mito Romántico: el concepto de España en el hispanismo británico contemporaneísta*, pp. 183-200; W.L. Bernecker and J.J. Carreras focussed on the German perspective, W.L. Bernecker, *La Historiografía Alemana sobre la Guerra Civil y el Franquismo*, pp. 237-266; J.J. Carreras, *Distante e Intermitente: España en la Historiografía Alemana*, pp. 267-278.

39 R. García Pérez, *Franquismo y Tercer Reich: Las Relaciones Económicas Hispano-Alemanas Durante la Segunda Guerra Mundial*, Madrid 1994.

40 García Pérez, *Franquismo y Tercer Reich* cit., p. 576. The work is opposed in some of its conclusions to the summary of Ángel Viñas's articles on the topic, written 10 years before. A. Viñas, *Guerra Dinero y Dictadura, Ayuda Fascista y Autarquía en la España de Franco*, Barcelona 1984. In the same line of interpretation as García Perez, see S. Payne, *La Política*, in J.L. García Delgado (ed.), *El Franquismo, el Juicio de la Historia*, Madrid 2000. For an analysis of the families that supported the Franco regime, see A. de Miguel, *Sociología del Franquismo*, Barcelona 1978.

41 J. Tusell, *Franco, España y la Segunda Guerra Mundial, entre el Eje y la Neutralidad*, Madrid 1995. Tusell not only uses the documentation of the Archive of the Ministry of Foreign Affairs but also official Italian, French and American documentation, as well as private archives.

42 Tusell's works likewise impact on an accusatory tradition against the minister and Franco's brother-in-law who, due to his distancing from the regime after the War, his ideological evolution and his intellectual baggage, enjoyed (until his death) prestige in the intellectual circles of the country.

43 Tusell, *Franco, España* cit., p. 646.

44 *Ibid.*

45 Coinciding with the publication of Tusell's work, in May and June, 1995, the Spanish Commission for the History of International Relations, in collaboration with UNED, organized a cycle of conferences with the title of *España y la II Guerra Mundial. 50 años Después*. The proceedings of the conferences were published in the *Bulletin d'Histoire Contemporaine de l'Espagne*, University of Bordeaux, no. 22 (December, 1995) and no. 23 (March, 1996).

46 This sector, during the 1990s, was already frankly in a minority in the field of contemporary history.

47 L. Suárez, *España Franco y la Segunda Guerra Mundial. Desde 1939 hasta 1945*, Madrid 1997.

48 M. Ros Agudo, *La Guerra Secreta de Franco*, Barcelona 2002. From this perspective, it shows the sometimes excessively tremulous prudence of Spanish historiography that the reissue of a work more than ten years old (P. Preston, *Franco, Caudillo de España*, Barcelona 2002.) had a greater impact that the publication of the brand new and top-quality work by Ros Agudo. Unfortunately it seems that for studies on Franco's regime, the foreign, fundamentally Anglo-Saxon origin, of a work is still a guarantee of quality. In the same line as Ros Agudo we can place the latest study on the Blue Division. X. Moreno, *La División Azul, Sangre Española en Rusia, 1941-1945*, Barcelona 2004. In 2004, Ignacio Merino published the novelized biography of Ramon Serrano-Suñer which, by its approach, lacks significant value to advance in the knowledge of the character. I. Merino, *Serrano-Suñer, Conciencia y Poder*, Madrid 2004

49 See Ros Agudo, *La Guerra Secreta* cit., p. XXVI.

50 E. Moradiellos, *Franco frente a Churchill*, Barcelona 2005; R. Wigg, *Churchill and Spain. The Survival of the Franco Regime, 1940-1945*, Oxford 2005.

51 This historiography, until now focused on a review of the causes and process of the Civil War, already aims at an interest in the political development of Franco's regime. Such is the case of Pío Moa: P. Moa, *Franco, un Balance Histórico*, Madrid 2005.

52 It is necessary to emphasize that African policy (which is not included in this section) had a special relevance in the context of Spanish diplomacy during World War II. Spain considered building an African empire at the cost of the French empire (these were, succinctly, some of Franco's principal requests to Hitler in Hendaye); on the other hand, from autumn 1942, the War moved with full force to North Africa, so that Spanish policy in the protectorate of Morocco was converted into a question of the first order for Spanish diplomacy. In any case, African policy is understood as a colonial process in which what is in play is the administration of territories that are considered as part of the nation in question, so that the works covered in the previous section inevitably tend to mention the African dimension in the Spanish politics. Morales-Lezcano is the greatest expert on the topic. See: V. Morales-Lezcano, *España y el Norte de África (1912-56). El Protectorado en Marruecos*, Madrid 1986. The same must be said of the United States. The relations with North America appear intimately involved in the aforementioned works.

53 L. Delgado, *Diplomacia Franquista y Política Cultural Hacia Iberoamérica, 1939-1953*, Madrid 1988.

54 *Ibid.*, p. 73. Thus, by the United States the Consejo was seen as an instrument of fifth-columnism of the Falange in America.

55 *Ibid.*, p. 77.

56 L. Delgado, *Imperio de papel. Acción Cultural y Política Exterior Durante el Primer Franquismo,* Madrid 1992. While the work continues to give preferential attention to the Latin-American environment, Delgado also directs his gaze to other zones of the European continent whose characteristics are still known almost exclusively through his references. This is case of Romania, Andorra or the north of Africa.

57 *Ibid.*, p. 385.

58 L. Delgado analyzed the gradual substitution of the concept of Spanishness for that of the Hispanic World in L. Delgado, *El Recurso al Mundo Hispánico, Elaboración y Trayectoria de Una Política de Sustitución*, in *El Régimen de Franco 1936-1975* cit., pp. 515-533.

59 R. Pardo, *¡Con Franco hacia el Imperio! La política Exterior Española en América Latina 1939-1945*, Madrid 1994.

60 *Ibid.*, pp. 340-341. Serrano tried, according to Pardo, to revitalize the Falangist affiliates without success, *ibid.*, p. 343.

[61] *Ibid.*, pp. 344-345.

[62] R. Ortega, *La proyección del Franquismo Hacia América Latina. La Política de Hispanidad a través del Ejemplo Chileno (1936-1957)*, in *El Régimen de Franco 1936-1975* cit., pp. 535-545.

[63] M. Quijada, *España y Argentina Durante la II Guerra Mundial*, "Espacio Tiempo y Forma (Serie Historia Contemporánea)", 7, 1994, pp. 256.

[64] R. Pardo, *"Leales, Tibios y Contrarios": El Ministerio de Asuntos Exteriores y las Colonias Pro-Republicanas en América, 1939-1945*, in *El Régimen de Franco 1936-1975* cit., pp. 579-595. On the republican exiles in Mexico, see also: A. Mateos, *Los Republicanos Españoles en el México Cardenista*, "Ayer", 47, 2002, pp. 103-128; D. Pla Brugat, *El Exilio Republicano en Hispanoamérica: Su Historia e Historiografía*, "Historia social", 42, 2002, pp. 99-122

[65] Pardo, *"Leales, Tibios y Contrarios"* cit., pp. 583-587. It was proposed, according to the author, to inform the other American republics that the Spanish Republican community in Mexico was organizing a communist network whose target was the whole continent; *ibid.*, p. 585.

[66] F. Rodao, *Franco y el Imperio Japonés, Imágenes y Propaganda en Tiempos de Guerra*, Barcelona 2002.

[67] The professor of the Imperial University of Kyushu, Fujisawa Chikao, was the principal mouthpiece of Spanish culture in Japan. Rodao, *Franco y el Imperio Japonés* cit., p. 135. The use of Japan in Spanish totalitarian propaganda has been analyzed by F. Rodao in: *Japón y la Propaganda Totalitaria en España, 1937-1945*, "Revista Española del Pacífico", 8, 1998, pp. 435-455.

[68] In the line of European conservative thought from the second half of the XIX century.

[69] Rodao, *Franco y el Imperio Japonés* cit., p. 133.

[70] *Ibid.*, p. 231 and 241. Japan was another motive for conflict between Falangists and traditional conservatism.

[71] *Ibid.*, p. 269.

[72] *Ibid.*, p. 406.

[73] *Ibid.*, pp. 506-507.

[74] *Ibid.*, pp. 165-166.

[75] Wang Jingwei, one of the principal leaders of the Guomingdang, would be enlisted to lead the pro-Japanese government, after being displaced from the leadership of the nationalist band by Jiang Jieshi.

[76] *Ibid.*, pp. 173-192.

[77] *Ibid.*, pp. 167.

[78] *Ibid.*, pp. 198.

[79] *Ibid.*, pp. 212-214 and 218. Recall in this respect that Chase's work, *Falange, el Ejercito Secreto del Eje en América*, was alluding in first place to the activities of the Falange in the Philippines. Rodao has studied monographically the development of the Falange in Asia. F. Rodao, *Falange en Extremo Oriente, 1936-1945*, "Revista Española del Pacífico", 3, 1993, pp. 85-112.

[80] Rodao, *Franco y el Imperio Japonés* cit., pp. 406-416.

[81] *Ibid.*, pp. 416-417.

[82] *Ibid.*, pp. 416-418. See also F. Rodao, *El Trampolín Tecnológico. El Incidente Laurel y España Durante la Segunda Guerra Mundial*, "Espacio Tiempo y Forma (Serie Historia Contemporánea)", 7, 1994, pp. 387-413.

[83] The consequences of Franco's policies during the War for Spanish culture in the Philippines have been analyzed by Rodao in: *Lo que Perdió También España en la Batalla de Manila*, "Revista Española del Pacífico", 6, 1997, pp. 145-149. F. Rodao, *La Cultura Española en Oceanía Después de 1898*, "Revista Española del Pacífico", 7, 1997, pp. 30-43.

[84] As a highlight in the field of significant unpublished and unknown documents referring to the period: E. Sáenz-Francés, *Las Memorias Secretas del Embajador von Moltke. Un Estudio Peliminar*, "Letras de Deusto", 110, 2006, pp. 85-134..

Bibliography

Areilza J.M. de - Castiella F.M., *Reivindicaciones de España*, Madrid 1941.

Beaulac W.L., *Franco, Secret Ally in Second World War*, Carbondale 1986.

Cava M.J., *Los Diplomáticos de Franco, José Félix de Lequerica*, Bilbao 1984.

Chase A., *Falange, The Axis Secret Army in the Americas*, New York 1943.

Cierva R. de la, *Francisco Franco, Un Siglo de España*, 2 vols., Madrid 1973.

Id., *Historia del Franquismo I, Orígenes y Configuración*, Barcelona 1975.

Cortada J.W., *United States-Spanish Relations, Wolfram and World War II*, Barcelona 1971.

Delgado L., *Diplomacia Franquista y Política Cultural Hacia Iberoamérica, 1939-1953*, Madrid 1988.

Id., *Imperio de papel. Acción Cultural y Política Exterior Durante el Primer Franquismo*, Madrid 1992.

Detwiler D.S., *Hitler, Franco und Gibraltar*, Wiesbaden 1962.

Doussinague J.M., *España Tenía Razón*, Madrid 1949.

Feis H., *The Spanish History, Franco and The Nations War*, New York 1948.

García Delgado J.L. - Tuñon de Lara M. (eds.), *El Primer Franquismo, España Durante la II Guerra Mundial*, V Coloquio de Historia Contemporánea de España, Madrid 1989, pp. 245-268.

García Delgado J.L. (ed.), *El Franquismo, el Juicio de la Historia*, Madrid 2000.

García Pérez R., *Franquismo y Tercer Reich: Las Relaciones Económicas Hispano-Alemanas Durante la Segunda Guerra Mundial*, Madrid 1994.

Halstead C.R., *Spain, the Powers and the Second World War*, Virginia 1962.

Hayes C.J.H., *Wartime Mission in Spain: 1942-1945*, New York 1946.

Id., *The United States and Spain, an Interpretation*, New York 1951.

Hoare S., *Ambassador on Special Mission*, London 1946.

Miguel A. de, *Sociología del Franquismo*, Barcelona 1978.

Moradiellos E., *Franco frente a Churchill*, Barcelona 2005.

Morales-Lezcano V., *Historia de la No-beligerancia Española Durante la Segunda Guerra Mundial (VI, 1940-X, 1943)*, Valencia 1980.

Id., *España y el Norte de África (1912-56). El Protectorado en Marruecos*, Madrid 1986.

Pardo R., *¡Con Franco hacia el Imperio! La política Exterior Española en América Latina 1939-1945*, Madrid 1994.

Parr E., *The Relations of General Franco and the Spanish Nationalists with the Axis Powers*, Aberystwyth (Wales) 1956.

Proctor R., *Agony of a Neutral: Spanish-German Wartime Relations and the "Blue Division"*, Moscow (Idaho) 1974.

Quintana F., *La Historia de las Relaciones Internacionales en España, Apuntes para un Balance Historiográfico. in La Historia de las Relaciones Internacionales: Una visión desde España*, Madrid 1996.

Rodao F., *Franco y el Imperio Japonés, Imágenes y Propaganda en Tiempos de Guerra*, Barcelona 2002.

Ros Agudo M., *La Guerra Secreta de Franco*, Barcelona 2002.

Ruhl K.J., *Franco, Falange y III Reich. España Durante la Segunda Guerra Mundial*, Madrid 1986.

Serrano Suñer R., *Entre Hendaya y Gibraltar*, Madrid 1947.

Id., *Memorias: Entre el Silencio y la Propaganda, la Historia como Fue*, Barcelona 1978.

Suárez L., *España Franco y la Segunda Guerra Mundial. Desde 1939 hasta 1945*, Madrid 1997.

Tusell J. - García G., *Franco y Mussolini. La Política Española Durante la Segunda Guerra Mundial*, Barcelona 1985.

Tusell J. (ed.), *El Régimen de Franco 1936-1975: Política y Relaciones Exteriores*, Madrid 1993.

Id., *Franco, España y la Segunda Guerra Mundial, entre el Eje y la Neutralidad*, Madrid 1995.

Viñas A., *Guerra Dinero y Dictadura, Ayuda Fascista y Autarquía en la España de Franco*, Barcelona 1984.

Wigg W., *Churchill and Spain The Survival of the Franco Regime, 1940-1945*, Oxford 2005.

Journals

Botti A., *El Franquismo en la Historiografía Italiana y la Mirada del Otro Sobre los Relatos de Otras Miradas*, "Ayer", 31, 1998, pp. 127-148.

Collado C., *¿De España a San Francisco? Londres y Washington contra Franco y la Falange (1942-1945)*, "Espacio Tiempo y Forma (Serie Historia Contemporánea)", 7, 1994, pp. 51-85.

Digón, P., *El Hispanismo Británico y la Historiografía Contemporánea en España*, "Ayer", 31, 1998, pp. 163-182.

García Pérez R., *España en la Europa Hitleriana*, "Espacio Tiempo y Forma (Serie Historia Contemporánea)", 7, 1994, pp. 35-51.

Gómez de las Heras M.S., *España y Portugal ante la II Guerra Mundial desde 1939 hasta 1942*, "Espacio Tiempo y Forma (Serie Historia Contemporánea)", 7, 1994, pp. 165-181.

Mateos A., *Los Republicanos Españoles en el México Cardenista*, "Ayer", 47, 2002, pp. 103-128.

Moradiellos E., *Más allá de la Leyenda Negra y del Mito Romántico: el concepto de España en el hispanismo británico contemporaneísta*, "Ayer", 31, 1998, pp. 183-200.

Pla Brugat D., *El Exilio Republicano en Hispanoamérica: Su Historia e Historiografía*, "Historia social", 42, 2002, pp. 99-122.

Quijada M., *España y Argentina Durante la II Guerra Mundial*, "Espacio Tiempo y Forma (Serie Historia Contemporánea)", 7, 1994, pp. 256.

Rodao F., *Falange en Extremo Oriente, 1936-1945*, "Revista Española del Pacífico", 3, 1993, pp. 85-112.

Id., *El Trampolín Tecnológico. El Incidente Laurel y España Durante la Segunda Guerra Mundial*, "Espacio Tiempo y Forma (Serie Historia Contemporánea)", 7, 1994, pp. 387-413.

Id., *Lo que Perdió También España en la Batalla de Manila*, "Revista Española del Pacífico", 6, 1996, pp. 145-149.

Id., *La Cultura Española en Oceanía Después de 1898*, "Revista Española del Pacífico", 7, 1997, pp. 30-43.

Id., *Japón y la Propaganda Totalitaria en España, 1937-1945*, "Revista Española del Pacífico", 8, 1998, pp. 435-455.

Sáenz-Francés San Baldomero E., *Las Memorias Secretas del Embajador von Moltke. Un Estudio Preliminar*, "Letras de Deusto", 110, 2006, pp. 85-134.

Saz I., *El Objeto Cercano: La Dictadura Franquista en la Historiografía Italiana*, "Ayer", 31, 1998, pp. 149-162.

Schulze I., *La propaganda Alemana en España, 1942-1944*, "Espacio Tiempo y Forma (Serie Historia Contemporánea)", 7, 1994, pp. 371-387.

Sueiro S., *España en Tánger Durante la Segunda Guerra Mundial: La Consumación de un Viejo Anhelo*, "Espacio Tiempo y Forma (Serie Historia Contemporánea)", 7, 1994, pp. 135-165.

Velasco C., *Propaganda y Publicidad Nazis en España durante la II Guerra Mundial: Algunas Características*, "Espacio Tiempo y Forma (Serie Historia Contemporánea)", 7, 1994, pp. 85-109.

Whose History is History? Singularities and Dualities of the Public Debate on Belgian Colonialism

GEERT CASTRYCK
Ghent University

In deze bijdrage wordt ingegaan op verantwoordelijkheden in het debat over de Belgische koloniale geschiedenis. Het gaat daarbij om de historische verantwoordelijkheden van koning Leopold II, het Belgische kolonialisme of de Belgen, maar vooral ook om de verantwoordelijkheden van historici.

Naar aanleiding van enkele ophefmakende publieke manifestaties (boeken, films, tentoonstellingen) kende België de voorbije jaren een Congo-opstoot. Het begin ervan viel min of meer samen met de verschijning van de boeken van Adam Hochschild, De geest van koning Leopold II en de plundering van de Congo (1998), en van Ludo De Witte, De moord op Lumumba (1999). Deze brachten het duistere hart van het Belgische optreden in Centraal-Afrika onder het voetlicht. Er barstte een debat los in de academische wereld, in de media en in de politiek. De parlementaire onderzoekscommissie naar de moord op Lumumba (1999-2002) en de televisiedocumentaire door Peter Bate, White King, Red Rubber, Black Death (2004), vonden de meeste weerklank en lokten ook politieke reacties uit.

Het Koninklijk Museum voor Midden-Afrika te Tervuren wou met haar tentoonstelling Het geheugen van Congo: de koloniale tijd (2005) een genuanceerde en in tijd en ruimte gecontextualiseerde versie van de Belgische koloniale geschiedenis brengen, en zo het woedende debat modereren. Ze bereikten echter enkel dat het in alle hevigheid opflakkerde en niet minder gepolariseerd is dan tevoren.

Het debat kent tegenstellingen tussen een generatie die door de koloniale mythologie is gevoed en een die nooit over de koloniale geschiedenis heeft gehoord, tussen een groep die het kolonialisme verdedigt en een groep die het verwerpelijk vindt, tussen Belgen die het debat voeren en Congolezen die uit het debat geweerd worden, tussen Vlaanderen en Franstalig België, en tussen historici en het brede publiek.

Twee dominante standpunten in het debat zijn dat de koloniale schandalen opgeklopt worden om België en het koningshuis te schaden, en dat Belgische historici de heikele thema's uit hun geschiedenis uit de weg gaan of toedekken. Deze twee benaderingen vallen opvallend samen met de Belgisch-Franstalige respectievelijk de Vlaamse teneur van het debat, en staan in feite in dialoog – of dovemansgesprek

Historici lijken veel te lang afwezig gebleven uit dit debat, maar bij nader toezien, blijken de versies die het publiek uiteindelijk wel hebben bereikt, vrijwel uitsluitend te putten uit het werk van Belgisch historisch onderzoek. Dit brengt mij tot de conclusie dat historici niet zozeer zijn tekort geschoten in het onderkennen en onderzoeken van delicate thema's, maar wel in het kenbaar maken van hun onderzoeksresultaten en in het opleiden van nieuwe onderzoekers. Deze vaststelling maakt het probleem niet minder acuut, maar impliceert integendeel dat het eigen is aan een actuele academische attitude en zich niet beperkt tot het domein van de koloniale of Afrikaanse geschiedenis.

Introduction

In February 2005, *The Memory of Congo: the Colonial Era*, a much debated exhibition on the colonial history of the Belgian Congo, opened at the Royal Museum for Central Africa in Tervuren (RMCA). The museum itself is part and parcel of this history and is without any doubt the single most important relic or witness to Belgian colonialism in the public sphere. Therefore, the exhibitioner is implicitly and symbolically also the exhibited. This apparent ambiguity is at the same time a unique opportunity, and the current management of the museum is well aware of this. Already at the time of a previous exhibition in 2001, *ExItCongoMuseum*, the RMCA combined its double identity of exhibitioner and exhibited with a modest touch of exhibitionism, in showing the historical layeredness, the social life and the moral implications of their own collection. This caused internal protest against any form of self-criticism, whereas external critics welcomed the initiative but thought it was too little, too late. In the 2005 exhibition, a less articulate reminder of this self reflection was exhibited, though stuck away in a corner and reduced to a display that stressed the prestigiousness of the collection rather than the contestation of how it had been acquired, decontextualised and recontextualised. This case is in a way a small-scale example of the colonial debate in Belgium. It is about the "other" but above all about the "self", it involves internal discordances and external interferences, it includes questions of layeredness and moral responsibilities, and it is an issue of struggle nicely put away in the corner of an old building.

In this contribution I shall analyse different ways in which colonial history is remembered and not remembered in Belgian public spheres. The public debates during the first years of this century surrounding the monograph by Adam Hochschild, *King Leopold's Ghost: A Story of Greed, Terror and Heroism in Central Africa* (1998), the television documentary by Peter Bate, *White King, Red Rubber, Black Death* (2004), and the exhibition by the RMCA, *The Memory of Congo: the Colonial Era* (2005), offer plenty of insights into the character of these remembrances and memories[1]. These issues were almost exclusively debated by journalists, politicians, academics and (former) colonials, but over the years the debates became ever more public, both in style and in scope. On the reverse side of the debates, however, there are some remarkable instances of indifference and of difference that deserve closer attention. Especially the relative absence of Congolese in the debates, the superficial or lethargic attitude of 'the public', and the generational, (sub)national, (inter)national, ideological, and professional cleavages are at least as revealing about the position of colonial history in the Belgian public spheres, as the actual debates on the surface.

White King, Red Rubber, Black Death

In April 2004, a documentary by Peter Bate on the cruel history in King Leopold II's Congo Free State was broadcast by both the Flemish and the Belgian-francophone public television stations. This event was the culminating point of a controversy that started in 1999 after the sensation surrounding the Dutch and French translations of Hochschild's monograph. In both the book and the documentary, the story is told of how King Leopold II of the Belgians obtained the Congo as a personal possession and how he earned huge amounts of riches by the brutal exploitation of rubber and people. The Belgian support for and interest in the king's colonial endeavours were derisory, and initially he had difficulties in avoiding bankruptcy. However, after the invention of the rubber tyre and the automobile, and the discovery of natural latex in the Congolese rainforest, he organised a reckless rubber harvest in which he actually preferred derisory interest. The campaign was based on forced labour, harvest quotas, and excessive measures of punishment and terror, including chopping off hands, killing people, destroying plantations and villages... The cruel intimidations drove rubber harvesters deeper and deeper into the forest, exposing them to hardship, hunger, danger, and disease. Their relatives were weakened by lack of food and labour, which drove them to hunger and disease as well. In the end, the combination of murder and torture, death by starvation and disease, and the disruption of demographic reproduction caused a steep fall in the population figures... or rather a dramatic decline of the population, since actual figures are not available. Micro research in a few villages severely affected by the rubber terror has shown that in that area at least half of the population disappeared[2]. It is difficult to extrapolate these figures to the Congo as a whole, but there is no doubt whatsoever as to the massive terror that took place under the personal responsibility of King Leopold II of the Belgians.

However, a debate between believers and disbelievers is raging around the figures, around the use of the words 'genocide' or 'holocaust', about the question if the king actually *knew* what was happening under his responsibility, and about the wider context of this horror. Adam Hochschild, and Peter Bate with him, adheres to estimates that the rubber terror caused a demographic deficit of 10 million people out of a total population of 20 million[3]. The RMCA on the occasion of their 2005 exhibition, accepted an approach that hypothesises a demographic regression of 20% for the whole of the Congo, due to a combination of epidemics, forced labour, mass migration, slave trade, and the Leopoldian terror. They refrain from using absolute figures, because it is impossible to know how many people lived in the Congo at the beginning of colonisation, and they accept implicitly that some regions were more heavily affected than this 20% average[4]. Hochschild also accepts that we will never know for sure, but nevertheless sticks to a regression of approximately 50% without making a distinction between different regions within the Congo[5]. At the other end of the debate, we find a calculation by (former) colonials, who claim that the number of people involved in the rubber regime remained *bien en dessous des cent mille* [well under 100,000][6]. Their calculation is completely implausible, since it ignores 'collateral damage' by hunger and disease, and since it naively believes that – later – laws were always in vigour and, moreover, effective. Nevertheless, their caricaturist stance is important, because they took sides with the RMCA, who in fact replied to the same statements. Hence, the defensive attitude at Tervuren is contaminated by a denial – which may have been the intention of some of them in the first place.

Anyway, whatever the estimate one follows or does not follow, the record remains horrific. Even if one believes the preposterous abstraction that less than 100,000 Congolese were involved in the rubber episode and that many of them died as a consequence, then this still is the single most deadly page in the history book of the Kingdom of the Belgians – at least, if it were in it – leaving both World Wars, including the mass murder of the Jews during the Second, far behind. As a matter of fact, this comparison with the genocide of the Jews is a strong emotional argument in the debate. Nobody really claims that what happened in Leopold II's Congo Free State was genocide. There was no intention "to destroy, in whole or in part, a national, ethnical, racial or religious group"[7]. The intention was to obtain riches and the execution was arbitrary and not aimed against a specific group[8]. Nevertheless, the number of casualties leads Adam Hochschild and others to comparisons with the Holocaust – with capital a 'H' – and to the use of the term holocaust, meaning massive destruction, but automatically alluding to the mass destruction of Jews in Europe. The subtitle of the French translation of *King Leopold's Ghost*, even contains the word *holocauste* [holocaust][9]. On the other side of the debate, people object to the use of the word "holocaust" or the suggestion of a genocide – or "genocidal scale" – in much the same way as they object to the claim that 10 million Congolese died. The francophone Belgian historian Jean-Luc Vellut, who is a renowned expert in the historiography and the political economy of the Belgian Congo, responded to Hochschild's book by declaring to the British newspaper "The Guardian" that "to compare it [the violent history of Leopold II's Congo] with the Holocaust or Auschwitz is an insult to the truth"[10]. At the time of the broadcast of Peter Bate's documentary, the director of the Royal Museum for Central Africa, Guido Gryseels, reacted in similar fashion by questioning the accuracy of the '10 million'-estimate and by assigning the brutal practices in Leopold II's Congo Free State – which neither he nor Vellut deny as such – to limited areas and a limited number of perpetrators[11]. In other words, they accept that extreme violence did occur and even on a massive scale, but they refute the idea that this was part of a system instead of unacceptable and unaccepted excesses. They also contest that this brutality was more excessive in the Congo than in other colonies. In short, they play down the Belgian and royal responsibilities.

In the same message, Gryseels also claimed that there is no reason to believe that King Leopold II ordered the use of violence. This brings yet another element of discord to the fore: was Leopold II aware of what happened, could or should he have known, did he care at all, and how far reaching was and is the royal and/or the Belgian responsibility? The historical record is quite clear that Leopold II ordered to harvest as much rubber as possible, and that he established a reward system that directly provoked all kind of abuses. He also was very well informed about all the proceedings in the Congo, and he did not pay much attention to the human cost. There is, however, no evidence that he ordered the actual killing of thousands or millions of people. Most certainly no one gave such an order, but he did cause it and was absolutely accountable. Of course, this does not turn the perpetrators in the field into innocent executors, but the final and paramount responsibility of the king of the Belgians is undeniable.

If one is to understand why this issue is so very sensitive for some and sensational for others, one has to look at the context of all these statements and at 20th-century Belgian history, and Belgian colonial history in particular. The context of Hochschild's statements, for instance, is that of a human rights' activist. Therefore, the more gruesome and unique the abuses are, the more heroic its contesters. It is, undoubtedly, not a coincidence that the word "heroism" figures in the title of his book. However, with respect to the subject of this contribution it is more important to find out the motivations of those people who consistently try to adjust – not necessarily without good arguments, by the way – the number of victims, the radius of cruelty, the deliberateness of crime, and the role of the king. By reducing the extent of the accusations, they seem to believe they can tear down the pervasiveness and trustworthiness of the accusation as such. In so doing, they make it very tempting to draw comparisons with the Holocaust and its negationists... There is, however, a reason for all of this: just like every nation in the world, Belgium has been built on myths[12], and the civilising genius of Leopold II is one of them. The unifying force and fairy story appeal of the royal family as a whole is another one. In this respect, it is striking to notice that the above statements by Gryseels were pronounced on the occasion of a visit to the museum by the present king of the Belgians, Albert II. These myths are especially strong for people who identify with Belgian colonialism[13]. They consider Leopold II as their founding father and the myth of his civilising mission as their single most important – and, again, heroic – paradigm. Criticism of Leopold II is considered as criticism of their own life and work, of their sincere – though misguided – idealism, of their royal family, and of Belgium as a whole.

The debate may appear to be a struggle with external contesters, like the American journalist Adam Hochschild or the British director Peter Bate, but the real fear is internal. In fact, Adam Hochschild and Peter Bate add virtually nothing to the historiography on the Congo. As far as contents are concerned, all had already been written before. In a review of the Dutch translation of *King Leopold's Ghost*, the expert in Belgian foreign politics Rik Coolsaet wrote: *Wat nieuw is voor Hochschild is hier intussen al lang bekend. [...] de werkelijkheid achter het patriottische discours over het Belgisch kolonialisme [is] al lang doorprikt* [What is new to Hochschild is already known over here. (...) the reality behind the patriotic discourse on Belgian colonialism has already been exposed for a long time][14]. In fact, the Belgian researchers Jules Marchal (under the pseudonym A.M.

Delathuy), Daniel Vangroenweghe, Jean Stengers, Jan Vansina and Jean-Luc Vellut had already uncovered many details in the 1980s. Hochschild, by the way, draws most of his information from Jules Marchal, but both he and Bate did add something to the historical debate: they made it public.

King Leopold's Ghost

A remarkable aspect of the controversy following the publication of the Dutch and French translations of Hochschild's book was the anger and the shock. Although there was nothing new in this monograph – apart, maybe, from its eloquence – it was new to the readers, who were either baffled by it or furious. Apparently, Belgians did not know or did not want to know what historians – so they pretend – already knew for ages. The myths surrounding Leopold II were at stake. It was as if his ghost came to life, which is either horror or desecration, and in any case lese-majesty.

In fact, the publication of *King Leopold's Ghost* triggered two debates: one in academic circles about the accuracy of Hochschild's allegations, and one in the media and public spheres, in which academics participated as well, about the double shame – of what happened and of not knowing. At the time, however, scholars in African studies were more interested in what would come out of the research on the assassination of Congo's first Prime Minister Patrice Lumumba, than in a book that only repeated what they already knew. The contrast between the public and academic reactions was so absolute that it became obvious that there is a serious problem in the communication of research results to the public. This problem is threefold: (1) the silent majority is basically not interested – and never was – in Congolese or colonial affairs, (2) African studies in Belgium are extremely minimal and the academic attitude in general attaches little importance to informing broader society, and (3) the political situation causes a preference for keeping history unknown. Moreover, these three aspects are closely intertwined.

Contrary to most nation-states, Belgium survived the past few decades by *not* constructing a national identity, by avoiding national history. Recently, *belgitude* is cultivated again, and, ironically, the absence of nationality is now praised as typically Belgian, hence as the national identity[15]. Nevertheless, the neglect of history has been a conscious policy for a long time, and in the 1970s the then Belgian government even seriously considered abolishing the teaching of history altogether. Since history historically is the science of the nation-state, history becomes useless or even embarrassing when the nation virtually collapses, or when several nations live side by side in an ambiguous mix of conflict and connivance as is the case in present-day Belgium. It has not always been like this. After World War I, Belgian nation-building was in a winning mood and the then Belgian colony was part of the propaganda. In 1908, after a fierce international and national campaign against the abuses in the Congo Free State, Leopold II handed over – or sold – his personal possession to the Belgian state, and from that moment onwards the Congo was a Belgian colony. Belgian propaganda and policy never drew a line between the two eras, but on the contrary organised a collective amnesia on the pre-War scandals[16]. At the same time, and more than ever, king Leopold II was honoured as the genial founder of the Congo. Even on the day of Congolese independence, on June 30th 1960, the then Belgian king, Baudouin I, uttered a perfect summary of the Belgian colonial idea, including an extensive celebration of Leopold II. On that same day, a speech by Prime Minister Lumumba gave a completely opposite perspective, which condemned Belgian colonialism altogether. The Belgian king and his establishment were "scandalised", quite as much as they had been at the beginning of the century because of the international human rights campaign against the Leopoldian abuses, and as they would be again at the beginning of the next century when Bate's documentary was broadcasted.

Lumumba did not survive his appraisal of colonial history very long: within weeks he was dismissed as Prime Minister and by early 1961 he was murdered. What happened in these crucial months was the subject of the book written by Ludo De Witte, in which he established the responsibilities of some Belgian politicians, colonial administrators and the king. In the year of publication, 1999, the Belgian government, the first one without Christian Democrats since 1954, made the surprising decision to start a Parliamentary Commission to investigate the events of 1960-1961. Four Belgian historians, nicely picked from different language and ideological groups but excluding Congolese participation[17], were allowed to do research using hitherto closed archives. Avoiding the reprimanding tone of De Witte, they pretty much came to the same conclusions, accepted by the Belgian parliament in February 2002.

Thus, between 1999 and 2002, both the beginning and the end of Belgian colonial history lost its mythical aura, and twice the Belgian establishment, including the equally mythical royalty, bore a dazzling responsibility. In a political context where Belgium as a whole and the monarchy in particular are often questioned, this entailed emotional reactions. (Former) colonials, understandably, felt as if their life and work was reduced to the temporal and moral extremes of colonialism, with which these men, who mostly worked in the Congo between 1930 and 1960, had little to do – at least in a direct way. Less understandably, they nevertheless felt as if these crimes concerned them personally. They – that is, (former) colonials who still today build their identity primarily on their former career – may have had good, even idealistic intentions in colonial times, maybe they even sincerely believed in the paternalistic and patriotic project, and they may have accepted the mythology around the founding father and royal protection, but it is surprising that they cannot or do not want to draw a distinction between their own job and the wrongs of predecessors and superiors. Apart from possible present political preferences, this is a consequence of two related facts. First, the Belgian colonial world view, on which (former) colonials had built their identity, was grounded in myths which had never been questioned before – except by Lumumba in 1960, but he was considered a 'communist' and hence not trustworthy by definition. Both an accepted 'truth' and the basis of their identity were now being questioned, and therefore this forcibly had to be false. A second fact is the genuine traumatic experience of many colonials when they fled the Congo in 1960, when they received an often hostile reception upon arrival in Belgium, and when they perceived that their beloved Congo endured ever harder times or, put another way, that their work in the Congo was ruined. Their side of the story, so they feel, is neglected and has been ever since their forced return in 1960. This explains the enthusiasm of (former) colonials when their experiences find their way into monographs and oral history projects. It is definitely not a coincidence that such books and projects emerged together with the (anti)colonial controversies of the past few years[18]. There is, by the way, some ground for the feeling that their side of the story has been neglected, but then again, this is because the colonial story has been neglected altogether after 1960.

After Congolese independence, the Belgian expertise on Central-Africa – whether biased or not – was largely dismantled. Research institutes were either abolished (Colonial University in Antwerp, Scientific Research Institute on Central Africa IRSAC-IWOCA, Afrika Insituut in Leuven...) or contained in politically harmless – at least so it seemed in pre-postmodernist times – fields like linguistics, geology, or agricultural sciences (Universiteit Gent, the scientific sections of the Royal Museum for Central Africa...). African history was still pretty much considered a *contradictio in terminis*[19], and colonial history was hardly included in Belgian national history either. The colonial endeavour had never caused much zeal in Belgium, which explains both the rather hostile reception of former colonials and the rapid elimination of expertise. In short, there were no chairs in African or Belgian imperial history at Belgian universities and as a lasting consequence no Belgian historians were trained in this field for decades[20]. There were, however, some Belgian historians who used to work at the IRSAC-IWOCA or who worked at the Congolese universities of Lovanium (Kinshasa) and Elisabethville (Lubumbashi), and some notable exceptions at Belgian universities who showed a certain interest in Belgian colonial history as a corollary of their research. Jan Vansina, Jean-Luc Vellut and Jean Stengers even built an international reputation as leading scholars in their fields, but within the Belgian context there seemed to be no popular interest in their findings. This problem, however, is not limited to colonial or African history.

The main gateway to bring the results of historical research to the public is schools, but since even the teachers did not take courses on African or colonial history at university, they were not in a position to integrate the latest research results in their own teaching. Schoolbooks continued to give the colonialist mythology on Belgian heroism, until Congo disappeared from history courses altogether[21]. The reason for this omission is partly that knowledge about the Congo and Belgian colonialism had no direct 'use' anymore, but it was also a consequence of internal political evolutions. Belgium, being a bi-national state, started to disintegrate at about the same time it lost its (African) colonies, and education was one of the first domains to be split. To say the least, stressing Belgian unity and pride is no longer an unquestioned priority in history courses. History, as I already mentioned before, was even considered completely superfluous and there were serious plans to proclaim the end of history 15 years before Fukuyama. As a result, there is a generational difference in Belgium concerning knowledge of colonial history: the youngest half of the population does not know colonial history because they never learned about it at school, and the oldest half of the population... does not know colonial history because they only learned the colonialist propaganda.

D-Bate

The publications of Hochschild's and De Witte's monographs, the parliamentary commission to investigate the assassination of Lumumba, as well as the Rwandan genocide and the Central African World War, caused debates in academic circles, in the media and in politics. The documentary directed by Peter Bate on king Leopold's looting massacre in the Congo Free State put this part of the story into a mass format and, therefore, the day it was broadcasted can be considered D-Day in the Belgian public confrontation with (its own?) colonial past.

On the occasion of the broadcast Louis Michel, who was then Belgian Minister of Foreign Affairs and who is now European Commissioner of Development and Humanitarian Aid, sent a communiqué after seeing *fragments* of the documentary (29/03/2004). In it, he wrote that he "normally would prefer to leave the debate to historians", but he meaningfully did not stick to his normal preferences this time. He stated that he was "shocked" and that it was a "partisan work giving a completely one-sided image of Leopold II and his era". He also mentioned that "all the positive contributions that are recognised by our Congolese partners" were omitted. Michel is clearly a member of the oldest half of the population. I, on the contrary, wonder what the positive contributions there could possibly have been during the period under scrutiny in the documentary (approximately 1895-1905). Again, we witness someone who is not able to draw a distinction between the utter looting at the early stage of colonialism, and the – more ambiguous – mix of exploitation, domination, infrastructural works, hospitals, schools... afterwards. It is symptomatic and revealing that a lot of people seem unprepared and incapable of distinguishing between Leopold II and Belgian colonialism as a whole – or between the royal family and Belgium as a whole.

This royal family also notified that it was "scandalised" by the documentary[22], and the equally royal Museum for Central Africa criticised the documentary and linked their objections to the exhibition *The memory of Congo: the colonial era* that was then in preparation[23]. Two years before, the same exhibition had already been announced as a reaction to Hochschild's book[24]. When the exhibition finally opened in February 2005, as a component of the celebrations of the 175th anniversary of the Belgian state, the director of the RMCA all of a sudden claimed that it is not their duty to make political statements...[25]. A fourth official Belgian protest against Bate's documentary was posted on the website of the Belgian embassy to the United Kingdom of Great Britain and Northern Ireland, and is still online today[26].

The broadcast also evoked a heated media debate, and the difference between the Flemish and the Belgian-francophone debates was staggering. The francophone media shared the scandalised feeling of their king and minister. The broadcasting company created a package deal consisting of a historical contextualisation of the documentary, then the documentary itself, and finally a debate about the documentary. The francophone press in Belgium overtly questioned the credibility of the historians who were interviewed in the documentary. With regard to the Congolese historian Elikia M'Bokolo, "La Libre Belgique" declared that he is not one of the experts on Belgian colonialism, and *parmi les autres intervenants, tous néerlandophones, figurent notamment le journaliste Marc Reynebeau ("Knack") ainsi qu'un missionnaire. Les spécialistes qui font le plus autorité sur notre passé africain, tels Ginette Kurgan (ULB) ou Jean- Luc Vellut (UCL), n'ont pas été rencontrés par l'équipe anglaise. On les entendra, en revanche, dans le débat qui suivra la diffusion* [among the other discussants, all of them Flemish speaking, are notably the journalist Marc Reynebeau ("Knack") as well as a missionary. The most renowned experts on our African past, like Ginette Kurgan (ULB) or Jean-Luc Vellut (UCL), were not contacted by the English team. We will hear them, in return, during the debate following the broadcast][27]. Another Brussels-based francophone newspaper, "Le Soir", was even more explicit in its paranoia and suggested that the fact that only Flemish historians took part in the documentary was part of a Flemish-nationalist plan to hit Leopold II and the royal family, and to undermine the Belgian union[28].

The Flemish press also questioned the credibility of the historians, but in quite the opposite way. The prevailing question was why Belgians did not know about this[29]. Ironically, the journalist who was discarded by "La Libre Belgique", is the main proponent of the claim that Belgian historians failed to study the controversial aspects of colonial history. Already in January 2003 Marc Reynebeau, who is in fact a qualified historian, blamed Belgian historians for not paying attention[30] , and he reiterates this charge unabatedly[31]. His statement is that all the controversial parts of Belgian colonial history have been studied by non-historians and/or non-Belgians, and this allegation has been picked up by others, either to demand that Belgian historians write their 'own' history[32], or to minimize the credibility of the work by so-called "amateur-historians"[33]. But is Reynebeau's statement correct? Without any doubt, it is at least partly true, but every half-truth is also a half lie. When we look at research by Belgian historians, we notice that a lot has been done already. The non-Belgian non-historians that Reynebeau seems to admire, draw almost all their facts from this research. However, it is a bitter reality that this research hardly reached the public: not through widely accessible and marketed books, not through education, not through the training of historians. Not only research, but also spreading the results is an academic responsibility, and in this respect Reynebeau and his adherents are right in blaming historians. In the remainder of this contribution, I shall give a short overview of the research that *has* been done by Belgian historians, and of the acute deficiencies that have to be remedied.

We already mentioned that after Congolese independence there was no chair in African history at any Belgian university. When, eventually, the Catholic University at Louvain-la-Neuve did establish an African chair, its consecutive holders, Louis Jadin and Jean-Luc Vellut, did an excellent job in making text editions, bibliographies, research guides, and the like[34]. They thus enabled historical research by others, as is what one can expect from the only chair available. Facilitating research and training researchers are, by the way, as important among the responsibilities of academic historians as conducting research properly. They conducted research, however, as well, and especially Vellut was prolific and influential with his work on the political economy of colonial Congo. He is not the kind of historian who looks for controversies, but he did not avoid contentious topics either. He did, amongst other things, write about violence in the Congo Free State[35], and Hochschild used Vellut's writings on colonial violence in his monograph.

When we take a closer look at Hochschild's *King Leopold's Ghost*, we notice that almost his entire work is based on research by Belgians, especially Jules Marchal, Daniel Vangroenweghe, Jan Vansina, and Jean Stengers. Stengers, professor at the *Université Libre de Bruxelles* [Free University Brussels], was an expert in, among other things, Belgian institutions and kings. He studied Leopold II's dealings with colonialism in general and with the Congo in particular; he furnished a wealth of information, but he believed he could and should avoid moral judgements[36].

Vansina is probably the world's most famous scholar in African history. He never hesitated to study controversial themes and to make controversial statements[37], but he is not always included in overviews of Belgian historians because he could not find an assignment at a Belgian university. According to Reynebeau, this is due to his controversial attitude[38]. It is also amazing to see how many people consider Jan Vansina, who holds a Ph.D. in history and is professor emeritus of history and anthropology at the University of Wisconsin, Madison, as anything but a historian: I have seen him labelled Africanist[39], ethnographer[40], anthropologist[41], linguist[42]... In the end, the Belgian historian Jan Vansina becomes a non-Belgian non-historian. One can wonder if this happens despite the fact that he does what one expects from a Belgian historian, or rather because what he does is not at all what one expects a Belgian historian to do.

Similar twists can be observed in the way Vangroenweghe is presented. He holds a Ph.D. in cultural anthropology and is guest professor in African history at Ghent University. He was the first Belgian scholar to study the Leopoldian rubber terror in depth [43]. He is rarely considered a Belgian historian[44], but rather an anthropologist[45], non-historian[46], amateur-historian[47], teacher[48]... Of course, Vangroenweghe *is* an anthropologist, but anthropology has its history. Throughout the colonial era African cultures and societies were the realm of anthropology. Anthropology and history share a colonial legacy of denying history to Africa, either by not including change and time in their research, or by not studying African cultures and societies altogether. When this "denial of coevalness" gradually lost – or loses – its allure, both disciplines became closely intertwined[49]. Hence, it is not a coincidence that Vansina combines a chair in history and anthropology, and that that the anthropologist Vangroenweghe lectures on African history.

Finally, Jules Marchal (under the pseudonym A.M. Delathuy), who has a degree in philology and made a diplomatic career, has less affinity with professional historiography than the other Belgian researchers of the history of the Congo Free State. As a consequence, he is often referred to as an "amateur-historian"[50]. He was the most prolific writer on Leopold's exploitation and the main source of information for Adam Hochschild[51]. In short, the allegation that Belgian historians avoid controversial topics is overstated, and that they avoid controversial statements is true for some but not for all.

However, there is some truth in the charge that historians do not live up to expectations. The main shortcoming, as far as their research attitude is concerned, lies in the assertion that what happened in the Congo under colonialism is African history and not Belgian history. The historians dealing with 19th- and 20th-century Belgian history, apart from Stengers, barely paid attention to what happened in the Belgian Congo. At the same time, and equally damaging, except in one Belgian University no historians of Africa were trained. It is distressing to notice that even the chair in African history at Louvain-la-Neuve was abolished when Vellut retired, and it is not yet clear if the recent establishment of African history at Ghent University will be enduring. However, the public debates of the past decade have prompted historians at least to realise that colonial history is part and parcel of Belgian, and not just of African history. Hence, colonial history is now better entrenched than the frail field of African history, which could turn out to be the drawback of recent evolutions.

Apart from the research situation, there remains a huge communication problem. Historians claim they already knew about Leopold's Congo, but they did not succeed or maybe did not even try to bring their findings to the public. The intermediate level of history teachers were not encouraged to utilise research findings either. Only recently are there clear signs of improvement, with reference material on the subject, seminars, and teaching ideas provided to history teachers. On the university front, however, the spur of the moment does not encourage communication with society at all, but rather forces scholars to climb up the ivory tower of global scholarship[52]. This is a huge societal problem, but alas not restricted to the field of African or colonial history.

Conclusion: the Memories of Congo

When the exhibition *The Memory of Congo: the Colonial Era* opened in February 2005, it caused a strong outburst of public debate, and it was at the same time a component of the festivities to celebrate the 175th anniversary of the Kingdom of the Belgians. This Belgian nationalist frame is in fact an age-old singularity of Belgian colonial history. It seems rather cynical to integrate colonial history in a celebration, and it is also ironic to view Belgian-nationalism at work in contrast to the accusations in the Belgian-francophone press one year before. All of this shows that colonial history has reached a stage at which it has become unavoidable in the Belgian public memories.

These memories, however, are full of dualities. Apart from the Belgian (sub)national duality, there is also a generational contrast, between those who studied colonial heroism and those who did not study colonial history at all. The current focus on cruelty entails a different effect on both groups. For the older generation, provided that they accept the historical record, this may be an adjustment of previous one-sided ideas, for the younger generation this may create a new one-sidedness. Another contrast, between those who defend their personal colonial identity, and those who condemn colonialism, is aggravated by the focus on colonial crimes. As long as the former deny these crimes, no reasonable conversation is conceivable, but those who admit the criminal and oppressive foundations of (Belgian) colonialism, do have a point in asking consideration for their experiences and the presumed accomplishments of colonialism. They – and all of us – must be prepared, however, to discover the paternalistic, exploitative and oppressive singularities of both 'their' colonialism and 'our' capitalist world-system, both in the past and the present, both in Belgium and in the entire world. This brings us to a further duality: the one between Belgium and the Congo, between Belgians and Congolese. It is amazing how little Congolese (are allowed to) take part in the public debates about our common history. A blatant example of this duality was in the composition of the Parliamentary Commission to investigate the assassination of Prime Minister Patrice Lumumba. Belgian paternalism decided that no Congolese historian was able to be neutral in this matter... as if Belgians are. This clearly illustrates that Belgium still has not recognized the Congolese as equal partners.

A final duality is history itself. Whose history is history? Is it the history of professional historians with university assignments, or the history of so-called "amateur-historians"? Is it the history of sensational horror or the history of systems and structures? Is it history as researched or history as taught? Historians have urgent responsibilities, but these are not necessarily what the public or the media expect. Belgian – but also other – historians especially need to research how colonialism worked in every-day life, what mechanisms enabled excesses and control, and if this history is perhaps not past but still present. Belgian universities need to train historians in the field of African history, and need *not only* to research what the public asks or expects, but also what the public is not aware of or would prefer not to be confronted with. Moreover, historians in general have to address the public with their findings, especially when these are not concurrent with the mainstream of the day. Finally, the most urgent need of the moment is probably to oppose the hegemonic academic thought that scholars have to work for the benefit of their peers only, and not of society. The allegations against historians may be not completely accurate, but they are absolutely appropriate: if historians are not able to communicate their findings, they become meaningless. Accommodating to the current isolationist trend would hasten the end of history after all.

Notes

1 Another case in point was the debate following the publication of the monograph by L. De Witte, *De moord op Lumumba* [The assassination of Lumumba], Leuven 1999, a Belgian parliamentary research commission in 1999-2002, and a movie by R. Peck, *Lumumba*, 2001.

2 D. Vangroenweghe, *Rood rubber: Leopold II en zijn Kongo*, Leuven 2004.

3 A. Hochschild, *De geest van koning Leopold II en de plundering van de Congo*, Amsterdam 1998.

4 The argumentation was exhibited on a bill board named *Genocide in the Congo?* in the section *Hierarchies* of the exhibition *Memory of Congo: the colonial era* at the RMCA in Tervuren. Also see: J.-L. Vellut, *Inleiding: Beelden van de koloniale tijd*, in *Het geheugen van Congo: de koloniale tijd*, Tervuren-Gent 2005, pp. 11-21; P. Marechal, *Kritische bedenkingen bij de controverses over Leopold II en Congo in de literatuur en de media*, in *Het geheugen van Congo: de koloniale tijd*, Tervuren-Gent 2005, pp. 43-49.

5 *De Congo-tentoonstelling in Tervuren liegt: Adam Hochschild over de strijd tegen de slavernij en hoe België met Congo omgaat*, "De Standaard", 1 October 2005.

6 *A un journaliste*, http://www.urome.be/fr/journ.htm [retrieved on 30 January 2006].

7 The definition of 'genocide' can be found in the Convention on the Prevention and Punishment of the Crime of Genocide, article 2, http://www.unhchr.ch/html/menu3/b/p_genoci.htm [retrieved on 30 January 2006].

8 One could argue that colonialism as a whole was based on racist grounds and hence that the brutal exploitation of the Congo was aimed against a racial group.

9 The title of the French translation is: *Les fantômes du roi Léopold II: Un holocauste oublié*, Paris 1998.

10 *Belgium exhumes its colonial demons: Historians vow to unearth truth about allegations of genocide in Congo*, "The Guardian", 13 July 2002.

11 *Afrikamuseum wil hogere dotatie*, "De Standaard", 24 June 2004.

12 E. Hobsbawm - T. Ranger (eds.), *The Invention of Tradition*, Cambridge 1983; B. Anderson, *Imagined Communities: Reflections on the Origin and Spread of Nationalism*, London 1983.

13 People who identify with Belgian colonialism are often former colonials, but not all former colonials continue to identify with colonialism. Some are really *former* colonials. When I write about '(former) colonials', I refer to the nostalgic ones who continue to identify with colonialism.

14 R. Coolsaet, *Adam Hochschild over het Congo van Leopold II: Een land waar de tien geboden niet gelden*, "De Standaard", 18 April 2000.

15 *Les petits Belges*, "De Morgen", 20 July 2005.

16 The 2005 exhibition of the RMCA mentioned the organised amnesia on the billboard *'Brutalities and acts of barbarism'* in the section *Transactions* of the exhibition *Memory of Congo: the colonial era* at the RMCA in Tervuren. Also scholars and journalist made reference to the Belgian amnesia in recent articles: A.T. Kongolo, *Colonial Memories in Belgian and Congolese Literature*, in C. Labio, *Belgian Memories*, "Yale French Studies", 102, 2002, pp. 79-93; M. Ewans, *Belgium and the Colonial Experience*, "Journal of Contemporary European Studies", 11, 2003, pp. 167-180; *Toen het nog onze Congo was: blank en zwart in Belgisch Congo*, "De Standaard", 2 June 2005.

17 It is remarkable that no Congolese historian was included. Jean Omasombo, the author of a biography of Patrice Lumumba, was a so-called ad hoc member but not a full member of the commission. He writes about his experience: *J'ai fait formellement partie de l'équipe avec le titre fort ambigu d'expert 'ad hoc' et/ou 'adjoint'. En ce qui me concerne [...] la raison de ce traitement particulier est qu'on estimait qu'en tant que congolais je ne pouvais être objectif. Ainsi bien qu' 'expert', il me sera fixé pour les quelques minutes que j'ai pu rencontrer les 'vrais experts' une 'méthodologie' faite surtout par des interdits: pas question de travailler avec le groupe et de 'toucher aux archives belges', ceci me dira-t-on afin de 'me protéger'! [...] Ce fut pour moi l'occasion de faire l'expérience d'être un Nègre, d'être perçu comme n'ayant pas de personnalité propre, par simple déterminisme biologique, représentant d'une région du monde et porte-parole de son opinion. J'ai pu vraiment ressentir combien était pesant le regard colonial encore bien présent dans les comportements* [I was officially part of the team with the ambiguous denomination of 'ad hoc' and/or 'deputy' expert. As far as I was concerned (...) the reason for this treatment was that they thought that I, as a Congolese, could not be neutral. Though I was 'expert', during the few moments I was permitted to meet the 'real experts' I was imposed a 'methodology' consisting above all of interdictions: I could not work with the group and I was not permitted to 'touch Belgian archives' in order to 'protect me', so

they said! (...) It was for me the occasion to feel being a Negro, being perceived as having no proper personality, because of biological determinism, representing a part of the world and being its spokesman. I really could feel how much the colonial view was still heavily present in the conduct], "Forum - Nieuwsbrief van de Belgische Vereniging van Afrikanisten / Bulletin de l'Association belge des africanistes", 22, 2002, pp. 11-12.

18 Another reason for the current revival of testimony efforts by (former) colonials is probably age. Books from the perspective of (former) colonials: P. Verlinden, *Weg uit Congo: het drama van de kolonialen*, Leuven 2002; UROME, *La colonisation belge: une grande aventure*, Bruxelles 2004; F. Ryon, *De laatste kolonialen: Vlamingen in de Congo 1950-1960*, Leuven 2005. Registration projects by (former) colonials: *Mémoires du Congo* (for Belgian francophone former colonials) and *Afrika Getuigenissen* (for Flemish former colonials). Two more scientific projects, including the registration of testimonies of (former) colonials, are conducted by SOMA-CEGES: *Het sociale geheugen van de Belgische koloniale / La mémoire sociale des coloniaux belges, 1945-1960*, and by the KULeuven under the auspices of the Flemish Government: *Afrika vertel(t)(d): de immateriële weerslag van het koloniale verleden in Vlaanderen.*

19 E. Said, *Orientalism*, Harmondsworth 1978; J. Fabian, *Time and the Other: How Anthropology Makes its Object*, New York 1983; J. Vansina, *Living with Africa: Reminiscences and Historiography*, Madison 1994.

20 See, e.g., the reprimand by W. Blondeel, *De jongste Congo-opstoot: mag het ietsje meer zijn?*, "Forum - Nieuwsbrief van de Belgische Vereniging van Afrikanisten / Bulletin de l'Association belge des africanistes", 23, 2002, pp. 5-7.

21 In the programmes of the four main educational nets in Belgium (Catholic and community / Flemish and French), only the Flemish community net, the former state schools in Flanders, demands one hour in the entire school curriculum to be spent on *Het Belgische koloniale avontuur in Kongo* [The Belgian colonial *adventure* in the Congo (italics by the author)] and another hour to deal with both the Balkan wars and colonial conflicts – combined. The other nets do not demand this one hour and a half, but then again, they do not incite these preposterous approaches and combinations either. To avoid misinterpretations, this does not mean that Congo is excluded from other nets in an absolute way, since the other nets only impose goals and allow their history teacher to choose their topics. But since the teachers are mostly not familiar with African or colonial history, the average will probably be not above the allotted time in the Flemish community schools.

22 *Un film sur Léopold II scandalise le Palais*, "Le Soir", 24 March 2004.

23 *Afrikamuseum wil hogere dotatie*, "De Standaard", 24 June 2004.

24 *Onderzoek naar koloniaal geweld in Congo*, "De Standaard", 15 July 2002.

25 Interview: *Er wordt wat onzin verteld over Leopold II*, "De Standaard", 1 February 2005 [this interview was part of a supplement to the daily newspaper De Standaard, entirely dedicated to the exhibition].

26 *Congo under King Leopold II*, http://www.diplobel.org/uk/pages/news/newsletters/LeopoldII.pdf [retrieved on 30 January 2006].

27 Épinglé - *Ce qu'on verra ce soir*, "La Libre Belgique", 8 April 2004. At that time, Marc Reynebeau was no longer a journalist of "Knack" but of "De Standaard".

28 *Un film sur Léopold II scandalise le Palais*, "Le Soir", 24 March 2004.

29 *De blinde vlek Congo Vrijstaat: Waarom moet een Britse tv-maker Belgiës duistere verleden uitspitten?*, "De Standaard", 1 April 2004.

30 *Een detail van de geschiedenis: Schrijven over Congo's verleden: tussen polemiek en wetenschap*, "Knack", 29 January 2003.

31 *België vergeet zijn koloniale verleden*, "De Standaard", 30 March 2004; M. Reynebeau, *Het einde van de vriestijd*, "De Standaard", 7 February 2005.

[32] K. Hemmerechts, *Liefde voor het leven: het turbulente leven van een Belgische prinses*, "De Standaard der Letteren", 14 April 2005.

[33] Interview: *Er wordt wat onzin verteld over Leopold II*, "De Standaard", 1 February 2005.

[34] J.-L. Vellut, *Guide de l'étudiant en Histoire du Zaïre*, Kinshasa 1974; J.-L. Vellut - F. Loriaux - F. Morimont, *Bibliographie Historique du Zaïre à l'Epoque Coloniale (1880-1960)*, Tervuren 1996.

[35] J.-L. Vellut, *La violence armée dans l'état indépendant du Congo: ténèbres et clarté dans l'histoire d'un état conquérant*, "Cultures et Développement", 16, 3-4, 1984, pp. 671-707; J.-L. Vellut - D. Vangroenweghe (eds.), *Le Rapport Casement*, Louvain-la-Neuve 1985.

[36] J. Stengers, *King Leopold's Imperialism*, in R. Owen - B. Sutcliffe (eds.), *Studies in the Theory of Imperialism*, London 1972; J. Stengers, *Belgian Historiography since 1945*, in P.C. Emmer - H.L. Wesseling (eds.), *Reappraisals in Overseas History*, Leiden 1979; J. Stengers - J. Vansina, *King Leopold's Congo, 1886-1908*, in R. Oliver - G.N. Sanderson (eds.), *The Cambridge History of Africa, Volume 6: From 1870 to 1905*, Cambridge 1985; J. Stengers, *Congo: Mythes et Réalités: 100 Ans d'Histoire*, Paris 1989. See also: J. Stengers, *Quelques réflexions sur le jugement moral en histoire*, "Académie Royale de Belgique - Bulletin de la Classe des Lettres et des Sciences Morales et Politiques", 58, 5, 1972 [1975], pp. 189-205.

[37] J. Vansina, *The Children of Woot: A History of the Kuba Peoples*, Madison 1978; Stengers et al., *King Leopold's* cit.; J. Vansina, *Paths in the Rainforest: Toward a History of Political Tradition in Equatorial Africa*, Madison 1990.

[38] For a full account of Vansina's professional wanderings, see his memoirs: J. Vansina, *Living with Africa: Reminiscences and Historiography*, Madison 1994. In his memoirs, one can understand why I call him 'Flemish' rather than 'Belgian'.

[39] *Een detail van de geschiedenis: Schrijven over Congo's verleden: tussen polemiek en wetenschap*, "Knack", 29 January 2003; M. Reynebeau, *Het einde van de vriestijd*, "De Standaard", 7 February 2005; *De Congo-tentoonstelling in Tervuren liegt: Adam Hochschild over de strijd tegen de slavernij en hoe België met Congo omgaat*, "De Standaard", 1 October 2005.

[40] L. De Witte, *De rush naar Congo*, "De Standaard", 9 February 2005.

[41] P. Verlinden, *Rwanda / Burundi: mensen - politiek - economie - cultuur*, Brussels 1996, p. 7.

[42] Verlinden, *Rwanda* cit., p. 59.

[43] Vangroenweghe, *Rood* cit.; Vellut e.a., *Le Rapport* cit.; D. Vangroenweghe, *Voor rubber en ivoor: Leopold II en de ophanging van Stokes*, Leuven 2005.

[44] *Een Afrikaanse holocaust?*, "De Standaard", 1 February 2005.

[45] *Een detail van de geschiedenis: Schrijven over Congo's verleden: tussen polemiek en wetenschap*, "Knack", 29 January 2003; *Een Afrikaanse holocaust?*, "De Standaard", 1 February 2005.

[46] Marc Reynebeau, *Het einde van de vriestijd*, "De Standaard", 7 February 2005.

[47] Interview: *„Er wordt wat onzin verteld over Leopold II"*, "De Standaard", 1 February 2005.

[48] Ludo De Witte, *De rush naar Congo*, "De Standaard", 9 February 2005.

[49] Fabian, *Time* cit. Also see Said, *Orientalism* cit. and Vansina, *Living* cit..

[50] Interview: *„Er wordt wat onzin verteld over Leopold II"*, "De Standaard", 1 February 2005.

[51] A.M. Delathuy, *E.D. Morel tegen Leopold II en de Kongostaat*, Berchem 1985; A.M. Delathuy, *De geheime documentatie van de Onderzoekscommissie in de Kongostaat*, Berchem 1988; A.M. Delathuy, *De Kongostaat van Leopold II, 1876-1900: het verloren paradijs*, Antwerp 1989.

[52] Jan Blommaert, *Kennis boven nostalgie*, "De Standaard", 11 February 2005.

Bibliography

Anderson B., *Imagined Communities: Reflections on the Origin and Spread of Nationalism*, London 1983.

Delathuy A.M., *E.D. Morel tegen Leopold II en de Kongostaat*, Berchem 1985.

Id., *De geheime documentatie van de Onderzoekscommissie in de Kongostaat*, Berchem 1988.

Id., *De Kongostaat van Leopold II, 1876-1900: het verloren paradijs*, Antwerp 1989.

De Witte L., *De moord op Lumumba*, Leuven 1999.

Ewans M., *Belgium and the Colonial Experience*, "Journal of Contemporary European Studies", 11, 2003, pp. 167-180.

Fabian J., *Time and the Other: How Anthropology Makes its Object*, New York 1983.

Hobsbawm E. - Ranger T. (ed.), *The Invention of Tradition*, Cambridge 1983.

Hochschild A., *King Leopold's Ghost: A Story of Greed, Terror and Heroism in Central Africa*, Boston 1998 [Dutch translation: *De geest van koning Leopold II en de plundering van de Congo*, Amsterdam 1998].

Id., *Leopold's Congo: a Holocaust We Have Yet to Comprehend*, "Chronicle of Higher Education", 46, 36, 2000.

Kongolo A.T., *Colonial Memories in Belgian and Congolese Literature*, in Labio C., *Belgian Memories*, "Yale French Studies", 102, 2002, pp. 79-93.

Marechal P., *Kritische bedenkingen bij de controverses over Leopold II en Congo in de literatuur en de media*, in *Het geheugen van Congo: de koloniale tijd*, Tervuren-Gent 2005, pp. 43-49.

Ryon F., *De laatste kolonialen: Vlamingen in de Congo 1950-1960*, Leuven 2005.

Said E., *Orientalism*, Harmondsworth 1978.

Stengers J., *The Congo Free State and the Belgian Congo before 1914*, in Gann L.G. - Duignan P. (eds.), *Colonialism in Africa 1870-1960*, volume 1, Cambridge 1969.

Id., *King Leopold's Imperialism*, in Roger Owen, Bob Sutcliffe (ed.), *Studies in the Theory of Imperialism*, London 1972.

Id., *Quelques réflexions sur le jugement moral en histoire*, "Académie Royale de Belgique - Bulletin de la Classe des Lettres et des Sciences Morales et Politiques", 58, 5, 1972 [1975], pp. 189-205.

Id., *Belgian Historiography since 1945*, in Emmer P.C. - Wesseling H.L. (eds.), *Reappraisals in Overseas History*, Leiden 1979.

Id., *Congo: Mythes et Réalités: 100 Ans d'Histoire*, Paris 1989.

Stengers J. - Vansina J., *King Leopold's Congo, 1886-1908*, in Oliver R. - Sanderson G.N. (eds.), *The Cambridge History of Africa, Volume 6: From 1870 to 1905*, Cambridge 1985.

UROME, *La colonisation belge: une grande aventure*, Brussels 2004.

Vangroenweghe D., *Rood rubber: Leopold II en zijn Kongo*, Brussels 1985 [new edition Leuven 2004].

Id., *Voor rubber en ivoor: Leopold II en de ophanging van Stokes*, Leuven 2005.

Vansina J., *The Children of Woot: A History of the Kuba Peoples*, Madison 1978.

Id., *Paths in the Rainforest: Toward a History of Political Tradition in Equatorial Africa*, Madison 1990.

Id., *Living with Africa: Reminiscences and Historiography*, Madison 1994.

Vellut J.-L., *Guide de l'étudiant en Histoire du Zaïre*, Kinshasa 1974.

Id., *La violence armée dans l'état indépendant du Congo: ténèbres et clarté dans l'histoire d'un état conquérant*, "Cultures et Développement", 16, 3-4, 1984, pp. 671-707.

Id., *Inleiding: Beelden van de koloniale tijd*, in *Het geheugen van Congo: de koloniale tijd*, Tervuren-Gent 2005, pp. 11-21.

Vellut J.-L. - Loriaux F. - Morimont F., *Bibliographie Historique du Zaïre à l'Epoque Coloniale (1880-1960)*, Tervuren 1996.

Vellut J.-L. - Vangroenweghe D. (eds.), *Le Rapport Casement*, Louvain-la-Neuve 1985.

Verlinden, P., *Rwanda / Burundi: mensen - politiek - economie - cultuur*, Brussels 1996.

Id., *Weg uit Congo: het drama van de kolonialen*, Leuven 2002.

The Historiography of Belgian Colonialism in the Congo

Guy Vanthemsche

In dit artikel worden de belangrijkste etappes van de historiografie van de Belgische kolonisatie onderzocht. Van bij het begin van de 20e eeuw werd de figuur van de stichter van Congo, koning Leopold II, het voorwerp van een ware cultus binnen het Belgische establishment, hoewel het regime dat hij installeerde in Congo in het buitenland (terecht) hevig op de korrel werd genomen. Pas in de loop van de jaren 1950-1960 werd de Belgische historiografie over Congo uit de apologetische sfeer gehaald, dank zij de fundamentele studies van de Brusselse historicus Jean Stengers. Toch bleef de gechiedschrijving over het kolonialisme in België weinig beoefend. Samen met Stengers zorgde enkel Jean-Luc Vellut ervoor dat die activiteit niet helemaal van de horizon verdween in België. Vanaf de jaren 1960 werden tal van belangrijke studies over het koloniale Congo dan ook door buitenlandse (waaronder Congolese) historici geproduceerd. Pas tijdens de laatste 15 jaar is er een "revival" te noteren oor de geschiedenis van het kolonialisme binnen de Belgische historische wereld. Recente polemieken over het Belgische koloniale verleden (rond het "rode rubber" van Leopold II en over de moord op de Congolese Eerste Minister Lumumba in 1961) hebben hiertoe bijgedragen".

Introduction

> When the Belgians arrived in the Congo, they found a population that was victim of bloody rivalries and slave trade. Belgian civil servants, missionaries, doctors, colonists and engineers civilized the black population step by step. They created modern cities, roads and railroads, harbours and airports, factories and mines, schools and hospitals. This work greatly improved the living conditions of the indigenous people.

This is how colonialism in the Congo is presented to Belgian 12-year old primary school children in 2006, almost half a century after the end of colonial rule in this African country[1]. The rhetoric used in (some) contemporary schoolbooks has not changed significantly since the early 20th century, when the official propaganda discourse on colonialism took form. The remarkable stability of pedagogical clichés not only tells us something about the way school programs are elaborated, but also about the *diffusion* of historical knowledge in society – which is an important, even crucial aspect of its *production*. In this chapter, I would like to analyze how historians have studied Belgian colonialism. Since the study of historiographical developments requires far more than the enumeration of authors' names and titles of books and articles, I intend to link this scientific production with the general social, political and institutional setting. Even if historical research is not 'steered' directly by political guidelines, it is always embedded in a societal context that pervades its activity.

Needless to say, the above apology of the many blessings of Belgian colonialism is a classical (but nevertheless excellent) example of selective reading of the past. Repression, murder, forced labour, racism and exploitation were intrinsic dimensions of the Belgian rule in the Congo, as they were in all colonial enterprises. This is not to deny the fact that the Belgians effectively did build roads, schools and hospitals and even raised the living standards of some of their colonial subjects. Moreover, the 'dark' and 'bright' sides of colonialism were not present in the same proportions during the different phases of foreign rule in the Congo; in fact, their 'mix' changed as time went by. But anyway, understanding the colonial past (like any historical phenomenon), has nothing to do with an 'arithmetical' addition of 'negative' and 'positive' aspects, since historical research is not concerned with ethical verdicts about 'good' and 'bad'. It is about explaining how a society changed in all its aspects, regardless of how its actors evaluated the moral qualities of some of these. So it is necessary to present the essential features of the Congo's colonial history, in order to grasp the evolution and the significance of historiographical production.

The history of Belgian colonialism in a nutshell

The origins of Belgian colonialism in central Africa were rather peculiar. Although the leading economic and political forces of his country were opposed to any colonial 'adventure', Leopold II, the king of the Belgians (1835-1909), relentlessly tried to get control of some overseas region which would enable him to develop a lucrative commercial business. This would not only enrich the king himself, but also, so he said, Belgium itself. After many fruitless and often unrealistic efforts in the most diverse and remote parts of the world (in East and South Asia, in the Pacific, in the Middle East and in many parts of North and Black Africa), the king finally succeeded in realizing one of his overambitious projects. Thanks to his immense personal fortune and to his (sometimes bold, even adventurous) diplomatic skills, he managed to exploit the colonial rivalries between Great Britain, France and Portugal in the heart of Africa. In 1885, the participants of the Berlin Conference (but not the Conference as such) agreed to recognize him as the sovereign of a "Congo Free State" (CFS or Independent State of Congo, *Etat Indépendant du Congo*). Apart from the fact that its king was also the head of state of a newly created political entity, Belgium officially had no relation whatsoever with this Free State (although unofficially Belgian diplomats and officers had helped Leopold to create it). The first years of the CFS were characterized by heavy financial difficulties, but from 1895 onwards, it became a very lucrative business, thanks to the ivory trade and, above all, to the large scale collecting of wild rubber. The local population was forced to work in a most inhumane way in order to boost rubber 'production' and export. Arbitrary executions, repression and even mass killings were common things in Leopoldian Congo. This soon became known outside the CFS, thanks to the denunciations of foreign missionaries and other witnesses of these cruelties. The publication of a report by Roger Casement, a British consul in the Congo who confirmed the existence of these atrocities, had great effect. An international protest campaign, led by E.D. Morel, originated in Great Britain and gained a wide audience, mostly but not exclusively in the Anglo-Saxon countries. Leopold came under heavy pressure, even in his own country where he faced severe criticism from progressive liberals, socialists and some Catholics. But in the meantime, a colonial lobby had been formed in Belgium, and the main Belgian capitalist groups had (although somewhat reluctantly) started investing in important colonial projects (mainly in railroad building and in mining). So from the Belgian point of view, it seemed inconceivable that the Congo would be handed over to some other European power. Consequently, international pressure finally led to the take-over of the CFS by Belgium as an outright colony in 1908. This solution had to be imposed upon the old, obstinate and embittered king, even though the Congo's transfer to the Belgian State had already been envisaged many years before.

From that date on, the Belgian authorities tried to eliminate the worst Leopoldian excesses. But forced labour did not disappear as such; till the very last years of colonial rule, the Congolese had to work 'for free' for at least some days or weeks each year (e.g. for road maintenance); they were obliged to cultivate some cash crops (e.g. cotton); they were subjected to harsh forced recruitments, because the European plantations and the large mining enterprises badly needed labourers. In the 1920s, Belgian capital flowed into the colony, creating an impressive infrastructure and an extensive network of large enterprises (some of them co-financed by public capital and most of them belonging to a few powerful private holding companies). During the Interwar period, the Belgian Congo became one of the world's largest primary commodity producers. After the Second World War, a new inflow of public and private capital boosted economic activity. Colonial authorities also launched a Ten Year Plan in order to modernize the country. They stepped up their efforts in the social, medical and educational sector: Belgian Congo was presented as a 'model colony', where primary schooling and medical treatment was more widely developed than in other colonies. But Belgian authorities anxiously avoided the formation of a Congolese social, political and intellectual elite; only a tiny minority of so-called *évolués* adopted Western habits and acquired a secondary school or technical training. When the colonial bond was suddenly severed in 1960, after an outburst of nationalism in the black population, the country had to face independence completely unprepared. This partly explains Congo's many misfortunes in the next decades.

Politics, institutions and the history of Belgian colonialism

The particular context in which Belgian colonialism was born influenced the first writings on its origins and development. Although he was surrounded by a group of devoted collaborators and although some leading Catholic politicians, who were in charge of the government, had more or less willingly supported his endeavours (mostly from a *donnant donnant* perspective), high-handed, ruthless and stubborn Leopold II was quite unpopular in his own country during his lifetime. But one thing was clear enough: without his obsessive quest for a colony, Belgium would never have become a colonial power (with all the national pride attached to that status); big capitalist groups would never have made their lucrative investments in the Congo; and the Catholic Church would never have found such an extensive missionary area. In an effort of self-justification and retrospective gratefulness, the Belgian political, economic and cultural elites therefore developed an outright Leopoldian cult immediately after the King's death in 1909 – even if many politicians, business leaders, clerics and other opinion leaders were perfectly aware of the 'dark' sides of his personality and actions (see below). Moreover, this cult contributed to the formation of a true 'colonial spirit' in the Belgian population, an attitude which had been largely absent before the take-over of the Congo. This colonial ideology in turn became a new tool in the forging of a lively Belgian patriotism (we must not forget that Belgium had been created as recently as 1830). Consequently, the King was presented as a visionary, an extraordinary genius who (so the story goes) had fought against the indifference and the indolence of his fellow citizens. The latter had not grasped the 'generosity' and the 'farsightedness' of his actions, all of them directed to one single goal: the gift of a prosperous colony to his beloved Belgium. The King, so official discourse added, also had to sustain the envious attacks of foreign countries, especially of Great Britain, which had 'invented' (or at least grossly exaggerated) the so-called "red rubber" atrocities in order to get hold of this rich colony. This interpretation had been the line of defence adopted by Leopold himself in the last decade of his personal rule over the Congo; it was adopted by Belgian authorities and immediately became the orthodox position of Belgian diplomacy. This was to have some effect on the historiography of colonial Congo, as we shall soon see.

The Leopoldian cult pervaded not only official discourses, but also most of the writings concerning the origins and the history of colonial activity in this region. Publications looking back into the (then still recent) past originated almost from the start of European penetration in central Africa. Of course, these writings cannot be labelled 'historical' in the true sense of the word, but they are important because many 'scientific' studies, later on, relied heavily on them. On coming back to Europe, many explorers and pioneers of the Congolese 'adventure' wrote extensive books recalling their African adventures, either in order to benefit from the financial advantages of what often became real bestsellers, or to contribute to the internal and external propaganda effort launched by the CFS, or else in an effort of self-glorification. It is known that Leopold II carefully watched and even guided these writings. Most famous in this category are of course the books written by Henry Morton Stanley, whom the King had hired after his first east-to-west crossing of the African continent in 1877, in order to help realize and organize his Congolese project. Other Belgian pioneers, mostly officers "on leave" from the Belgian army and collaborators of Stanley, also put their memoirs on paper. This literature was fundamentally apologetic. From then on, the tone was set for the description of the deeds of missionaries, administrators, businessmen, doctors or scientists who followed in the footsteps of these first pioneers. Heroism, unselfishness and unbridled thirst for action became the standard descriptors for Belgian activities in the colony, also in the works of professional historians. Private journals, notes and correspondence, where the actors and first-hand witnesses of the Leopoldian period plainly laid down their sometimes horrendous deeds and/or observations, only recently divulged their secrets. Since the 1970s, historians painstakingly began to sort out fact from fiction and to fill the gaps left by the founders of the CFS, whose semi-official and auto-celebrative works were, for many decades, the only source used to tell the story of the breaking up of the Congolese interior.

Not only the 'men on the spot', but also some of Leopold's close collaborators and admirers soon looked back on the origins and first developments of the CFS. Amongst them: some of his personal secretaries, a few journalists or diplomats, pseudo-scientific biographers. Their main setting is not the African *brousse* (this was only known through the above mentioned pioneers' memoirs), but the royal and ministerial offices and the Western chanceries. Their perspective was decidedly European: the focus of their "history of colonization" was reduced to the diplomatic scene or even to the mind of the "great man". In some of these writings, the cult of the King reached extraordinary, even preposterous proportions. "The birth of the Congo Free State is a fairy tale realized by the Leopold II, a colonizer with a touch of genius"[2], wrote Edouard Vandersmissen, a professor of the University of Liège, in 1920. In 1948, the *Biographie coloniale belge*, a (still used... because not yet replaced) reference work published by the *Institut Royal Colonial Belge* (to which we will come in a few moments), opens its first volume with a panegyric overloaded with superlatives and capital letters:

> Three aspects dominate the glorious life of Leopold II in its colonial aspect: political and diplomatic genius, nobility of sentiments, disinterestedness. (...) He had achieved the work of a Titan; He took rank amongst the greatest Statesmen of History. (...) This builder of Empire, this Gatherer of Lands ("Rassembleur de Terres") for the benefit of Fatherland and Civilization (...) [always] said that He wanted to give a colony to his country, to open up central Africa to Civilization[3].

This rhetoric is all the more *piquant* since the author of this eulogy admitted, in a private letter, that he had witnessed the "rubber atrocities", adding immediately that one should conceal this episode; he also told his correspondent that Leopold was "in some aspects a bad administrator [and] too much dominated by the material problem"[4] and even that he had become "megalomaniac" in his old days. It is difficult to find a more telling example of the abyss separating the inside of some people's minds and the official discourses they have to produce.

Disseminated and repeated time and again through the school system, textbooks, museums, exhibitions, public statements, etc, this view became the standard interpretation of the Leopoldian past – the generation of Belgians that did not witness this period believed, supposedly in all sincerity, that the CFS and the King had been victim of foreign slander, and that the colonization of the Congo had started as a humanitarian enterprise, the starting point of the 'model colony' that was Belgian Congo. But outside of Belgium, this consensus concerning the CFS's past did not exist. Regularly, journalists or general writers came back to the horror stories concerning Leopoldian Congo. The anti-Congo campaign had deeply influenced the minds of people and its effects lasted for many decades after the facts. From their foreign posts, Belgian ambassadors always carefully took note of these writings, despatching them to Brussels with some anxiety and/or indignation (See sourcesfor: some examples of the 'Congo atrocities' in foreign opinion and the Belgian reactions). Indeed, Belgian authorities always were extremely sensitive about these allegations. In their opinion, the Congo still was coveted by other powers; their sovereignty in central Africa always seemed weak and threatened. In their eyes, the "slander" concerning "red rubber" was more than just a disagreement about a historical event. It was seen as a threat for the foundations of Belgian colonial rule and even as an attack on the country's national honour.

The Belgian Ministry of Foreign Affairs, who kept (and still keeps) the diplomatic archives, also had at its disposal a History Counsellor (*Conseiller Historique*), whose duty it was to watch over the historical documents, but also to formulate advice concerning all retrospective questions the Department was confronted with. As late as the end of the 1950s, the orthodox and "negationist" view on Leopoldian Congo was still in force, as is shown by a note written by the then *conseiller historique*, Jacques Willequet, also a professor at the Université Libre de Bruxelles and author of an otherwise excellent book on *Le Congo belge et la Weltpolitik (1894-1914)*[5]. This is what he writes when Leopold's policy was once more was attacked in the foreign press by a journalist, H.D. Ziman, who spoke of "the disgraceful maladministration which he [Leopold] ultimately permitted in the Congo"[6]: "*Parler de 'disgraceful maladministration', c'est évoquer un fantôme dissipé depuis 50 ans: la campagne anticongolaise. (...) Le vrai et le faux, l'exagération et le mensonge s'y mêlaient inextricablement, avec bien entendu le minimum de dates, de lieux et de noms*". The fact that both leaders of the anti-Congo campaign, Morel and Casement, had been convicted of intelligence with the German enemy during World War I, is telling enough, according to Willequet: "*Ces faits, néanmoins, devraient inciter à la prudence ceux qui, aujourd'hui, continuent à colporter des affirmations systématiquement désobligeantes*"[7]. In other words: the Belgian Ministry of Foreign Affairs had developed a 'standard version' of the CFS's history, based first on minimizing, and later on denial and outright rejection of the "accusations" concerning the Congo atrocities. This orthodox view was at same time shared and fed by the 'scientific' caution of the renowned professional historians that worked for the Department.

Another institution has played a still more important role in the shaping of colonial historiography in Belgium: the Colonial Academy, or *Institut Royal Colonial Belge* (IRCB), founded in 1928. Originally, the IRCB (renamed *Académie Royale des Sciences Coloniales* (ARSC) in 1954 before adopting its present name of *Académie Royale des Sciences d'Outre-Mer* (ARSOM) in 1959) was essentially composed of prestigious colonial figures: former or actual politicians, administrators, business leaders, missionaries, and leading scientists. It was wholly devoted to the enhancement of colonial action: it would improve Belgian rule in the Congo by the scientific examination of questions related to an extensive range of domains (engineering sciences, agronomy, biology, geology, anthropology, medicine, etc., not to forget the political, economic and even the so-called 'moral' aspects). The spirit in which the IRCB worked is well reflected by the citation given above and taken from the introduction to the *Biographie coloniale belge*, a long-term scientific enterprise conceived in 1941[8] – and which is still going on[9].

The initiative of publishing this huge reference work on the history of Belgian overseas activity was not an isolated fact. As early as 1925, the Minister of Colonies had created an official commission, whose task it was to write an official history of the Belgian colonial empire (Royal Decree of 16.03.1925). Nothing came out of this project; the commission itself was dissolved in 1928, when the IRCB was founded. Somewhat exasperated, the Minister of Colonies said that the new Institute should take over the commission's task, since "it was somewhat humiliating to see that the best historical works on the Congo have been written by foreigners"[10] – quite a few books on the Congo Free State had indeed been written by British, American or French authors[11] A touch of historiographical 'nationalism' or even 'protectionism' certainly was present in the officials' minds at that time. At the foundation of the IRCB, this same Minister had also donated important archives of Leopold II, entrusted to the new Ministry in 1909, after the King's death, by his former secretaries[12]. These were all the more precious since Leopold reputedly had destroyed many documents of the CFS before his decease. It nevertheless took some years before the IRCB resumed the 1925/1928 historiographical project. Only in 1952 did it create a "Commission of Belgian colonial history". This commission did not have the intention of writing an official history itself; it only wanted to stimulate individual research initiatives in this field. An urgent task, so it seemed, was to explore the Leopoldian archives it had possessed since 1930. Quite tellingly, the commission did not want to make these documents publicly available ("too many documents are of a personal nature and concern too recent personalities")[13]. Only persons with due scientific credentials could have access to them. Where colonial matters were concerned, Belgian authorities always displayed some kind of fear and adopted a culture of secrecy – an attitude which has not completely disappeared, even at the beginning of the 21st century.

Jean Stengers and the birth of scientific colonial history in Belgium

In this context, the IRCB elected in 1952 as one of its members a young and talented historian of the *Université Libre de Brussels*, who was to influence deeply the development of Belgian colonial historiography: Jean Stengers (1922-2002)[14]. Only a few articles on early Belgian (i.e. Leopoldian) colonial policy, written since 1949, had established him as an authority in this field. During the 1950s, the IRCB/ARSC started publishing numerous studies concerning the early history of the history of the CFS and its antecedents, either as articles in its *Bulletin des séances*, or as monographs in its *Mémoires in-8°* series. Stengers was the author of many of these publications, but he was by no means the only professional Belgian historian related to the IRCB/ARSC. Other scientists also devoted themselves to early colonial history, most notably Auguste Roeykens, a Catholic priest, who published several (essentially document-oriented) volumes concerning Leopold's African initiatives. Still others, like Louis Jadin (1903-1972) (also a priest), specialized in the history of the ancient Kongo kingdom and in the early history of Christian missions in this region[15]. Another important cultural establishment in the colonial sphere, the Museum of Tervuren (now *Musée Royal d'Afrique Centrale (MRAC)*, Royal Museum of Central Africa) also contributed to the development of historical studies on colonialism. One of its directors, Marcel Luwel (1921), for example, wrote several studies concerning the first expeditions in and administrators of the Congo. Not surprisingly, the Tervuren Museum later acquired (and still keeps) the complete Stanley Papers.

Nevertheless, Stengers' significance for the development of Belgian colonial historiography surpasses that of his fellow members of the Academy or of other Belgian colonial historians of the 1950s and early 1960s. There are several reasons for that, apart from his sheer longevity (he continued publishing on the Congo for more than half a century after his first articles appeared). First of all, he changed the historiographical attitude towards Belgian colonial history. While some Belgian historians, even during the 1960s, still wrote within the context of the Leopoldian cult (Roeykens, for example, maintained the King on a pedestal, using terms such as "Leopold's genius" as late as 1976)[16], Stengers eliminated the hagiographical elements still pervading most studies on the CFS. He was clearly fascinated by Leopold's character and actions, but he never indulged in eulogy or apologetic discourse (only some expressions in his first writings could possibly be interpreted as a sort of 'admiration'). Some of his studies, for example on Leopoldian finances, even aroused the anxiety of his fellow IRCB members[17]. As the immense majority of Belgians in the 1950s, he supported Belgian colonial rule in the Congo – one of his interventions in the IRCB/ARSC discussions is telling[18] – but this positive attitude towards colonialism never directly transpired in his historical work. In that sense, he 'depoliticized' Belgian colonial historiography and gave it a real scientific content.

The second of Stengers' merits is to be found in the link he immediately established with colonial historians of the neighbouring countries. The 1950s were characterized by a growing scientific interest in the history of 19th-century European imperialism. The new generation of historians had of course noticed the importance of Leopoldian Congo in the development of overseas empires. This trend even somewhat alarmed Belgian diplomatic authorities. They feared unpleasant echoes concerning the CFS. In 1959, the Foreign Minister discreetly suggested that a renowned scholar as Ronald Robinson – who, of course, could not be 'influenced' in too crude a way – should nevertheless be brought in contact with Belgian historians such as Stengers and Willequet, in order to avoid some possible "incident" (see Sources, document 17). It is doubtful whether Stengers needed such an introduction, since he had already established some fruitful international contacts. He was not only doing intensive research in foreign archives (particularly in Great Britain); he had also attended international conferences since the beginning of the 1950. Stengers personally got to know very well such leading British, French or Dutch colleagues as Roger Anstey, William Roger Louis, Henri

Brunschwig and Henk Wesseling. He often invited them to contribute to the IRCB/ ARSOM's activities and had them publish important articles in the *Revue Belge de Philologie et d'Histoire*, of which he was a director. Some of these foreign researchers were among the first to publish up-to-date, unbiased and scientific syntheses on the history of colonial Congo, most notably Ruth Slade's *King Leopold's Congo* (1962) and Roger Anstey's *King Leopold's Legacy* (1966)[19]. Stengers himself became a member of the editorial board of the *Journal of African History* and contributed to many classic international publications on the history of colonialism, such as the *Cambridge History of Africa*. In short: his own research was the Belgian 'variant' of the broad historiographical current originating in the 1950s and focusing on the European diplomatic and political origins of late 19th-century imperialism.

In an impressive series of books and articles[20], Stengers managed, with great subtlety, accuracy and clarity, to unravel the complex and intricate machinery of Leopoldian action in and around the Congo. In doing so, he shed a crude light on the real nature of the King's methods and also demolished, *en passant*, some official Belgian myths concerning the CFS. He most notably demonstrated that the anti-Congo campaign of Morel and Casement had nothing to do with slander, and that the "red rubber" atrocities were genuine. But this "cleaning up" was done discreetly and without sensationalism. In Belgium, Stengers never was considered an 'iconoclast' or a 'radical' (which he most certainly was not); consequently, he never lost the esteem he had gained in the Belgian intellectual and even political establishment.

During the 1950s and 1960s, Stengers had guided Belgian colonial historiography out of apologetic waters into the currents of modern science. He continued publishing important studies during the 1980s and 1990s, but he never wrote a full-scale synthesis on the CFS (or even on Leopoldian action as a whole). His numerous other studies, some of them of book-length, on different aspects of Belgian contemporary history and on historical methodology (the World Wars, diplomacy, the monarchy, etc.), probably help to explain this fact. Only in 1989 did he agree to publish a collection of his main articles on the Congo[21]. This option somewhat limited the popular audience of his works on the colony; except for academics and some specialists, most Belgians still clung to the old mythical images of colonialism. Moreover, Stengers focused on the 'European' and political/diplomatic, and not on the 'African' aspects of colonialism. Finally, he never analyzed the history of Belgian colonialism from 1908 onwards (except for a few general overviews and some detailed articles on the decolonization).

In other words: two huge fields were still left untouched at the end of the 1960s: first, the evolution of colonial Congo itself during the CFS, and, second, both sides of the colonization (the Belgian *and* the Congolese one) after 1908. Indeed, before Congo became independent in 1960, no Belgian or foreign historian ever made any significant contribution to the study of a phenomenon that *was still going on*, i.e. Belgian colonial rule in the Congo. The archives of the Ministry of Colonies were of course inaccessible to research concerning the post-1908 period. All this would change in the next decade: these gaps were to be filled, piece by piece, from the 1970s onwards.

Belgian historians and the history of Belgian colonialism since Congolese independence

How did Belgium study the history of colonial Congo after this county's independence in 1960? Part of this historiographical work was produced in an institutional setting. From the 1960s onwards, the Royal Academy of Overseas Sciences (ARSOM) had changed quite a lot since the old days of the IRCB/ARSC. After the loss of the colony, this venerable institution quickly lost its political and 'utilitarian' dimension; logically, its composition also changed. Former politicians, businessmen and administrators disappeared gradually from this cenacle. By the 1970s and 1980s, it was composed exclusively of Belgian and foreign academics. The ARSOM extended its scope to the whole of the so-called "Third World" and thereby shifted its attention away from the Congo, Rwanda and Burundi, which originally had been its predominant centre of interest. Nevertheless, since the Independence days, the Academy still continued to publish numerous monographs and articles concerning the history of the Belgian Congo. Many of these contributions found their origin in initiatives by Jean Stengers, who regularly organized important colloquia under the ARSOM's aegis[22], and who invited Belgian or foreign scholars as guest speakers at the Academy's habitual *séances*. Needless to say, the public echo of these scientific activities was quite limited. Other works published on the 'history' of colonial Congo were far more successful in this respect. Journalists or other persons who had known colonial Congo personally published some books pertaining to the ex-colony, not without the zest of nostalgia and retrospective eulogy[23]. Some former colonial civil servants wrote their memoirs, mostly concerning the turbulent decolonization[24] or persons who had been engaged personally in the colonial adventure started to produce 'historical' studies on their previous domain of action (for example André Lederer, a former transport specialist, published extensively on the history of colonial transport[25]; Louis-François Vanderstraeten, a former officer of the colonial army, published several studies on the history of the Force Publique[26]; medical doctors produced a huge work on the history of medicine[27] and agronomists did so for their own field[28]; railroad amateurs published a extensive work on colonial railroad history[29]). In the eyes of the general, uniformed public, this kind of books "told the history of the Congo"; the important advances in historiography went largely unnoticed.

Indeed, some Belgian scholars made remarkable contributions to the history of colonial Congo. Teaching or research assignments in late colonial or in independent Congo played an important part in the orientation of their scientific activity. The Brussels historian Pierre Salmon (1926-2005), for example, originally trained as a scholar of ancient Greek history, became involved in African history because of his appointment in different central African universities in the late 1950s and early 1960s. He specialized in the publication and analysis of diaries and correspondence of early European travellers, pioneers and colonial administrators in the Congo[30]. Léon de Saint-Moulin (1932), professor at the University of Kinshasa, wrote many studies on Congolese demographic and urban history. Jacques Vanderlinden (1932), a brilliant ULB jurist, originally studied traditional and modern African law systems, but also became interested in the history of colonization. Among his many books, one notices a history of Congolese uranium diplomacy in 1940-1955, an edition of diplomatic documents concerning the Belgian Congo and an extensive biography of an important governor general of the Belgian Congo, Pierre Ryckmans – the first study of this kind to be published[31]. In 1992, Philippe Marechal, a historian of Ghent University who became head of the History Department of the above mentioned Tervuren Museum, published a remarkable book on the history of the early military operations in the CFS, shattering the traditional *images d'Epinal* that till then dominated the vision of the early occupation of the Congo[32].

Historians were not the only scholars to look back into the colonial past. Some economists also did so, using statistics and official published documents, most notably Gaston Vandewalle (Ghent University) and André Huybrechts, Jean-Louis Lacroix and Jean-Philippe Peemans (all three graduates from the Catholic University of Louvain, albeit from different theoretical perspectives)[33]. Every overview of Belgian historiography concerning the Congo should also mention the important contributions made by missionaries living or having resided for many years in this country. A wealth of knowledge was thus accumulated by such *érudits* as, for example, Frans Bontinck (who was professor at the University of Kinshasa)[34], Léon Verbeek and Honoré Vinck. Their work is concerned, *inter alia*, with pre-colonial Congo, church and missionary history, and the history of education in the Congo.

But the most important contributions to the history of colonial Congo undoubtedly came from Jean-Luc Vellut (1936), a historian trained at the Université Catholique de Louvain (UCL) (amongst his teachers was the above mentioned Louis Jadin) and at the Australian National University (Canberra). After his PhD in 1965, he obtained teaching appointments at the still young and expanding Congolese universities, first in Kinshasa and then at the University of Lubumbashi. There he not only helped to create a thriving History Department, which was to produce excellent Congolese historians (see below), but he also came into contact with the local written sources and with the Congolese dimension of colonial history. He not only thoroughly researched the archives of the former Belgian Ministry of Colonies (which, by now, had been opened to scientific research, albeit with an annoying 50-year limit to accessibility, somewhat tempered by possible derogations), but he also has visited indefatigably foreign archives mainly in France, Great Britain and Portugal. On coming back to Belgium in 1972, he became Professor of African History at his *Alma Mater*, the UCL. Up to this day, he has published extensively on a wide range of subjects, starting from pre-colonial structures[35], over the economic[36], social[37], religious[38] and diplomatic[39] aspects of both the CFS and Belgian colonial period, to basic reference tools such as research guides and bibliographies[40]. His perspective is all-round: he not only focuses on the Belgian face of colonialism, but also on what happened on the Congolese terrain. Moreover, being always in touch with the main research trends abroad, his work has gained a widespread international diffusion and reputation. The synthesis on Congolese colonial history he is currently preparing will no doubt be a landmark in the historiography of Belgian colonialism.

But apart from the work of Stengers and Vellut (and of the handful of colleagues we just mentioned), Belgian interest in colonial historiography cannot be described as overwhelming. In fact, the great majority of Belgian professional historians showed no real interest in this subject, or at least did not deem it necessary to devote part of their own research activity to it. Colonial history was considered 'exotic' and was never really "integrated" into the course of Belgian history. Colonial and, even more, non-European or world history only occupied a marginal place in the curricula of the history departments. The history of Congo itself (be it colonial or pre-colonial), never attracted much attention from the public or even academic authorities. A telling example of this neglect was the fact that the anthropologist Jan Vansina (1929), since the 1950s author of many important studies on traditional African societies, was not given the opportunity of continuing his research and teaching career in a Belgian university; consequently, he left Belgium and started to work at the University of Wisconsin, becoming one of the world's greatest authorities on pre-colonial African history. The conclusion seems obvious: the Belgian historical milieu missed an extraordinary opportunity to stimulate colonial history from an anthropological perspective. Meanwhile, the Belgian public's view on the Congo remained largely unchanged, shaped by school reminiscences, clichés and popular 'history' books.

The contribution of foreign historians to the history of Belgian colonialism

During the 1970s and 1980s, several important contributions to Belgian and Congolese colonial history originated in other countries than Belgium. While interest in this subject was waning in the latter country, it steadily grew abroad. Indeed, probably no other field of Belgian history attracted so many non-Belgian authors. Some of these new studies continued the rather "classical" approach of the 1950s and early 1960s, focusing on institutional and diplomatic history (see, for example, the work on *The Rulers of Belgian Congo* by Gann and Duignan, published in 1979; Emerson's biography of Leopold II; Collins's study on Leopold and the Upper Nile; Cookey's book on *Britain and the Congo Question 1885-1913*; etc.[41]). The synthesis of Congolese history written by the French historian Robert Cornevin, *Histoire du Congo (Léopoldville)*, which went through successive reprints, also offers a very classical, even "conservative" view of the subject – in fact a rather uninspired and uninspiring compilation[42]. Others books on the contrary, some of them written by non-historians, inaugurated a tradition of critical writings and stressed the negative aspects of Belgian colonization. One should mention here Ascherson's recently reprinted biography of king Leopold II, *The King Incorporated*[43], but also two syntheses on the history of the Belgian Congo written from a Marxist perspective: the stimulating book by the French author Auguste Maurel (under the pseudonym, Michel Merlier), and more recently, Jacques Depelchin's work [44].

But the main advances in our knowledge came from professional historians, who shunned large-scale syntheses, but explored new paths, with original approaches: they produced extremely valuable studies on some aspects of colonial Congo. Many of these books and articles were published by US historians (just as other scholars from that same country – political scientists, anthropologists, sociologists – also made some fundamental contributions to the study of independent Congo: Young, Turner, Weiss, J. and W. MacGaffey, Lemarchand, Gould, Callaghy, Schatzberg, etc. – but this aspect is beyond our scope). Thanks to these scientists we now know a great deal more on subjects as: city development (Bruce Fetter)[45]; railways and British interests (S.E. Katzenellenbogen)[46]; colonial labour policy (John Higginson, David Northrup, Samuel Nelson and William Samarin)[478]; Christian missions (Marvin Markowitz)[48], medical practices and gender aspects (Nancy Hunt)[49]; etc. A historian of Polish origin, who has taught in Lubumbashi for a while, and now is at Laval University in Quebec, Bogumil Jewsiewicki, has intensively published on class structure and economic activities in colonial Congo (from a Marxist perspective), before turning, in most recent years, to the analysis of contemporary social and cultural practices in Congo[50]. The German anthropologist, now at the University of Amsterdam, Johannes Fabian, has published – *inter alia* – an important book on language problems and policy in Belgian Congo[51]. The crossroads between diplomacy and economic interests were not neglected either, the United States being the main protagonist in this research. The American historian Jonathan Helmreich studied the relations between the US, Belgium and the Congo (1940-1960); the uranium question figuring prominently in his research. Another US scholar, David N. Gibbs, also concentrated on US policy towards Congo and its mineral wealth in the decade before and after Congolese independence – more or less the same subject that was thoroughly analyzed by the German historian Gerhard Mollin[52].

Another important turn in the historiography of colonial Congo has occurred in the 1970s and 1980s. From then on, Congolese historians have begun to produce important contributions to the history of their own country. As we have said, the Belgian colonizer started creating universities only a few years before the end of his rule, but historical studies were not included in this educational program. The first full-fledged History department in Congo was created in 1966, at the Lovanium University of Kinshasa; two other university centres, in Lubumbashi and Kisangani, only offered the two first years of studies in history[53]. In 1971, all these history departments were merged into a single one, located at the National Congolese University at Lubumbashi. Inevitably, foreign (mostly Belgian) historians staffed these departments in the beginnings (and until ca. 1976); after the graduation of the first Congolese historians, in the late 1960s and early 1970s, the best elements soon joined the staff and made it up entirely since 1976. Some Congolese historians also obtained their doctoral degree in foreign countries such as France or the United States.

Understandably, the work of these Congolese historians focused on the aspects that largely were absent from the 'first generation' studies on colonial history produced in Belgium. The *vécu* of the Congolese population in the social, economic and cultural field figured prominently in their studies based both the local sources (including oral traditions) and the rich archives of the Ministry of Colonies in Brussels. To mention just a few of those Congolese historians who had the opportunity of publishing (part of) their work in Belgium, France, the US or in international journals: Jacob Sabakinu Kivilu (historical demography and social conditions), Tshibangu Kabet Musas (economic and social conditions during the crisis of the 1930s), Tshund'Olela Epanya (economic aspects), Donatien Dibwe dia Mwembu (social history of Katanga miner families), Jeannot Mokili Danga Kassa (agricultural history), Jean-Marie Mutamba Makombo (rise of independence movements), Osumaka Likaka (cotton culture), Busugutsala Gandayi (educational policies), Charles Tshimanga (youth and education); Mulambu Mvuluya (forced cultures and revolts), Mumbanza Mwa Bawele (transition of social and cultural structures in the early colonial period), Khonde Ngoma Di Mbumba Côme (history of Congo's first capital, Boma), etc.

It is of course impossible to mention here the full titles of these studies: they can be found in Vellut's already mentioned reference work, but also – most significantly – in the extensive bibliography of Isidore N'Daywel's *Histoire générale du Congo*.[54] This book, almost 1000 pages long, is an important landmark in Congolese historiography, since it is the first general synthesis on Congolese history (from oldest times to the present) *written by a Congolese historian*. Of 'classical' facture[55], this book gives a wealth of factual information on this country's history; it, in a certain way, crowns the work of this first generation of Congolese historians. Another recent synthesis on Congolese history by a Congolese historian (Nzongola's critical book *The Congo from Leopold to Kabila*) is rather sketchy for the colonial period[56]. Still another overview of this subject history was also written by a Congolese historian, C. Didier Gondola. Unfortunately, this book, short and superficial, offers no new insights[57].

It nevertheless has to be admitted that this promising development lost some momentum in the last decade or two, because of Congo's catastrophic situation. Its formal economy has fallen into a deep crisis; the many years of squandering, corruption and maladministration under the Mobutu dictatorship and the civil war that has torn the country apart after its fall in 1997 have resulted in a grave paralysis of State functions. Universities are, of course, amongst the many victims of this tragedy, and so is scientific research. The many talented Congolese historians do not enjoy the normal material conditions that make historiography possible. They even have to fight hard to keep historical education and research going on a minimal level. Devoid of financial means, the Congolese national archives also struggle to survive, thanks to the efforts of their director, Antoine Lumenganeso, but the 'paper memory' of the colonial period is, in Congo itself, reduced to a minimum. Some archives of the Belgian local administration, most notably the massive document collection of the Governor General's services, were shipped to Belgium on the eve of independence ... and only recently have they been inventoried by the Archives of the Belgian Ministry of Foreign Affairs, where they finally found shelter. But in any case, visiting foreign archives is an almost impossible dream for most of the Congolese historians that have stuck by this rather unprofitable activity ...

Recent controversies on Leopoldian Congo

Only on a few rare occasions is historical research drawn into the limelight of public attention. This mostly happens when an author touches upon a controversial subject in a controversial manner. Recently, the history of colonial Congo enjoyed this rare privilege. A best-selling book by US writer Adam Hochschild, *King Leopold's Ghosts*, published in 1998, has triggered such a process. The turmoil caused by this book was not limited to Belgium (although the reactions there were, of course, more pronounced than elsewhere). On the contrary, it echoed through the media in most other European countries and even as far as Japan, where Belgian subjects rarely succeed in making the newspapers headlines ... To understand what happened, we have to come back to our (necessary) digression concerning Belgian official attitude towards the "red rubber" question. Despite Stengers' scientific work, the orthodox discourse (through statements, school books, etc.) as well as the general public view concerning Leopold's (and Belgian) rule in Congo had barely changed. This view can be summarized as follows: maybe some 'excesses' had been committed in the CFS, but they were excusable because of a whole range of elements (isolation of the colonial agents, financial weakness of the CFS, etc.); such abuses had also existed in other colonies, and they had only been temporary; the King was not aware of their existence, and he surely did not want them; etc. The essential conclusion remained unshaken: Belgium had brought progress and civilization to this unfortunate region.

But in the beginning of the 1980s, two researchers, neither of them 'professional' historians, dug into the archives (mainly of the Ministry of Foreign Affairs) in order to examine what really happened during the CFS period. Ironically, it was a Belgian diplomat (who had been posted, *inter alia*, in Africa), Jules Marchal (1924-2003), who was one of the first to do so. His interest in the subject had been awakened by an article published in a Liberian newspaper telling the story of the Congo atrocities. As so many of his predecessors (cf. the many examples we cited), he cabled this information to his Ministry in Brussels. Getting no reply, so he told later[58], he started to look for the truth on his own initiative. After painstaking research, he published a series of books under the pseudonym of A.M. Delathuy (1985-1989). Some years later, a French version of his books was published, now under his real name; moreover, this same author also published a series of books concerning the story of forced labour in Belgian Congo[59]. Even before the publication of Marchal's first book, a Flemish anthropologist who had done fieldwork in Congo, Daniel Vangroenweghe (1938), also got interested in the Leopoldian period in Congo. His research was also published in 1985, under the title *Rood rubber. Leopold II en zijn Kongo*[60]. That same year, he also published the original and integral version of Casement's report, in a university series directed by Jean-Luc Vellut[61]. Since then, Vangroenweghe has kept digging into the murky Leopoldian past, as shown by his most recent book, analyzing the infamous "Stokes affair" of 1895, one of the many examples of dysfunctions in the CFS[62].

These 1985-1988 books were important, because for the first time the Congo atrocities had become the subject of separate and in-depth monographs. They were carefully documented and analyzed the CFS atrocities in detail. So they did not pass unnoticed in Belgium. In a program on the Flemish television, for instance, Vangroenweghe was opposed to Stengers, who defended the position that the atrocities had not been as widespread as the author pretended. Overall, these books changed the view of a small part of Belgian public opinion, but without pervading the deeper strata of the population or changing the official position of Belgian authorities on the matter. On the other hand, professional historians, aware of previous scientific work on the CFS, were not surprised by the facts brought to light by these books; they only comforted their already established opinion on Leopold's regime in the Congo. Nevertheless, the Belgian historical establishment also had some objections against the *methodological* aspects of Marchal's work. His voluminous books essentially were indigestible compilations of documents, overloaded with lengthy citations. Synthesis, interpretation and contextualization – the essence of real historical analysis – were lacking. Consequently, the historical guild did not consider nor present his books as canonical historical research on the CFS, because historical analysis is something entirely different from 'prosecutor's work'...

The result of this situation was that apparently little had changed in Belgium's relation to its colonial past. There still lacked a large-scale, in depth historical work, treating all aspects of Leopoldian Congo (of which the atrocities were only one, albeit an important aspect) – a work that, so to say, could be "endorsed" by the Belgian scientific community and that might influence public authorities in their own discourses and statements. Seen from abroad, 'Belgium' as a whole still seemed to stick by its old 'negationism', refusing to face facts and deliberately organizing a "conspiracy of silence" – a view that was only partially correct, since such an attitude did not exist in professional historical milieus. Nevertheless, the difficulties in getting access to the archives of the former Ministry of Colonies and of the Ministry of Foreign Affairs in Belgium (partly due to understaffing), coupled with the heavy consultation procedures that still existed such as the 50-year rule, rightly or wrongly contributed to the impression that the Belgian authorities held to a culture of secrecy and did not want researchers digging into Belgium's colonial past. Consequently, the Congo atrocities remained an object of foreign indignation, reflected either in scientific publications, such as the 1990 article published by the Dutch anthropologist Jan Breman entitled "Congo, a state of terror"[63], or in more popular writings.

At the end of the 1990s, a foreign 'non historian', the American writer Adam Hochschild, once again took up this Belgian-Congolese subject, and denounced the Congo atrocities. He thus followed (maybe unknowingly) the long established tradition that we have documented above and that was never really extinguished, all efforts of the Belgian Foreign Ministry notwithstanding. He also continued the tradition of critical writings concerning the colony we mentioned above. But this time, the talented Hochschild produced a well researched, finely written and very readable book, which immediately became a world-wide best-seller (another book, in the same vein, written by the British author Evans largely passed unnoticed)[64]. For the *connoisseurs*, it contained few or no new things: not only Marchal's and Vangroenweghe's, but even Stengers' works were heavily relied upon. A polemic nevertheless arose concerning some of the author's objectionable statements, more particularly his use of the term 'holocaust' to describe what happened in the CFS, and, secondly, his 'educated guess' that Leopold's actions caused the death of 10 million Congolese. Belgian specialists such as Stengers and Vellut essentially (and, in my opinion, rightly) criticized these two elements, but unfortunately the discussion got entangled into these aspects, thereby missing what could have been (but still can become) a welcome 'wake-up' call for broader audiences, endorsed by the scientific community.

Indeed, Hochschild's book reached very large audiences, even (and foremost) in Belgium itself. Its effect was amplified by a broad echo in the written press and even by a much discussed television program, produced by the BBC. Peter Bates' film *White King, Red Rubber, Black Death* was broadcasted in many European countries, for instance in Great Britain, in France and Germany (Arte-TV), and of course in Belgium itself. It fuelled an already heated discussion in broad circles of Belgian public opinion[65]. An old reflex was awakened: Belgian official authorities were indignant; so were circles of ex-colonial civil servants or employees, some journalists, and many more or less patriotic Belgians. Some of them felt attacked in their national honour and reactivated arguments that, *in some cases,* showed *some* similarity with the ones that had been formulated by the Belgian diplomatic authorities since the early 1920's (if not by Leopold himself...).

In the meantime, Belgian public opinion and the political establishment had been confronted with yet another aspect of the colonial past. In 1999, the Belgian sociologist Ludo De Witte published a book that caused turmoil, not only in Belgium, but also in other countries[66]. Using important new documents found in the Archives of the Foreign Ministry, the author stated that the Belgian authorities had ordered the murder of Congo's first Prime Minister, Patrice Lumumba in January 1961. Strictly speaking, these events fall outside the scope of this chapter, since they have to do with *postcolonial* history. Nevertheless, they have to be mentioned, since they fuelled a heated debate in Belgium. In 2000, a Parliamentary Enquiry Commission was created by the House of Representatives. Political authorities made an appeal to professional historians in order to 'look for the truth' in this matter. After almost two years of research in hitherto inaccessible archives, these historians came to the conclusion that the 'moral responsibility' fell on the Belgian authorities of that time[67]. In short: at the turn of the century, Belgium was confronted twice with its colonial past. Newspapers, media and the general public showed more and more interest in their forefathers' actions in the Congo. The great public success of an exhibition on Belgium's colonial past, organized in the Tervuren Museum, which, at last, started to change its presentation after so many decades of immobility, was a clear sign of this growing overall interest in the colonial past[68].

A revival of Belgian historiography on colonialism?

This was only the most visible aspect of changing national attitudes. During the last ten or fifteen years of the 20th century, the Belgian historical world itself was shedding its indifference towards the Congo. A historian of Congolese origin, but who has been living in Belgium for many years, Mathieu Zana Aziza Etambala, has written many fine studies on the colonial period, mostly focused on the history of Catholic missions and on the contacts between Congolese and Belgians[69]. Very recently, race relations and gender aspects have inspired some innovative studies, such as those by the historians Valérie Piette and Catherine Jacques (Belgian women in the Congo), Lissia Jeurissen (mulattoes), Amandine Lauro (sexual relations between white men and Congolese women), and by the anthropologist Bambi Ceuppens (perceptions of the Congolese by the Belgians and vice versa)[70]. In this revival of colonial history cultural aspects figure prominently. The following aspects of this vast domain have been successfully been studied during these last few years: colonial architecture (Johan Lagae), colonial photography and colonial art (Françoise Morimont and Patricia Van Schuylenbergh), colonial film (Guido Convents), the history of colonial anthropology and museology in Belgium (Maarten Couttenier), the history of missions and propaganda (Luc Vints), the evolution of educational policy in the Congo (Marc Depaepe and Lies Van Rompaey)[71].

Other aspects were also being analyzed. The Belgian colonial world after 1908 (administration, enterprises, policies) still largely remains unknown. The author of these lines has tried to fill some of these gaps, by publishing a few contributions on Belgian colonial policy, on big business and on the impact of the colony on Belgium itself[72]. What happened on the colonial terrain itself has been analyzed by such authors as Bruno Demeulder (studying the labour policy of big enterprises[73]) and Marie-Bénédicte Dembour (studying the experience of Belgian colonial administrators, through an anthropological approach of their memories[74]). Hein Vanhee and Geert Castryck, two historians of the University of Ghent (who have also been trained in other disciplines, respectively in anthropology and Oriental studies), are currently working on some large-scale studies of Belgian colonial rule in the Congo.

A few years ago, these two authors produced a stimulating essay on the state of the art and the future perspectives of colonial historiography in Belgium, introducing a special issue of the Belgian review of contemporary history, consisting of several articles on Belgian colonial history[75]. This certainly is the symptom of the fact that something is indeed changing in the Belgian historical world. But in comparison to other former imperial countries, Belgian colonial historiography is lagging behind. The heavy institutional and political weight attached to the Leopoldian heritage had something to do with this. Much remains to be done, but luckily, new perspectives and approaches (anthropology, gender studies, cultural studies) undoubtedly will fertilize historical work on colonial Congo. The new generation of Belgian historians has never known colonialism. They do not want to "prove" anything and do not have any special feelings of guilt, nostalgia or justification towards what happened in the Congo under Belgian rule. In their eyes, there is only one thing left in eulogy and in national pride: these old fetters, which have influenced so deeply the beginnings of colonial historiography, have themselves become objects of scientific enquiry. Understanding and explaining colonialism, a complex phenomenon of societal contact: this is the huge task that lays ahead. If their new approach and the resulting new insights percolate through to public opinion, politicians and school children, these historians will not have wasted their time.

Notes

1 J.-P. Lefevre, *Une ancienne colonie, le Congo*, in *A la conquête du temps. Cycle 10/12*, Ransart, p. B9.

2 E. Vandermissen, *Léopold II et Beernaert d'après leur correspondance inédite de 1884 à 1894*, vol. I, Brussels 1920, p. 99.

3 O. Louwers, *Hommage au Roi Léopold II, fondateur de l'empire colonial belge*, in *Biographie coloniale belge*, vol. I, Brussels 1948, p. 5, p. 13, pp. 16-17.

4 Cited in G. Vanthemsche, *Belgique et Congo: empreintes d'une colonie (des années 1880 aux années 1980)*, Brussels 2006 (forthcoming).

5 J. Willequet, *Le Congo belge et la Weltpolitik (1894-1914)*, Brussels 1962, p. 499.

6 H.D. Ziman, *Stanley and King Leopold*, "The Daily Telegraph", 14 June 1957.

7 Archives of the Belgian Ministry of Foreign Affairs (AMFA), AF-I-26 (1957), J. Willequet to J. Delvaux de Fenffe (Director General of Political Affairs of the Ministry), 19 June 1957.

8 "Bulletin des Séances de l'IRCB" (hereafter "Bull. IRCB"), 12, nr. 1, 1941, p. 46.

9 Volume VIII of what is now called the *Biographie Belge d'Outre-Mer (BBOM)* has been published in 1998 (Brussels, ARSOM); the next volume is being prepared at the moment.

10 "Bull. IRCB", 1, nr. 1, 1930, p. 26.

11 See, for example, R.S. Thomson, *Fondation de l'Etat Indépendant du Congo. Un chapitre du partage de l'Afrique*, Brussels 1933, p. 354.

12 "Bull. IRCB", 16, nr. 3, 1945, p. 516.

13 "Bull. IRCB", 23, nr. 4, 1952, pp. 1064-1066 and 24, nr. 2, 1953, pp. 471-473.

14 Detailed biography and bibliography in J.-M. Duvosquel - A. Dierkens - G. Vanthemsche (eds.), *Belgique, Europe, Afrique. Deux siècles d'histoire contemporaine. Méthode et réflexions. Recueil d'articles de Jean Stengers*, Brussels 2005, (published also as a special issue of "Revue Belge de Philologie et d'Histoire", nos. 1-2, 2004). For his activities in IRCB/ARSOM see J. Vanderlinden, *Jean Stengers*, "Bulletin des Séances de l'ARSOM", 49, nr. 3, 2003, pp. 399-407.

15 A. Rubbens, *Jadin (Louis)*, in *BBOM*, Brussels 1977, vol. VIIb, col. 213-216.

16 A. Roeykens, *Le genie de Léopold II et la Conférence géographique de Brussels de 1876*, in *La Conférence de géographie de 1876. Recueil d'études*, Brussels 1976, pp. 375-413.

17 "The lucid exposé given by the author [Stengers] on the obscurities of this subject produces an almost painful impression: his paper projects a dubious light on certain actions of the King by putting into question their rectitude. We would like to attenuate this impression made upon the reader by [etc.]"; V. Gelders, *A propos de la communication de M. J. Stengers sur l'histoire des finances congolaises*, "Bull. IRCB", 25, nr. 1, 1954.

18 "We should state explicitly in the constitutional text our engagement (...) to exercise the rights [of sovereignty in Congo] that we have received, without renouncing them" – but this should be done "in the primordial interest of the Congolese population"; J. Stengers, *A propos de la révision de l'article 1er de la Constitution*, "Bull. IRCB", 25, nr. 5, 1954, pp. 1362-1363.

[19] R. Slade, *King Leopold's Congo. Aspects of the Development of race Relations in the Congo Independent State*, Oxford 1962, (she also authored a study on the history of the missions in Congo: *English-speaking Missions in the Congo Independent State*, London 1961); R. Anstey, *King Leopold's Legacy. The Congo under Belgian Rule 1908-1960*, Oxford 1966; see also Id., *Britain and the Congo in the 19th Century*, Oxford 1962.

[20] We will mention only a few of his books (for the articles see the above mentioned bibliography): J. Stengers, *Combien le Congo a-t-il coûté à la Belgique?*, Brussels 1957; Id., *Belgique et Congo. L'élaboration de la Charte coloniale*, Brussels 1963; J. Stengers W. Roger Louis, *E.D. Morel's History of the Congo Reform Movement*, Oxford 1968.

[21] J. Stengers, *Congo, mythes et réalités. 100 ans d'histoire*, Gembloux 1989, (second, enlarged edition in 2005).

[22] *L'expansion belge sous Léopold Ier (1831-1865). Recueil d'études*, 1965; *La Conférence Géographique de 1876. Recueil d'études*, 1976; *Le centenaire de l'Etat Indépendant du Congo. Recueil d'études*, 1988; *Le Congo Belge durant la Seconde Guerre Mondiale. Recueil d'études*, 1983; *Congo 1955-1960. Recueil d'études*, 1992.

[23] J. Kestergat, *Quand le Zaïre s'appelait Congo. L'aventure coloniale belge*, Brussels 1985; M. Massoz, *Le Congo de papa (1951-1960)*, Bressoux 1982; Id., *Le Congo de Léopold II (1878-1908)*, Liège 1989; Id., *Le Congo des Belges*, Liège 1994.

[24] E.g. A. Schöller, *Congo 1959-1960*, Gembloux 1982; G. Jacques, *Lualaba. Histoires de l'Afrique profonde*, Brussels 1995.

[25] E.g. A. Lederer, *Histoire de la navigation au Congo*, Tervuren 1965.

[26] E.g. L.F. Vanderstraeten, *La Force Publique congolaise de 1918 à 1960*, in *Actes du colloque d'histoire militaire belge (1830-1980)*, Brussels 1981, pp. 193-206.

[27] P.G. Janssensì et al. (eds.), *Médecine et hygiène en Afrique centrale de 1885 à nos jours*, 2 vols., Brussels 1992.

[28] V. Drachoussoff (ed.), *Le développement rural en Afrique centrale 1908-1960/1962*, 2 vols., Brussels 1991.

[29] C. Blanchart et al., *Le rail au Congo belge*, 2 vols., Brussels 1993, p. 400.

[30] See, for example, one of his last publications: P. Salmon, *Lettres et carnets de route de pionniers belges. Etude des mentalités colonials*, "Bull. ARSOM", 50, nr. 2, 2004, pp. 167-182 (of course with references to his own previous publications).

[31] J. Vanderlinden (ed.), *Documents diplomatiques belges 1941-1960. Tome VIII – Territoires d'Outre-mer*, Brussels 2004; P. Buch - J. Vanderlinden, *L'uranium, la Belgique et les Puissances. Marché de dupes ou chef d'œuvre diplomatique?*, Brussels 1995; J. Vanderlinden, *Pierre Ryckmans (1891-1959). Coloniser dans l'honneur*, Brussels 1994.

[32] P. Marechal, *De "Arabische" campagne in het Maniema-gebied (1892-1894)*, Tervuren 1992.

[33] G. Vandewalle, *De conjuncturele evolutie in Kongo en Ruanda-Urundi van 1920 tot 1939 en van 1949 tot 1958*, Gent 1966; A. Huybrechts, *Transports et structures de développement au Congo. Etude du progrès économique de 1900 à 1970*, Paris-The Hague 1970; J.-L. Lacroix, *L'industrialisation au Congo. La transformation des structures économiques*, Paris-The Hague 1967; J.-P. Peemans, *Diffusion du progrès et convergence des prix. Congo-Belgique 1900-1960*, Louvain-Paris 1968; Id., *Le Congo-Zaïre au gré du XXe siècle. Etat, économie et société 1880-1990*, Paris 1997 (collection of his most important historical articles on the Congo).

[34] Biographical sketch and bibliography in P. Mabiala Mantuba-Ngoma (ed.), *La nouvelle histoire du Congo: mélanges eurafricains offerts à Frans Bontinck c.i.c.m.*, Tervuren-Paris 2004.

[35] J.-L. Vellut, *Les bassin du Congo et l'Angola*, in J.F. Ade Ajayi (ed.), *Histoire générale de l'Afrique*, vol. VI: *L'Afrique au XIXe siècle jusque vers les années 1880*, Paris 1997, pp. 160-179.

[36] J.-L. Vellut, *Mining in the Belgian Congo 1910-1960*, in D. Birmingham - P.M. Martin (eds.), *History of Central Africa*, vol. II, London 1983, pp. 126-163; J.-L. Vellut, *Hégémonies en construction: articulations entre Etat et enterprises dans le bloc colonial belge (1908-1960)*, "Revue Canadienne des Etudes Africaines", 16, nr. 2, 1982, pp. 313-330.

[37] Id., *Rural poverty in Western Shaba, ca. 1900-1930*, in R. Palmer - N. Parsons (eds.), *The Roots of Rural Poverty in Central and Southern Africa*, London 1977, pp. 294-231.

[38] J.-L. Vellut (ed.), *Simon Kimbangu. 1921: de la prédication à la déportation. Les sources*, Brussels 2005.

[39] Id., *Un centenaire: 1885-1985. Les relations Europe-Afrique au ncrible d'une commémoration*, Leiden 1985.

[40] Id., *Guide de l'étudiant en histoire du Zaïre*, Kinshasa-Lubumbashi 1974; J.-L. Vellut - F. Loriaux - F. Morimont, *Bibliographie historique du Zaïre à l'époque coloniale (1880-1960). Travaux publiés en 1960-1996*, Louvain-la-Neuve-Tervuren 1996.

[41] L.H. Gann - L. Duignan, *The Rulers of Belgian Congo 1884-1914*, Princeton 1979; B. Emerson, *Leopold II*, London 1979 (French trans.: *Léopold II. Le royaume et l'empire*, Gembloux 1980); S.J.S. Cookey, *Britain and the Congo Question 1885-1913*, London 1968; R.O. Collins, *King Leopold, England, and the Upper Nile, 1899-1909*, New Haven 1968.

[42] R. Cornevin, *Histoire du Congo*, Paris 1963 (fourth edition: *Histoire du Zaïre des origines à nos jours*, Brussels 1989).

[43] N. Ascherson, *The King Incorporated. Leopold II in the Age of Trusts*, London 1963 (new edition: *The King Incorporated: Leopold the Second and the Congo*, London 1999, and translation in Dutch: *De Koning NV: de biografie van Leopold II*, Antwerp 2002).

[44] A. Maurel, *Le Congo de la colonisation belge à l'indépendance*, Paris 1992 (first edition under the pseudonym M. Merlier, Paris 1962); J. Depelchin, *De L'Etat Indépendant du Congo au Zaïre contemporain 1885-1974*, Dakar 1992.

[45] B. Fetter, *The Creation of Elisabethville 1910-1940*, Stanford 1976. Fetter has also contributed to general African demography: B. Fetter (ed.), *Demography from Scanty Evidence: Central Africa in the Colonial Era*, London 1990.

[46] S.E. Katzenellenbogen, *Railways and the Copper Mines of Katanga*, Oxford 1973.

[47] J. Higginson, *A Working Class in the Making: Belgian Colonial Labor Policy, Private Enterprise, and the African Mineworker, 1907-1951*, Madison 1989; D. Northrup, *Beyond the Bend of the River: African Labor in Eastern Zaïre 1865-1940*, Athens (Ohio) 1988; S.H. Nelson, *Colonialism in the Congo Basin 1880-1940*, Athens (Ohio) 1994; W.J. Samarin, *Black Man's Burden: African Colonial Labor on the Congo and Ubangi Rivers, 1880-1900*, Boulder 1989.

[48] M.D. Markowitz, *Cross and Sword: the Political Role of Christian Missions in the Belgian Congo, 1908-1960*, Stanford 1973.

[49] N.R. Hunt, *A Colonial Lexicon: of Birth Ritual, Medicalization and Mobility in the Congo*, Durham 1999.

[50] To cite only a few of his many publications on colonial Congo specifically (many other volumes edited by him concern Black Africa in general): B. Jewsiewicki, *Modernisation ou destruction du village africain: l'économie politique de la modernisation agricole au Congo Belge*, Brussels 1983 (Cahiers du CEDAF, n. 5, 1983); Id., *Zaïre enters the World System: its colonial incorporation as the Belgian Congo, 1885-1960*, in G. Gran (ed.), *Zaïre. The Political Economy of Underdevelopment*, New York 1979, pp. 29 53.

[51] J. Fabian, *Language and Colonial Power: the Appropriation of Swahili in the Former Belgian Congo 1880-1938*, Cambridge 1986.

[52] J.E. Helmreich, *Gathering Rare Ores. The Diplomacy of Uranium Acquisition, 1943-1954*, Princeton 1986; Id., *United States Relations with Belgium and the Congo, 1940-1960*, Newark 1998; D.N. Gibbs, *The Political Economy of Third World Intervention. Mines, Money, and US Policy in the Congo Crisis*, Chicago 1991; G.T. Mollin, *Die USA und der Kolonialismus. Amerika als Partner und Nachfolger der belgischen Macht in Afrika 1939-1965*, Berlin 1996.

[53] On the history of historical studies in Congo, see M. Mwa Bawele - S. Kivilu, *Historical research in Zaïre. Present status and future perspectives*, in B. Jewsiewicki - D. Newbury (eds.), *African Historiographies. What History for Which Africa?*, London 1986, pp. 224-234.

54 I. N'Daywel è Nziem, *Histoire générale du Congo. De l'héritage ancien à la République Démocratique*, Brussels-Paris 1998², p. 955 (first edition: *Histoire du Zaïre*, Paris 1997).

55 See the analysis by J.-L. Vellut, *Prestige et pauvreté de l'histoire nationale. A propos d'une histoire nationale du Congo*, "Revue Belge de Philologie et d'Histoire, " 77, no. 2, 1999, pp. 480-517.

56 G. Nzongola-Ntalaja, *The Congo from Leopold to Kabila: a People's History*, London 2002 (colonial period: pp. 13-93).

57 C.D. Gondola, *The History of Congo*, Westport 2002.

58 A. Hochschild, *De geest van koning Leopold II en de plundering van de Congo*, Amsterdam 1998. (Dutch translation of the author's original *King Leopold's Ghosts. A Story of Greed, Terror and Heroism in Colonial Africa*, 1998). The French version of the book used the controversial term "holocaust" in the title: *Les fantômes du roi léopold II: un holocauste oublié*, Paris 1998.

59 A.M. Delathuy, *E.D. Morel tegen Leopold II en de Kongostaat* (1985), *Jezuïeten met kruis en zwaard* (1986), *De geheime documentatie van de Onderzoekscommissie in de Kongostaat* (1988), *Missie en staat in oud-Kongo* (1992), all published at the Flemish left-wing publisher EPO in Berchem; *De Kongo Staat van Leopold II 1876-1900. Het verloren paradijs*, Antwerp 1989; French trans.: *L'histoire du Congo 1876-1900. L'Etat Libre du Congo: paradis perdu*, 2 vols., Borgloon 1996; *L'histoire du Congo 1900-1910. E.D. Morel contre Léopold II*, 2 vols., Paris 1996; *L'histoire du Congo 1910-1945. Travail forcé pour le cuivre et pour l'or, pour le rail, pour l'huile de palme*, 3 vols., Borgloon 1999-2001.

60 D. Vangroenweghe, *Rood rubber. Leopold II en zijn Kongo*, Brussel-Amsterdam 1985 (French translation: *Du sang sur les lianes. Léopold II et son Congo*, Brussels 1986).

61 *Le rapport Casement. (...) Introduction et notes de Daniel Vangroenweghe. Préface de Jean-Luc Vellut*, Louvain-la-Neuve 1985 (Enquêtes et Documents d'Histoire Africaine, vol. VI).

62 D. Vangroenweghe, *Voor rubber en ivoor. Leopold II en de ophanging van Stokes*, Leuven 2005.

63 J. Breman, *Een staat van terreur. Kongo rond de eeuwwisseling*, in *Amsterdams Sociologisch Tijdschrift*, 16, no. 4, February 1990, pp. 3-26.

64 M. Ewans, *European Atrocity, African Catastrophe. Leopold II, the Congo Free State and its Aftermath*, London 2002.

65 Overview of these reactions in M. Dumoulin, *Leopold II, un roi génocidaire?*, Brussels 2005; critical remarks on Hochschild in P. Marechal, *La controverse sur Léopold II et le Congo dans la littérature et les médias. Réflexions critiques*, in J.-L. Vellut (ed.), *La mémoire du Congo. Le temps colonial*, Tervuren-Gent 2005, pp. 43-49.

66 L. De Witte, *De moord op Lumumba*, Leuven 1999, (English trans.: *The Assassination of Lumumba*, London 2001; French tran.: *L'assassinat de Lumumba*, Paris 2000).

67 L. De Vos - P. Raxhon - E. Gerard - J. Gerard-Libois, *Les secrets de l'affaire Lumumba*, Brussels 2004 (see also www.lachambre.be).

68 See the catalogue published on that occasion: J.-L. Vellut (ed.), *La mémoire du Congo. Le temps colonial*, Tervuren-Gent 2005.

69 Z. Aziza Etambala, *Congo '55-'65. Van koning Boudewijn tot president Mobutu*, Tielt 1999; Id., *In het land van de Banoko. De geschiedenis van de Kongolese/Zaïrese aanwezigheid in België van 1885 tot heden*, Leuven 1993.

70 V. Piette - C. Jacques, *L'Union des Femmes Coloniales 1923-1940*, in A. Hugon (ed.), *Histoire des femmes en situation coloniale. Afrique et Asie XXe siècle*, Paris 2004; L. Jeurissen, *Quand le métis s'appelait "mulâtre"...: société, droit et pouvoir coloniaux face à la descendance des couples eurafricains dans l'ancien Congo Belge*, Brussels 2003; A. Lauro, *Coloniaux, ménagères et prostituées au Congo Belge 1885-1930*, Brussels 2005; B. Ceuppens, *Congo made in Flanders? Vlaamse koloniale visies op "blank" en "zwart" in Belgisch Congo*, Gent 2003 (English trans.: *From Home to Home? Flemish Discourses on Belonging and Difference in Belgian Congo and Flanders*, Oxford, forthcoming); Id., *Onze Congo? Congolezen over de kolonisatie*, Leuven 2003.

71 L. Vints, *Kongo made in Belgium: beeld van een kolonie in film en propaganda*, Antwerp 1984; L. Vints - Zana Aziza Etambala, *100 jaar Zusters van Liefde in Zaïre 1891-1991*, Leuven 1992; J. Lagae, *Kongo zoals het is. Drie architectuurverhalen uit de Belgische kolonisatiegeschiedenis (1920-1960)*, 3 vols., Gent 2002; M. De Paepe - L. Van Rompaey, *In het teken van de bevoogding. De educatieve actie in Belgisch-Congo (1908-1960)*, Leuven 1995; G. Convents, *Afrika verbeeld. Film en (de-)kolonisatie van de geesten*, Brussel-Berchem 2003,(on Belgian Congo: pp. 49-66 and pp. 94-109) (French trans.: *L'Afrique? Quel cinéma? Un siècle de propagande coloniale et de films africains*, Brussels 2003); M. Couttenier, *Congo tentoongesteld: een geschiedenis van de Belgische antropologie en het Museum van Tervuren (1882-1925)*, Leuven 2005; F. Morimont - P. Van Schuylenbergh, *Rencontres artistiques Belgique-Congo 1920-1950*, Louvain-la-Neuve 1995.

72 G. Vanthemsche, *Genèse et portée du "Plan Décennal" du Congo belge (1949-1959)*, Brussels 1994; Id., *Belgique et Congo* cit. (forthcoming).

73 B. De Meulder, *De kampen van Kongo. Arbeid, kapitaal en rasveredeling in de koloniale planning*, Amsterdam 1996.

74 M.-C. Dembour, *Recalling the Belgian Congo. Conversations and Introspections*, Oxford 2000.

75 H. Vanhee - G. Castryck, *Belgische historiografie en verbeelding over het koloniale verleden*, "Revue Belge d'Histoire Contemporaine", 32, nrs. 3-4, 2002, pp. 305-320.

Bibliography

Hochschild A., *King Leopold's Ghosts. A Story of Greed, Terror and Heroism in Colonial Africa*, New York 1998.

Marechal P., *De "Arabische" campagne in het Maniema-gebied (1892-1894)*, Tervuren 1992.

Mwa Bawelw M. - Kivilu S., *Historical research in Zaïre. Present status and future perspectives*, in Jewsiewicki B. - Newbury D. (eds.), *African Historiographies. What History for Which Africa?*, London 1986, pp. 224-234.

N'Daywel è Nziem I., *Histoire générale du Congo. De l'héritage ancien à la République Démocratique*, Brussels-Paris 1998 (first edition: *Histoire du Zaïre*, Paris 1997).

Peemans J.-P., *Le Congo-Zaïre au gré du XXe siècle. Etat, économie et société 1880-1990*, Paris 1997.

Stengers J., *Combien le Congo a-t-il coûté à la Belgique?*, Brussels 1957.

Id., *Belgique et Congo. L'élaboration de la Charte coloniale*, Brussels 1963.

Stengers J. - Wm. Roger Louis, *E.D. Morel's History of the Congo Reform Movement*, Oxford 1968.

Stengers J., *Congo, mythes et réalités. 100 ans d'histoire*, Gembloux, Duculot 1989 (second, enlarged edition in 2005).

Vanderlinden J., *Pierre Ryckmans (1891-1959). Coloniser dans l'honneur*, Brussels 1994.

Vangroenweghe D., *Rood rubber. Leopold II en zijn Kongo*, Brussel-Amsterdam 1985 (French trans.: *Du sang sur les lianes. Léopold II et son Congo*, Brussels 1986).

Vanthemsche G., *Belgique et Congo: empreintes d'une colonie (des années 1880 aux années 1980)*, Brussels 2006 (forthcoming).

Vellut J.-L., *Guide de l'étudiant en histoire du Zaïre*, Kinshasa-Lubumbashi 1974.

Vellut J.-L. - Loriaux -F. Morimint, *Bibliographie historique du Zaïre à l'époque coloniale (1880-1960). Travaux publiés en 1960-1996*, Louvain-la-Neuve-Tervuren 1996.

Willequet J., *Le Congo belge et la Weltpolitik (1894-1914)*, Brussels 1962.

Sources

The "Congo atrocities", foreign opinion and Belgian reactions, some illustrations

Document 1

In 1916, le Comte de Ramaix, high official of the Belgian Ministry of Foreign Affairs, writes to Baron Beyens, Minister of Foreign Affairs:

"Beaucoup de personnes même parmi les Anglais (...) se sont demandées si ces deux personnages [=Casement and Morel] n'étaient pas des agents aux gages de l'Allemagne dont la mission aurait consisté à nous brouiller avec l'Angleterre à propos du Congo. (...) Elles font remarquer que dès 1911, Morel qui se rendait compte que la Congo Reform Association devrait bientôt cesser sa campagne, les réformes si bruyamment revendiquées ayant été introduites par l'Administration Congolaise dès la reprise de la Colonie, commença à prôner un rapprochement anglo-allemand sur la base d'un partage du basin conventionnel du Congo".

"Many persons, even amongst the British (...) have asked themselves if both these persons (= Morel and Casement) were not German agent whose mission it was to arouse some quarrels with England concerning the Congo. (...) They noticed that from 1911 on, Morel, who was aware of the fact that the Congo Reform Association was soon to end its campaign, since the reforms that had been so loudly asked for, had been introduced by the Congolese Administration, began to defend and propose an Anglo-German alliance on the basis of a partition of the Congo conventional basin".

Source: *AMAE*, AF-I-26 (1876-1916), de Ramaix to Baron Beyens, 24.08.1916.

Document 2

In a report dating from January 1918, the Belgian consul in Johannesburg, Pierre Forthomme, wrote that some people once more had started to mention the "Congo atrocities". The Belgian Foreign Ministry gives the following guidelines:

"La plupart des abus invoqués contre l'EIC étaient, ou imaginaires, ou exagérés. [This sentence, mentioned in the first draft of the letter, was deleted from the final version, while the next sentence was added] *Il est désormais avéré que la campagne contre l'EIC n'était point inspirée par un souci désintéressé du sort des aborigènes. N'a-t-on pas appris depuis la guerre que les deux anciens chefs du mouvement anticongolais étaient deux séides de l'Allemagne et travaillaient dans son intérêt, qui était de nous brouiller avec l'Angleterre et d'entraîner celle-ci à provoquer un remaniement du statut territorial de l'Afrique. Malgré quelques abus inhérents à toutes les jeunes colonies et plus excusables pour l'EIC que pour toute autre étant donné les conditions de son existence et les faiblesses que lui imposait son statut international irrationnel, l'EIC peut se prévaloir d'une œuvre civilisatrice magnifique. (...) La Belgique n'a cependant pas à discuter le régime de l'EIC ni à se disculper de ses erreurs. Elle n'en était en rien responsable, car elle n'avait aucune part dans l'Administration de cet Etat. Bien mieux, quand elle a appris que tout n'y était pas parfait, elle a invoqué les droits que le Roi Léopold II lui avait accordés pour exiger d'en devenir maîtresse et d'en régler, désormais, les destinées".*

Most of the abuses invoked against the CFS were either imaginary or exaggerated. [This sentence, mentioned in the first draft of the letter, was deleted from the final version, while the next sentence was added] It is now evident that the campaign against the CFS was not inspired by a genuine concern for the fate of the aboriginals. Hasn't one heard since the war that both former chiefs of the anti-Congolese movement were in fact agents of Germany and worked in its interest, which was to generate some disagreement between us and Great Britain and to lead the latter into a new partition of Africa. Notwithstanding some abuses, inevitable in young colonies and all the more excusable in the CFS's case given the conditions in which it had to live and given the weaknesses imposed upon it by an irrational international statute, the CFS produced an wonderful civilizing activity. (...) Nevertheless, Belgium is not bound to discuss the CFS regime, nor to explain away its mistakes, since it had no part in its Administration. Even better: when Belgium saw that not everything was perfect over there, it has invoked the rights that King Leopold had given to it in order to become the full master of this territory and to henceforth guide its destinies.

Source: *AA*, AE-2, n. 364, Ministry of Foreign Affairs to P. Forthomme, 04.1918. *AMAE*, AF-I-26 (1917-1927), idem, 14.05.1918.

Document 3

In 1919, Pierre Daye, a Belgian journalist and colonial propagandist and former officer of the Belgian colonial campaigns in central Africa during World War I), is on a colonial propaganda tour in the United States:

"*Je suis actuellement persuadé qu'il n'existe aucun courant d'opinion hostile au Congo ou à son administration dans ce pays. Il m'arrive parfois – fort rarement – que des gens me demandent s'il est vrai que, du temps de l'Etat Indépendant du Congo (EIC), il avait été commis des atrocités au Congo*". In that case, he answered that they were "*des racontars favorisés par la propagande allemande*".

"I am presently persuaded that in this country, no opinion movement exists that is hostile towards Congo or its administration. Very rarely some people ask me whether it is true that atrocities have been committed in the Congo during the Free State period". In that case, he answered that they were "gossip stirred up by the German propaganda".
Source: *AA*, AE-2, n. 364, P. Daye to the Minister of Colonies, 04.01.1919.

Document 4

In September 1919, a German publication, the *Deutsche Kolonial Zeitung*, published an article on Congo, with a picture of two children with their hands cut off. The Director General of the Ministry of Colonies reacts as follows:

"*Je pense (...) qu'il est préférable de ne pas relever cette calomnie. (...) les faits allégués se se-*

raient produits il y a une vingtaine d'années: ils n'impressionnent plus. Il vaut mieux, s'il y a nécessité absolue, ne plus rouvrir ces discussions irritantes. Bien entendu, si une vraie campagne recommençait contre la gestion de l'Ancien EIC ou contre l'Administration Coloniale Belge, je soumettrai la question à un nouvel examen".

"I think (...) it is preferable not to react to this calumny. (...) the allegations are supposed to have taken place twenty years ago; they do not impress any more. If there is any absolute necessity, it is better not to reopen these irritant discussions. Of course, if a real campaign once again is being launched against the administration of the former CFS, than I will re-examine the question".

Source: *AMFA*, AF-I-1 (1920-1921), Halewyck, Director General of Ministry of Colonies, to the Director of the Bureau d'Information Belge, 23.01.1920.

Document 5

In 1920, Paul Hymans, the Belgian Foreign Minister, sends a note on colonial policy to the main Belgian ambassadors. They don't have to be afraid of the allegations concerning the so-called "Congo atrocities", he tells them:

"*Au contraire, cette question, n'ayez pas peur, à l'occasion, de la provoquer et de la rencontrer de front, elle ne gêne en rien le Gouvernement et il serait même bon que son opinion à ce sujet se répandît, afin de mettre fin à cette légende qui pèse si lourdement sur notre réputation».* The position of the Belgian governement is as follows: "*Le régime de l'EIC ne fut peut-être pas parfait: il compte cependant à son actif beaucoup de mérites qu'on a trop laissés dans l'ombre».* Those who attacked the CFS were in fact German agents. "*Quoi qu'il en soit, la Belgique ne doit pas être rendue responsable des erreurs de l'EIC*".

"On the contrary, don't be afraid, when necessary, to discuss this question and to handle it frankly. It does not embarrass the Government and it would be good if its opinion gets to be known, in order to put a halt to this legend that weighs so heavily on our reputation". The position of the Belgian government is as follows: "Maybe the CFS regime was not perfect: it nevertheless had many merits that went unnoticed". Those who attacked the CFS were in fact German agents. "Whatever it may be, Belgium must not be held responsible for the errors of the CFS".

Source: *AMFA*, AF-I-1 (1920-1921), P. Hymans, Minister of Foreign Affairs, to the Belgian ambassadors in Paris, London and Washington, 06.05.1920.

Document 6

In 1926, the Belgian consul general in Barcelona signals attacks on the atrocities in the CFS published in the Spanish press. The comments pretend that Belgium is incapable of running a colony.

Source: *AMFA*, AF-I-1 (1925-1926), Ch. Bastin, Belgian consul general in Barcelona, to Emile Vandervelde, Minister of Foreign Affairs, 06.10.1925.

Document 7

In 1928, Belgian authorities ask their consul general in Sidney to react against negative appreciations of Belgian colonial policy in Congo published in the Australian press, echoing the campaign against the CFS.

Source: *AMFA*, AF-I-1 (1927-1928), P. Hymans, Minister of Foreign Affairs, to Segaert, Belgian consul general in Sidney, 18.02.1928.

Document 8

In 1929, Octave Louwers, the Colonial Counsellor of the Belgian Ministry of Foreign Affairs, recommends great caution in handling the problems of forced labour on international discussion meetings:

"*La Belgique, sur qui pèse le souvenir du régime du caoutchouc, doit veiller d'une manière spéciale à échapper à toute critique. Il y a trop de puissances désireuses de pêcher en eau troublé*".

"Belgium, still haunted by the reminiscence of the rubber regime, must carefully watch not be the object of critic. Too many powers try to take advantage of the situation".

Source: *AMFA*, AF-I-17 (1926-1937), O. Louwers, *Note pour M. le Ministre*, 26.11.1929.

Document 9

In 1929, Prince Albert de Ligne, the Belgian ambassador in Washington, tells Foreign Minister Paul Hymans that the anti-Congo campaign has left deep marks in US public opinion. When speaking to a female journalist, the latter spoke of Leopold II as

'*un ogre*': "*elle m'avoua que, encore il n'y a pas longtemps, lorsqu'un enfant était méchant, on le menaçait d'appeler le roi Léopold II*". Now this negative attitude in the US towards Congo starts to change, he adds.

'an ogre' (=a man-eating monster): "she admitted that, not so long ago, when a child had been naughty, one tried to impress it by saying that King Leopold II would be called".

Source: *AMFA*, AF-I-17 (1926-1937), Prince A. de Ligne, Belgian ambassador in Washington to P. Hymans, Minister of Foreign Affairs, 10.12.1929.

Document 10

In 1930, the Dutch periodical *Licht* publishes an article on the CFS, with pictures of children with their hands cut off.

"La propagande anti-belge en Hollande, s'empare volontiers des critiques malveillantes et même des mensonges que l'on répand encore de temps à autre".

"Anti-Belgian propaganda in Holland readily takes advantage of the malevolent critics and even the lies that are still being disseminated once in a while".

Source: *AMFA*, AF-I-1 (1919-1930), E. Lauwers, Belgian consul general in Rotterdam to P. Hymans, Minister of Foreign Affairs, 04.01.1930.

Document 11

In the 1930s, the British press publishes several articles concerning the "scandalous" private life of Leopold II and mentions the CFS atrocities. These are also recalled in the British Parliament in 1937.

Source: *AMFA*, AF-I-26 (928-1947), diverse press cuttings.

Document 12

In 1944, a black American, Dr. Med. Joe T. Thomas, presenting himself as the "Representative of the Provisional Government of the Congo Free State" (founded in exile in 1906 in Birmingham, Alabama, and since then transferred to Cleveland Ohio, and to Detroit), writes a letter where he states that "the Belgian government does not own our territory. (...) Belgium stole our land and enslaved our native people. Belgian atrocities shocked the civilized world".

Source: *AMFA*, AF-I-1 (1943-1945), J. Jennen to P.H. Spaak, Belgian Minister of Foreign Affairs, 15.11.1944.

Document 13

In 1952, the former Belgian Minister of Colonies, Pierre Wigny, comes back from a visit in the US and recommends the launching of a propaganda campaign in order to gain some sympathy for the Belgian Congo.

"Au sujet du Congo, j'ai été étonné de constater combien les calomnies mises en circulation contre Léopold II restent vivaces. Partout on parle encore des mains coupées et du caoutchouc rouge. Les livres classiques qui traitent de l'histoire contemporaine rappellent ces atrocités. La littérature courante entretient ces souvenirs d'enfance. Le livre de Bertrand Russell qui vient de paraître contient à l'égard du Congo une allusion des plus déplaisantes".

"Concerning Congo, I was struck by the liveliness of the slander against Leopold II. Everywhere one still mentions the cut hands and the red rubber. The class books on contemporary history still mention the atrocities. The current literature keeps these recollections alive. Bertrand Russell's recently published book contains a most displeasing allusion concerning the Congo".

Source: *AMFA*, AF-I-17 (1948-1953), P. Wigny, *Voyage aux Etats-Unis 7 mars – 23 avril 1952. Rapport de mission*, p. 2.

Document 14

In 1958, Jacques Willequet, the *Conseiller historique* of the Ministry of Foreign Affairs, reacts to an article published in *The Times* of 27.10.1958, which, according to him, distorts reality.

"*Pourquoi certains abus inévitables de ce système furent-ils particulièrement reprochés à Léopold II, alors qu'ils étaient universels, et alors que le Roi, lui, avait été acculé par la détresse financière à un système que d'autres avaient adopté par pur égoïsme? La réponse est simple: le Congo était faible, vulnérable, mais riche, donc convoité (...) Et ainsi, quelques naïfs, souvent sincères, donnèrent à la campagne anticongolaise une façade idéaliste; derrière cette façade, des intérêts autrement palpables étaient en cause*".

"Why was Leopold II blamed in particular for certain inevitable abuses of this system? The latter were in fact universal; and sheer financial distress forced the King to adopt such methods that others introduced by sheer egoism. The answer is evident: the Congo was weak, vulnerable, but rich, and thus coveted. (...) A handful of naïve people, often sincere, gave an idealistic façade to the anti-Congolese campaign; behind this façade, material interests were at stake".
Source: *AMFA*, AF-I-1 (1958), J. Willequet, *Note pour P/Affaires coloniales*, 17.11.1958.

Document 15

In 1959, the British journalist, Peter Singleton-Gates, wants to publish the *The Black Diaries of Roger Casement*. The Belgian ambassador in London thinks that such a publication will be "particulièrement inopportune", considering the tense political situation in the Congo. It could "*servir d'aliment à une nouvelle campagne de calomnies*". Measures should be taken to combat the negative psychological effects of this publication. The Historical Counsellor of the Ministry finds that this document has no historical value whatsoever, since they mainly mention the author's homosexual adventures.

"*Un passionné, un malade, un anormal – un malheureux. Un malheureux, certes, comme il y en a beaucoup, mais son cas eût exclusivement relevé de la psychiatrie, s'il n'avait été mêlé, de façon bien discutable, à la campagne anticongolaise et au mouvement national irlandais. (...) Avec la même passion, avec la même absence d'esprit critique, Roger Casement devait projeter, cristalliser dans la question congolaise et dans le mouvement national irlandais tout l'envers d'un personnage hanté par ses perversions, torturé par ses complexes de culpabilité*".

"An emotional and sick man, an abnormal and unhappy person. Unhappy, certainly, as so many exist, but his case should have been treated by psychiatry, if he had not taken part, in a very disputable way, in the anti-Congolese campaign and in the Irish national movement. (...) With the same passion, with the same absence of critical mind, Roger Casement has projected, crystallized in the Congolese question and in the Irish national movement the dark side of his personality haunted by perversion, tortured by his guilt complexes".

Source: *AMFA*, AF-I-26 (1959), R. Van Meerbeke, Belgian ambassador in London to Pierre Wigny, Minister of Foreign Affairs, 02.02.1959; *AMFA*, AF-I-1 (1959), *Les "Carnets intimes" de Roger Casement*, note written by the "Service historique" of the Ministry of Foreign Affairs (= J. Willequet), 03.1959.

Document 16

In 1959, a meeting is being held at the Ministry of Foreign Affairs.
"*M. Xhronet rappelle qu'il a été entendu avec Inforcongo [the official information agency of Belgian Congo] qu'une étude serait établie avec des éléments de réponses que nos Chefs de poste pourraient opposer aux éternelles critiques de l'administration de Léopold II au Congo. N'y a-t-il pas lieu d'établir une collaboration entre le service historique du Département et Inforcongo pour cette étude?*".

"M. Xhronet reminds the fact that it has been agreed upon with Inforcongo [the official information agency of Belgian Congo] that a study should be made containing the elements of response that our diplomatic heads of post should oppose to the eternal critics of the Leopoldian administration of the Congo. Would it not be advisable to establish a collaboration between the History service of the Department and Inforcongo for this study?".

Source: *AMFA*, AF-I-1 (1959), "Compte rendu de la réunion tenue le 19.02.1959, au cabinet de M. J. Delvaux de Fenffe, Directeur général".

Document 17

In 1959, Pierre Wigny, the Belgian Minister of Foreign Affairs has heard that the historian Ronald Robinson intends to publish a book on the history of imperialism in Africa. Wigny writes to the Belgian ambassador in London:

"*Il faudrait éviter que ne soient répétées à nouveau, à propos de la période léopoldienne, les inexactitudes répandues par Bertrand Russell, entre autres. Il me paraît pourtant délicat d'approcher un homme de science pour l'"empêcher" de publier certaines choses; en revanche, il me paraît souhaitable de trouver une occasion permettant de signaler au Professeur Robinson qu'en Belgique, M. Jean Stengers, Professeur à l'ULB, est parmi d'autres, un spécialiste des questions africaines, que M. Jacques Willequet, Conseiller historique du Département, possède une gran-*

de connaissance de ces problèmes, et que l'un ou l'autre sont prêts à répondre à ses questions et disposés à lire, éventuellement, les passages de son manuscrit où il traite du Congo".

"One should try to avoid the errors being repeated once again, regarding the Leopoldian period, errors that have been uttered by Bertrand Russell, amongst others. It seems delicate to approach a man of science in order to prevent him from publishing certain things; on the other hand, it seems advisable to me to find an opportunity to say to Professor Robinson that in Belgium, Mr. Jean Stengers, Profesor at the ULB, is, amongst other things, a specialist in African affairs, and that Mr. Jacques Willequet, Historical Counsellor of the Foreign Department, knows a great deal about that matters, and that both of them are willing to answer his questions and to read, if necessary, the parts of his manuscript where he is referring to the Congo".
A similar letter was dispatched to Jan-Albert Goris, the official Belgian Commissioner of Information in New York.

Source: *AMFA*, AF-I-26 (1959), P. Wigny to R. Van Meerbeke, Belgian ambassador in London, 29.04.1959.

“Europe is irrelevant”: Redressing the Balance or the South African Ostrich Phenomenon

Donal P. McCracken
University of KwaZulu-Natal

Leli phepha libheka izinkinga ezikhungethe umlando waseNingizimu Afrika emva kombuso wobandlululo. Phambilini, ngaphansi kombuso wabamhlophe, umlando wawugxile kakhulu ezintweni eziwumthelela wesinqumo sokuthi abamhlophe bahlale eNingizimu Afrika. Kuliq iniso ukuthi kwakunezinkulumo mpikiswano phakathi kwabamhlophe abanesihe kanye nalabo abangabalandeli bakaMarx (abakholelwa ekutheni umnotho ngowabantu bonke) ngoshintsho kanye nokuguquka kwe-Afrika, kodwa ngonyaka we 1980 ukufundisa isifundo somlando emanyuvesi aseNingizimu Afrika kwakugxile kakhulu kwi-Yurophu. Leli phepha lizama ukuphendula umbuzo othi, kungabe sekukhona yini ukulingana noma mhlawumbe abahlaziyi bomlando baseNingizimu Afrika abayinakile yini ingxenye ebalulekile yemumva labo na?

In January 1977 Professor T.R.H. Davenport’s *South Africa: A modern history* was published by Macmillan South Africa[1]. After an initial scare that the apartheid authorities might ban the work by the then head of the Department of History at Rhodes University, Grahamstown, in the Eastern Cape Province, the book soon established itself as the leading undergraduate history textbook. This treatise, written from a South African white liberal perspective, not only confirmed Davenport as the leading South African historian but also confirmed a pattern that was already establishing itself in the English-medium white universities. It was clear that the future of historical enterprise lay in the study of African communities and African movements. Vasco da Gama, Diaz and van Riebeeck’s days were numbered.

This task or mission, however, was not easily accomplished and it continues to be fraught with pitfalls, present-mindedness, recrimination, and narrowness of approach that is both academically undesirable and conducive for the writing of bad history.

Davenport’s work itself suffered from one major flaw. It was essentially a history of the 20th century, with a substantial lead-in aimed at establishing a footprint for the dramatic and traumatic developments of the century of apartheid. His text ran to 432 pages. Of this, about two-thirds covered the post Anglo-Boer War (1899-1902) period. But equally dramatic was the down-playing of themes and events that had held centre stage since the great historians George Theal and George Cory compiled their multi-volume texts at the end of the 19th century and the beginning of the 20th century[2]. The Slagters Nek rebellion is not mentioned by name (interestingly an omission rectified in later editions) and the incident is passed over in a short paragraph. The Great Trek is rightly discussed in a much wider context than had been the practice. Detail of the two Anglo-Boer Wars is missing and indeed the first 'War of Freedom' is dismissed as 'engagements on the Drakensberg escarpment'.

What did the volume have within it instead? It was packed with details of chiefdoms, labour movements, the growth of a plural society, land issues and the white response to the liberation movement.

Davenport wisely retained a healthy balance of staff (albeit all white) in his department, between the young Turks and the empiricists. Southern, Elton, Trevor-Roper and the like were standard reading in an exacting and very impressive undergraduate programme. Roper's bitter tirade against African history – 'the gyrations of barbarous tribes' – was one not wholly dismissed by some associated with the department at that time.

The Rhodes postgraduate history honours class was monastic in its rigour, something inherited from, first, the formidable Professor Michael Roberts and then his successor, the great teacher Professor Winifred Maxwell[3]. The honours flagship programme was 'The Age of [Queen] Anne' and the Rhodes Library had a collection of texts relating to this period that would have put to shame most British university libraries.

In this milieu a balance existed between South African (not continental African) history and European history. The former was heavily weighted towards the white impact with some radical and recherché black South African history. The latter had an underlying, though not exclusive, regard for British history. In addition there were bits and pieces such as America, China, 'world civilisations' and so forth.

In the 1970s the balance tipped in favour of South African history. Some claimed that the syllabus was still dominated by contacts with Europe, colonisation, white settlement (not least the 1820 settlement of the Eastern Cape), white subjugation of the indigenous populations and constitutional history. This last was often taught in the context of what a generation before had termed 'the Native problem'. The course was exacting, especially at the honours level, where the 'Age of Anne' ruled supreme.

The result of the Rhodes fix was a generation of highly trained young white historians who were quickly snapped up for senior university administrative positions and corporations such as Anglo-American or who also helped staff in university history departments in South Africa and sometimes abroad.

But time and tide wait for no historian. Despite the excitement, zeal and (it has to be said) the anger Davenport's 'blue Bible' produced, there remained major problems in the South African history world in the last years of apartheid. These were simply that there were next to no African historians in the established universities. The concept of Africans writing their own history was to some whites an anathema and though to a larger number something they claimed to support only – "if standards are to be maintained, this has to be something for the future". This still remains the standard response of many to transformation to this day.

The upshot of this was as one might expect when no foundation had been laid. Change, when it came, resulted in a purposeful swing of the pendulum. This has produced two things: first, a downgrading in the themes and characters that once dominated history teaching in South African schools and universities. Second, there has been a consuming emphasis on the liberation movement and on African societies and African endeavour. This is hardly surprising in an immediate post-liberation phase, nor is it objectionable. What, however, has been unfortunate is that this period of readjustment has coincided with a dramatic decline in the fortune of history at schools and a commensurate collapse or decline of history departments in some universities. For example, the history section on the Pietermaritzburg campus of the University of KwaZulu-Natal, which once boasted six professors, is down to one professor and a lecturer. And at the University of South Africa History Department student numbers fell from approximately 7 000 in 1995 to 1 600 in 2005[4].

The introduction of a new matriculation examination process in 2008 may well reverse the decline in the fortunes of history in South Africa. History is to be one of a limited choice from which four subjects must be passed as core disciplines if matric exemption is to be certified. This will lead to an increased demand for history teachers which will impact favourably on the university history departments. But though this may affect numbers, whether or not this will influence the present trend in what is taught is another matter.

At the University of KwaZulu-Natal, history is included in a School of Anthropology, Gender and Historical Studies. This amalgam includes five disciplines: History, Anthropology, Gender Studies, Internet Studies as well as Cultural and Heritage Tourism. The school is situated on three campuses: Pietermaritzburg, Westville and the home campus at Howard College in Durban. The 2005 calendar entry for history reads:

> South Africa is changing fast, as is the global order in which we live. Understanding change, and managing it at personal and social levels, depends to a large extent on our appreciation and understanding of history. Courses and projects aim to help students to understand how major issues in today's world and in South Africa have come about – in the wider world, huge imbalances of power and wealth, skewed development, racial, gender and religious bigotry, rampant consumerism and environmental degradation; and in South Africa, the need to consolidate democracy, to expand urban and rural development, to raise levels of education and social welfare, to combat racism and other forms of discrimination and to promote a sense of national identity. This discipline gives students the opportunity to enter the exciting world of historical study and to apply what they learn to their own experience[5].

How does this translate on the ground for the approximately 300 undergraduates who register for history modules in the three-year Bachelor of Arts or Bachelor of Social Science degrees? The modules on offer include the following:

Change, revolution and the global world
Law and society
Conquest of the Indian and Atlantic Ocean world

Progress and paradox
Making of modern South Africa
Africa in crisis

Judging only from many university handbooks, though, it is very difficult to determine what exactly is being taught in history departments.

If South African universities slowly inched towards a new history for a non-racial South Africa, school history also had to make this leap. Their case is even more dramatic as, not surprisingly, for years the prescribed texts have been dictated by successive governments. Heavy emphasis was placed on just those things played down by Davenport and the new generation of historians: the impact of Europeans on the region in terms of 'discovery'; settlement and colonial politics; the Great Trek of the 1830s; the 'White' Anglo-Boer wars; the 1910 Union; dominion politics (Hertzog versus Smuts); the Second World War; the struggle against communism and so forth. In terms of secondary education, one can determine retrogression rather than an advance during the 20th century. A school text such as the 1897 *Natal: The land and its story* is, apart from being written in better English, also, within the confines of its day, better history than what was placed before many school learners during the apartheid years[6].

Then there are the international victims of the New University History. Medieval history in nearly all South African universities is not only dead and buried, but also forgotten. Economic history survives in pockets and social history has been fractured into a plethora of highly specialised themes. This balkanisation of history is reflected in the thematic approach: the family, gender, ethnicity, disease, health, holocaust/genocide studies.

These broad themes are complemented by broad sweeps of world history: from Saladin to Saddam Hussein; from Barbarossa to Bush. The niche role has been taken over by continental history, internationalism and a general shift into the 20th century and away from earlier periods (except the archaeological stuff). It is very unlikely that the majority South African history BA graduates have much inkling about what happened in the world prior to 1800, certainly prior to 1700. The post First World War human experience dominates.

But is this any different to a student sitting in a lecture theatre in Glasgow or Galway? The answer is probably, on the whole no. In that respect South African historians have achieved much over the last 20 years, though whether world trends in history teaching are a 'good thing' is another debate. In South Africa the historical handicaps remain: European settlement and its impact is a factor that may be unpopular in many history departments in South African universities today, but it is hardly something that can be denied.

The challenge is that one is faced with a generation that is rebelling, not without reason, against the legacy of 'the Whites made South Africa and this was a good thing' and embracing a new home truth – that 'White contact and settlement was both undesirable and detrimental (if not evil) to the region'. As a professor of history with an interest that is still regarded as somewhat quirkish in parts of the South African history world, it is fairly plain that what is needed in South Africa are considerably more young African historians trained in the tradition of von Ranke. They are the ones who must write the history of the European impact on southern Africa. As the Anglo-Irish historians have given way to an undoubtedly more nationalist generation of young Irish historians, so the Marxist and liberal white historians in South Africa will find themselves yesterday's chroniclers. The trouble is that in Ireland that process took 80 years to achieve.

Notes

1 T.R.H. Davenport, *South Africa: A modern history*, Johannesburg, 1977. Subsequent additions appeared in 1978, 1987, 1991 and 2000. The fifth edition was co-authored by the eminent South African historian Professor Christopher Saunders.

2 G. M. Theal, *History of South Africa*, 11 vols, 1888-1919 and G.E.Cory, *The rise of South Africa*, 5 vols, London 1910-1930.

3 Michael Roberts, an expert in Swedish history, following his sojourn at Rhodes was Professor of Modern History at Queen's University, Belfast in Northern Ireland. He subsequently retired to Grahamstown. For details on the Oxford-trained Winifred Maxwell, see J.A. Benyon - C.W. Cook, T.R.H. Davenport - K.S. Hunt, *Studies in local history:Essays in honour of Professor Winifred Maxwell*, Oxford 1976, pp. 7-14.

4 N.D. Southey to D.P. McCracken, 11 August 2005 and 10 January 2006.

5 *Faculty of Humanities, Development and Social Sciences: 2005*, University of KwaZulu-Natal Prospectus, 2005, p. 75.

6 R. Russell, *Natal: The land and its story: A geography and history for the use of schools*, Pietermaritzburg 1897.

Bibliography

Cobley A., *Does social history have a future? The end of apartheid and recent trends in South African historiography*, "Journal of Southern African Studies", 27, 3, 2001.

Cory G.E., *The rise of South Africa*, 5 volumes, London 1910-1930.

Davenport R.T.H., *South Africa: A modern history*, Johannesburg 1977 and 5th edition (Davenport and Christopher Saunders), Houndmills-London 2000.

Laurence P., *Nurturing ahistorical South Africans; declining numbers of history students*, "Financial Mail", 11 August 2000.

Nuttall T. - Wright J., *Probing the predicaments of academic history in contemporary South Africa*, "South African Historical Journal", 42, 2000.

Phillips H., *First Lessons in South African History: University teaching and writing of South African history, 1903- c.1930*, "South African historical journal", 34, 1996.

Polakow-Suransky S., *Reviving South African history: academic debate how to represent and teach the nation's past*, "Chronicle of Higher Education", 14 June 2002.

Sources

Extract from T.R.H. Davenport - C. Saunders, *South Africa: A modern history*, Houndmills-London 2000 (preface) pp. xxiii-xxiv.

The study of South African history, so dependent in the early part of this [20th] century on the work of George McCall Theal, has undergone two significant changes in the twentieth century and is now involved in a third. The first resulted from the work of what may be termed the 'Macmillan School' after W.M. Macmillan, who began to question the validity of earlier received versions above all presumption in favour of the 'colonial' as against the 'missionary' point of view in the inter-racial conflicts of the eighteenth and early nineteenth centuries. The second major change was a consequence of the revolution in the study of African history which accompanied the decolonization of tropical Africa in the 1950s and 1960s. This brought a new emphasis on the indigenous peoples of Africa, and the discovery that the history of the peoples of Africa could be written in greater depth by a reflective correlation, in the writings of historians, of the findings of anthropologists, ethnologists, archaeologists and linguists. Though African writers entered the field in growing numbers across the continent from the 1960s onwards, south of the Limpopo this process was solely hindered by restraints imposed on the training of blacks and other apartheid restrictions – an obstruction which happily no longer applies.

... The assumptions of the liberal Africanist school came under attack from Marxist historians who criticized the liberals for what they termed their inadequate conceptual framework, especially their reluctance to use class as a key category of analysis. But as time passed, liberal and Marxist historians set in motion a dialectic of scholarly discourse which exposed the limitation of both approaches and lifted the quality of debate to a new level.

... Conflicting versions of the historical story were pressed into the service of rival political power groups at a time of major confrontation in the country's history. On the one hand, the dogmatism of a white establishment assumed a perpetuation of racial differences to be part of a divinely inspired order, or at any rate a fixed point from which all policy calculations had to start. At the other extreme, a predominantly expatriate element saw as inevitable the revolutionary overthrow of the existing order, on the ground that the inherent logic of the situation ruled out the possibility of a peaceful transition to an acceptable social system.

Extract from Howard Phillips, *100 years old and still making history: The centenary of the Department of Historical Studies at the University of Cape Town*, "South African Historical Journal", 50, 2004, pp. 203-204.

From the mid 1980s, a combination of the growing influence of a new generation of staff in the department, more flexible academic framework at UCT, the impact of changing intellectual trends in Europe and the USA and the ongoing revolt against apartheid in the country-at-large, accelerated the changes of the previous decade ...

Courses thus proliferated in a host of new fields which spoke directly or indirectly to the past in the present: the history of work, cultural history, women's history, contemporary history, public history, film and history, medical history and environmental history, all of which offered yet wider visions of what constituted history. To these the incorporation of the Departments of Economic History in 1992 and of History of Art in 2000 added two further disciplinary dimensions to the department's range of teaching. To recognize the latter's inclusion, in 2000 the Department of History was renamed the Department of Historical Studies, an outward – and perhaps a postmodern – sign of one of the department's hallmarks in recent decades, adaptability and willingness – some felt an overwillingness – to innovate.

Crusades and Crusading in Hungarian Historiography

Attila Bárány
University of Debrecen

A tanulmány a keresztes hadjáratok magyarországi kutatástörténetét dolgozza fel, a 19. század eleji-közepi első, leginkább ismerettejesztő próbálkozásoktól egészen a modern, 20. század végi, 21. századi történetírás alapvető fontosságú, szakmailag megalapozott, forráskritikát alkalmazó műveiig. A cikk bemutatja azt a folyamatot, hogyan vált a keresztes háborúk kutatása a a hazai egyetemes történelem-kutatás szerves részévé, kiemelvén e folyamat nehézségeit és az egyetemes történeírás előtt tornyosuló problémákat. Áttekinti a periodizáció hazai specifikumait – a hazai történetírásban 1291, Akkon eleste jelenti a keresztes hadak történetének a végpontját – és összegzi, a modern kutatás hogyan, mi módon képes felülemelkedni a hagyományos történetírás sémáin, megcsökevényesedett konzervatív megítélésein, különleges figyelmet szentelve II. András király 1217 – es keresztes hadjáratának, amely sajnos sokáig a hazai medievisztika mostohagyermekének számított, és a hagyományos megítélése meglehetősen negatív. Végigkövetjük a magyarországi történetírás ideológiai meghatározottságának a hatásait: a keresztes háborúk kutatása igen nehézzé vált 1945 után, amikor a marxista tudományosságban az egyháztörténet nemcsak háttérbe szorult, hanem tiltólistára került, amely évtizedekig visszavetette a cruciata hazai kutatását. A tanulmány azokat a részterületeket szeretné kiemelni, amelyekben a hazai kutatás méltóképpen követni tudja a 19. század végének, 20. század elejének elődeit, és magas színvonalával a mai nemzetközi tudományosság fontos részét alkotja: például az egyházi lovagrendek tevékenysége Magyarországon; különös tekintettel például a Német Lovagrend erdélyi, barcasági szereplésére. E részterületeken a mai kutatás európai összehasonlításban is megállja a helyét, sőt, Magyarország nemzetközi konferenciák szervezésével, tanulmánykötetek kiadásával az egyházi és katonai lovagrendek (legfőképpen a johannita és a templomos rend) kutatásának egyik nemzetközi centrumává is vált az utóbbi években. Áttekinti a tanulmány a keresztes hadak története forrásainak hazai kiadásait, az első próbálkozásoktól Clairvaux-i Szt. Bernát művei (pl. De laudae novae militiae) kritikai kiadásáig.

Status of World History Research in Hungary: A Short Overview

Before turning to the issue of a sub-field of 'Europe and the World', the research on the crusades in Hungarian historiography, it is inevitable to summarize in a few words the present status of world history research in Hungary.

In the literal sense of the word, world history, as such – in the form, style and methodology that this scholarly sub-field of history is known and taught in for example the United States or in certain countries of Western Europe – does not exist in Hungary, or, rather, it embraces a very small percentage of the curriculum or of the research topics addressed by the academic personnel. This is for a number of reasons, though the most evident is that it has been a traditionally underrepresented subject both in university education and in scholarly research and this mainly derives from the traditional system of academics and university education in Hungary. Higher education, and in parallel, research in the fields of arts and humanities, and within that, in the subjects of literature and history, has been almost exclusively focused around national literature and history, and only a small proportion devoted to the study of the universal aspects of these subjects. Universal, as such, in the structure of the academy meant for the most part European, and had nothing to do with the parts of the world outside Europe. This is true even to a certain extent today. Furthermore, within the subject of European history, the term Europe was used for a long time to refer to certain central parts of the continent, and did not in any way include territories like Ireland and Portugal, which were seen as peripheral from the mainstream point of view.

Historical research and education was largely limited to those countries of Europe either that were categorized as central, such as Germany or the Holy Roman Empire, or whose historical development were closely related to Hungarian national history, e.g. Poland or Austria, maintaining that parallel historical-social-economic institutions were developed throughout our joint histories. Due to the long symbiosis between Hungary and the Austrian monarchy, the history of the Habsburg empire is not entirely seen as a field of universal history, but as one strongly connected to Hungarian national history in the Modern period, the knowledge of which is highly recommended or required for scholars of history even today. Therefore, in Hungary, the Austro-Hungarian monarchy has been researched and taught in a far greater proportion than any other field of European history.

We feel Austrian history as a part of our common historical heritage, and not that of a foreign country. The division of the research topics and the major emphases of education also follow that heritage: the dimension of the fields is still determined by the weight a topic is assigned in our traditional system, and courses and classes tend to cover issues like the conflict of the Papacy and the German Emperors or, the establishment of Modern Germany. The structure of higher education in Hungary is of the German-Austrian type, and this is largely reflected in the teaching of history. Consequently, areas traditionally judged as peripheral are still given less and less stress, or, even though history writing is changing, are treated as non-central, and thus not sufficiently represented in school curricula. Issues like the Scandinavian welfare state or the rapid industrial development of Ireland are of course known to be important ones in history research, but are not taken into consideration when compiling course plans, since teaching is still defined by the issues considered central for Hungary. Not to speak of the world outside Europe. There are underrepresented areas of European history, but I would say that whole areas of world history are not only neglected but also taken no notice of. World history is only taught in most Hungarian universities insofar as in certain respects it is unavoidably attached to the understanding of European history: e.g. colonial history. South-Africa or Modern India are mentioned as a part of the British colonial Empire, and nothing more. American Studies had long been a step-child of our history writing, and had long been a secondary field attached to British history, and it is only in recent times that it has gained a more established position in the curriculum.

Nevertheless, there are certain areas of world history that are given an exceptional prominence in education and research because they are adjacent to, or are on the edges of certain traditional fields of study, e.g. certain areas of Oriental studies or the history of Inner Asian peoples and cultures are on the boundaries of Hungarian pre- or ancestral history, and thus, Hungarian scholarship has been largely occupied in examining issues of traditionally non-European history like the history of Nomadic peoples and state formation, the steppe region cultures, the migration of Asian peoples, inner Asian nations and languages. These fields were not studied in their own right and significance, but just because of the fact that they were considered auxiliary or supplementary to the early history of the Hungarians, who, during their migration from the Ural mountains in the Pontic steppe to the Carpathian basin, were to supposed to have come across these nomadic warrior nations of mainly Turkic origin. The histories of the Huns, the Scythians and the Khazars were also investigated in detail in Hungarian academic scholarship, within the subject of *archaeology*, and these areas are also part of the university curriculum. The history of these nomadic populations, the Asian civilization of the 'Turkians', Huns or Khazars are thus taught widely in certain universities, and at our department at the University of Debrecen there have been times when *archaeological* research on the ancestral Hungarian tribal society and culture was of basic importance in the framework of Hungarian prehistory. There were a range of Hungarian scholars in Philology and Classics who largely contributed to the research in Oriental studies in Hungary.

Inner Asia is another area where World and European history adjoin one another: Russian studies including Russian history cannot be separated from the Inner Asian territories and nations, since throughout the Middle Ages Russia was for most of the centuries under threat of Asian invasion, namely through the Mongolian attacks that had their effect on Russian medieval and early modern history; while later, as the Russian empire extended its conquests further to the east, to Siberia and the Inner Asian territories, the history of these newly occupied provinces again became part of Russian history. This is also a point of contact between two fields: those interested in Russian history have knowledge of Russia's Inner Asian relationships and some of them have also dealt with Modern Chinese history through the study of Russian-Chinese relations and Russian foreign policy in the 19th and 20th centuries.

There are certain fields of European history, certain research themes or programs that are followed in European history as well; in such a way as to evolve in some cases into a comparative study. There were certain themes or paths of research that were set and methodology followed by the forefathers of our department in the mid-20th century, and since they were applied by generations of scholars they were adapted to European themes as well. For example, agrarian history began to be cultivated and then a research school for agricultural history and development of the peasantry was established by István Szabó and its research methodology was applied to European agrarian history. A comparative socio-economic historical analysis of those countries that had a parallel historical development was also launched and is still under way at the University of Debrecen, mainly on Eastern- or East-Central Europe or the Balkans. Comparative analyses on themes of economic history were carried out considering Hungary and Prussia from the 17th to the 19th centuries; or between the industrial development of 19th- to 20th-century Hungary and the Balkans and Eastern Europe. Another long-term research project initiated by György Ránki regards the stages of economic backwardness and industrial-financial underdevelopment. A major strength of present-day research is the comparative, socio-historical investigation of 19th- to 20th-century Hungarian and Eastern European Jewry. Constitutional history also determines the framework of medieval history: the parliamentary movement, the assemblies of the estates and constitutional privileges and grants throughout Europe are the major themes of university education.

Nevertheless, it has to be mentioned that the structure of Hungarian historical scholarship is not the result of a well-formulated, well-considered academic strategy: even though there were attempts to have a wider spectrum of world history topics and include African and Asian histories, the major emphasis in research and education still is within the boundaries of European history. In recent times, however, some fields of world history – such as American history and the history of the Middle East – are practiced to a much greater extent, although the latter is still attached to a traditionally European central research program, that of the Crusades.

The Crusades in Hungarian Historical Scholarship

The subject of crusades and crusading has never been treated as one of real world history but rather as one closely attached to and seen as part of European history. Frankly speaking, the Holy Land, Palestine and the Kingdom of Jerusalem have not at all been viewed as part of Asia, or belonging at all to another continent, but from a completely Europe-centred point of view, as territories having the same cultural heritage and political-social system as mainland Europe. In Hungary, crusading is traditionally not considered a non-European topic; this however is not an exception but the general case in most European countries.

The crusades as such have traditionally meant in Hungarian historical scholarship the period before the fall of Acre, and practically no one would treat any campaign or venture after 1291 as a 'genuine' crusade. It is traditionally held that the real era of the crusades ended in 1291. The period of the later crusades in the 14th and 15th centuries is not at all seen as part of the subject. In Hungarian historical literature there has long been the prevailing opinion that the conception of crusades disappeared from the horizon of European politics for good after the Christians lost Acre in 1291. This notion, however, has been confuted by the latest research results (and certain earlier works on this subject), pointing out that the failure of a vast crusade (*passagium generale*) after the fall of Acre did not mean waiving the claims for a war of revenge and the re-conquest of the Holy Land in Europe. Nevertheless, in Hungarian historical scholarship it is still more or less agreed that the campaigns denominated in international research and academia as "the later crusades" are not to be taken together with the pre-1291 'genuine' crusades.

The first piece of history writing on the crusades in Hungary was published in 1816 by Antal Pucz: a very brief summary of the major events and dates[1]. The second one was similarly not a scholarly enterprise, but rather a piece by a non-professional, enthusiastically committed to the subject[2].

It was at the beginning of the 20th century that the first primary sources were translated and published in Hungarian. A historian, Henriette Guizot (Mrs Witt) translated several of the most relevant narrative sources and devoted a whole volume to chronicle excerpts[3]. One had to wait more than half a century for this collection of sources to have a successor: it was only in the 1960s that László Mezey collected narrative source excerpts, but his volume on general medieval history had only one chapter devoted to the sources regarding the crusades[4].

Due to an unwise political-academic decision of the communist régime, the edition of sources soon diminished radically in Hungary. The direct consequences of this fact can be observed not only in the fall in scholarly production but also in the elimination of an entire generation of scholars of medieval church history. Up until the 1990s there was only one narrative source of the age of the crusades that was translated and edited in its entirety, Geoffroi de Villehardouin's *La conquête de Constantinople*[5]. At present we can appreciated the fact that the most significant sources of the crusades are starting to be published and translated into Hungarian: for example the *Gesta Dei per Francos* was published – a critical edition was provided together with a number of letters and charters from the age of the First and the Second Crusade – by László Veszprémy[6]

It is striking that no modern survey was completed in Hungarian historiography up until the very end of the 20th century. The first systematic treatment of the subject was not published until the middle of the 1920s when a leading historian of the age, though not an expert of the crusades, published a volume entirely devoted to the history of crusading[7]. There were general world histories written by Hungarian scholars, although it is conspicuous that even the one that has been taken as the outstanding piece of quality history writing, that is, the 700-page volume by Péter Váczy, a leading scholar of the period between the two World Wars[8] did not dedicate more than three (!) pages to the crusades, was confined to mere dates and events and did not attempt any kind of evaluation, not to speak of a conclusion. The same is true for another popularizing world history encyclopaedia of the early 20th century[9]. Another enterprise undertaken, a general synthesis of world history at the very beginning of the 20th century, but the field of the crusades was either rather neglected and pushed into the background, as the author was largely concerned with a descriptive relation of events[10].

Nevertheless, Áldásy's work is still of a unique character since it has not – not until the present day – been followed by any other work of scholarly quality on crusading written by a Hungarian historian. Unfortunately we must state that in the year 2006 Áldásy's work from 1924 is almost the only work of a native Hungarian historian to have produced a scholarly monograph partly based on primary historical sources and an up-to-date coverage of the secondary literature of the age. No one since that time in Hungarian academia has taken up the initiative to write a systematic work on the crusades: instead foreign studies were translated and published alongside a number of non-scholarly, nearly fictionalized publications of poor quality and popularizing character, mainly for the wider public; or even aimed at young readers[11]. Although these works were not born with the purpose of meeting any academic criteria, and were not written with the intention of their being used for university education, the fact that they were produced by well-known historians as well as the fact that there was a shortage of academic works of scholarly quality on the subject made it possible for these popularizing editions to be utilised in university curricula. They were also used as recommended reading material at in the University training of B.A. history majors at several departments of history. Up until the end of the 1980s these works were widely used as university course reading materials, notwithstanding the fact that they had neither any kind of scholarly documentation; nor a select bibliography; nor had they anything to do with academic style and format. They were of a very similar character, largely comprising a descriptive narration of events and military actions, concentrating on heroic deeds of legendary knights, giving these 'idols' an almost fictitious character. Unfortunately, Áldásy's work was stigmatized under the Communist regime by the leading figures of Marxist scholarship as being the product of bourgeois ideology, and thus it was not permitted to consult it in classrooms. University lecturers were forced to use the works of popularizing character, which were close to being documentary novels. These works are not to be treated as pieces of real historiography since they tried only to a very limited extent to examine the deeper layers of research on the crusades, very rarely studied the motivations of the crusaders and almost never raised the issue of the economic-political-spiritual causes of the crusading ventures. Their authors were satisfied with a brief, merely linear chronological description of sieges and battles. As far as secondary literature is concerned, they were mainly grounded on older 19th century and pre-1945 authorities, and very rarely tried to have their argumentation backed by the studies of more modern Western scholarship.

Under the Communist regime Marxism prevailed over historiography, and medieval ecclesiastical history, such as the crusades, was an unwanted step-child in the eyes of Marxist ideologies. The former Western, bourgeois concepts were to be expelled. Furthermore, local research and scholarship and in general national academic life had to observe the standards and cultivate the themes determined by Soviet academia. In the field of medieval studies there were a number of works by Russian historians that were to be translated into most of the languages of the Socialist countries and no other works could be used. In the case of the crusades, for decades there were only two books that could be consulted, one by a Soviet and one by a East-German historian[12]. The tone of these volumes was set by the major argumentation of Marxist historiography: in the field of the crusades the role of the Christian religion, the church, devotional factors were absolutely denied. As far as the reasons of the crusades are concerned, Marxist ideology emphasized the role of economic and social factors and refused the idea that personal devotion or individual religious considerations could be behind them. The campaigns had to be oversimplified as adventures of selfish, cruel conquerors, who had nothing to do with the Papacy; the only thing they wanted was to grab more and more land. This ideology of the Western 'colonists' and medieval colonization determined the overall view of the crusades for long decades. The role of the Holy See was seen as a part of an oppressive policy, with the popes making use of the crusades to increase their political power and material wealth. The reasons for taking up the cross were oversimplified, and declared to be materially determined: the major motive that led crowds to take up arms according to Marxist ideology was the failure of the succession system (*primogenitura*), overpopulation and other economic difficulties. Pious considerations, personal deep religiousness and individual mysticism were not at all mentioned. The ideology was most exclusive as for instance the works outside the Marxist sphere of academia could not be read and it was out of the question to have Runciman's outstanding work translated. It is emblematic that it was necessary to wait almost 50 years – until 1999 – to be able to read one of the best known historian of the crusades in Hungarian language. From the end of the 1940s until the early 1990s in the ideological cage of Marxist-ruled academia it was not possible to do any kind of genuine research on the crusades, since scholars had no access the major works of European scholarship.

As regards the spiritual background of crusading thought, it was not until the mid-1980s that the Hungarian public had an opportunity to get acquainted with the real role of the church and the papacy in the crusades. It was in 1984 that the first article was published on the Christian concept of war, the notion of just war[13]. After that time some of the most relevant theological tractates that formed the background of the crusading spirit could come out: the decisive work of St. Bernard of Clairvaux, *De laudae novae militiae* was translated into Hungarian by László Veszprémy in 1999.

As far as the military fields of the crusader studies are concerned, there was only one work that paid attention to the crusaders' campaigns and battles: Gyula Rázsó[14] devoted a chapter to the battle of Hattin.

The field of the relationship of Hungary and the crusades and the role and activity of the country in the crusading effort was for a long time almost entirely neglected. One had to wait until the late 1980s for a study on this subject be published, interestingly not from the pen of a Hungarian, but from that of an American historian[15]. In recent years considerable investigations have been carried out by András Borosy[16].

One had to wait until the mid-1990s for a new monograph on the crusades to appear in the realm of Hungarian scholarship[17]. Nevertheless, it was not one of the mainstream academic historians either from university departments or academic research institutes that undertook the decades-old task of writing a modern monograph in Hungarian, but a Franciscan friar: Bozsóky was only noted for his ecclesiastical and theological writings, and not at all for work of historical scholarship. This work of his, understandably, bears the signs of the author's deep commitment towards his subject. It is rather a devotional writing, full of tones of an emotional character, rather than being an objective historical study. In some places it is quite subjective. Nevertheless, this is the only piece of scholarship in Hungary in at least 60 or 70 years' time that has attempted at all to make use of modern international scholarship and to build on the results of the recent research of French, German and Anglo-Saxon historiography into the work. Bozsóky is the only historian in several generations to use and apply primary sources, and to try to draw conclusions based on archival, documentary and narrative source material. He is the only one to have systematically investigated the major narrative source editions in Hungarian scholarship (*Recueil des historiens des croisades*). He has a wide knowledge not only of the older, 19th century and early 20th century French, English and German literature of the crusades (A.S. Atiya, S. Runciman, Y. Le Febvre, P. Riant, P. Rousset, H. Prutz, Th. Wolff), but is familiar with the latest results of European scholarship, of the 1980s and 1990s (A. Maalouf, J. Richard, C. Cahen, F. Cardini). What is the most important, however, that Bozsóky is the first historian who does not neglect the spiritual-theological factor in analysing the reasons of the crusades, but renders the Church its rightful role. He is the first one in modern scholarship to have refused the Marxist approaches and ideological conceptions: he devoted a whole work to clarify the ideologically biased notions of earlier Marxist literature and he drew attention to the "civic", Western, "spiritually based" conceptions long denied by our national historiography as well[18].

In addition, Bozsóky published a work of specific interest within the field of the crusades: in 2004 he wrote a monograph on the Latin Kingdom of Jerusalem[19], which is another unique piece of Hungarian scholarship, giving new insights into a particular sub-field, also based on the most recent historiographic material (J. Prawer, J. Richard, P. Deschamps).

However, fortunately a new generation of medievalists in Hungary have started to do systematic research in the field since the late 1980s. László Veszprémy, who produced a great number of studies in medieval Hungarian military history, also touched the spiritual background of the birth of the crusading idea[20]. György Szabados published a study on a 'delayed' crusade, undertaken by King Béla III and King Imre of Hungary[21]. It is worth mentioning that there are now two scholars who chose to deal with the later crusades and the schemes – namely that of Pierre Dubois – for a *passagium generale* to recapture the Holy Land in the 14th century[22].

King Andrew II's Crusade of 1217

Hungary was one of the countries in the Middle Ages that organized a crusade to the Holy Land in 1217 and her monarch, Andrew II of the Árpád dynasty, led his own enterprise to Palestine. The dynasty and the kingdom was an active participant imbued with the crusading spirit and the Hungarian nobility of the age, full of spiritual fervour, responded to the call of Jerusalem. Unfortunately, no matter how actively the kingdom was involved in the crusading effort and how relevant the 1217 venture was within the history of the crusades, there has been no modern monograph of academic quality written on the subject by a Hungarian historian. It is very difficult to understand why, but apart from a brief study by a non-professional, Emília Vasshegyi in the early 20th century[23] there has been no real monograph of scholarly standards published in Hungary. Andrew II's campaign is totally neglected in our historiography. In the 21st century one is still bound to turn back to 19th century scholarship if he or she is interested in King Andrew's crusade. At the end of the 19th century two scholars took the initiative of doing research on Andrew's campaign, Ede Wilczek and László Kozics[24], although neither of them provided an extensive study, but summarized the major events of the crusade in articles for periodicals. No real monograph has since been published – King Andrew's crusade is still forgotten. After 1916 Hungarian history writing has not produced anything on the subject meeting the requirements of modern scholarship (except for a very brief non-scholarly approach by a retired army general, János Gabányi[25]). King Andrew's crusade has not only been neglected but also underestimated in historiography: even general works have not dedicated more than a few lines to the crusade, emphasizing its insignificance, and have taken every chance to stress its negative aspects, the shortcomings of the enterprise, and condemning the king for the failure of the campaign. The king's schemes are vehemently criticised in the general synthesis of Hungarian military history[26]. There were attempts in general works, in synthetic summaries, to approach the 1217 crusade by using the most important narrative sources, for instance József Breit-Bánlaky did in fact consult a few of the chronicles of the early 13th century Holy Land, but was far from applying the complete narrative material[27]. No scholar has so far utilised the source material on the 1217 crusade; apart from slight attempts no one has consulted the narratives of the *Gesta dei per Francos*, the *Historia Damiatina* by Oliver Scholasticus, the *Liber duellii christiani in obidione Damiatae*, the *Gesta obsidionis Damiatae*, the *Historia Iherosolominata* by Jacques de Vitry. It would be essential for Hungarian historiography that someone undertake to examine sources like John of Tulbia/Tolve, *De Domino Johanno rege Jerusalem*; or, the *L'Estoire de Eracles empereur*; or, the *Chronique d'Ernoul et de Bernard le trésorier*; or the chronicle of Aubrey of Trois-Fontaines or the *Chronica regia Coloniensis*. Until that happens, Hungarian scholarship will have to be content with foreign authorities: it is an unfortunate situation but if a Hungarian were to read about the 1217 crusade led by a Hungarian king, he could only refer to a German language study, written by an Austrian historian[28] since there is no work of that kind of Hungarian scholarship. Even the sources on King Andrew's campaign were collected by this Austrian authority and not by a Hungarian[29]. It is a pity that if one is interested in the 1217 crusade, one must consult either a 19th century German[30], or 20th century Anglo-Saxon scholars[31]. The only works on the Hungarian king's crusade that can be read in Hungarian, based on Hungarian scholarship, is an article by László Veszprémy[32], which is hopefully the beginning of a future project, and will be followed by extensive studies on the 1217 crusade.

Military and religious knightly orders

A certain sub-field of crusading, the military-religious orders and their activities, has already produced a great number of studies in Hungary historiography. Furthermore, this is the direction where current historical research in crusading is also very rapidly and fruitfully developing. The military orders are almost the sole area within crusading where Hungarian historiography has worked well and published works of real scholarly quality based on thorough historical research. Scholarly investigations in this sub-field started very early: the leading historians of the 18th century, the Jesuits, were also concerned in doing research on the military orders. They collected sources and published their findings in Latin-language volumes: Gabriel Kolinovich investigated the history of the Templars in Hungary[33] and Georgius Pray dealt with the major landed estates of the Templar, then of the Hospitaller Order[34]. In the early 19th century a general history of the Hospitaller knights was written, this time in Hungarian, by Mihály Kovacsóczy[35]. At the middle of the 19th century a noted church historian of monasticism, Antal Arzén Karcsú published a work of general, synthetic character[36]. This was followed in the second half of the 19th century by systematic approaches aiming to collect all possible data. Historians started to examining the history of particular knightly orders, either in general, or examining their activity in Hungary in particular. Nándor Knauz explored the Hospitallers in the capital of medieval Hungary, Esztergom[37]. Pál Oltványi gave an overview of the Order of the Holy Sepulchre[38]. The work that is still taken as authentic and of great authority was written by Frigyes Pesty on the Templars in Hungary[39].

The beginning of the 20th century saw the publication of two most relevant volumes on the Templars and the Hospitallers, both of which are still considered 'the' authoritative works: one by Ferenc Patek and the other by Ede Reiszig. In the period between the two World Wars there was a slight rise in ecclesiastical research in Hungary, which was reflected in the field of the military orders as well. The 1930s and early 1940s saw the publication of a synthetic work of scholarly quality, which was very highly considered in academic circles ever since: it was from the pen of a foreign historian who also worked in Hungary, Heribert Thierry. Thierry also compiled a bibliography of the Hospitallers[41].

This research were not followed by further systematic efforts since the subject of ecclesiastical history was not favoured in the Communist period; nonetheless certain studies were published, such as that of László Hársing and Károly Kozák, *A johanniták a középkori Magyarországon*[42]. However, the major works on the military orders were published by emigrant Hungarian historians living mainly in Western Europe such as Károly-György[43] As ecclesiastical research was not supported in Communist Hungary, it is emblematic that for example the sole study on the history of the Order of St. Lazarus could only be published in Germany by Tibor Buzády[44]. The historiography of the Templars and the Hospitallers has also been burdened with a serious conceptual problem for a long time. In contrast to the Western European context, Hungarian sources often use the term *crucifer* instead of the appropriate *miles Templi* or *frater hospitalis* possibly with reference to the cross depicted on their habits. This led to confusion, as many scholars treated the houses and the landed properties of other orders of similar status as belonging to the Temple or the Hospital, and vice versa. On the basis of this perception and through a close reading of primary sources as well as through the clarification of the notions and denominations applied in them, Karl-Georg Boroviczény discovered or, in fact, singled out in the late 1960s, a formerly unknown religious institution, the Order of Hospitaller Canons Regular of St. Stephen (often referred as Stephanites), founded by the Hungarian King Géza II (1141-1162)[45]. The members of this order were also called *cruciferi* in contemporary sources – they even used this expression in the inscriptions of their own charters – but they had nothing in common with either the crusaders or with the Hospital of St. John[46].

Recent years have seen almost an outburst of initiatives to explore the history of the knightly orders in medieval Hungary. After the fall of the Communist regime an outstanding summary of the monastic and knightly orders in Hungary was published by József Török[47]. It was the first to provide a modern, detailed and systematic study concerning the subject. Both of the rules of the orders of St. John and that of the Temple was published in Hungarian[48].

A few years ago an extensive study, the result of a more than decade-long research – including the Archives of the Maltese Order in La Valletta, Malta – Zsolt Hunyadi published a considerable work on the Hospitaller Order in medieval Hungary[49]. The study systematically covers the history of the Hospitallers in the medieval Kingdom of Hungary, enumerating their houses, dignitaries and personnel from the period of their appearance (c. 1150) up to the end of the 14th century, mostly on the basis of written sources. It is also to be noted that the Hungarian medievalist that first did research in the Maltese archives of the Order of the Knights of St. John and published charters of Hungarian reference was Pál Engel[50]. Hunyadi contributed to the research of medieval Hungarian military orders with numerous publications[51].

In recent years there have been extensive investigations about the Templars as well: a paper provided a detailed database of the landed properties of the order[52]. It has not only been local historians but also foreigners that have shown interest in studying the history of Hungarian knightly orders[53]. They too have carried out research and devoted excellent studies to the field.

In addition there has also been published a number of specific research projects concerning particular sub-sections within the religious orders: Adél Edelényi investigated the Templars and the attitudes towards them in European and Hungarian society from a cultural-anthropological and ethnographical point of view, examining the folklore reminiscences of the knights in European and Hungarian tradition[54].

A number of regional studies have come out recently, examining the role of the knightly orders in different areas, counties, cities etc.[55].

A certain sub-field of studies on military orders, and a field of an interdisciplinary character, on the boundaries of archaeology, art history and history, that of the castle-building activity of the orders in medieval Hungary, has also been thoroughly and systematically approached in Hungarian academic world[56].

In recent years studies have appeared on different specific sub-fields such as the heraldry and iconography of the knightly orders. Tamás Gömbös examined the heraldic representation of the military (and monastic) orders as well as giving an outline of their distinctive insignia, devizes, badges, attires etc. of theirs[57]. In recent years there have been initiatives to investigate the smaller religious knightly orders as well[58]. There have also been a good number of studies of general interest or popularizing character published mainly for the general public, for example by József Török and László Legeza[59].

The Teutonic Order in Hungary

There is a sub-field of the knightly orders with which Hungarian historiography has been particularly concerned, the Teutonic Order and its activity in Hungary. The reason for this increased scholarly interest is the fact that the Teutonic Knights, after they moved from the Holy Land to the European continent, were invited to Hungary and were granted substantial landed properties in the southern part of Transylvania, in the Barcaság region (*Burzenland, Bursia*). The knights received considerable privileges from King Andrew II in 1211 and were donated a distinct district, a *comitatus,* independent from the Hungarian administration, in order to protect the country from the invasions of the Cumans as well as to convert them to Christianity. Aside from the fact that the failure of the very rigidly interpreted conversion activity of the Order made the king expel it from Hungary, a number of the German villains of the knights stayed in the region and contributed to the settlement and development of Transylvania, making up the core of the German population of that country. That is why the topic of the German knights and their policy has always been approached with great attention in Hungarian – and in German and Austrian – historiography. In Hungarian scholarship, this is one of the fields of crusading where numerous thorough, detailed analyses, based on archival source backgrounds have come out since the 19th century[60]. Nevertheless, research in this respect is still going on fruitfully and there are new results presented by contemporary medievalists as well, who have now made use of the documentary sources of the Teutonic order in foreign archives[61].

NOTES

1 A. Pucz, *A' keresztes hadaknak rövid leirása* [A brief description of the crusade wars], Pest 1816.

2 A. Gyurits, *A keresztes hadak története* [The history of the crusade wars], vols I-II, Buda 1853.

3 H. Guizot, *A keresztes hadak története: középkori krónikákból* [The history of the crusading wars. Excerpts from medieval chronicles], Budapest 1905.

4 L. Mezey, *Krónikások, krónikák* [Chroniclers, chronicles], Budapest 1960.

5 G. de Villehardouin, *La conquête de Constantinople (Bizánc megvétele)*, Budapest 1985.

6 L. Veszprémy, *Az első és második keresztes háború korának forrásai* [The sources of the age of the First and Second Crusade], Budapest 1999.

7 A. Áldásy, *A keresztes hadjáratok története* [History of the crusades], Budapest 1924.

8 P. Váczy, *A középkor története* [The history of the Middle Ages], in B. Hóman - G. Szekfű - K. Kerényi (eds.), *Egyetemes történet: négy kötetben* [Universal history], vol. II, Budapest 1936.

9 K. Balla - L. Mangold - C. Horváth (eds.), *Tolnai világtörténelme* [Tolnai edition world history], vol. III/2: *A középkor története* [The history of the Middle Ages], Budapest 1991.

10 S. Mika, *A középkor* [The Middle Ages], in H. Marczali (ed.), *Nagy képes világtörténet* [Great illustrated world history], vol. II, Budapest 1899-1905.

11 I. Zombori, *Lovagok és lovagrendek* [Knights and knightly orders], Budapest 1988; J. Erdődy, *Keresztes lobogók alatt* [Under crusading banners], Budapest 1986; S. Szunyogh, *Jeruzsálem lovagjai* [Knights of Jerusalem], Budapest 1986.

12 M.A. Zaborov, *A keresztes háborúk* [Crusades] Budapest 1958; W. Zöllner, *A keresztes háborúk története* [The history of the crusades], Budapest 1980.

13 T. Somlyói Tóth, *Mennyei béke – földi háború. A háború keresztény megítélése a középkorban* [Heavenly peace – earthly war. The Christian conception of warfare in the Middle Ages], "Világosság", 25, 1984, pp. 98-105.

14 G. Rázsó, *A lovagkor csatái* [Battles of the knightly age], Budapest 1987.

15 J.R. Sweeney, *Magyarország és a keresztes hadjáratok a 12-13. században* [The Crusades and Hungary in the 12th and 13th centuries], "Századok", 118, 1984, pp. 114-124 (English translation: *Hungary in the Crusades, 1169-1218*, "International History Review", 3, 1981, pp. 467-481).

16 A. Borosy, *A keresztes háborúk és Magyarország I-II* [The Crusades and Hungary] "Hadtörténelmi Közlemények", 109, 1996, no. 1, pp. 3-41; no. 2, pp. 11-52.

17 P.G. Bozsóky, *Keresztes hadjáratok* [Crusades], Szeged 1995.

18 P.G. Bozsóky, *Igaz-e, hogy a keresztes hadjáratok gyarmatosítók voltak?* [Is it true that the crusaders were colonists?], Szeged 1995.

19 P.G. Bozsóky, *A jeruzsálemi latin királyság* [The Latin Kingdom of Jerusalem], Szeged 2004.

20 L. Veszprémy, *A keresztes eszme születése*, "Vigilia", 65, 2000, no. 11, pp. 832-836.

21 G. Szabados, *Egy elmaradt keresztes hadjáratról. Magyar-szentszéki kapcsolatok 1198-1204 között* [On a delayed crusade. Hungarian-Papal relations between 1198-1204], in *"Magyaroknak eleiről". Ünnepi tanulmányok a hatvan esztendős Makk Ferenc tiszteletére*, Szeged 2000, pp. 473-492.

22 M. Molnár, *Pierre Dubois terve a Szentföld visszaszerzésére* [Dubois's scheme to reoccupy the Holy Land], "Hadtörténelmi Közlemények", 116, 2003, no. 2, pp. 367-426; M. Sághy, *Keresztes háború és nemzeti propaganda. Pierre Dubois: "A Szentföld visszafoglalásáról"* [Crusade and national propaganda. Pierre Dubois "On the Reoccupation of the Holy Land"], in G. Klaniczay - B. Nagy (eds.), *A középkor szeretete. Történeti tanulmányok Sz. Jónás Ilona tiszteletére*, Budapest 1999, pp. 121-132.

23 E. Vasshegyi, *II. Endre keresztes hadjárata* [The crusade of King Andrew II], Budapest 1916.

[24] E. Wilczek, *II. Endre keresztes hadjárata* [The crusade of King Andrew II], "Századok", 28, 1894, nos. 7-8, pp. 592-608, pp. 697-713; L. Kozics, *II. Endre keresztes hadjárata* [The crusade of King Andrew II], "Katholikus Szemle", 1893, pp. 391-417.

[25] J. Gabányi, *II. Endre keresztes hadjárata* [The crusade of King Andrew II], in I. Zadrawecz (ed.), *Magyar Szentföld* [Hungarian Holy Land], Budapest 1931, pp. 177-192.

[26] J. Borus (ed.), *Magyarország hadtörténete* [The military history of Hungary], vols. I-II, Budapest 1984.

[27] J. Breit-Bánlaky, *A magyar nemzet hadtörténelme* [The military history of the Hungarian nation], vols. I-VIII, Budapest 1929-1934.

[28] R. Röhricht, *Studien zur Geschichte des fünften Kreuzzuges*, Innsbruck 1891.

[29] R. Röhricht, *Quinti belli sacri scriptores minores*, Genéve 1879; Id., *Testimonia minora de quinto bello sacro*, Genéve 1882.

[30] H. Hoogeweg, *Der Kreuzzug von Damiette, 1218-21*, "Mitteilungen des Instituts für Österreichische Geschichtsforschung", 1887-1888.

[31] J.M. Powell, *Anatomy of a Crusade, 1213-21*, Philadelphia 1986.

[32] L. Veszprémy, *II. András magyar király kereszteseinek létszáma* [The number of the crusaders of King Andrew II of Hungary], "Hadtörténelmi Közlemények", 107, 1994, no. 1, pp. 113-116.

[33] G. Kolinovich, *Chronicon militaris ordinis equitum templariorum*, Pestini 1751.

[34] G. Pray, *Dissertatio historico-critica de Prioratu Auranae*, Vienna 1773.

[35] M. Kovacsóczy, *Jerusálemi Sz. János Lovagrendje' története* [The history of the Order of St. John of Jerusalem], Kassa 1837.

[36] A.A. Karcsú, *Az egyházi és szerzetesi lovagrendek történelme* [A history of the military religious Orders], Pest 1867.

[37] N. Knauz, *A János lovagok Esztergomban* [The Knights of St. John in Esztergom], "Magyar Sion", 3, 1865.

[38] P. Oltványi, *A jeruzsálemi szent sír és lovagrendjének rövid története* [A brief history of the Order of the Holy Sepulchre in Jerusalem], Szeged 1882.

[39] F. Pesty, *A templáriusok Magyarországon*, "Akadémiai Értesítő", 2, 1861, pp. 30-152.

[40] F. Patek, *A magyarországi templárius rend felbomlása* [The dissolution of the Templars in Hungary], Budapest 1912; E. Reiszig, *A jeruzsálemi Szent János lovagrend Magyarországon* [The Order of the Knights of St. John of Jerusalem in Hungary], vols. I-II, Budapest 1925-1928.

[41] H. Thierry, *Jeruzsálemi Szent János [Máltai] Lovagrend. Múlt és Jelen* [The Knights of St. John of Jerusalem. Past and present], Budapest 1936; Id., *A Jeruzsálemi Szent János [Máltai] Lovagrend Magyar Bibliográfiája* [A bibliography of the Knights of St. John of Jerusalem in Hungary], Budapest 1941.

[42] L. Hársing - K. Kozák, *A johanniták a középkori Magyarországon* [The Knights of St. John in medieval Hungary], "Világosság", 20, 1979, pp. 692-699.

[43] K.G. Boroviczény, *Kommentierte Bibliographie der Kreuzherren- und Hospitalorden, sowie deren Krankenhaus- und Bädergründungen in Ungarn in der Zeit der Arpaden (X. bis XIII. Jahrhundert)*, Freiburg 1970; Id., *Die Hospitaller und Ungarn*, "Johanniter", 3, 1972; A. Radvánszky, *Ein Ritterwall Gegen die Türken. Geschichte des Johanniterordens in Ungarn*, "Johanniter", 2, 1986; A. Radvánszky, *A Szent János lovagrend története Magyarországon* [A history of the Knights of St. John in Hungary], Paris 1986; S. Vajay, *A Máltai Rend magyar lovagjai, 1530-2000. Militenses ex Hungarica stirpe: militum, capellanorum, dominarumque ex origine Hungarica Ordinis Hospitalis Sancti Johannis Hierosolymitani Militaris de Melita dictae ab anno 1530 ad annum 2000 Incarnationis Domini* [The Hungarian knights of the Order of St. John, 1530-2000], Budapest 2002; I.M. Tóth, *Die Ungarische Genossenschaft des Ritterlichen Ordens Sankt Johannis von Spital zu Jerusalem*, Munich 1959.

[44] T. Buzády, *A Lázár-lovagrend Magyarországon* [The Order of St. Lazarus in Hungary], Munich.

45 K.G. Boroviczényi, *Cruciferi Sancti Regis Stephani. Tanulmány a stefaniták, egy középkori magyar ispotályos rend történetéről* [On the history of a hospitaller order in Hungary, the Stephanites], "Orvostörténeti Közlemények. Communicationes de Historiae Artis Medicinae", 133-140, 1991-1992, pp. 7-48.

46 Z. Hunyadi, *Hospitallers in the Medieval Kingdom of Hungary, c. 1150-1387.* PhD-dissertation. Web: http://sol.cc.u-szeged.hu/~capitul/hzs_thesis.htm, 14 January 2006.

47 J. Török, *A szerzetes és lovagrendek Magyarországon* [Monastic and military religious orders in Hungary], Budapest 1990.

48 S. Homonnai - Z. Hunyadi, *A jeruzsálemi Szent János lovagrend regulája. Regula Hospitalis Sancti Johannis Jerosolomitani* [The Rule of the Order of St. John of Jerusalem], "Documenta Historica", 26, 1996; J. Pánczél Hegedűs (ed.), *A templomos lovagrend regulája. Regula Pauperum Commilitonum Christi Templique Salomonici* [The Rule of the Order of the Templars], trans. by B. Stossek, Budapest 2005.

49 Z. Hunyadi, *Hospitallers in the Medieval Kingdom of Hungary: Houses, Personnel, and a Particular Activity up to 1400*, in Z. Hunyadi - J. Laszlovszky (eds.), *The Crusades and the Military Orders: Expanding the Frontiers of Medieval Latin Christianity*, Budapest 2001, pp. 253-268.

50 P. Engel, *14. századi magyar vonatkozású iratok a johannita lovagrend máltai levéltárából* [14th century-documents from the Archives of the Order of St. John in Malta with reference to the History of Hungary], "Történelmi Szemle", 39, 1997, pp. 111-118.

51 Z. Hunyadi, *A székesfehérvári johannita konvent hiteleshelyi tevékenysége az Árpád-korban* [The Székesfehérvár convent of the Knights of St. John of Jerusalem as a place of authentication in the age of the Árpád dynasty], in L. Koszta (ed.), *Capitulum I. Tanulmányok a középkori magyar egyház történetéből*, Szeged 1998, pp. 33-65; Id., *A johanniták a középkori Magyarországon: az első évtizedek* [The Hospitallers in medieval Hungary: the first decades], in S. Homonnai - F. Piti - I. Tóth (eds.), *Tanulmányok a középkori magyar történelemről*, Szeged 1999, pp. 29-37; Id., *The Knights of St. John and the Hungarian Private Legal Literacy up to the Mid-Fourteenth Century*, in M. Sebők - B. Nagy (eds.), ... *The Man of Many Devices, Who Wandered Full Many Ways. Festschrift in Honor of János M. Bak*, Budapest 1999, pp. 507-519; Id., *Hospitallers in the Medieval Kingdom of Hungary*, "Melitensia", Summer and Fall, 2002, pp. 6-7; Id., *Military-religious Orders in the Medieval Kingdom of Hungary: a historiographical overview*, "Chronica", 3, 2003, pp. 50-57.

52 B. Stossek, *Maisons et possessions des Templiers en Hongrie*, in Hunyadi - Laszlovszky (eds.), *The Crusades and the Military Orders* cit., pp. 245-251.

53 K. Borchardt, *Military Orders in East Central Europe: The First Hundred Years*, in M. Balard (ed.), *Actes de Colloque de la Society for the Study of the Crusades and the Latin East, 'Byzantina Sorbonensia'*, vol. 14, Paris 1996, pp. 247-254; A. Luttrell, *The Hospitallers in Hungary before 1418: Problems and Sources*, in Hunyadi - Laszlovszky (eds.), *The crusades and the military orders* cit.

54 A. Edelényi, *Templomos lovagok az európai néphagyományban* [The Templars in European folk tradition], Budapest 2004.

55 T. Rászlai, *Johanniták a középkori Somogy megyében* [The Knights of St. John in the medieval Somogy county], "Somogy", 1986, pp. 77-84; I. Antics, *A Johannita-rend története és az újudvari convent* [A History of the Knights of St. John and the Újudvar Convent], Szeged 1992.

56 M. Horler, *A johanniták és a korai magyar vártípus* [The Knights of St. John and the early Hungarian castle-type], "Castrum Bene", 1, 1989, pp. 135-152; K. Kozák, *Constructions dans la Hongrie des XIIe-XVe siécles des ordres de chevalerie et d'Hospitaliers et leur influence*, "Acta Archaelogica", 34, 1982, pp. 71-130; K. Kozák, *Téglából épített körtemplomaink és centrális kápolnáink a XII-XIII. Században* [Brick-built rotundas and central chapels in the twelfth and thirteenth centuries in Hungary], "Móra Ferenc Múzeum Évkönyve", 1, 1976-1977, pp. 49-89. The castle building of the Teutonic Order in Transylvania was also studied by Romanian historians: A.A. Rusu, *Die Frage der vom Deutschen Orden im Südosten Siebenbürgens errichteten Burgen*, "Castrum Bene", 5, 1996, pp. 165-172.

57 T. Gömbös, *A szerzetes és lovagrendek címerei és viseletei* [Coat-of-arms and garments of the monastic and military orders], Budapest 1993.

58 B. Stossek - M. Kurecskó, *A Szent Sír Kanonokrend története Magyarországon* [The history of the Canons Regular of the Holy Sepulchre of Jerusalem], in L. Koszta (ed.), *Capitulum* cit., pp. 83-114.

59 J. Török - L. Legeza, *Máltaiak. Szerzetesrendek a Kárpát-medencében. Ordo Equitum Hospitalariorum Sancti Johannis de Jerusalem* [The Maltese. Orders in the Carpathian Basin], Budapest 1999; I. Marjai, *A kereszt és a kard lovagjai. (A máltai lovagrend)* [The Knights of the Cross and the Sword (The Knights of Malta)], Budapest 1990.

60 J. Illésy, *Törekvések a német lovagrend meghonosítására Magyarországon* [Endeavours to settle the Teutonic Order in Hungary], "Századok", 26, 1902, no. 3, pp. 234-48; K. Veszely, *II. András és a német lovagok a Barcaságban* [King Andrew II and the Teutons in the Barcaság region], "Magyar Sion", 1864, pp. 161-171; E. Reiszig, *A német lovagok a Barcaságban* [The Teutons in the Barcaság region], "Századok", 25, 1901.

61 L. Hanzó, *A Barcaság betelepítése és a Német Lovagrend* [The settlement of the Barcaság and the Teutonic Knights], "Századok ", 113, nos. 3-4, 1989, pp. 359-374; L. Pósán, *A Német Lovagrend története a 13. században* [The history of the Teutonic Order in the 13th century], Debrecen 1996; M. Font, *A német lovagrend alkonya* [The waning of the Teutonic Order], Pécs 1997. The subject is very popular in present-day Hungary, and in recent years researchers in this field has produced new insights: G. Frank, *Újabb nézetek a Német Lovagrend barcasági történetéről* [New views on the history of the Teutonic knights in the Barcaság region], in M. Fülöp - J. Vonyó (eds.), *Történeti tanulmányok Dél-Pannóniából*, Pécs 1994, pp. 38-48. The subject has always received international attention, since leading figures of the German academia have also been concerned with the Teutons in Hungary: H. Zimmermann, *Siebenbürgen und seine Hospites Theutonici*, Cologne-Weimar-Vienna 1996; Id., *Der Deutsche Orden im Burzenland: eine diplomatische Untersuchung*, Cologne 2000.

Bibliography

Áldásy A., *A keresztes hadjáratok története* [History of the crusades], Budapest 1924.

Antics I., *A Johannita-rend története és az újudvari convent* [A History of the Knights of St. John and the Újudvar Convent], Szeged 1992.

Balla K. - Mangold L. - Horváth C. (eds.), *Tolnai világtörténelme* [Tolnai edition world history], vol. III/2: *A középkor története* [The history of the Middle Ages], Budapest 1991.

Borchardt K., *Military Orders in East Central Europe: The First Hundred Years*, in Balard M. (ed.), *Actes de Colloque de la Society for the Study of the Crusades and the Latin East,* 'Byzantina Sorbonensia', vol. 14, Paris 1996, pp. 247-254.

Borosy A., *A keresztes háborúk és Magyarország I-II* [The Crusades and Hungary] "Hadtörténelmi Közlemények", 109, 1996, no. 1, pp. 3-41; no. 2, pp. 11-52.

Id., *Keresztes hadjáratok* [Crusades], Szeged 1995.

Id., *Igaz-e, hogy a keresztes hadjáratok gyarmatosítók voltak?* [Is it true that the crusaders were colonists?], Szeged 1995.

Id., *A jeruzsálemi latin királyság* [The Latin Kingdom of Jerusalem], Szeged 2004.

Boroviczény K.G., *Kommentierte Bibliographie der Kreuzherren- und Hospitalorden, sowie deren Krankenhaus- und Bädergründungen in Ungarn in der Zeit der Arpaden (X. bis XIII. Jahrhundert)*, Freiburg 1970.

Id., *Die Hospitaller und Ungarn*, "Johanniter", 3, 1972.

Id., *Cruciferi Sancti Regis Stephani. Tanulmány a stefaniták, egy középkori magyar ispotályos rend történetéről* [On the history of a hospitaller order in Hungary, the Stephanites], "Orvostörténeti Közlemények. Communicationes de Historiae Artis Medicinae", 133-140, 1991-1992, pp. 7-48.

Borus J. (ed.), *Magyarország hadtörténete* [The military history of Hungary], vols. I-II, Budapest 1984.

Breit-Bánlaky J., *A magyar nemzet hadtörténelme* [The military history of the Hungarian nation], vols. I-VIII, Budapest 1929-1934.

Buzády T., *A Lázár-lovagrend Magyarországon* [The Order of St. Lazarus in Hungary], Munich.

Edelényi A., *Templomos lovagok az európai néphagyományban* [The Templars in European folk tradition], Budapest 2004.

Engel P., *14. századi magyar vonatkozású iratok a johannita lovagrend máltai levéltárából* [14th century-documents from the Archives of the Order of St. John in Malta with reference to the History of Hungary], "Történelmi Szemle", 39, 1997, pp. 111-118.

Erdődy J., *Keresztes lobogók alatt* [Under crusading banners], Budapest 1986.

Font M., *A német lovagrend alkonya* [The waning of the Teutonic Order], Pécs 1997.

Frank G., *Újabb nézetek a Német Lovagrend barcasági történetéről* [New views on the history of the Teutonic knights in the Barcaság region], in Fülöp M. -Vonyó J. (eds.), *Történeti tanulmányok Dél-Pannóniából*, Pécs 1994, pp. 38-48.

Gabányi J., *II. Endre keresztes hadjárata* [The crusade of King Andrew II], in Zadrawecz I. (ed.), *Magyar Szentföld* [Hungarian Holy Land], Budapest 1931, pp. 177-192.

Gömbös T., *A szerzetes és lovagrendek címerei és viseletei* [Coat-of-arms and garments of the monastic and military orders], Budapest 1993.

Guizot H., *A keresztes hadak története: középkori krónikákból* [The history of the crusading wars. Excerpts from medieval chronicles], Budapest 1905.

Gyurits A., *A keresztes hadak története* [The history of the crusade wars], vols. I-II, Buda 1853.

Hanzó L., *A Barcaság betelepítése és a Német Lovagrend* [The settlement of the Barcaság and the Teutonic Knights], "Századok ", 113, nos. 3-4, 1989, pp. 359-374.

Hársing L. - Kozák K., *A johanniták a középkori Magyarországon* [The Knights of St. John in medieval Hungary], "Világosság", 20, 1979, pp. 692-699.

Homonnai S. - Hunyadi Z., *A jeruzsálemi Szent János lovagrend regulája. Regula Hospitalis Sancti Johannis Jerosolomitani* [The Rule of the Order of St. John of Jerusalem], "Documenta Historica", 26, 1996.

Hoogeweg H., *Der Kreuzzug von Damiette, 1218-21*, "Mitteilungen des Instituts für Österreichische Geschichtsforschung", 1887-1888.

Horler M., *A johanniták és a korai magyar vártípus* [The Knights of St. John and the early Hungarian castle-type], "Castrum Bene", 1, 1989, pp. 135-152.

Hunyadi Z., *Hospitallers in the Medieval Kingdom of Hungary: Houses, Personnel, and a Particular Activity up to 1400*, in Hunyadi Z. - Laszlovszky J. (eds.), *The Crusades and the Military Orders: Expanding the Frontiers of Medieval Latin Christianity*, Budapest 2001, pp. 253-268.

Id., *A székesfehérvári johannita konvent hiteleshelyi tevékenysége az Árpád-korban* [The Székesfehérvár convent of the Knights of St. John of Jerusalem as a place of authentication in the age of the Árpád dynasty], in Koszta L. (ed.), *Capitulum I. Tanulmányok a középkori magyar egyház történetéből*, Szeged 1998, pp. 33-65.

Id., *A johanniták a középkori Magyarországon: az első évtizedek* [The Hospitallers in medieval Hungary: the first decades], in Homonnai S. - Piti F. - Tóth I. (eds.), *Tanulmányok a középkori magyar történelemről*, Szeged 1999, pp. 29-37.

Id., *The Knights of St. John and the Hungarian Private Legal Literacy up to the Mid-Fourteenth Century*, in Sebők M. - Nagy B. (eds.), ... *The Man of Many Devices, Who Wandered Full Many Ways. Festschrift in Honor of János M. Bak*, Budapest 1999, pp. 507-519.

Id., *Hospitallers in the Medieval Kingdom of Hungary*, "Melitensia", Summer and Fall 2002, pp. 6-7.

Id., *Military-religious Orders in the Medieval Kingdom of Hungary: a historiographical overview*, "Chronica", 3, 2003, pp. 50-57.

Illésy J., *Törekvések a német lovagrend meghonosítására Magyarországon* [Endeavours to settle the Teutonic Order in Hungary], "Századok", 26, 1902, no. 3, pp. 234-248.

Karcsú A.A., *Az egyházi és szerzetesi lovagrendek történelme* [A history of the military religious Orders], Pest 1867.

Knauz N., *A János lovagok Esztergomban* [The Knights of St. John in Esztergom], "Magyar Sion", 3, 1865.

Kolinovich G., *Chronicon militaris ordinis equitum templariorum*, Pestini 1751.

Kovacsóczy M., *Jerusálemi Sz. János Lovagrendje' története* [The history of the Order of St. John of Jerusalem], Kassa 1837.

Kozák K., *Constructions dans la Hongrie des XII-XVe siécles des ordres de chevalerie et d'Hospitaliers et leur influence*, "Acta Archaelogica", 34, 1982, pp. 71-130.

Id., *Téglából épített körtemplomaink és centrális kápolnáink a XII-XIII. Században* [Brick-built rotundas and central chapels in the twelfth and thirteenth centuries in Hungary], "Móra Ferenc Múzeum Évkönyve", 1, 1976-1977, pp. 49-89.

Kozics L., *II. Endre keresztes hadjárata* [The crusade of King Andrew II], "Katholikus Szemle", 28, 1893, pp. 391-417.

Luttrell A., *The Hospitallers in Hungary before 1418: Problems and Sources*, in Hunyadi Z. - Laszlovszky J. (eds.), *The Crusades and the Military Orders: Expanding the Frontiers of Medieval Latin Christianity*, Budapest.

Marjai I., *A kereszt és a kard lovagjai. (A máltai lovagrend)* [The Knights of the Cross and the Sword (The Knights of Malta)], Budapest 1990.

Mezey L., *Krónikások, krónikák* [Chroniclers, chronicles], Budapest 1960.

Mika S., *A középkor* [The Middle Ages], in Marczali H. (ed.), *Nagy képes világtörténet* [Great illustrated world history], vol. II, Budapest 1899-1905.

Molnár M., *Pierre Dubois terve a Szentföld visszaszerzésére* [Dubois's scheme to reoccupy the Holy Land], "Hadtörténelmi Közlemények", 116, 2003, No. 2, pp. 367-426.

Oltványi P., *A jeruzsálemi szent sír és lovagrendjének rövid története* [A brief history of the Order of the Holy Sepulchre in Jerusalem], Szeged 1882.

Pánczél Hegedűs J. (ed.), *A templomos lovagrend regulája. Regula Pauperum Commilitonum Christi Templique Salomonici* [The Rule of the Order of the Templars], transl. by B. Stossek, Budapest 2005.

Patek F., *A magyarországi templárius rend felbomlása* [The dissolution of the Templars in Hungary], Budapest 1912.

Pesty F., *A templáriusok Magyarországon*, "Akadémiai Értesítő", 2, 1861, pp. 30-152.

Pósán L., *A Német Lovagrend története a 13. században* [The history of the Teutonic Order in the 13th century], Debrecen 1996.

Powell J.M., *Anatomy of a Crusade, 1213-21*, Philadelphia 1986.

Pray G., *Dissertatio historico-critica de Prioratu Auranae*, Vienna 1773.

Pucz A., *A' keresztes hadaknak rövid leirása* [A brief description of the crusade wars], Pest 1816.

Radvánszky A., *Ein Ritterwall Gegen die Türken. Geschichte des Johanniterordens in Ungarn,* "Johanniter", 2, 1986.

Id., *A Szent János lovagrend története Magyarországon* [A history of the Knights of St. John in Hungary], Paris 1986.

Rászlai T., *Johanniták a középkori Somogy megyében* [The Knights of St. John in the medieval Somogy county], "Somogy", 1986, pp. 77-84.

Rázsó G., *A lovagkor csatái* [Battles of the knightly age], Budapest 1987.

Reiszig E., *A német lovagok a Barcaságban* [The Teutons in the Barcaság region], "Századok", 25, 1901.

Id., *A jeruzsálemi Szent János lovagrend Magyarországon* [The Order of the Knights of St. John of Jerusalem in Hungary], vols. I-II, Budapest 1925-1928.

Röhricht R., *Studien zur Geschichte des fünften Kreuzzuges*, Innsbruck 1891.

Id., *Quinti belli sacri scriptores minores*, Genéve 1879.

Id., *Testimonia minora de quinto bello sacro*, Genéve 1882.

Rusu A.A., *Die Frage der vom Deutschen Orden im Südosten Siebenbürgens errichteten Burgen*, "Castrum Bene", 5, 1996, pp. 165-72.

Sághy M., *Keresztes háború és nemzeti propaganda. Pierre Dubois: "A Szentföld visszafoglalásáról"* [Crusade and national propaganda. Pierre Dubois "On the Reoccupation of the Holy Land"], in Klaniczay G. - Nagy B. (eds.), *A középkor szeretete. Történeti tanulmányok Sz. Jónás Ilona tiszteletére*, Budapest 1999, pp. 121-132.

Somlyói Tóth T., *Mennyei béke – földi háború. A háború keresztény megítélése a középkorban*, [Heavenly peace – earthly war. The Christian conception of warfare in the Middle Ages], "Világosság", 25, 1984, pp. 98-105.

Stossek B., *Maisons et possessions des Templiers en Hongrie*, in Hunyadi Z. - Laszlovszky J. (eds.), *The Crusades and the Military Orders: Expanding the Frontiers of Medieval Latin Christianity*, Budapest 2001, pp. 245-251.

Stossek B. - Kurecskó M., *A Szent Sír Kanonokrend története Magyarországon* [The history of the Canons Regular of the Holy Sepulchre of Jerusalem], in Koszta L. (ed.), *Capitulum I. Tanulmányok a középkori magyar egyház történetéből*, Szeged 1998, pp. 83-114.

Sweeney J.R., *Magyarország és a keresztes hadjáratok a 12-13. században*, [The Crusades and Hungary in the 12th and 13th centuries], "Századok", 118, 1984, pp. 114-124 (English translation: *Hungary in the Crusades, 1169-1218*, "International History Review", 3, 1981, pp. 467-481).

Szabados G., *Egy elmaradt keresztes hadjáratról. Magyar-szentszéki kapcsolatok 1198-1204 között* [On a delayed crusade. Hungarian-Papal relations between 1198-1204], in *"Magyaroknak eleiről". Ünnepi tanulmányok a hatvan esztendős Makk Ferenc tiszteletére*, Szeged 2000, pp. 473-492.

Szunyogh S., *Jeruzsálem lovagjai* [Knights of Jerusalem], Budapest 1986.

Thierry H., *Jeruzsálemi Szent János [Máltai] Lovagrend. Múlt és Jelen* [The Knights of St. John of Jerusalem. Past and present], Budapest 1936.

Id., *A Jeruzsálemi Szent János [Máltai] Lovagrend Magyar Bibliográfiája* [A bibliography of the Knights of St. John of Jerusalem in Hungary] Budapest 1941.

Török J., *A szerzetes és lovagrendek Magyarországon* [Monastic and military religious orders in Hungary], Budapest 1990.

Török J. - Legeza L., *Máltaiak. Szerzetesrendek a Kárpát-medencében. Ordo Equitum Hospitalariorum Sancti Johannis de Jerusalem* [The Maltese. Orders in the Carpathian Basin], Budapest 1999.

Tóth I.M., *Die Ungarische Genossenschaft des Ritterlichen Ordens Sankt Johannis von Spital zu Jerusalem*, München 1959.

Váczy P., *A középkor története* [The history of the Middle Ages], in Hóman B. - Szekfű G. - Kerényi K. (eds.), *Egyetemes történet: négy kötetben* [Universal history], vol. II, Budapest 1936.

Vasshegyi E., *II. Endre keresztes hadjárata* [The crusade of King Andrew II], Budapest 1916.

Vajay S., *A Máltai Rend magyar lovagjai, 1530-2000. Militenses ex Hungarica stirpe: militum, capellanorum, dominarumque ex origine Hungarica Ordinis Hospitalis Sancti Johannis Hierosolymitani Militaris de Melita dictae ab anno 1530 ad annum 2000 Incarnationis Domini* [The Hungarian knights of the Order of St. John, 1530-2000], Budapest 2002.

Veszely K., *II. András és a német lovagok a Barcaságban* [King Andrew II and the Teutons in the Barcaság region], "Magyar Sion", 1864, pp. 161-176.

Veszprémy L., *II. András magyar király kereszteseinek létszáma* [The number of the crusaders of King Andrew II of Hungary], "Hadtörténelmi Közlemények", 107, 1994, no. 1, pp. 113-116.

Id., *Az első és második keresztes háború korának forrásai* [The sources of the age of the First and Second Crusade], Budapest 1999.

Id., *A keresztes eszme születése*, "Vigilia", 65, 2000, no. 11, pp. 832-836.

Villehardouin G. de, *La conquête de Constantinople (Bizánc megvétele)*, Budapest 1985.

Wilczek E., *II. Endre keresztes hadjárata* [The crusade of King Andrew II], "Századok", 28, nos. 7-8, 1894, pp. 592-608, pp. 697-713.

Zaborov M.A., *A keresztes háborúk* [Crusades], Budapest 1958.

Zimmermann H., *Siebenbürgen und seine Hospites Theutonici*, Cologne-Weimar-Vienna 1996.

Id., *Der Deutsche Orden im Burzenland: eine diplomatische Untersuchung*, Cologne 2000.

Zöllner W., *A keresztes háborúk története* [The history of the crusades], Budapest 1980.

Zombori I., *Lovagok és lovagrendek* [Knights and knightly orders], Budapest 1988.

The Orient in 16th-Century Portuguese Historiography

ANA PAULA AVELAR
Open University, Lisbon

No nosso artigo sobre o modo como o Oriente foi historiografado no Portugal de Quinhentos, partimos da noção que então corria de Europa e de outros Mundos, analisando os textos que descrevem a presença nas paragens orientais e os processos narrativos seguidos para registar a História. Expomos como as novidades foram descritas e transmitidas não só em Portugal mas também no espaço europeu, assinalando, nomeadamente, os diferentes tipos de textos que são produzidos, desde as crónicas régias, às que narram a presença portuguesa no Oriente, passando por aquelas que descrevem cercos militares os as deambulações singulares dos portugueses que em Quinhentos partiram para outros terras por outros mares ao serviço d'el-rei.

O objecto primeiro deste trabalho é a construção da História e do seu narrar, naquele que foi o acto de descrever o espaço oriental, não deixando de reflectir as escolas historiográficas que em Portugal se debruçaram e debruçam sobre a historiografia portuguesa que no século XVI narrou a prresença em terras orientais.

When in the 16th-century Portuguese sailors built an oceanic path to India they felt the need to leave marks of their presence that would somehow distinguish and identify Portugal among the other European countries. These marks would also mean the building of a certain memory and the inscription of historical events. We find the landmarks of Portuguese presence in other spaces during the 16th century in the narratives that unfold oriental lands and seas. When we ponder on the Orient as a concept in Portuguese historical narratives, we feel the need to inscribe it in a larger geographical sense, the one used by Portuguese historians in Modern Age, namely in the 16th century.

The Orient is a geographically identified place where Europeans got the flavourful spices and the marvellous animals and artefacts that were shown or kept in the *studioli* and in the so-called cabinets of curiosities. The embassies to the Pope in Rome revealed those novelties from the new lands. One must bear in mind the embassy to Pope Leo X (1516), sent by the Portuguese king D. Manuel I, where he offered a rhinoceros which, in turn, was given him by Muzafar II, sultan of Gujarat. The peculiar description of this animal would be known all over Europe in engravings made by several artists, such as Albrecht Dürer. Dürer's woodcut actually reveals the influence of the descriptions of the animal's arrival in Lisbon in May 20, 1515. According to Erwin Panofsky: "(...)

Dürer stylized the creature, bizarre in itself, into a combination of scales, laminae and shells suggesting a fantastically shaped and patterned suit of armor"[1]. His description was enhanced by the word, not by the artist's direct observation.

Descriptions of a marvellous and unknown Orient run through Portuguese expansion chronicles. This space is conceived as a heterogeneous whole where one gradually recognizes successive parts, those touched by the sea routes. These parts were to be named using a Portuguese version of local language phonetics, e. g., Vijayannâgara was to become Bisnaga.

One must stress the fact that the Orient as an epochal and historical concept must accompany Europe which is also an epochal and historical concept: " It hardly needs to be demonstrated again that language itself is a highly organized and encoded system, which employs many devices to express, indicate, exchange messages and information, represent, and so forth. In any instance of at least written language, there is no such thing as a delivered presence, but, *a re-presence*, or representation"[2].

Before moving ahead, we must stress the fact that we are dealing with a specific concept, since Europe actually meant something different in the 16th century. Besides in Portuguese intellectual circles this word is used in a very specific context. In order to understand it we must recall its mythological background. The word "Europe" goes back to the continent-founding myth, deriving from Greek mythological narratives. Europe was the daughter of Aganor, King of Tirus. Zeus fell in love with her from the moment he first saw the young girl on a spring morning while she was walking through the fields. He decided then that he would come down to earth, disguised as a bull. When she looked at him she did not feel afraid; instead she jumped on his back and together they rode over the oceans. As soon as the young girl discovered Zeus' identity she was carried to Crete where she would bear his children.

This founding myth remains as a rather constant presence through the centuries in European arts and literature. In Classical Antiquity Europe is represented as a heroine of whom Moschus, Ovid, and Lucian sang in their lyrics. In the Middle Ages, Christianity deleted her kidnap, namely when Ovid was translated into different European languages. Europe would remain, then, as an icon of sacrilegious polytheism. In 16th and 17th centuries, when the *empire of signs* gave way to the *empire of princes*, illuminists, scribes, and printers portrayed her as a Christian goddess.

In Renaissance imagery classical myths remain as mirror-like presences, having Ovid's *Metamorphoses* as main literary background. Two issues should be stressed at this moment: 1. In the Modern era Europe's founding myth means a geographical environment 2. Christianity assimilated this space as a political concept. We must wait for the 17th century for Europe to mean both a geographical environment and a political concept. As Anthony Pagden states: "If 'Europe' had, or came to acquire, an identity as a place, it was always one which lived in the uneasy realization that not only were Europe's origins non-European, but that no one could establish with any precision where Europe stopped and Asia and Africa began"[3].

In the 16th century the encounter of new spaces in Africa, Asia, or America also meant for European countries a questioning of their own conventional identities. This becomes clear when we analyse the changes that take place in cartography, since didactic narratives of Christian history and places give way to *reality* as such. Urgency of information required a world wide rigorous configuration of oceanic expeditions routes. Earlier maps had a more local or regional dimension, demanded either by the need to claim a territory, or the celebration of battles or territorial disputes. In these maps signs dialogue with a specific finality; they are symbols of a certain event, and scale is definitely not a problem.

Later, in the 16th century, sailors would follow their paths far away from shore. This means that they needed a faithful representation of seas, oceans, and continents; besides the notion of earthly space had changed. In the early 16th century Europe controlled the seas, not the continents; this dominion would only be achieved a few centuries later, in the 19th century. European presence was nevertheless a worldwide reality since the early 16th century. However, even conflicts such as those that took place among Portuguese, English, and Dutch on the African coasts and in the Indies, never meant a significant move of European peoples towards these areas. European presence in Asia after the first Vasco da Gama's first voyage and in the 120 years that followed would only mean a concentration of communities of approximately 30000 persons, mainly along a total of 230000 Km of coastline.

Likewise, on the American continent the European presence did not increase much during the 17th century. Consider the Brazilian example with 57,000 inhabitants, 25,000 of whom were white, approximately ¼ of the 120,000 living in Spanish America. A Euro-centric point of view dominated other spaces. We were still far from those years of 1788 when the French Academy challenged French society in order to question American influence in politics, commerce, and costumes in Europe.

We must stress, along with Stuart B. Schwartz, that: "The very act of using concepts such as 'European' and 'other peoples' creates categories that determine the way in which we tend to approach the study of these topics (...)"[4] and we must be aware of this when we study the way 16th century Portuguese historians describe the presence of their *Kingdom* in other continents.

The *world* Europe *knew* turned out to be only a *part* of it; the desire to rule the world that was *missing* would guide the next move. In the early 16th century Portugal would play a significant part in the rigorous way this *new world* would be described. Description was then strictly connected with quality. A new mercantile mentality anchored in emerging techniques would provide a new quantitative approach.

Some historians actually consider that this worldwide approach is an early stage of a global economy[5] deeply based on a European economic framework.

Two books describing the Portuguese presence in the Eastern world were printed in the second half of the 16th century, both claiming priority, originality, and the King's protection. In 1551 Fernão Lopes de Castanheda's published the first, *História do Descobrimento e Conquista da Índia pelos Portugueses* [History of India Discovery and Conquest by the Portuguese]. Later João de Barros would publish *Ásia,...Dos feitos que os Portugueses fizeram* no *descobrimento e conquista dos mares e terras do Oriente* [Asia...Portuguese Deeds in the Discovery and Conquest of the seas and lands of the Orient] also known as *Décadas* [Decades].

Our analysis will focus on the two texts in order to understand the way those writers manipulated memory on their quest for knowledge and its transmission in this specific universe. We will conceive *memory* in its social function, as a tool for building a collective identity; as Jacques le Goff states: "The study of social memory is one of the fundamental approaches to the problems of time and history, in relation to which memory is sometimes retreating, sometimes overflowing"[6].

History also shows how collective memory has been part of the struggle for power: "oblivion and silence" *versus* "reference and remembering" have manipulated our collective memories. The importance of memory and its social function will be thus a relevant presence in the writing of History.

We shall not focus on memory as an intellective and rhetorical process, though we should recall that it is one of five instances of rhetoric, a key element for interpretation of speech. This means that memory stands as a rather functional instrument in terms of political strategy. However, in the 16th century the art of memory remains a residual presence in intellectual disputes[7], namely due to the printing press which would raise other issues such as those concerning the diffusion of the printed text and its audience. The *repetition* of a text, its reproduction in identical series, creates a uniform object[8], and raises the issue of its own conception. This text will cross its 'natural' linguistic borders, spreading through different circles through the translation process.

Humanist historiography writing synthesizes *self* and *eloquence*. This means that each element – word or sentence – must be analysed, since it may be either part of an anagogical strategy as in Gaspar Correia[9], or of a functional approach, as in João de Barros' Platonic concept. According to Plato, the word creates an illusion of life.

João de Barros develops his notion from an 'organic' point of view: speech and enunciation are generated in the palate, tongue, teeth, lips, and breath, which, according to him, the Latins called *affatus*. This process creates words, which are easily assimilated by the ear, *its natural object*, creating *different meanings and concepts according to its place in the sentence*. This chronicler develops his idea with a detailed analysis of the 'mechanical processes of reading'. One of his key-concepts deals with what he considers the arbitrary sequence each *nation* delineates for its alphabet. This sequence would derive, then, from each *national language*. Vision is an important element since it 'catches' each character thus forming the *essence of things* and the *rational concepts*. In a final stage, these will be transmitted by speech.

Barros takes a certain mechanics of the senses as a starting point for the analysis of communication and memory, as a repository of time. In all these issues the echoes of a Platonic conception prevail: "(...) artificial elocution precedes natural speech. Since the latter only lives during the enunciation, and flows away like time which has no turning back: being letters no more than dead characters they still retain the spirit of life (...)"[10]. Therefore Barros devotes his attention to the graphic forms of characters (namely Chinese), and signals them in his historical writings, in his chronicles. Even in his grammatical studies, *Cartinha Com os Preceitos e Mandamentos da Santa Madre Igreja* [Letter Containing the Holy Mother Church Precepts and Commandments]; *Gramática da Língua Portuguesa* [Grammar of Portuguese Language] and *Diálogo em Louvor da Nossa Linguagem* [Dialogue in Praise of Our Language], we find a rather constant concern with a logical-grammatical correspondence, which is part of his search of the nature of things[11].

Barros' studies on language may be understood in the broader context of Renaissance Humanism in its efforts to re-evaluate vernacular languages in the context of the canonical language, Latin. The press will play a significant part in the whole process of standardization of language. Besides, writing ought to be clear and legible for a wider audience, since it should function as an archive of memory for a great diversity of readers. A common memory, living together with different memories, provides the basis for communication, for an increasing sense of belonging[12]. Writing's social function depends on its ability to reach new horizons, new readers, and new geographical, namely European, frontiers.

Writing History in the 16th century means, among other things, a concern for vernacular language whose oral marks remain present. One must bear in mind that these texts deal with a first oral stage when they are read by the author having a Maecenas as private audience. In Portuguese Expansion Chronicles, the Maecenas is the King himself. In the Prologue to his first *Década* [Decade], João de Barros recalls a previous work, the *Chronicle of Emperor Clarimundo*. This *Chronicle* was meant as an essay, a starting point for his (relevant) work to come, the *Décadas* [Decades]. If the king accepted this book, then he would be able to write the *Décadas* [Decades].

In the late 16th century Manuel Severim de Faria praises Barros' classical way of writing History. This point of view derives mainly from Barros' ability to apply traditional rhetorical strategies, such as *deliberatio* and *demonstratio*, to the vernacular language[13].

A similar concern towards the vernacular language may be found in other chroniclers of the Portuguese Expansion, such as Fernão Lopes de Castanheda who stood against those who thought that Portuguese language was not appropriate for the writing of History. Castanheda supports his idea with the poems of Francisco Sá de Miranda who, in his words, had introduced Portuguese into a new era, and had become an icon of modernity[14]. Vernacular language became thus a sign of identity, a specific vehicle of memory, of singularity, among the multiplicity of Nations/States. Fernão de Oliveira, the author of the first Portuguese grammar, printed in 1536, also supports this idea[15].

Like the authors we have quoted, Fernão de Oliveira is a 'man of his time', dividing his writing into different works as *A Arte da Guerra e do Mar* [The Art of War and Sea] published in 1554, *O Livro da Fábrica das Naus* [The Book of the Vessel Factory] which remained unpublished until the 19th century, and an *História de Portugal* [History of Portugal], whose fragments lie in the *Bibliothèque de Paris*[16]. This Renaissance man defined what he considered to be the pragmatic application of vernacular language *vis-à-vis* memory. For him this meant a way of preserving a people's identity[17].

Either in the Royal Chronicles or in the Expansion Chronicles, writing History meant building and preserving a collective memory. The Royal Chronicles of those monarchs who played a significant role in the policies of Portuguese Expansion, namely D. Manuel and D. João III, mirror this strategy. In his Prologue to the *Crónica do Rei D. Manuel* [Chronicle of King D. Manuel], Damião de Góis identifies what he considers to be the right method for those who consider themselves History writers, and denounces those who have not fully related facts as they were[18]. Writing History meant for him, first of all, careful selection of facts, a detailed analysis of each action reported, and of each actor involved. Besides it also meant *decorum*, which should be stressed in the Prologues. An ethical issue is raised here: since History always surpasses its chronicler, facts are always more important than writing.

We find an identical point of view in Francisco de Andrada's dedication to Filipe III of Portugal[19]. His ethical claim for rigor and objectivity may be seen ironic since Andrada often quotes Gaspar Correia's *Lendas da Índia* [Tales from India] without mentioning his source. Nevertheless, we should recall that quoting previous testimony, even without referring to it explicitly as a source, was considered an example of rigor. This work actually provides an excellent background for his purpose, as Correia develops his History through those characters (personalities, heroes) whose image somehow typify and exemplify Christian morals and a Christian *ethos*.

As these examples show, writing History is obviously not an innocent issue. We should remember R. G. Collingwood's analysis of the way History is portrayed in the 16th century. For him, the Renaissance man is understood under a new paradigm clearly different from the one we find in ancient philosophy. In this new paradigm, Man emerges as master of actions and destiny. Collingwood underlines the fact that man is a passionate being, and this obviously echoes in the way History is written. Therefore, History can not be understood as a rigorous recording of facts, but, instead, as a (personal) narrative *of passions and urges*[20]. All this becomes clear when we look at Portuguese History written during the 16th century, either as Royal Chronicles, Expansion Chronicles, or any other historical Memories including such narratives, as Miguel de Castanhoso's *História dos Feitos de Dom Cristóuão da Gama em Etiópia* [History of Things Done by Dom Christovão da Gama in Ethiopia].

Memory naturally means a selection of facts. Besides, it functions as a way of defeating death, time, and oblivion. All the facts not reported, all the heroes' deeds unsung, in a certain sense, cease to exist, since they are lost in time. This attitude derives from a providential concept of the flow of history; this perspective also echoes in the writing of the past.

Supported by *Fama Bona* and *Fama Mala*, History stands as a tutelary figure mirroring Providence. Also supported by Experience and Truth, she wins over Death and Oblivion. We find this concept in Walter Raleigh's *History of the World* (1614), where he expresses a notion that was actually built during the Modern Age[21].

We should remember Diogo do Couto's wanderings in his *Soldado Prático* [Practical Soldier], namely his interpretation of what he saw as the "Sixth Age": The wars in Flanders, France, and England; the conflict between Christianity and Islam in Greece, Hungary, and Germany; Portuguese natural catastrophes – earthquakes, famine, plague; all these are seen as a sign of God's wrath due to Man's sins[22].

Portuguese chroniclers saw the recording and teaching of History as a way of preserving national tradition and national identity, therefore its importance in the education of the Prince. Castanheda thought that it also meant a sign of the vassals' worth. History provided examples both of the analogy between "great leaders and great vassals" – in Rome and Greece –, and of those deeds forgotten because the vassals did not prove to be worth of their leaders – "barbarians, Greeks, and Latins"[23]. For Castanheda this would not be a danger since the Portuguese vassals would be of great value in order to help to perpetuate the Portuguese Empire. His notion actually echoes Baldo's dispute on what the Emperor should be. Ernest Kantorowicz states that: "(...) The cause of corruption namely is, all by itself, Time... and although the empire is forever... it nevertheless does not remain in the same status because it dwells in continuous motion..."[24].

However, Portuguese chroniclers consider a wise government to be the key for perpetuity. In order to be wise, leaders should study History. António da Beja reminds his readers of Marcus Tulius Cicerus' three main elements of wise government: memory of things past, knowledge of present things, foresight of things to come[25]. This is the reason why Gaspar Correia stresses the importance of a rigorous record of historical events. According to him this had not been the case of earlier narratives of the Portuguese presence in India, when some authors had embellished certain events forgetting all the fighting and suffering that prevailed[26]. On the other hand, João de Barros thought that infamous facts, even when true, should be censured[27].

This is not, however, a common strategy for those who write History in Portugal during the 16th century, since, for them, recording a fact implied a dialogue with memory. In those days writing History was underlined by a common methodology whose main vectors were classical, although this did not mean that there was a single work synthesizing the proper method, such as Jean Bodin's *Methodus ad facilem historiarum cognitionem*, printed in Paris in 1566, where he stresses the connection between *Ars Memoria* and *Ars Historica*[28].

The connection between Memory and History has always been present in the conceptualization of historiographical writing, either meaning the building of a method, or its insertion in the narrative structure of a specific *History*. During the Renaissance, the delineation of historical narrative is deeply connected with the emphasis on a certain actor. This emphasis grows hand in hand with a broader context providing the main frame that explains the *Res Historica*. Quoting T.F. Earle: "Narrative, like description, also has a rhetorical function. It may form part either of deliberative discourse, designed to persuade the audience to some course of action, or of epideictic discourse, which attributes praise or blame"[29].

However, we must considerer two main groups of historiographical narratives, those printed during the 16th century and those that were not printed. This major distinction will determine the typification of the narratives describing Portuguese presence in other parts of the world, and unveiling the novelties of the new spaces, the marvelous wonders, the strange and different peoples and cultures, to the European reader/public.

We can map these 16th century Portuguese works in the following table:

Gaspar Correia's book, *Lendas da Índia* (Legends of India), follows this model. This book remained a manuscript from the 16th century until the 19th century, when it was printed for the first time. This fact does not mean that it was not known in earlier days, as demonstrated by its use in Francisco de Andrade's *Crónica de D. João III* [D. João III's Chronicle], printed in 1613.

We also must consider another kind of historical narrative written in the 16th century, those that were printed later, such as Duarte Barbosa's and Tomé Pires'. These Portuguese officers wrote books that functioned as sources for Fernão Lopes de Castanheda, João de Barros and Gaspar Correia. Written in the early 16th century, they described their travels in India and other parts of Asia, and the traditions and daily life of the people they met.

Portuguese Chroniclers of Expansion used other sources like letters, personal descriptions of battles or embassies, and ships' logs, among others. All these texts portrayed personal experiences and served specific purposes, such as getting the King's protection, the observance of orders, and the mere narrative of one's experience... Nevertheless these narratives did not aim at writing the History of the Portuguese Presence in other parts of the world.

The Chronicles of the Expansion, and specially the ones focusing Portuguese presence in India, actually are the main narratives on the 16th-century dialogue between Portugal and the World. One of the most interesting aspects of these narratives is that they have been studied either as literary documents, belonging to a specific genre, or as a source of true/false facts that have built History. So when a historian does his research on 16th Portuguese History, namely in a political, social, economical or cultural field, he cannot forget these narratives. More recently these narratives have been approached from a different angle, as unique documents that must be put in perspective. They have not been treated as mere subsidiary sources as happened until recently, but rather as the centre of the equation. Among the scholars who have carried out such studies one

16th-century Portuguese narratives concerning Portugal and the World (printed during the 16th century)

Date	Place	Title	Author
6 March 1551	Coimbra	"Liuro primeiro da historia da India…" [The First Book of the History of India…]	Fernão Lopes de Castanheda
20 January 1552	Coimbra	Liuro Segundo da Historia do Descobrimento e Conquista da India…" [The Second Book of The History of the Discovery and Conquest of India…]	Fernão Lopes de Castanheda
28 June 1552	Lisboa	"Ásia…fectos que os Portugueses fizeram no descobrimento & conquista dos Mares & terras do Oriente" [Asia…Portuguese Deeds in the Discovery and Conquest of the seas and lands of the Orient]	João de Barros
12 October 1552	Coimbra	Liuro Terceiro da Historia do Descobrimento e Conquista da India pelos Portugueses…" [The third Book of The History of the Discovery and Conquest of India by the Portuguese…]	Fernão Lopes de Castanheda
15 October 1553	Coimbra	Ho Quarto Liuro da Historia do Descobrimento & Conquista da India pelos Portugueses… [The Fourth Book of the History of the Discovery and Conquest of India by the Portuguese…]	Fernão Lopes de Castanheda
15 October 1553	Coimbra	Liuro Quinto da Historia do Descobrimento & Conquista da India pelos Portugueses… [The Fith Book of the History of the Discovery and Conquest of India by the Portuguese…]	Fernão Lopes de Castanheda
14 March 1553	Lisboa	Segunda Decada da Asia… dos feitos que os Portugueses fizeram no descobrimento& cõquista das Mares & terras do Oriente [The Second Decade of Asia …Portuguese Deeds in the Discovery and Conquest of the seas and lands of the Orient]	João de Barros
3 February 1554	Coimbra	Ho Liuro Sexto da Historia do Descobrimento & Conquista da India pelos Portugueses…" [The Sixth Book of the History of the Discovery and Conquest of India by the Portuguese…]	Fernão Lopes de Castanheda
20 June 1554 (reprinted)	Coimbra	Ho primeiro liuro da Historia do descobrimento e conquista da Índia pelos Portugueses… [The First Book of the History of the Discovery and Conquest of India by the Portuguese…]	Fernão Lopes de Castanheda
[1554]	Coimbra	"Ho Septimo liuro da Historia do descobrimento e conquista da Índia pelos Portugueses…" [The Seth Book of the History of the Discovery and Conquest of India by the Portuguese…]	Fernão Lopes de Castanheda
26 August 1561	Coimbra	Ho Livro oytavo liuro da Historia do descobrimento e conquista da Índia pelos Portugueses…" [The Eight Book of the History of the Discovery and Conquest of India by the Portuguese…]	Fernão Lopes de Castanheda
18 August 1563	Lisboa	Terceira decada da Asia… Dos feytos que os Portugueses fizeram no descobrimento & conquista dos Mares & terras do Oriente" [The Third Decade of Asia… Portuguese Deeds in the Discovery and Conquest of the seas and lands of the Orient]	João de Barros

finds both literary critics and cultural historians. Historians such as Vitorino Magalhães Godinho, Joaquim Veríssimo Serrão, Borges Coelho, Banha de Andrade, Diogo Ramada Curto, Maria Augusta Lima Cruz and Ana Paula Avelar have rediscovered these historiographical narratives. Although belonging to different generations and to different historiographical traditions, these Historians unveil the writing of History, the History of 16th century Portuguese perception of its country and its *world*.

Notes

1 E. Panofsky, *The Life and Art of Albercht Dürer*, Princeton-Oxford 2005.

2 E. Said, *Orientalism*, New York 1979, p. 21

3 A. Padgen, *Europe and the World Around*, in E. Cameron, *Early Modern Europe*, Oxford 2001, p. 4.

4 S.B. Schwartz, *Implicit Understandings-Observing, reporting, and reflecting on the Encounters between Europeans and other Peoples in the Early Modern Era*, Cambridge 1994, p. 6.

5 Cf. V. Magalhães Godinho, *Les Découvertes XVe-XVIe: une révolution des mentalités*, Paris 1992, pp. 61-72.

6 J. Le Goff, *History and Memory*, New York 1992, p. 54.

7 *Ibid.*, p. 82.

8 Cf. R. Barthes - E. Marty, *Oral/Escrito*, in *Enciclopédia Einaudi*, 11, Lisbon 1987, p. 55.

9 Cf. the first Prologue of Lendas da Índia where the author states the main vectors of his project: G. Correia, *Lendas da Índia*, Porto 1975, I, p. 2.

10 J. de Barros, *Ásia... Dos feitos que os portugueses fizeram no descobrimento e conquista dos mares e terras do Oriente*, Lisbon 1988, p. 2.

11 Cf. M.L. Buescu, *Textos Pedagógicos e Gramaticais de João de Barros*, Lisbon 1969.

12 Cf. H. Carvalhão Buescu, *Em busca do autor perdido*, Lisbon 1998, pp. 3-4.

13 Cf. J. de Barros, *Clarimundo*, Lisbon 1953, vol. I, p. 34.

14 Cf. F. Lopes de Castanheda, *História do Descobrimento e conquista da Índia pelos portugueses*, Porto 1979, vol. I, p. 494.

15 Some authors claim that the first grammar is actually Barros'. For a clearer view of this debate cf. M.L. Buescu, *A Gramática da linguagem Portuguesa de Fernão de Oliveira*, pp. 18-22.

16 *Ibid.*, p.18.

17 *Ibid.*, p.45.

18 Cf. D. de Góis, *Crónica do Felicíssimo Rei D. Manuel*, Coimbra, 1949, vol. I, p. 1.

19 Cf. F. de Andrada, *Crónica de D. João III*, Porto 1976, pp. LXXI-LXXII.

20 Cf. R.G. Collingwood, *A Ideia de História*, Lisbon 1978, p. 78.

21 Cf. B. Southgate, *History : What e Why?* London 1996, p. 4.

22 Cf. D. do Couto, *O soldado Prático*, Lisbon 1980, p. 136.

23 Cf. Lopes de Castanheda, *História do Descobrimento* cit., p.3.

24 E.H. Kantorowicz, *The King's two bodies*, Princeton 1997, p. 299.

25 Cf. F. António da Beja, *Breve Doutrina e Ensinança dos Príncipes*, Lisbon 1965, p. 152.

26 Cf. Correia, *Lendas da Índia* cit., p.1.

27 Cf. J. de Barros, *Prólogo*, Lisbon 1988.

[28] Cf. M.-D Couzinet, *Histoire et Méthode à la Renaissance*, 1996, p. 64.

[29] T.F. Earle - J. Villiers, *Albuquerque Caesar of the East- selected texts by Afonso de Albuquerque and his son*, Warminster 1990, p. 28.

Selected Bibliography

Banha de Andrade A.A., *Gaspar Correia - Inédito*, Lisbon 1977.

Id., *João de Barros: Historiador do Pensamento Humanista Português de Quinhentos*, Lisbon 1980.

Id., *Mundos Novos do Mundo* - Panorama da difusão, pela Europa, de notícias dos Descobrimentos Geográficos Portugueses, Lisbon 1972.

Avelar Menino A.P., *Figurações da alteridade na cronística da Expansão*, Lisbon 2003.

Barreto L.F., *Caminhos do Saber no Renascimento Português- Estudos de História e Teoria da Cultura*, Lisbon 1986.

Id., *Descobrimentos e saber: Formas de Ser e de Pensar nos séculos XV e XVI*, Lisbon 1982.

Bitterli U., *Cultures in Conflict*, Oxford 1989.

Breisach E., *Historiography: Ancien, Medieval, and Modern*, Chicago 1983.

Id., *On the Future of History - The Postmodernist Challenge and its Aftermath*, Chicago 2003.

Coelho A.B., *Quadros para uma viagem a Portugal no século XVI*, Lisbon 1986.

Id., *O Tempo e os Homens - Questionar a História III*, Lisbon 1988.

Id., *Tudo é Mercadoria - sobre o percurso e a obra de João de Barros*, Lisbon 1992.

Lach D.F., *Asia in the Making of Europe*, 8 vols. Chicago 1965-1993.

Lima Cruz M.A., *A primeira Viagem à Índia pela rota do Cabo* / The First Voyage to India by the Cape route, trad. R.A. Brown, Lisbon 1998.

Id., *As vozes da Índia nas 'Décadas da Ásia' de Diogo do Couto*, "Oceanos", 19-20, 1994, pp. 182-188.

Id., *Diogo do Couto e a Década Oitava, da Ásia*, 2 vols, Lisbon 1992-1995.

Id., *La vision de l'indien chez les premiers chroniqueurs portuguais de l'Asie: la fixation d'une image*, in Actas Colloque la découverte, le Portugal et l'Europe, Paris 1990, pp. 235-241.

Loureiro R., *A China na cultura portuguesa do século XVI - Notícias, Imagens e Vivências*, Lisbon 1995 (edição policopiada).

Id., *Fidalgos, Missionários e Mandarins - Portugal e a China no século XVI*, Lisbon 2000.

Id., *A Bibiloteca de Diogo do Couto*, Macau 1998.

Magalhães Godinho V., *Découvertes: XVe-XVIe- Une revolution de mentalités*, Paris 1992.

Id., *Entre o mito e a utopia: os descobrimentos, construção do espaço e invenção da humanidade nos séculos XV e XVI*, "Revista de História Económica e Social", 12, 1983, pp. 1-43.

Id., *Le Devisement du Monde- De la pluralité des espaces à l'espace global de l'humanité Xvème-XVI ème siècles*, Lisbon 2000.

Id., *Mito e Mercadoria - Utopia e Prática de Navegar século XIII -XVIII*, Lisbon 1990.

Munslow A., *Deconstructing History*, London 1997.

Ricoeur P., *La mémoire, l'histoire, l'oubli*, Paris 2000.

Rubiés J.-P., *Travel and Ethnology in the Renaissance – South India through European eyes, 1250-1625*, Cambridge 2000.

Schwartz S.B., *Implicit Understandings. Observing, reporting and reflecting on the encounters between Europeans and others peoples in the early modern era*, Cambridge 1994.

Serrão J.V., *A Crónica de D. João III de António de Castilho*, in Arquivos do Centro Cultural Português, II, Paris 1970, pp. 317-403.

Id., *A Historiografia Portuguesa - Doutrina e Crítica I - séculos XII-XVI*, Lisbon 1972.

Southgate B., *History: What & Why? - Ancient, Modern and Postmodern Perspectives*, London 1996.

Colonial Constructions of Tribe in India: the Case of Chotanagpur

Vinita Damodaran
University of Sussex

This chapter looks at the multiple strands in British policy towards tribes in Eastern India. It is concerned with revisionism in the context of tribal histories. Here, I will consider colonial narratives of representation. that have come in for criticism by revisionists, in particular, the idea of the ecological noble savage, pristine forests and isolated tribal people. The argument that earlier ethnographers and colonial administrators had mistakenly thought that "tribes" were static entities, leads many of the revisionist critics to conclude that distinct tribes never existed, and that the claims of indigenous people for autonomy must have no theoretical legitimacy or historical validity.

A closer look at the record reveals that we may be too hasty in dismissing colonial narratives in this summary fashion. Indeed I argue that earlier generations of ethnographers did actually very often understand the complexities of ethnic identity and cultural dynamics. In similar ways, colonial discourse did not just conjure up an imaginary landscape, but analysed real landscape differences. In fact, it can be said that the material and the imaginary landscape constituted one another in complex ways. Colonial administrators did participate and engage with the land and the people and were forced to contend with indigenous knowledge and ideas of place. The narratives of these travellers, surveyors and officials of the company raj were not merely a 'representation of place' that could be used to root colonial claims to possession, but a far more ambiguous relationship with the place and its native inhabitants[1]. The ambiguities, contradictions and often acute observations of colonial officials go unrecognized in such post-modern reading. It is against this background that colonial representations of customary rights and constructions of indigeneity need to be seen. In a recent article, Nancy Lee Peluso has criticised colonial constructions of customary rights as having little basis in reality and leading in the Indonesian context to the 'racialisation' of the landscape with 'ethnic access' to resource use[2]. This is a problematic position, for the history of debates on customary rights in the Indian context reveals quite clear colonial preoccupations with the detail of local rights and their practice, especially in the context of forest lands. Given the nature of the state and the dominance of the property interest, these rights proved difficult to recover and to legislate in favour of, because they belonged only to practise and to oral tradition. Despite this, genuine attempts were frequently made in the latter half of the 19th century to document local rights and land-use customs and to protect some customary practises. In the context of the discourse of indigeneity, these attempts are of enormous importance, although they are rarely given adequate attention. The recent extraordinary attempts of the Jharkhand government to award indigenous land claims not on the basis of oral evidence but specifically on the basis of colonial documentation dating back to the 1920s demonstrates the vital importance of understanding the colonial interpretation of customary rights.

James Bodley has recently observed that "the revisionists assault on the 'noble savage' and the wilderness idea come at the historical moment when the global culture's unsustainable cultural imperative of perpetual capital accumulation is reducing the earth's stocks of water, soil, forests, and fisheries to dangerously low levels and disrupting ecosystems and natural cycles on an unprecedented scale". Similarly as notions of indigeneity and customary rights come in for revisionist attack, the marginalisation and proletarianisation of many forest based communities and the demise of their traditional livelihoods gains pace all over the world[3].

Colonial policy in Chotanagpur

Links with the past

To be linked to the wilderness or the jungle, was by definition pejorative from ancient times down to the 18th century. It was not a recent phenomenon. It must be noted, and I fear that in their haste to dismiss the notion of the unchanging primitive tribe, revisionists do not sufficiently emphasise this, that colonial epistemology aligned itself with Brahmanical knowledge resulting specifically in the depoliticisation and emasculation of many communities which came to be later termed as *adivasi.* Sumit Guha's work for example in his recent book, *Environment and Ethnicity in India* seems to follow the line, criticised by Bayly[4] and O'Hanlon, that the British invented 19th-century caste and tribe. In order to challenge the notion of an ageless caste-based social order, Guha's argument may have been carried too far. Colonial regimes did not simply invent caste and tribe out of pre-colonial systems that were uniformly mobile and uncodified. The agency of Indians and long-term structural continuities need to be taken more into account in these studies. 19th-century preoccupations with caste needs to be understood in terms of continuity with precolonial Brahmanic and Kshatriya precepts and traditions. While one cannot deny the existence of powerful local ideologies and alternative forms of social organisation the growing dominance of Brahmanical ritual and scribal specialists in the immediate precolonial period needs to be sufficiently studied[5].

In Chotanagpur then, it is possible to argue that the categorising of the indigenous inhabitants of Chotanagpur as barbarous and in need of civilisation has a longer history than the colonial period. The idea of the Aryan invasion of India was an important premise in colonial writings which recorded the negative images of non-Aryan people that could be seen to date back to the first contacts of the non-Aryan peoples with the sanskrit speaking Arya peoples in the 1st century[6]. Evidence for this was recorded by 18th century British orientalists and later by 19th-century colonial and Indian ethnographers. Clearly the idea of the Aryan invasion of India is much disputed. The literature relies, as Trautmann notes, on an over reading of the Vedic texts. However it is less easy to dispute the fact that an analysis of these texts makes it possible to say there were clear markers of difference between the Aryans and the non-Aryans. Religion and language were seen as marking difference between the Aryas and the Dasyus[7]. The historian Romilla Thapar cautions us to stay strictly within the definition of *arya* from Sanskrit texts where it "is a linguistic and social qualifier without the overlay of nineteenth century theories". It is true that 19th-century colonial ethnographers including S.C. Roy, the Indian ethnographer drew heavily on these texts while recording the oral traditions of the Oraon and Mundas in the late 19th century[8]. Some of this evidence can be relied on though as Thapar argues the reconstruction of societies of an earlier period needs to rely also on archeological data. Such a change of focus, she notes, would require a search for a graduated interaction over many centuries between various settlements and cultures and where large scale violent conflict was not the norm. She agrees that the Rgveda refers to relations between the Arya-Varna and the Dasa Varna who were identified as distinct peoples. The later Vedic texts also refered frequently to differences between aryas and dasas in worship and rituals[9]. Thus while recent research shows that the relationship between Aryas and non-Aryas was more ambivalent than has been recognised so far, there is no disputing the idea of difference in early times. S.C. Roy noted that the Oraons community in Chotanagpur called themselves Kurukhs, a term which can be traced to their mythical hero king Karakh. In Hindu tradition the Kurukhs were compared to the legendary monster king Ravana of Ramayan fame. The Kurukhs with what appeared to the Hindu to be their "monstrously impure habits" came to be called *Raona put* or the progeny of Ravana[10].

Colonial epistemology thus built both on Brahamanical notions of caste and drew on 18th- and 19th-century ideas of race. How does this relate to colonial understandings of tribes? Some ethnologists viewed tribes in the north-eastern parts of India such as the Nagas and the Mizos as the "true wild tribes of India" and "unlike the broken tribes found in Chotanagpur". For these colonial administrators the 'tribal' model with its essential unity, clear body of customary law and unambiguous legitimacies was better suited to the task of maintaining public tranquility[11]. Victorian anthropology in this period was dominated by ideas of socio-cultural evolution. Indeed, as Stocking notes, by the time of the great Crystal Palace exhibition of 1851 a considerable body of British writing including utilitarianism had been concerned with the progress of civilisation[12]. As he notes,

> within the British tradition and Continental tradition civilisation was conceived: ideas about non-European 'savages' who defined 'civilisation' by contrast; ideas about the physical nature and differentiation of man, which raised the problem of its universality; ideas about the nature of social order, which defined the specific context of civilisation; and ideas about the methods appropriate to the study of human life and history, which defined the extent to which it might be subsumed within the rubric of natural science.

These constructions of difference and the rigid drawing of boundaries had important implications for the discourse on tribes. In the context of the increasing migration of Hindus into remote *adivasi* areas and as Brahmanical values acquired a legitimacy as a strategy for the exclusion and surbordination of tribals, British racial ideas acquired a new meaning. The British aided and abetted the process of subordination, as Chotanagpur was brought under administrative control in the late 18th and early 19th century, accompanied by projects for the classification of castes and tribes, the production of new regional histories and the *de facto* enshrining of Brahmanical law within the Anglo-Indian judicial system. The early ethnographic surveys of the 'tribes' were thus concerned with assigning them a social position in a Hindu social hierarchy. By the 19th century developments in thinking in Europe gave further impetus to these ideas. Human diversity was beginning to be conceptualised in rigidly hierarchical and physical terms due to new ideas in comparative physical anatomy and physical anthropology. The implications of all this for scientific conceptions of the mental characteristics of non-European peoples was profound. In the 18th century, 'savages' had been generally assumed to share essentially the same psychic nature as Europeans. In the first half of the 19th, this essential unity was eroded by a hereditary racialism[13]. European ideas on race were to change with the impact of Darwin's ideas which, while challenging polygenetic ideas, actually strengthened racial attitudes[14].

Indeed, the 19th century saw the emergence of a comprehensive Anglo-Saxon racialism. Though the biological elements in the race idea developed in a more gradual way a number of events sharpened the sense of separation of Europeans from the dark-skinned colonial peoples. By the 1850s, the sub discipline of ethnology had developed in Britain as the most general scientific framework for the study of the linguistic, physical and cultural characteristics of dark-skinned, non-European, 'uncivilised' peoples. For example, among the other exhibits of the newly established Natural History Museum in London there were 13 life size groupings of 'savages', the Eskimos next to the polar bear, the Red Indians next to the north American birds, the west African negroes next to the chimpanzee. The museum encased in time and space different cultures and civilisations within the "teleology of manifest destiny". In the case of the displays on native Americans, in America Hinsley notes that dehistoricization was the essence of the process. "World fairs, wild west shows, anthropology museums all provided public spaces for the safe consumption of a newly dehistoricized Indian; in most of them there was an element of theatre"[15]. In his study of Victorian anthropology in the period, Stocking has examined in some detail the attitudes of some of those who provided the data of Victorian ethnography: George Grey, Thomas Williams, Francis Galton and Alfred Russel Wallace[16]. He notes that though they were from different professional backgrounds they were all conscious of their racial and cultural superiority. Even humanitarian writers such as Evans Prichard, the father of ethnology in Britain, accepted many notions about the content of particular 'racial' characters.

By the time of the Sepoy Mutiny the same can be said about many colonial administrators, missionaries, gentleman explorers and scientific travellers in India. After Darwinian theories came into prominence dark-skinned peoples were assigned their proper place in the evolutionary timescale. They were the missing links in the evolutionary chain and could cast light on the processes by which the "ape had developed into the British Gentleman"[17]. It was through the census, map and museum that they were assigned their proper place[18]. The late 19th-century movement to conceptualise human diversity in rigidly hierarchical terms resulted in India in a spurt of ethnological conferences and published papers on the comparative physical characteristics of castes and tribes in India. It is important to note that in the same period the new teachings of evolutionary racial ideologists made India an important source of data for the supposed transition from the primitive to the advanced. For men such as W.W. Hunter, Herbert Risley and Forsyth, evolutionary racial ideas dominated their work on caste and tribe.

As Herbert Risley recorded, the ethnographic conference at Lahore in March 1885 hoped to built up the modern science of anthropology in India and it was believed "that it might be possible by careful observation and record of social practises, to arrive at fresh data throwing light on ethnological problems which scientific men John Lubbock, Henry Maine, and E.B. Tylor have discussed in Europe"[19]. Elsewhere he wrote that:

> the physical characteristics which distinguished the tribe tend on the whole to be preserved; it is this persistence of type which accounts for the differences of feature, which though only definable by scientific method, are marked enough to render it possible within certain limits to make a fair guess of a man's caste from his personal appearance.

The association of racial ideas with colonial constructions of caste and tribe received its scientific backing in the corpus of volumes on anthropometric studies in India. It was hoped thus to identify difference among the multiplicity of castes and tribes in India and to arrange them in rigidly physical terms. Amid the confusion caused by the staggering variety of communities in India, it was hoped that the disorderly nature of Indian society could be organised hierarchically and in racial terms. The search for 'true origins' and separateness among the castes thus became the central task of the ethnographic surveys. As Risley noted:

> the difficulty of throwing much light on the true origin of the lower and intermediate castes by collating customs and ceremonies which they have borrowed in the most liberal fashion from the higher castes suggested to me the possibility of applying to the leading tribes and castes of Bengal the methods of recording and comparing typical physical characteristics which have yielded valuable results in other parts of the world.

He hoped through these anthropometric methods to detach "the considerable body of non-Aryans from the general body of Hindus and to refer them to specific stocks as Dravidian, Lohitic, Tibetan and the like and through these methods to determine the divergence of each of these aggregates from known Aryan and non-Aryan types". Such an exercise, he had little doubt, would not only have the support of the scientific community in Europe but would also appeal to leaders of the Hindu community amongst whom the orthodox and advanced laid so much stress on the "purity of their Aryan descent".

As early as 1866, Dr. J. Fayrer C.S.I. submitted to the Asiatic Society of Bengal a proposal for the great Ethnological Congress in Calcutta which was to bring together in one exhibition "typical examples" of the races of the old world, to be made the subject of scientific study when so collected. The council of the society was unanimous in regarding the position as one highly calculated to advance the science of ethnology and in submitting it to the government of India warmly advocated its adoption, as an appropriate adjunct to the general industrial exhibition which it was then intended to hold in 1869-70. However, the scheme ran into difficulties. It was important that the wild tribes of India should be represented. Yet it was no easy matter to induce these "strange shy creatures to visit even the stations nearest to them and to induce them to proceed to a remote and unknown country for a purpose they could not be made to comprehend"[20]. The commissioner of Assam was more specific: "if specimens of the more independent tribes fell sick and died in Calcutta or on the journey it might lead to inconvenient political complications".

By 1865 in India ethnology was the most popular and rising science of the day – so much so that one commentator noted that:

> I soon expect to find that, instead of collecting postage stamps, young ladies of an intellectual turn will collect nice little cabinets of Crania for the inspection of their friends.

Views of comparative types, with a measuring pole diligently but uselessly placed in the background, demonstrate the approach of many of the soldiers and residents who utilised their photographic skills in the cause of ethnology[21].

It is in this context that sterotyped images of the tribe predominated in colonial discourse in the mid and late 19th century. Among the many stereotypes, images of the tribes as addicted to drink and merrymaking continued to proliferate. Most of the colonial officials reported the tribes were all addicted to drink. Reporting on the condition of the Gonds and Korkus of the Central Provinces Forsyth remarked that:

> until lately habits of unrestrained drunkenness have aggravated the natural obstacles to their improvement... it is this unfortunate want of steadiness that has led to most of the misfortunes of the race, to the loss of their heritage in the land, and in a great many cases practically even of their personal liberty. Inferior races gave way before superior whenever they meet; and whether, as here and in America, the instrument selected be 'fire-water', or as in New Zealand, it be our own favourite recipe of powder and lead, the result is the same[22].

W.W. Hunter writing in the *Annals of Rural Bengal* in 1897 recorded that:

> it was not difficult to understand the contempt with which the Sanskrit speaking conquerors regarded a speech squeezed into such narrow and so ignobly objective moulds as that of the ancient *dasyus* or their descendants the present hill tribes of the northern frontier... of this language the most striking features are its multitude of words for whatever can be seen or handled, and its absolute inability to express reflex conceptions of the intellect, the absence of terms representing relationships in general and conspicuously the relationship of cause and effect[23].

The Hinduisation of tribes was seen as improving these wild people and in the case of the Bhumij of Chotanagpur it was reported approvingly that "he was no longer the wild marauder of the 17th and 18th century"[24].

Similarly one can see ideas of environmental determinism and notions that a "jungly landscapes producing a jungly mind" surfacing in some of ethnographic writing on tribes[25]. The term jungle was not an unchanging one in the Indian context. As Zimmerman notes, the use of the term *jungle jangala* in Sanskrit is interesting. The Sanskrit Jangala (as a mental image) corresponds in many respects to the frontier. It was a land wild but fertile, good for hunting and fighting, "where the brave devour the cowardly". More importantly it was a land where noble kings and conquerors would expand their domains. Subtly he notes the value of the jangala to Indians themselves changed over time. Jangala lands were created, in reality, by a process of progressive deforestation, partial cultivation and abandonment of deforested territory. The non-Aryans practising slash and burn were driven back into the less inhabitable mountains and marshes[26]. In colonial discourse images of the tribes are replete with references to the forest environment. Ideas of savagery were associated with an inhospitable forest environment and tropes of wilderness. Shivaramakrishnan has argued that these tropes resulted in the production of "primitive places"[27]. However, the argument that colonial discourse tended to overemphasise the relationship of local communities with forests and tended to misread the landscape has to be examined more carefully. For example, S.C. Roy – the noted Indian anthropologist of the early decades of the 20th century – has recorded in some detail the migrations of the Mundas and Oraons. He records that at some stage the Mundas and the Oraons finally secluded themselves away from the attacks of the Aryans in the valleys and jungles of Chotanagpur[28]. He notes that it was in the "primeval forests" of Jharkhand that the first Munda immigrants made clearances in the jungles and established their villages in the north western parts of what is now Ranchi district and records that the Jharkhand Mundas "appear to have remained unmolested in their isolated mountain fastness. Walled off from the outside world by chains of wooded hills they had a long immunity from hostile disturbances which enabled them to build up their social and administrative organisation"[29]. These representations of a remote wooded landscape are in keeping with what Shivaramakrishnan has called "enduring tropes of wilderness" and one can argue that this idea of a pristine landscape is not borne out by the evidence. Indeed it is clear, that the landscape in Chotanagpur, even in the thickest jungles, was an anthropogenic one. This is in keeping with the numerous studies elsewhere that have argued that "there is no such thing as virgin forest"[30]. The forests that ecologists have assumed to be unchanged for centuries are being found to reveal, pot sherds, charcoal and the remains of ancient crop fields[31]. One can safely conclude that the forests of Chotanagpur constituted an anthropogenic landscape. However, to my mind, what is important is not whether ecosystems are untouched or unchanged by humans but whether there exist serious "quantitative and qualitative differences in human impact over time in relation to cultural, species and ecosystem diversity"[32]. The more serious threshold of human activity is the point when the natural regenerative capacity of the ecosystem is exceeded and ecological succession is halted as was beginning to happen by the late 19th century in Chotanagpur[33].

Similarly, while the argument for isolation is also not borne out by much of the 19th-century literature there is little doubt that distinctive cultures and ontologies were practised on the plateau. Many of these showed evidence of complex cultural exchanges from an early historical period distinguished by reciprocity not easily categorisable as Hinduisation or tribalisation. Valentine Ball in 1868 recorded ancient excavations, indicating human activity at the tops of the hills, in valleys, in the middle of cultivation and even in the thickest jungles of Chotanagpur. In Singhbhum, Colonel Tickell in 1840 noted the complex political economy of the region in the earlier periods and the fact that Singhbhum was in the hands of the Surawaks or Jains whose oppressions ended in their expulsion from the Kolhan[34]. O'Malley noted that in the ancient period the sravakas or lay Jains penetrated the jungles, where they were rewarded with the discovery of copper[35]. Dalton recorded in the 13th century that the north of the district came under the rule of the Singh family of Porahat, who claimed to be Rathor rajputs, whose ancestors were three brothers in the body guard of Akbar's general Man Singh who took the part of the Bhuiyas against the Hos and ended up conquering the country for themselves. At one time, the Singh rajas also ruled over the country now included in the states of Seraikela and Kharsawan and claimed suzereignity over the Kolhan, a claim which the Hos denied. According to Dalton, old Hos told him that they honoured and respected the Singh chiefs, but regarded them, until they quarrelled, rather as friends and allies than as rulers. Even if they ever were subjects they had achieved their liberty in various hard fought fields[36].

What is clear from these histories – many of them conjectural – is that the communities in Singhbhum and elsewhere were not in any sense 'isolated' but were constantly interacting with other groups from the north. However, one cannot simply reject of the notion of a cultural autonomy of, for example, the Hos in Singhbhum as some recent revisionist historians who record the complex process of migration and cultural transformation in Singhbhum and elsewhere have done[37]. As Stuart Hall has argued: "cultural identities come from somewhere, have histories. But far from being externally fixed in some essentialised past, they are subject to the continuous play of history, culture and power". Hall's argument, that identities are always about becoming as well as being, offers, it has been argued, a way out of the "impasse in which those who historicize the identities or traditions of others are accused of undermining political projects founded upon originary, perhaps essential truths"[38].

Indigenous agency and colonial discourse

Notwithstanding the rich and complex histories of acculturation and settlement of communities in Chotanagpur, colonial discourse tended to perpetuate stereotyped images of the tribe which had important implications. It is not surprising that racial and evolutionary ideas dominated given the global historical context and the dominance of racial ideas. It is important to note that, despite the often racial, evolutionary ideas of tribes, British attitudes towards indigenous peoples in India in the 19th century were not unchanging or homogenous. It is difficult in this chapter to completely unravel the multifarious skeins that made up British policy in the period. However, some main strands in the thinking of officials, administrators and anthropologists need to be identified in order to assess the overall impact of colonial interventions in the lifestyles of the 'tribes'.

The 19th century had seen the emergence of humanitarian sentiments about the future of aboriginal peoples. This trend in Victorian thinking developed in the 1830s with the Parliamentary Select Committee on Aborigines which was set up to inquire into

> the measures... to be adopted with respect to the native inhabitants of countries where British settlements are made, and to the neighbouring tribes, in order to secure them the due observation of justice and the protection of their rights, to promote the spread of civilisation among them, and to lead them to the peaceful and voluntary reception of the Christian religion[39].

Even among writers such as W.W. Hunter the ethnological vision of partnership between the colonial state and non-Aryan groups is evident. Throughout East Bengal, he noted "Santhals and other hill men may be found living apart from the Hindu's and preserving their national customs... patient of labour at home with nature, as pioneer cultivators, seasonal indigo workers, such people furnish the sinews by which English enterprise is carried on in Bengal"[40]. The Santhal in much of colonial ethnology functions as a sort of 'noble savage' with all its associated stereotypes. The idealised concept of the 'noble savage' was a counter to the most pejorative characterisations of foreign peoples as barbaric and fundamentally inferior. As David Brion Davis has plausibly speculated, the celebration of so-called primitives may well have partially weakened Europe's arrogant ethnocentrism and created at least a momentary imbalance about the human cost of civilisation. Yet as Muthu notes, as much as this may have helped to elicit the intellectual groundwork for the humanitarianism of anti-slavery thinking a rejection of noble savagery was necessary before a more meaningful and substantive moral commiseration with non-Europeans could develop. The peculiar understanding of the relationship between human nature and culture in noble savage writings yielded a virtually dehumanising exoticism despite the best intention of thinkers who chose to celebrate what they saw as the 'purely natural' specimens of humanity in the new world.

Despite this criticism, it was these ideas that allowed a nascent humanitarian discourse to develop in India about the position of tribes in the mid 19th century which we will discuss in a later section of the chapter. In order to understand this complex colonial discourse on tribes we will have to take into account indigenous agency and ideas of place.

I have noted the complex history of migration into Chotanagpur from a very early period rendering the whole idea of 'isolated' tribes questionable. What cannot be disputed however is the fact that that while many of these developments did lead to a complex acculturation process it gradually resulted in the spread of hierarchy and differentiation and the increasing loss of status of these communities. Increasing inroads by a money lending, landlord class gradually intensified the decline of these groups. The increasing marginalisation started in the pre-colonial period and was aided and abetted by the British in the 18th century. In the Ranchi region, by 1585, the Mughal empire succeeded in making inroads into the region and imposing revenue demands for the first time on Munda and Oraon village communities. On their failure to oblige, the king Durjan Sal was imprisoned by Jahangir in 1616 for twelve years. On his return to Chotanagpur Durjan Sal became progressively Hinduised and acquired a retinue of Brahmin priests and Rajput courtiers. These outsiders gradually attacked the Munda and Oraon communities imposing *rakumats* and cesses as they acquired *jagirdari* rights. The introduction of hordes of strangers into the country and the creation by the raja of a class of middlemen brought changes in the communal system of the majority of Mundari villages[41]. The system of service grants was an exotic idea introducing a class of *jagirdars* into the villages under various denominations such as *Bhaiyes, Baraik, Pandey, Jamadars*, *Ohdars* and so on. Gradually some Munda and Oraon settlements came under the onslaught of these new class of exploiters[42]. In Ranchi, the *Khuntkatti* nature of a number of villages hitherto held by the descendants of the original settlers in common ownership was beginning to be impaired and in some villages the tribesmen were reduced to the ranks of an agricultural labourer. In the *rajhas* lands the *jagirdars* and later the *thikadar* laid hold of some of the finest plots in the village and began to cultivate it through farm servants. Some of the Mundas appear to have retreated to the jungles further south rather than submit to such ruthless exploitation. Thus we hear of Gaasi Munda of the Purthu Kili then living in Hasa village not far from Khunti emigrating to the mountainous and jungly tract further to the south east and his descendants founded villages all around them, where the *Khuntkatti* system was still in full vigour at the time of the East India Company. It is clear that the social downgrading of these communities quickly followed military marginalisation by the Mughals in the 17th century. In the region of Singhbhum, the advent of outsiders had resulted in a growing unrest among the surrounding Ho population. Here, the interventions of East India Company in the 18th century unleashed other forces of change[43]. As the company got a foothold in Dhalbhum and started interfering in the affairs of the local zamindars with an eye to subduing them, local government in the region was severely weakened, though overall control of areas of areas such as Kuchang was given up as it was seen as encroaching on the rights of the independent raja of Mayurbanj[44]. However, in the following seventy years increasing inroads by an 'outsider class' resulted in growing unrest. The Kol rebellion of 1830 was the culmination of the period of change.

The period of the 18th century and certainly the 19th century had seen an invasive colonial policy in Chotanagpur in the interests of "good rule and government". The early incursions into the region had resulted in the formation of a district in about 1780 known as the Ramgarh Hill Tract, and magisterial courts were held first at Shergati to the north west of Hazaribagh. At Hazaribagh was stationed the local force of infantry under a European commander. At first there was only one officer who performed the duties of judge, magistrate and collector and the region was only gradually brought under the control of the British. The British had tried to enforce control through the local chief but by 1800 this policy was abandoned in favour of more direct control which was implemented militarily and the whole region was placed under the magistrate of Ramgarh in 1816 and the district was governed in accordance with ordinary regulations in force in Bengal. The effects were immediate and most visible in Tamar where the exploitation of Hindu moneylenders, whose activities were bolstered by colonial courts, resulted in widespread protests which continued unabated until the 1830s[45]. As the tribes were introduced to the idea of 'good government', they had to wend their way long distances to Shergati in land disputes which resulted from the seizure of Munda lands by Pathan money lenders[46].

When the courts failed to redress their grievances protest seemed the only answer. British administrative reports in the early 19th century show bewilderment at the hostility of the tribes to 'good government'. The commissioner of Circuit in 1830 reported colourfully on the Munda rebellions of 1830. They were, he noted:

> Restless, wild and furious... they rushed into an insurrection scarcely paralleled for ferocity. Eager for plunder and universally prone to inebriation and infuriated by real or imaginary wrongs, the whole population yielded to the unobstructed tide of rebellion – fire, rapine and murder marked their paths; nor was their vindictive spirit confined to those to whom their injuries were ascribed[47].

This was the language of savagery and rebellion that it has been argued helped in the "production of primitive places through their influence on images, ethnology and administrative policy"[48]. Elsewhere the language was subtly different as in this oft quoted statement of Bindrai Manki that figures in several reports on the 1830 rebellion:

> We complained to the raja of the *munshi* having sided with his father-in-law and deprived my wife of her chastity and of the Singh having forcibly taken and kept my sister. When we told the Raja our grievances we returned home. We four were subsequently sent four by Krishna Dewan who told us that as we were *Kols* we might do as we pleased, but be careful not to involve Raja Achet Singh in any difficulties in our conduct. We returned home. We returned home, invited all the kols our brethren and caste to assemble at the village inn where we had a consultation. The Pathans had taken our honour and the Singh our sisters and the Kuar Harnath Sahi had forcibly deprived us of our estate of twelve villages which he had given to the Singh. Our lives we considered of no value and being of one caste and brethren it was agreed that we should commence to cut, plunder, murder and eat. We said if any were hanged it would be us four. If any put in irons it would be we should be the four. We four should be answerable and if the gentleman sent for any it would be us, who were ready to submit to whatever might be the sentence. It is with this resolution that we have been murdering and plundering those who have deprived us of both honour and homes that committing such outrages our grievances would come to light and that if we had any master notice would be taken of them and justice rendered[49].

That these rebellions forced colonial policy to contend with 'indigenous' ideas of place and being is not in doubt. Native resistance to European land claims forced a recognition of Munda rights and highlighted the limits of colonial power. The process revealed the ambivalence of the colonial state and the "interaction of indigenous narratives of resistance with narratives of power"[50]. Some representations of rebellions also make the case for indigenous agency quite strongly. Here, we see a doctrine of human nature where the savages are bestowed with moral judgement, and a sharp sense of injustice which stands in contrast to ideas of the 'noble' or 'ignoble' savage. Through the conscious use of their will to transform their unhappy circumstances into a better social condition the tribes are seen as active agents of their own future. In these accounts which see 'tribes' as cultural beings, they are afforded more genuine respect as human

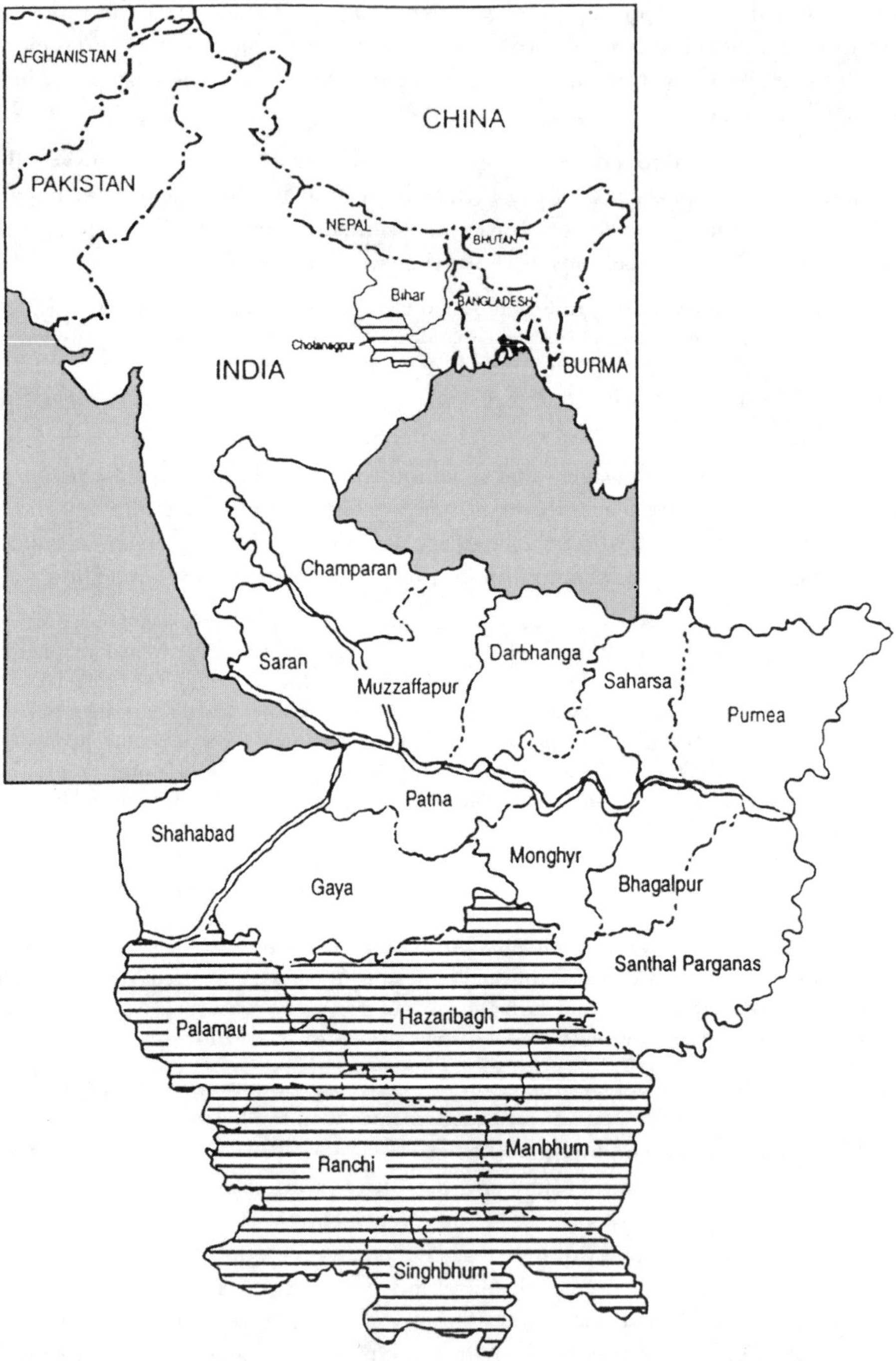

Fig. 1.
Chotanagpur.

beings, resulting in a critique of British imperial policy from within the system which is brutalising fellow human beings and destroying their culture.

In the context of the Munda and Santhal rebellions in Chotanagpur in the 1830s and 1850s these humanitarian sentiments found expression in the writing of administrators, missionaries and ethnologists of the time. One report in the aftermath of the Santhal rebellion of 1851 noted that "the Santhals were excessively simple and quite unacquainted with or unable to comprehend the most simple accounts and the mahajans and zamindars... take advantage of their defects of character in this respect by cheating them both in money transactions and arrangements for holding their land"[51]. While the repression of the rebellion was extreme, a growing perception of the plight of the 'indigenous' inhabitants who were threatened by the ruthless interventions of moneylenders from the plains and colonial institutions begins to become more evident in the writings of administrators from about the 1850s. It was reported that the "keen-eyed Hindu merchants from the north were quick to gauge the simple character of the primitive peoples"[52]. H. Ricketts, a member of the board of Revenue, noted in 1854 that "there seems reason to apprehend that the people of the district, the coles suffer much injustice at the hands of the foreign middleman introduced by the *raja*, their *zamindar*", while Davidson who studied the condition of the province in 1839 noted: "In point of fact there is no regular police or administration of justice in Nagpur till the present agency was established in 1834, that the coles are frequently imposed on by their landholders is not for want of comprehension, but they have been so long completely left to their mercies and so entirely deprived of any protection from them that it is difficult to resist". He further stated: "efficient administration in this part of the country will be impracticable until the rights of the people have been authoritatively recorded and steps been taken to secure them in the enjoyment of their rights by comprehensive legislative enhancement"[53]. In 1854 another fair minded official, Major Hannyngton, agent to the governor general in 1849 and the first district commissioner of Chotanagpur, in 1850 noted the ways in which *dikus* had tried to rob tribals of land, "in Chotanagpur, the *bhooi* has lands which exist in every village have been exposed to the rapacity of the middlemen, aliens who are hated by the people and who to obtain these lands, spare no species of force or fraud"[54].

This perspective of fair minded officers and commentators was to continue until the late 19th century when Birt noted that "the new-comers had under-rated the risk. The Kols and Oraons they so much despised were dangerous foes when pushed too far. Fire and sword struck terror into the hearts of *zamindars* and interlopers and taught the British government that special cases needed special laws and that a backward people at the mercy of unscrupulous adventurers called for timely assistance and protection"[55].

The sentiments expressed in this writing by Bradley-Birt in 1907 illustrates the different levels of thinking among British administrators in the latter half of the 19th century. That the tribes were 'backward' and 'primitive' was clearly felt. However, it was realised as early as the 1830s that the way of life of the indigenous inhabitants of Chotanagpur was being gravely threatened by the incursions of a Hindu landlord and money lending community aided by colonial institutions and bolstered by colonial law. The production of what has been called the colonial stereotype of the "simple innocent tribal people who needed protection from non tribal merchants and money lenders" had a basis in the existing reality of tribal oppression and found voice in indigenous narratives of resistance to such oppression. In the context of widespread rebellion and protest by the tribes these ideas were taken seriously by the administrators and significant attempts were made to make Chotanagpur a non-regulation province of Bengal and one where colonial institutions would function keeping in mind the different character and problems of the region.

Such a perspective allows us to move away from the revisionist view that colonial rulers were merely conjuring up tribes as 'isolated', 'difficult' and essentially 'different' to an understanding of the ways in which colonial rulers were forced to participate and engage with the land and its people and to contend with indigenous ideas of place and being. Many of those cited, Davidson, J.C. Hannyngton and Ricketts, between the 1830s and 1850s had tried to carefully document the history and land rights of local communities and were strongly critical of colonial courts and administration. As Ricketts noted: "It appears to me that the system existing is the most mischievous that could be followed, that any change would be for the better"[56].

The importance of resistance and the idea of Munda and Ho exclusiveness

After the Munda rebellion of 1830, the government put the entire province of Chotanagpur under the charge of an officer designated 'Agent to the Governor-General'. The first legislation implemented for Chotanagpur was the introduction of the "Wilkinson rules" under regulation 13 of 1833 which made Chotanagpur a non-regulation province of the South-West Frontier Agency after abolishing the military collectorship of Ramgarh Hill Tract[57].

In Singhbhum, the Munda rebellions helped the company in their 'expansionist goals' and a major portion of the territories of Porahat, Seraikela, Mayurbanj and Kharsawan were put together under the charge of a British officer and given the name Kolhan, 1955 sq. miles in all[58]. Major Wilkinson, the Governor General's Agent of the South West Frontier Agency recorded the reason for taking over these areas owing

> to the inability of the chiefs of the estates to keep control of the Lurkas... the strength and resources of the Kuar of Seraikella (being) exhausted by the constant necessity... to repel the attacks of the *coles*, that our Dak runners on the Bombay road throughout Baumghatty and from thence to Kutkurinjhea, will always be liable to interruption; and that many murders will be annually committed on suspicion of witchcraft[59].

In Kolhan, therefore the Kol rebellion had made it possible to render Ho exclusiveness a fact with the "amputation of the Ho tracts of the Kolhan" from Seraikella, Kharsawan and other Oriya states[60]. For the adminstration of justice, the district of Lohardugga was constituted as a centre for dispensing justice over 12,500 sq. miles. Wilkinson tried to pacify the tribes by granting the village headmen or Mundas and *mankis* of certain areas official documents confirming their title to the land and fixing the rent in perpetuity. But his reforms were based on a fundamental misunderstanding. As a result of this misunderstanding and the granting of land titles to village headmen, several villages fell into the hands of *diku* landlords for arrears of rent. British courts participated in this dispossession as Mundas of villages had no title deeds to their land and could not prove ownership in British courts[61]. As there was no proper record of rights, land grabbing by *dikus* in cahoots with the courts continued to an unparalleled degree. E. Dalton was to note in 1890 that "it was during the administration of the south western agency that the greatest disturbance of peasant proprietary tenure occurred"[62].

The agency administration was abolished under Act 20 of 1854 and the powers of the agency were vested in an officer appointed by the local government known as the 'Commissioner' who was placed under the Lieutenant Governor of Bengal. In 1869 the Chotanagpur Tenures Act was passed to redress some of the grievances of the peasantry[63]. One could say that the act was a case of too little too late. It recognised *Bhuinhari* tenures and as these lands were subject to such dispute the act was passed providing for the demarcation of such tenures and lands and the preparation of registers to record them with rights, privileges, immunities and liabilities affecting the holders thereof[64]. As a result of the *Bhuinhari* act the Lieutenant-Governor was empowered to appoint one or more persons as special commissioners to carry out the provisions of the act[65]. Each special commissioner was to investigate claims to the tenures and demarcate the lands, and then make for each village an accurate register of all the tenures. He was also authorised to restore to possession all persons or their heirs who had been wrongly dispossessed within two years of the passing of the act, and to enter their names as occupants of lands in the village register[66]. It is important to point out that while this act seemed specifically designed to end disputes at the village level, in practice it succeeded it restoring only very limited areas of land to the dispossessed tribals and did not demarcate all the traditional tenures. In fact it completely left out other tenures, in particular Mundari *Khuntkhatti* tenures. Thus, in examining the nature of the special laws on Chotanagpur we need to keep in mind the fact that they had a limited impact and did not dramatically change the predicament that the local people found themselves in.

It is interesting to note that these partial legislative attempts to check obvious exploitation by outsiders developed alongside the notion of 'civilising' the tribes. This was made most clear in the debate on shifting cultivation. Richard Temple, for example, argued strongly in favour of ending the practice of shifting cultivation. *Jhuming* was said to be wasteful and to threaten the jungles in the remoter parts. It was reported that the Kharia tribe of Dhalbhum who lived on fruits available from trees and jungle produce, raised a few precarious crops on patches of jungle which they cleared for the purpose by burning the trees. After reaping their harvest, they shifted to another area of jungle and returned to the same patch after 8-9 years. The language of settling and improving these groups was always in evidence[67].

It is also important to note that the legislative exercise of the latter half of the 19th century which was aimed to redress the most pressing grievances of the tribes in Chotanagpur did not fail to rouse debate on the merits of a policy that provided for an 'excluded' or 'partially excluded area'. Forsyth, the administrator of the Central Provinces, was vociferous in his criticism of colonial policy regarding these tracts. He proposed that the Mandla plateau, or *savannahs* as he called it, should be opened up for permanent cultivation. "We have here a tract eminently fitted to yield results from the application of European energy, intelligence, and capital to the supervision and direction of native labour... none but a capitalist can now practically occupy the waste lands so as to secure a legal proprietary title; and the aborigine never has such capital as would enable him to do so"[68]. Edward Dalton, the former commissioner of Chotanagpur, was of the opinion that the complicated machinery of civilised laws was unsuited to the backward tribes and that the government was "inclined to treat them with favour bordering on partiality"[69]. But the debate was won by those who believed in some form of protection for the tribes.

In the early part of the 20th century the Chotanagpur Tenancy Act of 1908 attempted further to define and record tenures and to "register... rights, privileges, immunities and liabilities affecting holders". This legislation, the reasons for which were given in a Bengal government resolution in 1880, aimed to put an end to disputes which had assumed "so chronic a character in connection with these special tenures". It is important to note that while the act recognized *Khuntkhattidar* rights it gave no privilege to *khuntkhattidars* to entitle them to retain possession against the wishes of the landlord. The limitations of the act could be clearly seen[70].

All this does not detract from the fact that some effort was made to record and protect customary rights by the colonial state. Often misjudged, but sometimes appropriate, the protection of these customary rights helped to institutionalise the fact of tribal autonomy. The move to protect these rights was fuelled by resistance movements of the 19th century, and by the fact that colonial administrators were forced to contend with indigenous knowledge and ideas of place. As I have noted, we thus need a more sophisticated understanding of colonial ethnography that takes into account various strands of thinking and the great variety of imperial agents involved in the process of colonisation. A whole generation of ethnologists and administrators in the nineteenth and early twentieth century had systematically studied 'tribal culture'. Starting with the work of Colonel Tickell and Ricketts in the 1840s and 50s to W.W. Hunter and E. Dalton in the late 19th century to S.C. Roy in 1910 the idea of a distinct tribal Munda, Ho or Oraon culture had been given textual force and meaning which was to be translated to legislative protection of sorts. S.C. Roy, the Indian anthropologist whose early work according to Sangeeta DasGupta followed in the footsteps of Victorian evolutionary anthropologists such as Tylor and Morgan, while continuing to describe Oraons in racial terms systematically mapped Oran culture through meticulous field work, becoming a champion of tribal protection and precursor to Verrier Elwin[71]. In his study of the Mundas and their country published in 1912 he is greatly interested in the land system of the Mundas and in recording their customary social and religious practices. In recording the folklore and songs of the Birsa Munda movement Roy gave legitimacy to the loss of dignity and economic injustice suffered by the Mundas. He noted how the Mundas had reacted against the interventions into their daily life and portrayed their dispossors as "men of mean blood". In their songs they pilloried them,

> owls pose as lords, the owls of low birth, struts the vain peacock in glory of plumage. Look how the crow rules as digaur over each village. Peacocks are grown great beings on earth. Rules the vile crow as kotwal all over. Now hath each village for *digaur* a crow. Mundas of hamlets now tremble and shiver. Terror supreme does reign the land over. Mundas of hamlets have lost their old cheer[72].

By recording these songs, Roy revealed the strong sense of fear and hatred by Mundas of outsiders. They were perceived as destroying the happy life style of the indigenous peoples and as a proud, vain and parasitical class imposing their administrative structures on hitherto autonomous Munda villages. In songs composed later in the 19th century the extent of the destruction is made more apparent and they talk of death and famine stalking the land as in *"horrible death from hunger prevails, oh! for the days when man knew no cares... woe to this age when men on earth below do daily die of famine"*. This was a reference to the results of dramatic changes brought by British land revenue policy and increasing emigration into the region of outsiders in the wake of colonial rule[73].

We also need to locate the work of administrators like Davidson, Hannyngton and Ricketts in the 1850s or ethnologists like S.C. Roy in 1900 and others within a broader framework of 19th century humanitarianism. In an important article, Alan Lester has argued that humanitarian ideology can be traced to the late 18th - early 19th century when a sense of responsibility for distant human suffering was created in western Europe when these societies became entwined within global networks of exchange and exploitation. He challenges the notion of a singular metropolitan centered colonial discourse and suggests instead a complex network of discursive exchanges in a globalised field[74]. In fact, the young science of ethnology owed its institutional origins to the humanitarian impulses embodied in the Aborigines Protection Society, founded in 1833 "to promote the spread of civilization and the protection of their rights". The 19th century, had seen the emergence of humanitarian sentiments about the future of aboriginal peoples. Stocking argues that in the period 1830-1870, the organisation and the ideology of empire were in a state of irresolution as humanitarians, colonists, colonial reformers and free traders pushed their respective concerns in the metropolitan political arena. This trend in Victorian thinking manifested itself in the 1830s with the Parliamentary Select Committee on Aborigines which was set up to inquire into "the measures... to be adopted with respect to the native inhabitants of countries where British settlements are made, and to the neighbouring tribes, in order to secure them the due observation of justice and the protection of their rights, to promote the spread of civilisation among them, and to lead them to the peaceful and voluntary reception of the Christian religion"[75]. The story of missionaries such as Hoffman and Leivens is important in this context.

Important new work is allowing us to reassess the work of missionaries. While it has been argued that from the start missionaries provided a more authoritarian instrument for the attempted control of indigenous communities in India and Africa, it is recently been argued that missionaries played an ambivalent role both in Britain's imperial expansion and in local power struggles. In a recent important work E. Elborne has shown that the religious 'conversation' between the missionary and his parishioners resembled more the ministrations of the Good Samaritan than a dichotomous clash of cultures. According to her, the London Missionary Society missionaries in South Africa were not simply cogs in the imperial wheel. She emphasizes the poverty, eccentricity, and alienation of the missionaries from their own European background. One lived in a windowless "straw hut... about 9 feet square", which the people had helped him build. Another frequently went shoeless for want of money to afford a new pair[76]. Many of them married Khoe women and these interracial marriages scandalized white settlers for many generations to come.

Similarly in India, missionaries were sometimes an important critic of colonial policy and attacked an indifferent or even greedy administration[77]. Along with the reverend J. Parry, A.F. Lacroix and J. Wenger and other colleagues with experience of work in other areas, James Long of the Church Missionary Society in Bengal was for example fiercely critical of the effects of the landlord or zamindary system. In the 1850s, referring to the case of Spain under Arab rule during the middle ages, he remarked that "there are certain stages in society when the government of enlightened foreigners is better for a nation than that of her own rude chieftains... the doctrine avowed in various quarters that India is to be ruled not for the benefit of the 200 millions, but in the interests of a few foreigners". And then again in 1856:

> The peasant has no real protection by law. It is a mere protection on paper... his spirit is cowed down by centuries of oppression and the courts are such a network of bribery, that the poor ryot never thinks of seeking redress. The zamindar tortures and imprisons him in order to extort the last anna from him... wherever I go I see grog shops authorised by the government for the peasant, but no schools for the peasant. The grog shop and the gallows are at present almost the only signs of interest the peasant sees the government take in him... compel by force of public opinion the Indian government to do something for the enlightenment of the masses[78].

In Chotanagpur, four missionaries of the Gossner Mission came to Ranchi in 1845. They were Germans who had been invited to preach in Chotanagpur by the first commissioner of Chotanagpur, J.C. Hannyngton. They had become acquainted with the 'kols' while in Calcutta where they came across "black children engaged in mean works like sweeping the roads and carrying the goods... the young missionaries were at once struck by these dark skinned, bright merry faced people, who presented in every way a marked contrast to the decidedly handsome, fair skinned indolent Bengalees and the rather martial looking up-country men"[79]. They settled in Ranchi in 1845 where progress was slow and "at the close of day of weary, fruitless toil they might have been seen again digging on their own little garden plots, to raise up a few vegetables for the supply of their common table or working with hatchet and plane squaring timber for their dwelling houses and schools with their own hands raising the walls, or laying on the roof of their godly church"[80]. As a result of their work, four Oraons were baptized in 1850 and the first church was founded; and two Mundas were baptized in 1851. The Anglican Mission established its work in Ranchi in 1869 and the Roman Catholic mission started work in Chotanagpur soon after. I will concentrate here on the work of the Jesuit mission which has a long and rich tradition of involving itself in tribal land struggles. It would be interesting to compare the work of the Protestant with the Catholic missions though this is outside the scope of this chapter. Work on Protestant missionaries elsewhere has argued for the close association of Protestantism with empire and the fact that Protestantism was an important element of the constitution of 'British' identity in the 19th century and as such helped to unify diverse communities. Jesuit radicalism on the other hand developed in Chotanagpur as an important critic of colonial state policy – a tradition that continues to this day.

The first Jesuit missionary in Chotanagpur, Stockman, settled in Chaibasa in 1869. The early Jesuits did not believe that they had to help the local people against oppression by landlords[81]. Until the 1880s they had few tribal converts. Between the years 1880-1885, more converts were made as a result of the efforts of Mullender who helped a few people in court cases in Bandgaon and Burudi[82]. In March 1885 with the arrival of Father Lievans, a young Jesuit missionary, things moved at a dramatic pace. He was given the charge of the whole area between Sarwada and Badagaon in the south and south west part of Munda territory. Leivens believed that ordinary preaching would not work given the growing crisis in the agrarian scene. He came to study and understand the traditional rights of the Mundas and began to develop a strategy to help them[83]. He believed that only a policy that would not unduly antagonise the government but invoke the power of its laws would work. He refused for this reason to have anything to do with the *sardari* agitation which he regarded as socialistic. He loaned money for poor tribals to hire lawyers and pointed out their rights to them[84]. It can be argued that by helping mainly Christians and getting entire villages to convert that Leiven's motives were primarily that of conversion. He may have been focussed on turning indigenous people into civilised Christians. However, equally important was the role of missions in the eyes of local communities as "vectors of contact" with the British imperial centre. In the southern African case Elbourne argues, that, "missionaries were sources of useful information about European technology, culture and religion. Such information could be used to protect societies against imperialist incursions, as much as, to internalise the dictates of cultural colonialism"[85].

Frequently Lievens travelled to the Ranchi court. At the Ranchi court he got his clients to meet lawyers and court employees, who according to a special arrangement took up the causes of the people for a moderate fee. Lievens himself supplied the magistrates with information regarding the many ways in which the villagers were being harassed. Exaggerated statements of false witnesses of the landlord party were detected in court. By December 1887, many of the lawsuits undertaken or contested on the missionaries advice were successful[86].

The number of converts seems to have increased rapidly. In September 1886, there were 200 followers. By October 1888 these had increased to 56,000. It has been argued that Mundas began to look at Catholicism as a society wherein they could be protected. It was believed, and this is in line with Elbourne's argument, that as the Jesuit missions were in the good books of the government, the people hoped that the missionaries would help win over the government to their side.

The landlords reacted by complaining to the government that the people were preparing for rebellion as a result of mission activities, were "illegally combining against the landlords by gathering in large numbers, carrying battle axes, cutting the rice of these gentlemen, refusing to work for them, preventing others from working, forcing people to become Christian, even rescuing people imprisoned by police and beating constables".

The commissioner of Chotnagpur sent two officials – Renny, the acting DC of Lohardugga, and Patch, the Superintendent of police – to investigate in 1889. Both blamed the missionaries for fomenting rebellion[87]. As a result of "the disgraceful and deceptive conduct of these missionaries a large number of tenants have become Christians and in consequence they have been doing lawless acts". Despite the fact that the missionaries had only a limited effect on the overall agrarian crisis, they were important critics of colonial policy towards tribes and perceived as such by administrators such as Renny and Patch.

By the 1890s the anger and resentment of the Mundas had erupted once again into the Munda rebellion. The rising was put down by the government, but it was renewed in 1899. Birsa was an ex Lutheran who put himself at the head of a new religion in which elements of Christianity were to be found. The risings were against the government, but there were also attacks against the missionaries. Thus the people, after trying various forms of adaptation, resorted once again to open rebellion. They seem to have felt that the government and the Christian missions had let them down. Limited agrarian legislation in the form of the Chotanagpur tenures act of 1869 extended only to the survey of *bhuinhari* (ancestral) lands and the *manjihas* tenures. No attempt was made to deal with the disputes about *rajhas* (ordinary raiyati) lands which comprised the great bulk of the cultivated area.

This was the context for the arrival of the next important missionary to involve himself with agrarian affairs in Chotanagpur, John Baptist Hoffmann, a German Jesuit who became a strident critic of colonial policy towards tribes. On his arrival, he viewed the local district commissioner, Gordon, in 1893 as a

> man of little intelligence, incapable and lazy, who because of his illustrious family connections was shifted from military to civil administration so that he could build a fortune. Because of his laziness in administration he left the whole job in the hands of his Bengali assistants. One of them a very clever man but bought by the zamindars so controlled him that out of all the cases brought to trial before him in five years he awarded all but one to the zamindars. He was extremely hostile to the missionaries and so ignorant of the state of the region that he said it was the tribals who were persecuting the zamindars rather than the other way around[88].

Hoffmann was perturbed by the anger and the hostility of the Mundas who were preparing under Birsa to launch their attack on the government and the missionaries by secretly plotting their rebellion in the hills and the forests. His writings clearly ascribe more agency to the communities whose unhappiness was fuelled by the neglect of grievances by the state. Birsa persuaded his followers that God had given him the task of liberating the tribals and instituting a new religion. Hoffman noted that the religious gatherings,

> gave a harmless appearance to the numerous *sardar* meetings in which the intended rising was settled without arousing any serious suspicions in either government or missions. It facilitated the gathering of about 6,000 armed men around Birsa in Chalkad in August 1895, after which it was announced that he would call fire from heaven to destroy the aliens... then a few young men who were still wavering between Christianity and the new religion came in and begged Hoffmann to leave immediately for Ranchi, because the very next morning the armed men with Birsa would start to massacre all the foreigners, adding that I as the nearest European to Chalkad was already designated as the first victim. Since I refused to move, they gave me up for lost and went away.

The Birsa movement forced missionaries such as Hoffmann to recognise the strength of local grievances and the inability of the colonial state to deal with the grievances of the communities. For tribal converts like Birsa then the reimagination of community through the use of invented and traditional symbols became more potent weapons than loyalist Christian discourse. It was in this context that the missionaries also came under attack because they were no longer 'vectors of contact' with the British imperial centre. In this past these connections with the missionaries had helped to challenge in a limited way the overwhelming incursions of the colonial state and the zamindars. Hoffmann was deeply aware of the social and economic problems in Chotanagpur and gradually evolved a strategy to rectify legally through the laws the injustice done to the Mundas by zamindars, thikadars and moneylenders. His years in the Serwada mission were to make him a great missionary, a philologist, anthropologist and social reformer[89]. Hoffmann seized the opportunity to propose to the government, through the commissioner, a scheme for amending the laws, because as he had said so often concerning the rebellion, many of the complaints of the tribals were just. Hoffmann's detailed research into the Munda land system was consulted by Lister during the survey and settlement operations in 1902.

In August 1899 when Sir John Woodburn the Lieutenant-Governor of Bengal visited Ranchi, the question of the settlement operations came up again. As J. Reid noted, the discussions regarding the bill to consolidate the law of landlord and tenant in 1899 showed clearly that there was a considerable divergence of opinion regarding local customary agrarian rights and customs and a record of these rights and customs was evidently necessary to supply the data for agrarian legislation. The Lieutenant Governor, in the first place, considered it inadvisable to proceed with the bill, because after the Birsa movement, the Mundas were seen as still being very disturbed; secondly he thought that until the record of rights for the whole district was prepared, it was difficult to say what provisions of law were suitable for Chotanagpur.

The Lieutenant-Governor had sought advice of the local officials, zamindars and missionaries. He was afraid that the proposed law would give rise to quarrels between the zamindars and the tribals and rebellion. Hoffmann tried to argue that codification and land measurement were the only way of preventing a rebellion. Streatfield, the judicial commissioner, and Taylor were of the opinion that until a survey and a record of rights were undertaken, at least in Munda country, disaffection and discontent will continue. On 2 February 1902, the government of India sanctioned the inception of the survey and settlement operations, beginning with the Munda country and eventually extending to the whole of the district. The government of India undertook to bear 1/4 of the cost and the remaining 3/4 was supposed to be borne by zamindars and tenants. The correspondence and control with regard to the survey and settlement operations were referred to Lister the settlement officer and John Reid director of land record.

The survey operations began on 8 March 1902 in the police stations of Khunti and Tamar under Lister. When it was carried out Hoffmann was at Sarwada. He was closely associated with Lister in this important work, so that many provisions in the Act that relate to the aborigines were the draft of father Hoffmann himself. It is recorded that Lister and Hoffmann talked far into the night with Hoffmann rendering valuable assistance to Lister with regard to the Munda land system and local customs. Tete notes that it was Hoffmann who drafted the special laws in connection with Mundari *Khuntkhatti* which appeared in appendix one of the Chotanagpur Tenancy Act of 1908. As Hoffmann noted,

> It is no exaggeration to say that the state of insecurity of nearly all kinds of tenures and titles to possession was so universal as to seriously depreciate the value of lands and cripple agriculture. This insecurity was not limited to the raiyats holdings, but extended to the zamindar's as well. So much so that it was common belief that any man with a little audacity and a little money might take possession of what lands he pleased. The courts, having little or noting to go upon but oral evidence were in practice not merely powerless, but were in a way bound to assist rather than to check spoliation. This I know is a startling statement... consider how legal records of tribal rights and customs in the absence of all legally fixed and demarcated boundaries of villages as well as fields, among an ignorant people, who could neither understand the court language, nor make themselves understood except through interpreters, how easy it was I say in these circumstances for them to prove in court any claim they might choose to make. In their bewilderment and despair, the aborigines were driven to attempts at risings and in fact always lived in a state of disaffection. In such a state of affairs, a general settlement was a necessity. Now that it has been completed, it has, in the course of years furnished the plainest proof of its importance and utility[90].

In 1908 the Chotanagpur Tenancy Act was passed with the aim to "supersede and consolidate the Act in force in Chotanagpur... to improve the procedure... to complete and improve substantive law, by embodying in it certain necessary provisions borrowed from the Bengal Tenancy Act of 1897 in connection with praedial dues and services. The government had been forced to make a survey of *khuntkhatt*i in order to bring out peace and tranquillity among the Mundas in particular and in Chotanagpur in general. But it was felt that the survey was not enough to secure this finality; it was also necessary to protect the Mundas in their possession of the land. Hence the restrictions that were embodied in the Chotanagpur Tenancy Act. Legal provisions were made within the act to protect Mundari *khuntkhatti*. It could not be transferred by sale except in special circumstances. In other words, where the record of rights had been prepared, a suit for the recovery of rent was not maintainable in any court unless it was sanctioned by the zamindar. If he refused the sale he had the right to liquidate the arrears of rents. A mortgage of any Mundari *khuntkhatti* was prohibited. Bhugut bhanda was allowed but was not supposed to exceed seven years"[91]. No transfer of a Mundari *Khuntkhatti* was valid unless in accordance with the provisions of the Act.

The Chotanagpur Tenancy Act aimed to amend the laws and codify them according to custom and usage. However, when the act came into force there were only 156 villages registered as having full Mundari *khuntkhatti* rights and 203 sq. miles as *bhuinhari* fields. It was found that out of 3614 sq miles of cultivated land only 405 sq. miles were registered as ancestral property. From this we can say that the Act came too late. However, it had great significance for the Mundas as it recognised the Munda land system itself, for which they had been struggling for more than a 100 years. Hoffmann himself was optimistic about the impact of the Act;

> for more than a hundred years the Mundas were calumniated as savages or semi-savages, whose claims were too exorbitant and absurd to be listened to as stubborn rebels whom nobody could satisfy and therefore justly subjected to severe military reprisals as the Kols who were fit for nothing, but carrying burdens and being serfs. And now after a cruel martyrdom that has lasted all too long, their claims have been recognised officially as having been perfectly right and their land system appears as one of the wisest creations of pre-historic times. So after all they are neither savages nor semi-savages, but a race of martyrs most deserving of the sympathy and respect of all right minded men. Therefore the Act is a justification and a rehabilitation of the highest moral value[92].

Hoffmann clearly followed the tradition of Lievens who preceded him. But he also promoted a method of dialogue with the government officials and persuaded them to protect the rights of the tribals. For him personally this was a rewarding exercise for as he noted:

> Thus the settlement literally resembled a calm sunny morning after a long destructive hurricane, which had reduced all the Mundas to extreme poverty and had thrown hundreds of thousands far away from their own dear country. For those remaining it brought peace and security. To me, who had been forced to witness and feel horrid sufferings of the Mundas for many years, it afforded one of the greatest joys of my life[93].

The discourse of tribal protection was to come to full term in the debates around the statutory commission in the 1920s.

Protectionist policy further enshrined

When the Indian Statutory Commission visited India in 1928, the various provincial governments submitted their memoranda and their proposal for further changes. The Bihar government, reporting on the Backward Tracts, agreed that protection for the tribes was still needed. However, as the Statutory Commission noted, some members were anxious that careful enquiries should be undertaken to determine whether it was "possible to make some further advance in dispensing with special forms of protection then in force"[94]. The commissioners, therefore, concluded that the Backward Tracts, with one or two exceptions, must be excluded from the general constitutional arrangements and that "special provision must be made for their administration". They also suggested that the Backward Tracts were to be called 'excluded areas'. Their grounds for the exclusion of these territories were that "the stage of development reached by the inhabitants prevented the possibility of applying to them methods of representation adopted elsewhere" and that the people wanted freedom for the "reasonable exercise of their ancestral customs, freedom in the pursuit of their traditional methods of livelihood and security of land tenure. Their contentment does not depend so much on rapid political advance as on experienced and sympathetic handling, and on protection from economic subjugation by their neighbours". For financial reasons and the nature of the suggested provincial government, they came to the conclusion that the responsibility for the administration of these tracts should rest on the central government.

The commission further distinguished the tracts into those wholly excluded and those not wholly excluded. The Assam tracts belonged to the first category while Chotanagpur, Sambalpur, the Santhal Parganas and the Madras Agency Tracts belonged to the latter. These partially excluded tracts were to return representatives to the provincial legislatures and the revenues raised within their borders were to be spent on them, additional funds being allocated by the central government. The governor as the agent of the governor-general in council, was to administer the tracts with some latitude allowed to him by the rules to act in consultation with other ministers. The wholly excluded tracts were to be administered by the governor general in council using the agency of the governors. In the Federal Assembly the inhabitants of the excluded areas were to be represented through nomination by the governor general. They were to be eleven in a house of 250 to 280 members. It must be noted that the political exclusion of these areas was justified on the grounds of "the stage of development reached by the inhabitants".

In the succeeding decades the debate on these issues was to grow stronger. Under Gandhi the movement for political representation for Indians had reached new heights. The 1920s and 1930s had seen a sharpening of the national struggle and in Bihar the Congress succeeded in mobilising large sections of the population to the movement. In Chotanagpur, Congress activities had resulted in popularising the name of the party in an area which was hitherto quite remote. In the neighbouring Central Provinces the Congress, by taking up issues relevant to the Gonds, such as the movement against forest laws, enabled the civil disobedience movement in the region to achieve substantial success. There was a growing belief among the nationalist intelligentsia that the British policy of exclusion was intended to render these areas immune to the political activities of the Congress. In the discussion in the House of Commons on the provisions of the Government of India Bill of 1935 these issues came to a head. In the discussion on section 92 of the act which provided for the governor's special powers Wedgwood pointed out that more tribes should be protected. He noted that "all that was required was that for another twenty or thirty years we should have an administration by anthropologists and people whose whole trend is to preserve and develop all that is best in these native tribes". He was against any policy that would allow them to be governed by educated Indians who merely wanted to exploit them and "get them as cheap labour"[95].

Mr Clement Attlee, who was another signatory to the report of the Indian Statutary Commission, supported the amendment for enlarging the schedule. The people in these areas needed to be specially treated or they would be exploited. He also pointed out that these backward areas should be directly administered by Europeans or by Indians only under European supervision. The parliamentary debate on the excluded areas highlighted the significance of the colonial discourse on tribes in the 1930s. At one level there was a perception that the influx of outsiders into the hitherto remote regions inhabited by the 'indigenous' people had led to serious exploitation and alienation of tribal lands. Colonial institutions had aided and abetted this exploitation and the legislative measures that were introduced in the 19th century to slow the pace of change had addressed the problem only partially. These measures were given constitutional status under the 1919 act and the 1935 Government of India Act. The Government of India (Excluded and partially excluded areas) Order, 1936 stated that as regards these areas the Governor "shall exercise his functions at his discretion". Under section 92 of the Government of India Act, no act of the federal or the provincial legislature applied to the excluded or to a partially excluded area unless the governor directed its application by notification. At another level there was recognition that the creation of these excluded and partially excluded areas strengthened the powers of the British crown as these areas were directly adminstered by the centre[96]. In the context of the devolution of power to Indians under the 1935 Government of India act, the benefits of such an exclusion for colonial policy were enormous.

The policy of exclusion in effect meant excluding Indians from administering these areas which could be adminstered in the "interests of the indigenous inhabitants only by Europeans"[97].

An examination of the colonial discourse on tribes thus reveals that views on the assimilation and civilisation of 'backward peoples' which had been vehemently expressed in the early and mid-nineteenth century were giving way to more humanistic considerations which started to be expressed in the middle and latter half of the nineteenth century in the reports of fair minded officers, missionaries and through special legislation. By the 1930s these debates had culminated in the Excluded Areas Order which went some way to protecting the tribal communities. By the 1950s, the debates in the Constituent Assembly and the Report of the Thakkar commission further ensured that this legislation was to remain in force in the constitution of the newly created Indian State[98].

Notes

1 Such a post modern reading of colonial narratives of a place and its people tends to establish an easy coincidence between an aesthetic appreciation of the landscape, geographical science and colonial ap-

propriation. That maps were a fundamental tool of colonial conquest cannot be denied but that the trope of conquest was wholly accepted by natural historians, scientists, artists and other imperial agents is more difficult to establish. To see all colonial images as constitutive of the colonial identity of India and as part of the regime of colonial control does not allow for individual agency to emerge and tends as Dane Kennedy notes to "essentialise the west as an undifferentiated, omnipotent entity... imposing its totalising discourse on the rest of the world without check or interruption... a discursive practice no less distorting than the west's tendency to essentialise the orient". See D. Kennedy, *Imperial history and post colonial history*, "Journal of Imperial and commonwealth History", 24, 1996, p. 3.

2 N.L. Peluso, *Fruit trees and family trees in an anthropogenic forest: ethics of access, property zones and environmental change in Indonesia*, "Comparative studies in society and history", 38, 3, 1996, pp. 510-548; and *Genealogies of the political forest and customary rights in Indonesia, Malaysia and Thailand*, "Journal of Asian Studies", 60, 3, 2001, pp. 761-812.

3 J. Bodley, *Comment*, in Th. Headland, *Revisionism in ecological anthropology*, "Current Anthropology", 18, 4, 1997, pp. 611-613.

4 C. Bayly, *Indian society and the making of the British empire*, Cambridge 1988.

5 Brahamanical theories of society that had long been propounded in the ancient centres of Hindu scholarship became, more widely influential, with the growing power of Brahmin ritual in the seventeenth and eighteenth centuries. As the surrounding Hindu caste society became less mobile and more codified under colonial institutions, these older images of the tribes received a new impetus. In Guha's work, he himself notes that in western India, little trace could be seen in the more modern epigraphs of Bhar chiefs, the Tharu gentry or Bhil kinglets. Social downgrading quickly followed military marginalisation and the turn of the eighteenth century saw severe Maratha reprisals against the Bhils in Khandesh What needs to be examined more carefully therefore, is the way in which, Brahamanical and Kshatriya values seemed to acquire a more exclusive dominance. As Rosalind O'Hanlon notes, citing Christopher Bayly, "what brought these Brahmanical values into wider currency was not some extraordinary piece of colonial conjuring. It was rather a complex set of processes to which British and Indian alike contributed, and some of which, such as, the association of Brahmins with newer pre-colonial dynasties were already in train during the seventeenth and eighteenth centuries". With the emergence of a more settled and homogenous peasant society and the increased pressure on land, the exclusion of potential competitors became a more appropriate strategy. She argues that "where the British did contribute to the processes it was to stimulate them indirectly, in their project for the classification of castes, in their production of new regional histories and in their enshrining of what was in effect Brahamanical precept and custom as law within the anglo-Indian judicial system". See R. O'Hanlon, *Cultures of rule, communities of resistance: gender discourse and tradition in recent South Asian historiographies*, "Social analysis", 25, 1914, pp. 94-114.

6 Notions of cultural primitivism in Europe can be traced back to classical Greece and Rome. Similarly it can be seen that Brahmanical attitudes towards the other were constructed over time. However, this is not to say that the images were unchanging. See G. Boas - A. Lovejoy, *Essays on primitivism and related ideas, in Antiquity*, Baltimore 1935.

7 T. Trautmann, *The Aryans in British India*, California 1997, p. 214.

8 Roy's analysis of the Mundas is based on the premise of the Aryan invasion of India a topic that is still debated. He notes for example, that in the course of their migration across India, the Mundas and the Oraons along with other non Aryan tribes encountered the wave of Aryan immigration. Accounts of this encounter between the advancing Aryan races and the retreating non Aryan tribes abound in ancient Sanskrit literature. The Rigveda Samihita of the Aryan victors tells us of numerous conflicts of the invading Aryan warriers and the despised Dasyus. According to Mundari tradition the Mundas appear to have migrated from northern India southwards to modern Bhundelkhand and central India and then across eastern Rajputana back again to north western India and then through modern Rohilkhand and Oudh to Berar and finally Chotanagpur. In the course of their retreat they met with and were

characterised as demons by the Aryans in their literature. S.C. Roy argued that among the names of the hostile Dasyu leaders are a few bearing a close resemblance to the names still in use among the Mundas. Ancient sanskrit literature is replete with encounters between the invading Aryans and the indigenous Dasyus. Hermits living in the forests of Bhundelkand where the Mundas resided for a time in the course of their migration complained to Ram Chandra of Ayodhya who visited here during his exile of the harassment of the Anarya savages. Their descriptions of the non-Aryan races are recorded as important. "Men-devouring rakshas of various shapes and wild beasts, (or serpents) which feed on blood, dwell in this vast forest. They harass the devotees who reside in the settlements and slay them in the forest. Repress them, Raghava". The Rishis go on to describe these black denizens of the woods as "shapeless and ill looking monsters", "anarya wretches uttering frightful sounds". And Rama is warned that it is not expedient for him to wander alone with Sita in the neighbourhood of these cruel Rakshasas, for though he is indeed able to destroy them, he should not be too confident, for they are a treacherous race. In the account of the Kuru Panchala war in the Mahabharata the description of the Kaurava army names the Mundas and they are compared to demons. The Aryan warrior Satyaki boasts "I shall kill these Mundas even as Indra killed the Danavas. The Mundas ranged themselves on the side of the Kurus against the army led by Krishna the great foe of the non-Aryan races. It was Krishna who slew the asuras Pitha and Mura and the rakshasa Ogha". See S.C.Roy, *Mundas and their country*, Calcutta 1912.

9 R. Thapar, *The theory of Aryan race and India: History and Politics*, in Id., *Cultural Pasts. Essays in Early Indian History*, Delhi 2000, pp. 1134-1135.

10 S.C. Roy records that in 1915 Oraons still remembered being called Raona put by their Hindu neighbours. Roy, *The Mundas and their country* cit.

11 I. Kopytoff, *The African Frontier: The Reproduction of Traditional African Societies*, Indiana 1987.

12 G.W. Stocking Jr., *Victorian Anthropology*, London 1987, p. 9.

13 Stocking, *Victorian Anthropology* cit., p. 142.

14 Darwin for example argued in the decent of man that he would rather descend from a heroic monkey than a negro savage. Cf. C. Darwin, *The descent of man*, New York 1871.

15 C.M. Hinsley, *Zunis and Brahmins, cultural ambivalence in the gilded age*, in G.W. Stocking (ed.), *Romantic motives, essays on anthropological sensibility*, Madison 1996, p. 170.

16 Stocking, *Victorian Anthropology* cit., p. 80.

17 *Ibid.*, p. 185.

18 B. Anderson, *Imagined communities, Reflections on the Origin and Spread of Nationalism*, New York 1983.

19 Maine had hoped to render available for the use of scientific men in Europe "the large body of barbarous or semi-barbarous custom both Aryan and non-Aryan which still survives in India" quoted in E. Dalton, *Descriptive ethnology of Bengal*, Calcutta 1872.

20 *Ibid.*, p. 1.

21 J. Falconer, *Ethnographical Photography in India 1850-1900*, "Photographic Collector" 5(1), 1984, pp. 16-46.

22 *Ibid.*

23 W.W. Hunter, *The annals of rural Bengal*, Calcutta 1897, pp. 29, 114.

24 District Gazetteer of Manbhum, p. 79.

25 A. Von Humboldt similarly talked of the native americans by proclaiming "that a savage landscape produces a savage mind". Id. *Personal narrative of travels to the equinoctial regions of America 1799-1804*, London 1908.

26 F. Zimmermann, *The jungle and the aroma of meats, the ecological theme in Hindu medicine*, Delhi 1999.

27 K. Shivaramakrishnan, *Modern Forests, state making and environmental change in colonial eastern India*, Stanford 2002.

28 Roy, *The Mundas and their country* cit.

29 In the last stage of their journey the Oraons went up the valley of the Koel which fell into the Son not far from Rohtasgarh and finally entered Chotanagpur plateau. On their way, they passed through vast jungles, where with the help of iron tipped arrows they secured plenty of game for their food. When they reached Chotanagpur they found the Mundas already in occupation of the country.

30 There are of course important qualifications to be made, which many revisionists ignore. As Leslie Sponsel argues, the speculation that humans have had an impact on the ecosystem for millenia must be tempered by other considerations.For example, 1/3 of the land of the planet is may be termed 'wilderness', and while 12% of the interior forest of the Brazilian Amazon is anthropogenic, 88% is certainly not by any definition. Quoted in Headland, *Comment* cit., p. 621.

31 C.K. Yoon, *Rain forests seen as shaped by human hand*, in Headland, *Revisionism in ecological anthropology* cit., p. 608.

32 L. Sponsel, *Comment*, in Headland, *Revisionism in ecological anthropology* cit.

33 *Ibid*., p. 621.

34 S.R. Tickell, *Memoir on the hodesum*, "The Journal of the Asiatic society of Bengal", IX, 9, 1840, p. 690.

35 L.S.S. O'Malley, *Bengal district Gazetteers,* vol. XX, p. 25.

36 *Ibid*., p. 26.

37 T.N.N. Singh Deo, *Singhbhum - Seraikella - Kharsawan, Through the ages*, Calcutta 1940, p. 41; more recently see the work of A.K. Sen, *Text and beyond Text; essays on the history of the Ho of Singhbhum during colonial rule* (unpublished manuscript).

38 S. Hall quoted in T. Murray Li, *Environment, indigeniety and transnationalism*, in M.J. Watts - R. Peet (eds.), *Liberation ecologies*, London 1996, pp. 342-343.

39 Stocking, *Victorian Anthropology* cit., p. 241.

40 S. Muthu, *Enlightenment against Empire*, Princeton 2003.

41 See J.A. Reid, *Final report on the survey and settlement operations in Ranchi, 1902-1910,* Calcutta 1912, p. 129.

42 It needs to be pointed out that the incursions by an outsider class was made possible in a context where older images of the Mundas, Oraons and Hos as inferior received a new lease on life. These formed the basis of increased interventions into tribal society. Brahmanical theories on society became more widely influential with the growing power of Brahmin ritual in the 17th and 18th centuries. As the surrounding Hindu caste society became less mobile and more codified under colonial institutions these old images of the tribes received a new impetus. Migration of plains Hindus into the area increased, and the interventions of a new outsider class and of the colonial state became more invasive. It was in this context that colonial epistemology lined up with Brahmanical knowledge resulting in the depoliticisation and emasculation of the adivasi communities. The process by which the sub-continent was gradually domesticated by Brahmanic thought and practice has only recently become a subject of scholarship. This process was a very complex and gradual one but its effects on the tribes and their way of life was catastrophic. The upper caste Hindus were contemptuous of the tribes and this can be seen by the names that they were called them by in the 18th and 19th centuries. The name Kol which was applied indiscriminately to both the Oraons and the Mundas by the Hindu immigrants into Chotanagpur was a pejorative appellation. Oraon labourers were called Danghars as they became the first members of the group that Hindus came into contact with. The Danghars were considered impure as unconverted Mlecchas. Oraon laboureres interviewed by S.C. Roy in 1915 recorded being called as *Ravana put* or the sons of Ravana by their Hindu neighbours. See Roy, *The Mundas and their country* cit.

43 See Reid, *Final report* cit.

44 L.S.S. O'Malley, *Bengal district Gazetteers*, Calcutta 1914, p. 29.

45 See file on Tamar disturbances, *Hazaribagh District Collectorate Records*, 1819.

46 Report of the Munda rebellions in the 1830s in Dalton's, *Ethnology of Bengal* cit.

47 F.B. Bradley-Birt, *Chota Nagpur: a Little Known Province of the Empire*, reprint: first published in 1903, p. 21.

48 Shivaramakrishnan, *Modern Forests* cit.

49 Cited in Roy, *The Mundas* cit., p. 201.

50 *Ibid.*

51 Letter 184 of 1857, Hazaribagh District Collectorate Records, 1856-57.

52 Bradley Birt, *Chota Nagpur: a little known province of the British Empire* cit., p. 5.

53 *Ibid.*

54 Cited by H. Ricketts in *Selections from the records of the Bengal government*, no. XX, Calcutta 1855, pp. 14-15.

55 *Ibid.*, p. 6.

56 *Ibid.*, p. 10.

57 Regulation XIII of 1833 exempted certain areas, among them Chotanagpur from the regulations and placed them under special new rules for the administration of civil and criminal justice and for the superintendence of police, land revenue etc.

58 Singh Deo, *Singhbhum* cit., p. 47.

59 Major T.S. Wilkinson, no 36 to RD Mangles, ESQ Secretary to Government, Fort William, 22 August 1836.

60 See criticism of this position, Singh Deo, *Singhbhum* cit. According to one historian, K. Sahu, the British introduced a system of administration that consolidated its grip over the Kolhan. In this way, the Kolhan became politically and administratively part of the Indian empire. He notes that the attempt of the British to prevent land alienation was caused by the growing problem of dikku penetration. "The policy was praise worthy inasmuch as without this the entire tribal community would have been swept away by the Diku influx". See K. Sahu, *The Kolhan under the British rule*, Calcutta 1985.

61 J.B. Hoffmann, *Encyclopaedia Mundarica*, vol. VIII, Calcutta 1906, p. 2400.

62 Sahu, *The Kolhan* cit.

63 The operations under the Act though successful to some extent in the areas in which they were carried out were a mere palliative of the disorders. There was a failure to even define *bhuinhari* or *Khuntkhatti* which was perpetuated when the rent act of 1879 was enacted. The provisions related to *bhuinhari* and khuntkhatti; "no lands known as bhuinhari or *khuntkhatti* shall be liable to any enhancement of the rent previously paid by him for such lands unless it be shown that the tenure has been shown before the institution of the suit to enhance rent of said lands and when the enhancement of the rent of such tenures is decreed the rent assessed shall not exceed one half of the rent paid by the ordinary raiyats with a right of occupancy in the same class of land with similar advantages". Local courts were said to be in ignorance of local customary rights attached to this class of tenancy and failed to give effect to these provisions. The provisions of the law were in fact disregarded until Lester started the settlement operations in Munda country and rediscovered that one of the most common tenures in that part of the country that was been excluded from the scope of the *bhuinhari* survey was *Khuntkhatti* tenure.

64 Bhuinhari tenures were those which were reclaimed and held by persons claiming to be descendants of the original founders of the village in which such lands were situated.

65 Only one special commissioner was appointed: Rakhal Das Haldar, a Calcutta barrister. Roy notes that

the investigations began on 1 April, 1869 and went on until 31 March, 1880, *The Mundas and their country* cit., pp. 272-273.

66 The Chota Nagpur Tenancy Act, 1908, pp. 22-23.

67 In the Central Provinces the activities of the shifting cultivators was criticized with vigour. Forsyth reported "the Byga (Baiga) is the most terrible enemy to the forests we have anywhere in these hills. Thousands of square miles of sal (shorea robusta) forest have been clean destroyed by them in the progress of their cultivation... in addition to this, the largest trees have everywhere been girdled by them to allow the gum resin of the sal to exude... the improvident wild man will cut down the whole tree to save himself the trouble of climbing". The fact that much of the destruction of the forest resulted from the activities of merchant capital and the opening up of the region by railways was mentioned by many of the settlement officers only in passing. See J. Forsyth, *The highlands of central India,* London 1871, pp. 96, 364, 367.

68 *Ibid.*, p. 163.

69 Dalton, *Descriptive ethnology of Bengal* cit., p. 3.

70 The Chotanagpur Tenancy Act, 1908.

71 S. DasGupta, *The journey of an anthropologist in Chotanagpur,* "Indian economic and social history review", 41, 2, 2004, pp. 165-198. DasGupta could usefully develop this aspect of Roy's work more elaborately.

72 Roy, *Mundas and their country* cit.

73 In this context, we can note that revisionist writers like Guha may be right in arguing as they do in the case of western India that the Bhils and the Kolis were not "isolated remnant populations savagely defending themselves against encroaching civilisation rather they were deeply integrated into the political economy of medieval India". However, the declining status of groups like those of the Mundas, Hos and Oraons in the eighteenth and nineteenth centuries, the force of their resistance and the processes involved in their proletarianisation needs to be the focus of much more analysis. Despite the validity of Guha's thesis for western India that "the wanderers may settle and the settled wander; forests might be cleared and forests grow, ploughshares might be beaten into swords and vice versa" the problem remains of explaining the spread of principles of hierarchy and real differentiation. While the evolution of Munda and Ho identity did not occur in complete isolation from developments outside Chotanagpur, the complex historical and political processes resulting in the creation of their identity does need to be delineated and explained historically. The history both of acculturation and resistance to outside cultural and economic agency is vitally important, in understanding identity formation and ideas of difference. But in defining the terms of this historical development of difference. the intervening agency of tribal communities needs to be taken more into account. Furthermore, nineteenth century preoccupations with caste and tribe need to be understood in terms of continuity with pre-colonial Brahmanic and Kshatriya precepts and traditions. Munda and Ho resistance to colonial policy is an important part of the story of identity formation and one that is neglected by revisionists.

74 A. Lester, *Observing the due observance of justice: the geographies of colonial humanitarianism*, "Environment and planning: society and space 2002", vol. XX, p. 277.

75 Stocking, *Victorian Anthropology* cit., p. 241.

76 E. Elbourne, *Blood ground, colonialism, missions and the contest for Christianity, 1799-1853*, Montreal 2002, p. 214.

77 See P. Anderson - S. Ross, *Christian missionaries and orientalist discourse*, in R.E. Frykenberg (ed.), *Christians and missionaries in India*, London 2003, p. 313.

78 G. Oddie, *Missionaries, rebellion and proto nationalism, James Long of Bengal, 1814-87*, London 1999, p. 183.

79 See A. Nottrott, *The Gossner mission under the kols and Chatterton, the story of fifty years mission in Chotanagpur*, cited in S. Mahato, *A hundred years of Christian missions in Chotanagpur, since 1845*, p. 21.

80 *Ibid.* p. 29.

81 F. De Sa, *Crisis in Chotanagpur*, Bangalore 1975, p. 117.

82 P. Tete, *The kharias and the history of the catholic church in Biru*, Armidale 1990, p. 61.

83 *Ibid.*, p. 66-67.

84 De Sa, *Crisis in Chotanagput* cit., p. 124-25.

85 Elbourne, *Blood Ground* cit., p. 13.

86 Tete, *The history of the Catholic Church in Biru* cit., p. 78-79.

87 De Sa, *Crisis in Chotanagput* cit., p. 207.

88 P. Tete, *A missionary social worker in India*, Rome 1984, p. 29.

89 *Ibid.*, p. 46.

90 J.B. Hoffmann, cited by J. Reid, *Survey and settlement operations in Ranchi*, Calcutta 1912.

91 This was the transfer of interest of tenancy for the purpose of securing payment of money advanced or to be advanced by way of loan, upon the condition that the loan with all interest thereon shall be deemed to be extinguished by the profits arising from the tenancy during the period of the mortgage. J. Reid, *The Chotanagpur Tenancy Act* (1910).

92 Hoffmann, *Encyclopaedia Mundarica* cit., p. 2402.

93 *Ibid.*, pp. 2403-2404.

94 Report of the Indian Statutory Commission, vol. XII, p. 361.

95 Parliamentary Debates, 5th series, vol. 299, cols. 1550, 1548, 1549; vol. 301, col. 1418.

96 The excluded areas proposed were (I) the north east frontier (Sadiya, Balipara, amd Lakhimpur) (II) the Naga hill districts (III) the Lushai hills and (IV) the Chittagong Hill tracts. The partially excluded areas included (I) the North Cachar Hills (II) the Mikir hills (in Nowgong and Sibsagar districts) (III) the British portion of the Khasi and Jaintia Hills District (V) the district of Angul (VI) the Chotanagpur division (VII) the district of Sambalpur (VIII) the Santhal Parganas district (IX) the Darjeeling district (X) the Lacadive Islands including Minicoy and (XI) the Ganjam, Vizagapatnam and Godavari Agencies.

97 Samuel Hoare's intervention in the parliamentary debate in answer to Wedgewood's assertion that only Europeans could administer these areas was to argue that there were among Indians a school of administrators sensitive to the problems of the tribes. However this was disregarded.

98 Constituent Assembly debates official report, 1946-50, vol. 1, p. 139.

Bibliography

District Gazetteer of Manbhum.

The Chota Nagpur Tenancy Act, 1908.

Report of the Indian Statutory Commission, vol XII.

Constituent Assembly debates official report, 1946-50, vol I.

Anderson B., *Imagined communities, Reflections on the Origin and Spread of Nationalism*, New York 1983.

Id., *Genealogies of the political forest and customary rights in Indonesia, Malaysia and Thailand*, "Journal of Asian Studies", 60, 3, 2001, pp. 761-812.

Anderson P. - Ross S., *Christian missionaries and orientalist discourse,* in Frykenberg R.E. (ed.), *Christians and missionaries in India*, London 2003.

Bayly C., *Indian society and the making of the British empire*, Cambridge 1988.

Boas G. - Lovejoy A., *Essays on primitivism and related ideas in Antiquity*, Baltimore 1935.

Bodley J., *Comment,* in Headland Th., *Revisionism in ecological anthropology*, "Current Anthropology", 8, 4, Aug.-Oct. 1997, pp. 611-613.

Bradley - Birt F.B., *Chota Nagpur: a little known province of the Empire*, reprint, first published in 1903.

Dalton E., *Descriptive ethnology of Bengal*, Calcutta 1872.

Darwin C., *The descent of man*, New York 1871.

DasGupta S., *The journey of an anthropologist in Chotanagpur*, "Indian economic and social history review", 41, 2, 2004.

Elbourne E., *Blood ground, colonialism, missions and the contest for Christianity, 1799-1853*, Montreal 2002.

Falconer J., *Ethnographical Photography in India 1850-1900*, "Photographic Collector" 5(1), pp. 16-46.

Forsyth J., *The highlands of central India*, London 1871.

Headland Th., *Revisionism in ecological anthropology*, "Current Anthropology", 18, 4, Aug-Oct 1997.

Hinsley C.M., *Zunis and Brahmins, cultural ambivalence in the gilded age*, in Stocking G.W. (ed.), *Romantic motives, essays on anthropological sensibility*, Madison 1996.

Hoffmann J.B., *Encyclopaedia Mundarica*, vol. VIII, Calcutta 1906.

Humboldt A. von, *Personal narrative of travels to the equinoctial regions of America 1799-1804*, London 1908.

Hunter W.W., *The annals of rural Bengal*, Calcutta 1897.

Kennedy D., *Imperial history and post colonial history*, "Journal of Imperial and commonwealth History", 24, 1996.

Kopytoff I., *The African Frontier: The Reproduction of Traditional African Societies*, Indiana 1987.

Lester A., *Observing the due observance of justice: the geographies of colonial humanitarianism*, "Environment and planning: society and space 2002", vol. XX, p. 277.

Murray Li T., *Environment, indigeniety and transnationalism* in Watts M.J. - Peet R. (eds.), *Liberation ecologies*, London 1996.

Muthu S., *Enlightenment against Empire*, Princeton 2003.

Nottrott A., *the Gossner mission under the kols* and Chatterton, *the story of fifty years mission in Chotanagpur*, in Mahato S., *A hundred years of Christian missions in Chotanagpur, since 1845*.

O'Hanlon R., *Cultures if rule, communities of resistance:gender discourse and tradition in recent South Asian historiographies*, "Social analysis", 25, 1914.

O'Malley L.S.S., *Bengal district Gazetteers*, vol. XX.

Oddie G., *Missionaries, rebellion and proto nationalism, James Long of Bengal, 1814-87*, London 1999.

Peluso N.L., *Fruit trees and family trees in an anthropogenic forest:ethics of access, property zones and environmental change in Indonesia*, "Comparative studies in society and history", 38, 3, 1996, pp. 510-548.

Reid J.A., *Final report on the survey and settlement operations in Ranchi, 1902-1910*, Calcutta 1912.

Ricketts H., *Selections from the records of the Bengal government*, n. XX, Calcutta, 1855

Roy S.C., *Mundas and their country*, Calcutta 1912.

Sahu K., *The Kolhan under the British rule*, Calcutta 1985.

Sen A.K., *Text and beyond Text; essays on the history of the Ho of Singhbhum during colonial rule* (unpublished manuscript).

Shivaramakrishnan K., *Modern Forests, state making and environmental change in colonial eastern India*, Stanford 2002.

Singh Deo T.N.N., *Singhbhum, Seraikella and Kharsawan, through the ages*, Calcutta 1940.

Sponsel L., *Comment*, in Headland, *Revisionism in ecological anthropology* cit.

Stocking G.W. Jr., *Victorian Anthropology*, New York 1987.

Tete P., *The kharias and the history of the atholic church in Biru*, Armidale 1990.

Id., *A missionary social worker in India*, Rome 1984.

Thapar R., *The Theory of Aryan race and India: History and Politics*, in Id., *Cultural Pasts. Essays in Early Indian History*, Delhi 2000.

Tickell S.R., *Memoir on the hodesum*, "The Journal of the Asiatic society of Bengal", IX, 1840, p. 690.

Trautmann T., *The Aryans in British India*, California 1997.

Yoon C.K., *Rain forests seen as shaped by human hand*, in Headland Th., *Revisionism in ecological anthropology* cit, p. 608.

Zimmermann F., *The jungle and the aroma of meats, the ecological theme in Hindu medicine,* Delhi 1999.

The Views of the Young Turks and the Conservatives about Foreign and Domestic Politics before the Balkan Wars

GÁBOR DEMETER
University of Debrecen

A tanulmány célja, hogy bemutassa az ifjútörök mozgalom megítélését és annak változását az európai, török és magyar történetírásban. A közös elképzelések valamint eltérő álláspontok felvázolása, illetve ezek okainak és eredetének megvilágítása mellett szerepet kap annak vizsgálata, hogy a különböző európai felfogások és trendek hatása hogyan jelenik meg a magyar történetírásban az egykorú reakcióktól a legújabb kutatásokig. A magyar történetírásban az ifjútörök mozgalom önálló kutatási területként sohasem szerepelt: a keleti kérdés részeként csupán a diplomácia- és politikatörténeti vonatkozásai kerülnek említésre, a mozgalom előzményeivel, ideológiájával, céljaival, azok megvalósulásával, társadalmi hátterével magyar szerzők nem foglalkoztak, és a külföldi művek hozzáférhetősége is korlátozott maradt. Ezzel szemben a források zömének birtokában lévő török történetírás az 1970-es évek végéig éppen ezekre a kérdésekre fókuszált a nemzeti történelem részének tekintve a problémakört, és elhanyagolta a mozgalom nemzetközi vonatkozásainak tanulságait. A nemzetközi folyamatokra gyakorolt hatást illetően a magyar történészek nincsenek lemaradva a nemzetközi trendektől. Nyugat-Európában az ifjútörök mozgalomnak éppen azon vonásait érte kritika, melyekre a török történetírás annak erényeként tekint. A mozgalom ideológiájának gyökereit és társadalmi támogatottságát illetően máig nincs egyetértés a két csoport között, miként Törökországban is vita folyik arról, hogy az ifjútörökök elgondolásainak megvalósítása jelentette-e az egyetlen kiutat a helyzetből. 1908-1913 között ez nem volt olyan egyértelmű, mint 1918 után, éppen ezért vizsgálódásainkat az előbbi időszakra helyeztük, mely sokak szerint éppenhogy oka volt a későbbi szituációnak.

THE PROBLEMS OF EUROPEAN, TURKISH AND HUNGARIAN HISTORIOGRAPHY

This contribution aims to examine the transformation of the interpretation of the Young Turk reform movement in European historiography by comparing the different approaches and their evolution. The common ideas and counterpoints of the Turkish and Western European authors are also investigated, as well as the influence of their interpretations on Hungarian historiography. Since the latter lacks separate, modern works based on reliable sources concerning this period, we also tried to compare the older opinions, contemporary to the movement itself. Our investigation mainly focuses on the period between 1908-1913, in order to examine a situation where the positive effect of the Young Turk movement on the survival of Turkey was at least questionable. The positive political role played by Young Turks can be verified after 1923, but before it was more dubious. In order to differentiate between the origins of different political groups and their ideas about modernization, constitutionalism, liberalism and nationalism and their instruments, it is necessary to observe briefly the Young Ottoman period, 1876-1878.

Kemal H. Karpat claimed in 1975 that the Young Turks remained the least studied and understood power group in the history of the Balkans and the Middle East, though the movement itself was not negligible[1]. It was the first case of seizure of power in an Eastern country by a young, westernized generation, the first defeat inflicted by an energetic and radical intelligentsia upon the Islamic 'ancien régime'[2].

As the original sources were usually written in Turkish language this gives a great advantage to Turkish historians. Therefore the Young Turk period is often regarded merely as a part of the national history of Turkey – even some Turkish historians think the same, although the CUP was established as a multi-ethnic and multicultural organisation in the Balkans[3]. Until this fact was realized, mainly Turks dealt with the issue. As the Young Turks after 1923 cut off the connections between the old Empire and the modern Turkish State, so Turkish historians tended to forget about the periphery and they considered the activity of the early Young Turks as the sole solution to save Turkey – just because that is what later events eventually seemed to show. Actually the activity of CUP in 1908-1913 was also responsible for the forthcoming events. The major early works in Turkish on this subject are written by A. B. Kuran. Kuran sympathized with the so-called liberals and conservative-liberals led by Prince Sabaheddin – influenced by the ideas of August Comte – and showed a strong bias against the CUP[4].

Until the 1970s, Turkish scholars and researchers produced little on very late Ottoman histories because of the existence of an official state-sanctioned thesis of history that imposed ideological interpretation on this point. The authors avoided the objective discussion of sensitive subjects. These issues, like international reception and relations towards other Muslims were left almost entirely to foreign scholars, while the evolution of the movement was at the centre of interest according to M. S. Hanioglu[5]. Very little has been written about CUP policy towards the Balkan states. Over the last decades a new philosophy emerged to challenge these traditions (H. Ünal, A. Özcan)[6].

According to Karpat, in Western Europe it was E. E. Ramsaur in 1957 (*The Young Turks: Prelude to the Revolution*) who rekindled some kind of interest in this period. This work was criticized by Turks as it did not use most of the available Turkish sources, and dealt with the activity of Young Turks in exile, exaggerating their role in forming the ideology of the movement. Turkish authors often questioned the role of the West in forming the ideas of Young Turks. It is claimed that while Young Ottomans and early Young Turks (1908) were driven by western liberal ideas, nationalism – which finally *saved* Turkey from total dismemberment, was adopted from the nationalism of the Balkan countries as a result and a response to this challenge. Many of the books published before 1970 on this period fail to take into account and contrast the conflicting nationalism of Balkan peoples with the similar ideologies that appeared among the Muslim groups in the Young Turk era. In the early years a debate began between Turkish and European scholars.

Now both sides tend to accept that the Muslims' original anti-imperialistic self-defensive nationalism which culminated in the Pan-Islamism of Abdülhamid II was replaced by an aggressive linguistic and ethnic nationalism under the CUP and that the latter is partly responsible for the partial disintegration of the Ottoman State – though it was called to life to hinder, not to promote this process. The early books often fail to take into account the developing political conflict between the bureaucratic elite and the economic middle class, the pressing demand for development and education that played a mobilizing role among the population. These processes need further investigations.

Before examining the situation and role of Hungarian historiography, recent major European trends and works which are available in English in this topic are worth mentioning too. A general history covering Turkey in this period is written by B.Lewis, *The Emergence of Modern Turkey* (1968), and updated by E.J. Zürcher, *Turkey: A Modern History* (1993), and by F. Ahmad, *The Making of Modern Turkey* (1993). B. Niyazi in *The Development of Secularism in Turkey* (1964), covers similar ground, but concentrates on the development of ideas. An attempt of R.E. Ward and D.A. Rustow (eds.), *Political Modernization in Japan and Turkey* (1964), to use a comparative method to understand the distinctive but successful modernization induced by the pressure of Powers, has valuable essays on general themes. W.F. Weiker in *The Modernization of Turkey* (1981) covers the period beginning in 1923. R.H. Davison, *Reform in the Ottoman Empire, 1856-1876* (1963, reissued 1973); and C.V. Findlay, *Bureaucratic Reform in the Ottoman Empire: The Sublime Porte, 1789-1922* (1980), discuss the Tanzimat era. R. Devereux, *The First Ottoman Constitutional Period* (1963), is a careful study of the 1876 crisis and the establishment of the first Ottoman parliament and S. Mardin in *The Genesis of Young Ottoman Thought* also studied the Young Ottomans; studies of the Young Turks include E.E. Ramsaur, *The Young Turks: Prelude to the Revolution of 1908*; F. Ahmad, *The Young Turks: The Committee of Union and Progress in Turkish Politics, 1908-1914* (1969); E.J. Zürcher, *The Unionist Factor: The Role of the Committee of Union and Progress in the Turkish National Movement 1905-1926* (1984); and M.S. Hanioglu, *The Young Turks in Opposition* (1995); *Preparation for a Revolution: The Young Turks, 1902-1908* (2001). In the 1970s Ahmad's book, relying mainly on the consular reports of the British Public Office but also including Turkish sources, was the best according to Karpat, although his work paid scant attention to social, economic and ideological currents[7].

Uriel Heyd published *The Foundations of Turkish Nationalism* (1950). David Kushner in *The Rise of Turkish Nationalism, 1876-1908* (1977) has won acclaim for its consideration of ideological aspects. Hasan Kayali – investigating the transformation of Middle Eastern political identities from empire to nation-states in his work *Arabs and*

Young Turks: Ottomanism, Arabism, and Islamism in the Ottoman Empire, 1908-1918 (1997) – deals with the ideological opposition between the Islamic centre and periphery. Kayali denies that schism between Turks and Arabs arose because of the attempt to Turkify the population. Instead, he argues, that the CUP dismissed Arabs from administrative positions in order to get rid of incompetent leaders and the supporters of the old regime. The weakness of the author's case – according to Commins – is that Hanioglu quotes the private correspondence of Turkish leaders, which is contrary to Kayali's opinion[8].

The Hoover Library in the USA has numerous works on the topic[9]. Among these books only the ones written by Mardin, Zürcher, Lewis, Kayali (internet) Hanioglu (internet) and Niyazi are – in a limited way available for researchers in Hungary. Nor can we find a concise history at least of the Eastern Question or the Balkans written by Hungarians from the period after 1945, and only one concise history of the Balkans is translated into Hungarian language – the one written by Jelavich, which does not focus on the question that concerns us here. Though the Eastern Question – or at least its independent part, the Balkans – has already been conscientiously examined in Hungary by Horváth, Balanyi and Lajtor just after the first World War, due to the context in which they wrote, they are not impartial. Their descriptive works, based on the news of daily press witnessing the events, met the standards of higher education, but they are now forgotten.

In comparison to Western Europe and especially to Turkey the question of Young Turks' reform movement remained underestimated, underexamined and almost unrepresented as a separate research area in the last eight decades of Hungarian historiography. Hungarian books about Young Turks are not based on original sources, they are compilations. The authors usually give a short description of events without evaluating them, rarely is there an attempt at synthesis. Nonetheless a comparison with foreign works might be interesting in order to investigate their influence and also to measure the lag with respect to mainstream studies and new results. As the number of works written in Hungarian is quite limited, as is the number of books translated into Hungarian, foreign works available in Hungary (i.e. H.A. Gibbons) had to be taken into consideration in order to collect the necessary data to examine the differences between interpretations appearing in the Hungarian works. This topic has always been treated as part of the wider problem of the Eastern Question. This was a consequence of the fact that historians in Hungary examined Turkey (and the Balkans) merely in the context of the Balkan policy of the Monarchy and not as a separate unit. The latest Hungarian works proved to be usable for higher education and comparative history-teaching[10], sometimes far-sighted, but these are still general works based merely on some well-selected publications, without the deeper knowledge and use of other important and specific works.

The fate of Turkey might have been a lesson for the Dual Monarchy and for Hungarian national development – concerning both the problems of nationality and the failure of different solutions adopted to keep the state together – but these lessons were neglected. However, early in the 19th century the conservative politician Gentz had warned the Hapsburgs, that after the fall of Turkey the Monarchy would be the next victim, because with the collapse of Turkey the circumstances which allowed and made necessary the existence of the Monarchy would disappear – but no comparative work about the two empires was published.

This underestimation in Hungary is partly because the leftist historical tradition claims that the modern democratic Hungary is not the successor of Austria-Hungary: it is held that it is a brand new state formed together with Czechoslovakia and Yugoslavia, in order to avoid being considered as a defeated country. But cutting all connections and common responsibility with the past of the Monarchy meant that it was considered merely as an imperialistic state, therefore the examination of Balkan policy was not seriously studied in the communist period, unlike domestic policy. The national movement of small states in the Balkans was considered positive in comparison to the role played by Habsburg Monarchy and Turkey. This also meant that if Young Turks ever appeared on the pages, they were considered as oppressors with respect to the role of the small Slavic states engaged in building Yugoslavia, – and sometimes as victims, if the Monarchy or Power Policy appeared on the other side. So judgements on the Young Turks were ambivalent – at least they enjoyed positive features in comparison to conservatives and liberals. The decentralising-federalistic tendencies of the latter were also underestimated (in case of the Slavs in Yugoslavia they were welcomed), since they promoted the interference of the Grand Powers.

The conservative historical tradition in Hungary also neglected the Young Turks. Those who estimated highly the role of the Monarchy and agreed with its Balkan policy, considered the Young Turks' constitutionalism as a challenge to the Monarchy's political claims. Those conservatives who opposed the Balkan policy that they identified merely with the interests of Austria and Germany, also underestimated the Young Turks as they proved to be too weak to stop the events in the Balkans (indeed, they were accused of promoting them because of their acts), therefore giving space to the imperialistic ambitions of the Monarchy.

These statements can be corroborated by some examples. In the work of Horváth, the Turkish reform movement does not appear in a separate chapter, but it is divided between different events considered as foreign policy. The crisis of 1908 is incorporated in the problem of the Sanjak Railway, which not only induced the Powers to oppose the Monarchy, but also spurred the action of Young Turks. The annexation crisis and the declaration of independence in Bulgaria were responses for the Turkish reform movement according to the author.[11] The second time the Turkish political situation is mentioned, it is incorporated into an illustration of the consequences of the Bosnian crisis, which led to the crisis of the Turkish government.

Balanyi was of the opinion that the second meeting at Reval in 1908 led to the activity of Young Turks. He claimed that the Memorandum of Curzon had revealed that the Triple Entente intended to reorganize the Asian parts of Turkey with a centre in Mecca, while the European parts would have been split between the Powers, although the Triple Entente claimed that the talks had been about giving international forces to strengthen the position of Hilmi Pasha against the bands of Macedonia and to carry out reforms[12]. Lajtor – contrary to Balanyi – thinks that the CUP feared the success of the Macedonian reform movement, which would have resulted in creating an autonomous province and thus the possibility of permanent intervention of the Powers. This would have led to the total independence of the province as the example of Eastern Rumelia showed, and therefore – unlike Turkish authors – he claimed that the Young Turks had shown centralist tendencies from the beginning of their movement in 1908. Lajtor wrote that the Young Turks' movement had intended to form a nationalist and democratic constitutional monarchy from the feudal and clerical Empire. This movement – since the Empire lacked a bourgeoisie – could not aim to achieve the results of the European revolutions of 1648 and 1789. The movement of the Young Turks was not supported by huge masses, it was the consequence of the debut of some idealist intellectuals[13]. Lajtor also tended to call the Young Turks anti-Islamic in the sense that they were not only anticlerical but also non-religious. This might be because the Young Turks disliked the idea of Pan-Islamism, that Abdülhamid used to gain support.

Balanyi claimed that the Young Turks originally represented democratic tradition against Abdülhamid's despotism. The author thought that Turkey would be able to solve her problems without foreign intervention thus stabilizing her position. In his work, the problem of modernization in Turkey is considered in the context of international affairs. The successful boycott against Austrian merchandise was the only case when Balanyi admitted that the CUP had support from broad classes of society. The latest books published in Hungary concerning the history of Eastern Europe in the early 20th century did not even mention the events in Turkey between 1908-1913. The books used in higher education also omit this period: 20th-century World History has a separate chapter about Turkey only after 1945. The latest sourcebook also lacks sources on Turkey, although events in the Balkans are involved, while older sourcebooks have separate volumes on the Balkans and Turkey[14].

The internal aspects of the reform movement

The Young Ottomans – who were both constitutional reformers and revolutionaries, but not nationalists – are considered as the predecessors of Young Turks, and although they had different ideas on modernization, the two groups are usually fused together in Hungarian historiography. For the period of Tanzimat the only book available in the Hungarian language is written by Ilber Ortayli. The author claims that the constitution of 1876 was established due to internal pressure and not as a result of external political events – contrary to the opinion of Davison[15]. Young Ottomans were not necessarily friendly to ideas of western nations, but at least they knew them and prepared to respond to the challenge. When they started their constitutional reform movement, they wanted the renewal of the whole Empire, not only of Turkey, as it exists today. But many Turks thought then that constitutionalism would be Turkey's gravedigger[16] and some Turkish historians – knowing the results of the futile efforts – believe that the Young Ottomans should have dealt only with the central areas.

The Hamidian regime was not receptive to bourgeois, nationalist ideas, as it lacked a bourgeoisie[17]. Ortayli recognised that the reforms were initiated by a narrow group of idealists, noblemen working in the bureaucracy – the same happened in the East European societies, where revolutionary movements were often led by the elite of the old regime. Unlike the, at least declaredly, democratic Young Turks, the Young Ottomans did not want universal suffrage, but the two movements had a common idea, that they must fight against despotism and foreign intervention, not against the Sultanat. According to Ortayli, Europe was not interested in Turkish constitutionalism in 1876: its reception in Austria and Russia was hostile, France and England thought that it would not be suitable for Turkey. Constitutional government did not hold back small states and Russia (which did not have a constitution) from declaring war on Turkey. Moreover, Europe supported Turkey not because of its constitutional regime, but to stop Russia[18].

Hungarian historiography (and Gibbons) – with the exception of Matuz – did not judge correctly the significance of the liberal groups between Old Turks and Young Turks, and usually it considers them together with conservative elements. Liberals were considered renegades, who came from the conservative bureaucracy, and became supporters of the Young Turks in order to save their own power, then to return to their roots. Although in 1911 when the secession between the liberals and the "main stream" of the CUP occurred, the former included many educated members from different Balkan nations fighting for decentralism, parlamentarism, constitutionalism against the increasing chauvinism and centralisation of the CUP. Those liberals, who originated from the common intellectual heritage of the CUP, and then joined to the conservatives, are judged in the same way[19]. According to Kuran this is a misinterpretation. For many historians, liberalization and modernization are parallel and complementary concepts, and any trend of liberalization is accepted by them as a pledge to modernization, whereas any restrictive measure is seen as an expression of traditionalism[20]. Kuran, Lewis and Balanyi consider Küçük Said Pasha – who persuaded the Sultan to restore constitutionalism instead of initiating a civil war in 1908 – as a conservative who was a modernist too[21]. Therefore the above mentioned approach of Hungarian historians to the liberals is not correct – it is still misleadingly confused by searching for a 'good guy' and a 'bad guy' in the story of 1908-13.

In 1877 Said opposed the implementation of reforms urged by Midhat Pasha because he thought it would hasten the disintegration of the Empire, and he further remarked that the satisfactory operation of a constitutional regime necessitated the existence of large group of well-educated deputies having enough knowledge. In 1908 he might have thought that time had come for parliamentarism. His concept is worth further investigation, because the Young Turks were driven by just the opposite opinion, that only *reforms could have hindered the dismemberment* of the Empire. Young Turks thought that decentralization urged by the liberal flank would hasten disintegration, while secessionist liberals thought the same about centralization. Among Turkish historians both concepts appear.

Said Pasha seemed to have been the first statesman who realized that the policy of Ottomanism, aiming to create an Ottoman nation (including not only ethnic Turks) through a fusion of different ethnic communities, was doomed to failure. Therefore two other ways seemed to be applicable: creating a homogenous Turkish state (with the constant threat of losing the periphery), or favouring a policy based on strengthening the loyalty of Muslims subjected to the Sultan as Caliph. Accepting the latter strategy Said became the precursor of Pan-Islamism, though he opposed Abdülhamid's plan to make Arabic the official state language[22]. The other "conservative" (also Grand Vizier in the era of the CUP), Kiamil Pasha, refused the despotism too, but sympathized more with the decentralising ideas of liberals[23].

According to recent Turkish opinion, Özcan's analysis shows that Ottoman Pan-Islamism was not an aggressive ideology created by Abdülhamid II and there is no evidence that he ever claimed political sovereignty over the Muslims outside his dominion. It was an important device in the Ottoman state's relation to those Powers that had Muslim subjects, and a tool to unite Arabs, Turks and Albanians among whom nationalist sentiments were also growing.

Like the ideological bases, Turkish constitutionalism is not much researched in Hungary. While in 1876 the Parliament recognised the Sultan as the Supreme Executive, in 1908, he had to take an oath to preserve the constitution, and when he objected to it in 1909, the Sheik-ul Islam forced him to resign. This was a real constitutional revolution: a member of the ancien regime used his constitutional and traditional power to defend the constitution. Lajtor constantly uses the term revolution for the events of 1908, counter-revolution for 1909 and military mutiny for the events of 1912, which means that first the Young Turks were accepted with enthusiasm in Hungary, but all the other events are considered coups d'état. This decline in acceptance and evaluation of the events symbolises that the Young Turks lost the benevolence of foreigners. The same opinion can be traced and derived from the daily press[24].

Concerning the relationship between Muslims and Christians before 1908 the following facts can be stated. Christians absorbed western ideas of liberty and nationality first, therefore they were always viewed with suspicion; several Great Powers acted as traditional protectors of the Christians thus interfering into the internal affairs of the Empire, which also angered Muslims. So Christians were not trusted but were also fond of modern ideologies, which helped the Young Turks[25]. The Young Turks might have thought that if Christians preserved their special rights or gained more, it would further encourage the Powers to interfere, thus decreasing the stability of the state. The constitution of 1876 affirmed, that "all Osmanli are equal before law... without distinction to religion". But Christians did not want to be called Osmanli, they felt that they were Greeks, Bulgarians etc. They thought that constitutionalism was the beginning of some kind of homogenization. Therefore, from 1876 western ideas of the liberalism of Young Ottomans and the nationalism of Christians were necessarily opposed to each other. Ottomanism, the brotherhood of imperial subjects, was refused by most non-Muslim peoples. Although in 1876 these peoples became equal with the ruling elite, they lost their nationality, their self-identification. The demand e.g. in Crete was basically for autonomy or for union with Greece, not for equality. When Midhat Pasha began to work on the scheme of a federalist State in 1872, the Balkan nations refused his plan. The ecclesiastical hierarchies that ruled a Christian millet also refused equality: for them Ottomanism would have meant a decrease in their authority and income. Nationalism, fed by the self-supporting statehood of peoples subjected to the Empire, proved too strong to be contrasted by liberal efforts. This challenge called into life the Turkish nationalism manifested in the Young Turks' activity.

Cavour declared nationality to be the most potent force in the political world of the 19th century and the political weakness of the Treaty of Berlin seems to derive from the fact that its authors failed to recognise this truth[26]. Early in 1904 Y. Akçura pointed out that both Pan-Islamism and Ottomanism had already failed as Christians did not respect equality, nor the modern State as the successor of the Empire. For them both meant oppression. Turkish nationalism was the logical choice for survival and modernization against the nationalism of Balkan peoples[27]. Even the early Ottomanists concealed the idea of Turkish superiority. "The Turkish nation – wrote the Tanin, the paper of the CUP in 1908 – is and will remain the ruling nation"[28].

Until the defeat of 1912-1913 Anatolia was neglected in the movement, which concentrated on the European territories. Arabs, Vlachs, Jews and Greeks were also the members of the CUP. The Jews of Saloniki and Freemasonry played an important role, the Vlachs cooperated with the Turks, because the small scattered nation feared the nationalism of Greeks and Bulgars[29]. But the fanatism of Young Turks unified the Balkan Peoples against the Turks in a way unimaginable few years before. It may be true, as Batzaria, one of the Christian leaders of the CUP believed, that whenever Christians cooperated with Muslims and Turks in the framework of the CUP, they did so with the hope that this cooperation would hasten the downfall of the Ottoman State, and promote their own nationalist aspirations more rapidly. Liberalism was a device used by each ethnic group merely to fulfil its own political ambitions, although Batzaria himself believed that if the Young Turks had remained faithful to their original programme they might have succeeded in holding the state together. According to him, as a witness, after the revolution of 1908 the Christians soon began to feel that the constitution was only a device to hinder the political interference of the Powers without real contents. The policy of denationalization arrived too late: the old system of tolerance and privileges had already developed strong national consciousness among the nationalities[30]. Turkification was doomed because the Turk was the weakest element of the Empire culturally.

External factors in the Turkish reform movement and their influence on domestic policy

As Hungarian authors consider the domestic policy of Turkey too as the part of the Eastern Question, and deal with Eastern Question only when it has a connection with the Monarchy, we must discuss two questions briefly: first we must place the Young Turks in the context of the Eastern Question, and then present an overview of the aims of and reasons for Turkish domestic policy. Apart from tracing the historiographic background, this contribution examines the attitude, strategies and tactics of the leading Parties in trying to create circumstances which would allow Turkey to survive, while including both the European and Asian parts of the Empire. The statesmen of Turkey from 1856 saw two ways to counterbalance the challenge caused partly by the Powers and partly by the Balkan States and the unrest of Christians subjected to the Turkish yoke: first, by initiating new waves of reforms or, second, through a permanent alliance with a Great Power – which definitely meant economic subjection too in order to make such a Power interested in financing and supporting Turkey. These were the solutions to legitimate the existence of the state. The latter proved to be impossible, since if, in the tense situation after the establishment of the two rival European blocks, the militarily weak Turkey had joined with one of these blocks, the other block would have considered this a hostile step, and would have tried to hinder economic penetration even in the cost of a war. Therefore economic subjection and peaceful competition within Turkey among one another was better for Germany, Britain and France than an alliance. The Hungarian historian Elek Fényes wrote in 1854 about the Crimean War that, the Powers "are not worrying because they like the Turks so much ... but because they instinctively feel that the forthcoming partition of the heritage of the dead (Turkey) might cause a world war ..."[31].

So conservatives had to give up the idea of gaining a faithful ally. Abdülhamid promoted the idea that the controversies between the two groups of Powers would enable Turkey to survive as the Powers were afraid of disrupting the equilibrium. The Turks did not believe that there would be war. "Italy will not draw the sword, because she knows that, if she does attack us, all Europe will be eventually drawn into the bloodiest struggle of history – a struggle that has always been certain to follow the destruction of the integrity of the Ottoman Empire", pointed out Hakki Pasha, Grand Vizier, in 1911. Mahmud Shevket also joined this optimistic opinion which exaggerated the importance of the Ottoman state in maintaining equilibrium: "the million bayonets of Turkey will decide the fortunes of Europe"[32]. Abdülhamid incorrectly thought that the existence of Turkey ensured the balance, but the truth was that Turkey was considered only as a prey.

Young Turks chose a different way. Both parties wanted Turkey to survive, but the different instruments and tactics they used caused rivalry and as a consequence, there was unrest and a lack of stability in domestic policy. For the Powers and the small states, events suggested just the opposite of what the Turks wanted to emphasize: the collapse and unsustainability of the Empire was near, thus they became more aggressive and impatient. The constant internal fights promoted the development of the Balkan League which proved that the conservative Turkish calculations concerning external relations were wrong.

As the opposition between the Young Turks and conservatives deepened, the methods applied in the fierce fight for political predominance sharpened further including genocide and coups d'état. After the victory of the revolution, the liberals, who seceded from the moderate wing of the Young Turks because they refused violent methods, became the real opponents. They announced decentralisation in order to correspond to the wishes of Europe, and to save the integrity of Turkey. Decentralisation met with the approval and support of France and England because a weak and partially disintegrated Turkey was in their interests. in order to exploit and maintain the possibility of economic subjection. Till 1918 the Powers agreed that a dismembered Turkey was bad, and a strong one is even worse. The Young Turks, on the contrary, insisted on centralisation and, by making the Turkish element predominant, on the homogenisation of the Empire, which induced the resistance of Christians and Muslim Arabs. Centralisation applied by Young Turks was suitable for the German economic and railway interests, though the latter did not believe that the periphery could be saved, but hoped that the central Turkish areas could be maintained. Therefore Germans supported the Young Turks while England and France supported the liberals[33]. As a consequence, the different ideas of modernisation not only set the two parties against each other but domestic policy was also influenced by the Powers, and it also deepened further the existing fault line in Power policy between the Triple Alliance and the Triple Entente, according to Hungarian historians.

The Balkans became important because the Powers were afraid that the 'balance of power' would suffer because of the decision of the small states, that is to which party they want to belong in order to obtain territorial and economical advantages. Winning the whole of Turkey to one of the European Power groups would have forced the other group to insist on the dismembering of the country, while in case of the Balkan League the confrontation between the Powers was not necessary. This was a further factor which the Turks had to deal with. Contrary to the expectations of the conservatives, Turkey felt the Great Powers lining up. According to the new policy of Great Britain, Grey in 1906 gained Sinai Peninsula from the Ottoman Empire, then in 1907 divided Persia with the Russians into spheres of influence. Grey declared war on the Mürzsteg programme of Austria and Russia, demanding that the Turkish army leave the three Macedonian vilayets.

Bulgaria, the Hapsburg Monarchy and Greece were afraid of the rejuvenation of Turkey; if thanks to constitutionalism Turkey was able to maintain administration and win the benevolence of the population in those provinces which were about to secede, these states would have had to abandon their claims or give back territories[34]. This fear resulted in the annexation of Bosnia, the declaration of independence in Bulgaria, and a revolt in Crete. But the Powers did not want Turkey to lose three provinces at the same time, so they refused to accept the union of Crete and Greece. The crisis, which the Young Turks tried to face, is not comprehensible without taking into consideration the importance of the Albanian, Cretan and Macedonian and the Straits Questions; just as the date of the outburst of tensions is not understandable without taking into account the penetration of the alliance systems into the peninsula, established and fueled by the divergences between the Great Powers. The symbolic meaning of the Tripolitanian War, which must be added to the list, was not only a fight for a useless province, but in fact, a precedent for the disruption of the status quo by a Power that had previously promised to maintain the integrity of Turkey. This event meant that if a state was allowed to violate the integrity of Turkey *by force* (in 1908 this did not happened), then others could also attempt to insult it. That was a great opportunity and an excuse for Balkan States to settle the bill. The danger coming both from the small states and from the intervention of the Powers forced the Young Turks to turn to the programme of centralisation. Among them the European element was dominant , therefore they considered the Balkan provinces to be part of the homeland. Originally, centralisation did not appear in their programme, so at an early stage they were able to win over those who later seceded as liberals.

Exposed to the partly external and partly internal problems mentioned above, it was hard to initiate real reforms. As usual in the Eastern part of Europe, external problems could not unite the state or the nation, and the parties in opposition always tried to exploit the situation against the ruling party to bid for power in these difficult times. Although Lybia was not an important province of Turkey – especially since Egypt de facto was under English rule – the Young Turks could not abandon the fight and surrender, because in this case they would have been accused by betrayal by the other side. After the July 1912 mutiny when the conservative-liberal coalition came into power, it insisted on carrying on the struggle because of ideological reasons. The Lybians were Muslims and the Sultan was the caliph of all Muslims, it was his duty to take care of his subjects. If conservatives had surrendered, they would have lost their ideological base and the support of the 'public opinion', as actually happened in January 1913 when they decided to accept the peace terms dictated by the Balkan League. When Enver Bey's coup d'état succeeded and the Young Turks removed the conservative-liberal coalition from power, they did not make the same mistake: they insisted on waging war against the "infidels" to save sacred Edirne. Thus they were able to mobilize the religious Turks and those officers who sided with the conservative-liberal coalition and to continue the war.

According to the opinion of some Hungarian daily papers the main reason for continuing the war was to stabilize their internal position: during the battle of Bulair Young Turks managed to get rid of some officers who formerly supported the liberals as they died under the fire of Bulgarian machine guns. After only one month of fighting, as they had got rid of the dangerous political elements, in March the Young Turks asked for peace too, accepting most of the terms including the loss of Edirne. Matuz claims that the assassination of Mahmud Sevket Grand Vizier in June was a revenge of the liberals for making peace.

The CUP was divided between those who worshipped England and those who worshipped Germany, according to many authors. Ünal denies this: the CUP mistrusted all Grand Powers and the assumptions many researchers have made about the Young Turks' Anglophilia are over-simplifications. The CUP did not prefer either group. It has been suggested that the counter-revolution constituted a watershed in Britain's relations with Turkey marking the end of the honeymoon[35]. In fact, the CUP may have taken power in 1908 with greater anti-British and anti-French leanings than any other Ottoman government[36]. These tendencies were identified by Hungarian authors early in the 1980s; they tended to judge the late Young Turks as Germanophiles.

Hungarian researchers cannot get rid of the suspicion that if the Powers had not been so cruel to Turkey between 1903-1908, the Young Turks would not have chosen the path toward homogenisation that ended in genocide. Leftist tradition considers the Monarchy partly responsible for the subsequent events (and this might be an other reason for neglecting Turkey). In this period the Powers tried to solve the antagonism between the will of small states and the needs of Turkey by forcing Turkey to reform, rather than by exerting pressure on the small states. This solution was chosen because Turkey could not be won over to a system of alliances, because the other alliance system would have opposed it, but the small states could have been won over, partly by fulfilling their demands and partly – by reforming Turkey – by making their demands, as weapons of interference into Turkish internal policy, irrelevant.

The contradiction between ideas and action of the Young Turks

The upsurge of enthusiasm soon disappeared as the Young Turks in power initiated their new programme, which, especially after their return in 1909, differed markedly from that of drawn up while they were in exile and under persecution. They wanted total unity and reform in the Western European meaning of this term, in a country which due to its origin lacked Western European traditions[37]. The Young Turks studied in Western European universities, but they had to face the fact that probably only 5% of the population of the Empire had ever known what a constitutional regime meant[38]. Democratic elections were only a piece of theatre to amuse Europe. In Hungary this movement of 1908 is sometimes taught as the blossoming of the reform process, a reform coming from below, deriving from the pressure of society contrary to the constitution established in 1876 and its predecessors of 1839 and 1856. The latter came from above, from the Sultan, forced to act by external political events (the attack of Muhammad Ali of Egypt, the Crimean War, the Turco-Russian War of 1877-1878). We saw the latter challenged by many writings (i.e. Ortayli). And the support of broad classes of society is also questionable [see Source 1, Part 1]. The CUP lacked the support of social classes and relied only upon the Army. (Staff officers led the military revolution in 1960, too). They stood at the peak of the military elite, differing from the corrupted civil bureaucracy[39]. In Turkey, intellectuals could only make a career in the army or in the bureaucracy, where people had enough power to bring about their ideas. "From the very beginning the genuine Young Turks who were honest and consistent in their idealism had to make a compact (and a compromise) with the higher army officers and with the corrupt civil officials of Abdul Hamid. When the real Young Turks controlled the Cabinet, disasters were those of theorists (not terrorists) and visionaries. When they yielded the control of affairs to men more experienced than they, it was simply the renewal of the tyranny of Abdülhamid" – wrote Gibbons[40]. The radicalism of the Young Turks was influenced by the permanent threat of counter-revolution[41]. The threats to the new regime came from different directions as had already been predicted in 1909 [Source 1, Part 2]. Of the two possibilities delineated by Trotsky neither became reality: the Young Turks tried something different. A democratic Balkan Federation remained a dream.

In 1909 a law concerning the freedom of assembly and union came into effect, but with this act all kind of movement based on the principle of nationality too was forbidden [Source 2, §§ 9-10] Contrary to these rights, to defend the new regime the movement of conservatives to grab power was smashed by 60 arrests in July 1910. Participation of soldiers in political activity was punished with dismissal and 2-4 months imprisonment for the officers. A tax paid by Christians as a military contribution (kharadj) was abolished, but from that time Christians who had earlier been excluded from being soldiers were also enlisted in the army[42]. It is true that the older solution was not the best choice: because of military service the Turkish peasant was kept in a condition of economic serfdom while his Christian neighbours progressed. It is also true however that Turks thought that Christians could not be trusted.

Hungarian authors, like Kayali, admit that the Young Turks, as they tried to create a state in which Turkish was the official language both in offices and schools, lit the flames of nationalism [Source 2, §§7 and 17] even in Muslim places where earlier it had seemed impossible for such a thing to happen (i.e. Yemen)[43]. It further strengthened the opposition, which was formerly ideological between the Muslim caliphate and the secular state: from 1910 on the same forces (Muslim nationalism based not only on religion) appeared in the other side. Young Turks pointed out that every European country had gone through the process that they had just initiated in Turkey, and that this was the only way in which a strong nation could be built[44]. But in Europe the processes of centralization and homogenisation took hundreds of years to reach success – not 2 or 3 years – and besides European states had been unable to avoid revolutions and counter-revolutions, while the entire process was coupled with the enrichment of the existing bourgeoisie.

The nationalism of Young Turks alienated the Albanians too, though formerly they had been considered the main supporters of the Empire. According to the leftist politician Pogány, the behaviour of Albanians was fully acceptable: Albanian autonomy meant tax immunity and the refusal of military service and any other obligations. In Pogány's view, theirs was an instinctive revolt of a nation which gained nothing from the Turkish nation and state[45].

The Young Turks also claimed that ecclesiastical autonomy was necessary under despotism, but the constitution guaranteed equal rights irrespective of religion. Therefore, the

Greek Church, which gave protection to the Greeks and had been treated as a permanent threat because of the Megali Idea, must resign from its prerogatives of a political nature. What the Turks truly attempted was to destroy the privileges of the Orthodox Church (in contradiction to §10). No religious organisation was allowed, under a constitutional regime, to be a state within a state and enjoy peculiar privileges and immunities, but this demand of the Young Turks contradicted their own previous proclamation.

In 1909, the cabinet, with a mixture of shortsightedness and modernity, nationalism and liberalism, abolished the possibility of creating societies based on the principle of nationality at the first sight with the intention of modernization and egalitarianism according to Balanyi. With that step, they were successful in destroying the legal basis of the Macedonian paramilitary organisations (i.e. IMRO) too, but not the organisations themselves. These responded with terrorism in order to provoke the intervention of the neighbouring states between 1911-1912; the massacres at Shtip, Kochane, Doyran and Kichevo committed by Muslims were provoked by Christian terrorists/freedom fighters. As the Turkish constitution indicated that the state should control schools (which was a natural step, the same happened in whole Europe), with that act the Turks prohibited the operation of schools organized on national basis, especially if the money to maintain them arrived from foreign Balkan countries. The state bought up arable lands to distribute them to Muslim muhadjirs who settled down and formed paramilitary organizations in order to counterbalance the similar activity of Christian komitadjis. In November 1909 laws against banditry were born, which made possible to accuse whole villages and deport the population if one of them was suspected of supporting an IMRO terrorist. The Young Turks and conservatives tried to use the "divide et impera" principle against Greek and Bulgarian bands, which resulted in banditry becoming more common. Instead of giving preference to commercial interests and an outlet for Bulgaria to the Aegean Sea as England proposed, the Porte insisted on sharpening the rivalry of Balkan States against each other's claims, knowing that they would thwart each others' plans[47]. This strategy might have been successful, except for the fact that it did not take into account the capability of these states to cooperate against their common enemy, despite the hatred among them.

According to Karpat the Balkan Wars of 1912-1913 had a profoundly demoralizing effect on the Young Turks, not because they ended in a defeat, but primarily because the defeat was inflicted on them by the former subject peoples who started work together with them. Their victory was convincing proof that nationalism and modernization had to carry on, and this led to the Arabian revolt and the loss of peripheries after 1918.

Notes

1 K.H. Karpat, *The Memoirs of N. Batzaria: the Young Turks and Nationalism*, "International Journal of middle east Studies", 6, 3, 1975, pp. 276.

2 S.A. Zenkovsky, *The Young Turks – Prelude to the Revolution of 1908* (Review), "American Slavic and East European Review", 17, 2, 1958, pp. 254-256.

[3] Karpat, *The Memoirs* cit., p. 279.

[4] A.B. Kuran, *Inkilap Tarihimiz ve Jön Türkler* (1945); *Inkilap Tarihimiz ve Ittihad ve Terakki* (1948); and *Osmanli Imparatorluğunda Inkilap Hareketleri ve Milli Mücadele* (1959). Other important older works are: T.Z. Tunaya, *Türkiyede Siyasi Partiler 1859-1952* (1952) and S. S. Aydemir: *Makedonya'dan Orta Asya'ya: Enver Paşa* (1970-1972) include sources from the diary of Enver Pasha. C. Bayar, *Ben de Yazdim* (1967-1972), 8 vols; Y.H. Bayur, *Türk Inkilâbi Tarihi I-II*, (1940-1943); K.N. Duru, *Ittihad ve Terakki Hatiralarim* (1957); *Arnavutluk ve Makedonya Hatiralarim* (1959); A.F. Türkgeldi, *Görüp Işittiklerim* (1951); H.C. Yalsin, *Talat Paşanin Hatiralar* (1958); A.C. Emre, *Iki Neslin Tarihi* (1960); H. Ertürk, *Iki Devrin Perde Arkasi* (1969); S. Külce, *Firzovik Toplantisi ve Meşrutiyet* (1944); H. Amca, *Dogmayan Hürriyet* (1958); M. Selahattin, *Ittihad ve Terakki Cemiyetinin Maksadi Tesis ve Suretli Teşkili*. The memoirs of Djemal, Mukhtar Pashas are published in English, German or French.

[5] M.S. Hanioglu, *Pan-Islamism: Indian Muslims, The Ottomans and Britain (1877-1924)*, Review of the book of A. Özcan, "International Journal of Middle East Studies", 31, 1, 1999, pp. 145-147.

[6] See H. Ünal, *Ottoman Policy during the Bulgarian Independence Crisis 1908-9: Ottoman Empire and the Outset of the Young Turk Revolution*, "Middle Eastern Studies" 34, 1, 1998.

[7] Karpat, *The Memoirs* cit., p. 278.

[8] D. Commins, *Arabs And Young Turks: Ottomanism, Arabism and Islamism in the Ottoman Empire, 1908-1918*, "The American Historical Review", 104, 1999, pp. 1041-1042. and M.S. Hanioglu, *The Young Turks and the Arabs before the Revolution of 1908*, in R. Khalidi et. al. (eds.), *The Origins of Arab Nationalism*, New York 1991.

[9] S.J. Shaw - E. Kural, *History of the Ottoman Empire and Modern Turkey, Volume II: Reform, Revolution, and Republic: The Rise of Modern Turkey, 1808-1975*; D. Fromkin: *A Peace to End All Peace: The Fall of the Ottoman Empire and the Creation of the Modern Middle East.* A. Mango also wrote about Young Turks ("Middle Eastern Studies", 8, 1, 1972, pp. 107-117); V.R. Swenson, *The Young Turk Revolution*, Phil. Diss. 1968. Among Russians we have to mention A.F. Miller, *Pjatidesjatiletije Mladotureckoj Revoljucii*, Moscow 1958; E.I. Hasanova, *Ideologija Burzhuaznogo Nacionalizma v Turcii*, Baku 1966; H.Z. Gabidullin, *Mladotureckaja Revoljucija*, Moscow 1936; A.N Mandelstam, *Mladotureckaja Derzhava*, Moscow 1915; G, Aliev, *Turcija v period pravljenija Mladoturok*, Moscow 1972; and the Bulgarian T. Vlakhov, *Balgarija i Mladoturskata Revoljutsija*, "Godishnik na Sofijskija Univerzitet", 59, 3, Sofia 1960, pp. 1-80.

[10] Especially J. Matuz, *Az Oszmán Birodalom története*, Budapest 1990.

[11] J. Horváth, *A Balkáni kérdés utolsó fázisa 1895-1920. Külügyi könyvtár II.*, Budapest 1921, pp. 57-61.

[12] Gy. Balanyi, *A Balkán-probléma fejlődése a párisi kongresszustól a világháború kitöréséig 1856-1914*, Budapest 1920, p. 230.

[13] L. Lajtor, *A keleti kérdés története*, Budapest 1940, pp. 112- 113.

[14] E. Palotás, *Kelet-Európa története a XX. század első felében*, Budapest 2003; I. Diószegi et al. (eds.), *XX. századi egyetemes történelem I. (1890-1945)*, Budapest 1999; I. Diószegi (ed.), *Egyetemes történeti szöveggyűjtemény. XIX. század*, Budapest 2001.

[15] R.H. Davison, *Turkish Attitudes Concerning Christian-Muslim equality in the Nineteenth Century*, "The American Historical Review", 59, 1954, p. 850

[16] I. Ortayli, *Az Oszmán Birodalom leghosszabb évszázada*, Budapest 2004, pp. 245-248.

[17] D. Kushner, *The Rise of Turkish Nationalism 1876-1908*, London 1977.

[18] Ortayli, *Az Oszmán* cit., pp. 245-248.

[19] H.A. Gibbons, *The New Map of Europe*, London 1914, p. 174.

[20] E. Kuran, *Kücük Said Pasa as a Turkish Modernist*, "International Journal of Middle East Studies", 1, 2, 1970, pp. 124-132.

[21] B. Lewis, *The Emergence of Modern Turkey*, London 1968. p. 179.

[22] Kuran, *Kücük Said Pasa* cit., p. 131.

[23] A.H. Lybyer, *The Turkish Parliament*, "Proceedings of the American Political Science Association", 7, 1910, p. 72.

[24] *Reichspost*, 26 July, 1908; and 22 July, 1912

[25] R. Davison, *Turkish Attitudes Concerning Christian-Muslim equality in the Nineteenth Century*, "The American Historical Review", 59, 4, 1954, pp. 844-864.

[26] *The Balkan Situation*, "The American Journal of International Law", 3, 3, 1909, pp. 688-690.

[27] Karpat, *The Transformation* cit., p. 280.

[28] R.G. Suny, *The History of the Armenian Genocide: Ethnic conflict from the Balkans to Anatolia to the Caucasus.* (Review), "Slavic Review", 55, 3, 1996, pp. 676-677.

[29] F. Ahmad, *The rise of Turkish Nationalism 1876-1908*, "International Journal of Middle East Studies", 12, 4, 1980, pp. 552-553; and E. Kedourie, *Young Turks, Freemasons and Jews*, "Middle Eastern Studies", 7, 1, 1971, pp. 89-104.

[30] Karpat, *The Memoirs* cit., p. 289-292.

[31] E. Fényes, *Az orosz-török háború*, Pest, 1854, p. 6.

[32] Gibbons, *The New Map* cit., pp. 231-234

[33] Matuz, *Az Oszmán* cit., pp. 200-202.

[34] Lajtor, *A keleti* cit., p. 113.

[35] H. Ünal, *Britain and Ottoman Domestic Politics: From the Young Turk Revolution to the Counter-Revolution 1908-1909.*, in "Middle Eastern Studies", 2001, 37, 1

[36] H. Ünal, *Young Turk assesment of international politics 1906-9*, "Middle Eastern Studies", 32, 1, 1996.

[37] Balanyi, *A Balkán-probléma* cit., pp. 255-256.

[38] Lybyer, *The Turkish* cit., pp. 65-77; and Gibbons, *The New Map* cit., p. 173.

[39] K.H. Karpat, *The Transformation of the Ottoman State, 1789-1908*, "International Journal of Middle Eastern Studies", 3, 3, 1972, 3, p. 277.

[40] Gibbons, *The New Map* cit., p. 174.

[41] Balanyi, *A Balkán-probléma* cit., p. 259. The danger of abolishing the constitution in 1909 was the only factor which united the Young Turks and other opponents of Abdul Hamid in the Osman Union for a short time and even the conservative Mohamedan Union claimed that the existance of the constitution was not against the spirit of the Islam. As the counter-revolution was overcome, thousands of soldiers were sent to Macedonia to build railways. Those who work, have no time to think of revolts while promoting the economic development.

[42] Gibbons, *The New Map* cit., p. 195.

[43] Balanyi, *A Balkán-probléma* cit., p. 264.

[44] Gibbons, *The New Map* cit., pp. 185-186.

[45] J. Pogány, *A Balkán-háború és az osztrák-magyar imperializmus*, Budapest 1913, p. 19.

[47] Gibbons, *The New Map* cit., p. 164.

Bibliography

Ahmad F., *The Young Turks: The Committee of Union and Progress in Turkish Politics, 1908-1914*, Oxford 1969.

Id., *The rise of Turkish Nationalism 1876-1908*, "International Journal of Middle East Studies", 12, 4, 1980, pp. 552-553.

Balanyi G., *A Balkán-probléma fejlődése a párisi kongresszustól a világháború kitöréséig 1856-1914*, Budapest 1920.

Commins D.D., *Arabs And Young Turks: Ottomanism, Arabism and Islamism in the Ottoman Empire, 1908-1918*, "The American Historical Review", 104, 3, 1999, pp. 1041-1042.

Dadrian V.N., *The History of the Armenian Genocide: Ethnic Conflict from the Balkans to Anatolia to the Caucasus*, Providence 1995.

Davison R.H., *Turkish Attitudes Concerning Christian-Muslim equality in the Nineteenth Century*, "The American Historical Review", 59, 4, 1954, pp. 844-864.

Fényes E., *Az orosz-török háború*, Pest 1854.

Gibbons H.A., *The New Map of Europe*, London 1914.

Hanioglu Ş.M., *The Young Turks and the Arabs before the Revolution of 1908*, in Khalidi R. et. al. (eds.), *The Origins of Arab Nationalism*, Istanbul 1991.

Id., *The Young Turks in Opposition*, Istanbul 1995.

Id., *Pan-Islamism: Indian Muslims, The Ottomans and Britain (1877-1924)*, Review of the book of Azmi Özcan, "International Journal of Middle East Studies", 31, 1, 1999, pp. 145-147.

Id., *Preparation for a Revolution: The Young Turks, 1902-1908*, Oxford 2001.

Horváth J., *A Balkáni kérdés utolsó fázisa 1895-1920. Külügyi könyvtár II.*, Budapest 1921.

Karpat K.H., *The Transformation of the Ottoman State, 1789-1908*, "International Journal of Middle East Studies", 3, 3, 1972, pp. 243-281.

Id., *The Memoirs of N. Batzaria: the Young Turks and Nationalism*, "International Journal of Middle East Studies", 6, 3, 1975, pp. 276-299.

Kayali H., *Arabs and Young Turks: Ottomanism, Arabism, and Islamism in the Ottoman Empire, 1908-1918*, Berkeley-Los Angeles 1997.

Kedourie E., *Young Turks, Freemasons and Jews*, "Middle Eastern Studies", 7, 1, 1971, pp. 89-104.

Kuran E., *Kücük Said Pasa (1840-1914) as a Turkish Modernist*, "International Journal of Middle East Studies", 1, 2, 1970, pp. 124-132.

Kushner D., *The Rise of Turkish Nationalism, 1876-1908*, London 1977.

Lajtor L., *A keleti kérdés története*, Budapest 1940.

Lewis B., *The Emergence of Modern Turkey*, London 1968.

Lybyer A.H., *The Turkish Parliament*, "Proceedings of the American Political Science Association", 7, 1910, 7th Annual Meeting, pp. 65-77.

Mardin S., *The Genesis of Young Ottoman Thought*, Syracuse 2000.

Matuz J., *Az Oszmán Birodalom története*, Budapest 1990.

Niyazi B., *The Development of Secularism in Turkey*, London 1998.

Ortayli I., *Az Oszmán Birodalom leghosszabb évszázada*, Budapest 2004.

Palotás E., *A nemzetállamiság alternatívái a Balkánon a 19. század végén-20. század elején*, Budapest 1999.

Id., *Kelet-Európa története a XX. század első felében*, Budapest 2003.

Pogány J., *A Balkán-háború és az osztrák-magyar imperializmus*, Budapest 1913.

Ramsaur E.E., *The Young Turks: Prelude to the Revolution of 1908*, Princeton 1957.

Stewart-Robinson J,, *The Young Turks: Prelude to the Revolution of 1908* (Review), "Journal of the American Oriental Society", 78, 4, 1958, pp. 311-312.

The Balkan Situation, "The American Journal of International Law", 3, 3, 1909, pp. 688-690.

Zenkovsky S.A., *The Young Turks – Prelude to the Revolution of 1908* (Review), "American Slavic and East European Review", 17, 2, 1958, pp. 254-256.

Zürcher E.J., *The Unionist Factor: The Role of the Committee of Union and Progress in the Turkish National Movement, 1905-1926*, London 1984.

Id., *Turkey: A Modern History*, London 1998.

Sources

Source 1

Part I

"...But what is the secret of victory and what is the explanation of this astonishing success? ... In its real significance, a revolution is a fight for control of the State. That rests directly on the Army. This is why all revolutions in history sharply raised the question: on whose side is the army? In the case of the revolution in Turkey – and that gives it its specific features – it is the army itself which put forward these liberating ideas. Consequently, a new social class did not have to overcome the armed resistance of the Ancien Régime ... The unimportance of Turkish industry and low level of urban culture left the Turkish intelligentsia with hardly any other choice than a military or civil service career. So the State organized at its centre the militant vanguard of the bourgeois nation in process of formation: the critical and dissatisfied intelligentsia. The last few years have seen an uninterrupted series of disorders in the Turkish army due to non-payment of salaries or delays in promotions. ... Regiment after regiment, the army was taught in the school of rebellion... After the success of the revolt, numerous European politicians and journalists spoke of a mysterious ambience of brilliant organisation created by the Young Turks ... In fact, as Niazy Bey and Enver Bey themselves admitted, the revolt broke out when the Young Turks were "largely unprepared" for it. What helped them, was the automatic organization of an army ... The mechanical discipline of the army was transformed naturally into the internal discipline of the revolution. A collapse of the bureaucratic machine combined with the revolt of the army..."

Part II

"... After the success of revolution the different classes of the country had jointly fought to preserve the existing economic hierarchy, the economically dominant classes thus preserving their hegemony over the masses in the revolution – from whose efforts victory had come. ... Only a single state of all the Balkan nationalities, on a democratic and federal basis similar to the Swiss or United States model, can bring internal peace to the Balkans and ensure the conditions for a broad development of its productive forces... The "Young Turks" for their part definitively rejected this approach. Representing the dominant nationality and having their own national (muslim-Turkish) army, they remain national centralisers. The right wing consistently opposes self-government, even at the provincial level ... the right wing of the "Young Turks" will openly move to the side of counter-revolution...
A fifth of the peasants are landless, ... reforms are urged by the Macedonian group of Sandanski and the Armeniains... the party of "Young Turks", in which Beys and landowners dominate, with a national-liberal blindness denies that there ever existed an agrarian question.

Obviously, the "Young Turks" hope that handing-over to a new administration, using the forms and procedures of parliamentarism, will be enough to satisfy the peasants. They are so wrong. Dissatisfaction... will find a greater reflection within the army which consists of peasants. And if a party which is based on officers, ... it could easily happen that the soldiers rise once again but this time against their officers...
Of the 240 deputies, the "Young Turks" have support from approximately 140. About 80 deputies, primarily Arabs and Greeks, form the block of the "decentralizers". Prince Sabah-ed-Din seeks influence and a political base by an alliance with them... On the extreme left, are the Armenian and Bulgarian revolutionists who include in their rows some social democrats. ...This is why I maintain that the military revolt in Macedonia of last July, which led to the calling of Parliament, was only the prologue to the revolution: the drama is still before us. ... Victory for the revolution will mean the victory of democracy in Turkey, democratic Turkey would be the foundation of a Balkan Federation ... The restoration of the Sultan and his despotism would mean the end of Turkey, leaving the Turkish State to the mercy of those who want to carve it up".

From: L. Trotsky, *The Young Turk*, "Kievskaya Mysl.", 3, 3 January 1909.

Source 2

The Young Turks:

Proclamation for the Ottoman Empire, 1908

§7. The Turkish tongue will remain the official state language. Official correspondence and discussion will take place in Turkish. ...
§9. Every citizen will enjoy complete liberty and equality, regardless of nationality or religion, and be submitted to the same obligations. All Ottomans, being equal before the law as regards rights and duties relative to the State, are eligible for government posts, according to their individual capacity and their education. Non-Muslims will be equally liable to the military law.
§10. The free exercise of the religious privileges which have been accorded to different nationalities will remain intact".
§17. All schools will operate under the surveillance of the state. In order to obtain for Ottoman citizens an education of a homogenous and uniform character, the officials schools will be open, their instruction will be free, and all nationalities will be admitted. Instruction in Turkish will be obligatory in public schools. In official schools, public instruction will be free. Secondary and higher education will be given in the public and official schools indicated above; it will use the Turkish tongue. Schools of commerce, agriculture, and industry will be opened with the goal of developing the resources of the country".

From: *The Young Turks*, trans. A. Sarrou, in Rondo Cameron (ed.), *Civilization since Waterloo*, Paris 1912, pp. 40-42.

The American Revolution in Hungarian Historiography during the Socialist Regime

Csaba Lévai
University of Debrecen

A tanulmány azt vizsgálja, hogy milyen történetírói vélemények fogalmazódtak meg Magyarországon az 1949 és 1989 közötti időszakban az amerikai forradalom értékelésére vonatkozóan. 1949-re teljessé vált a kommunista párt (Magyar Dolgozók Pártja) hatalomátvétele az országban. Ezt követően csakis olyan mûveket lehetett publikáni, amelyek az amerikai forradalmat a hivatalos marxista-leninista forradalom-felfogának megfelelően értelmezték. A problémát csak az jelentette a marxista történészek számára, hogy az amerikai forradalmat nehezen lehetett beilleszteni a marxista-leninista forradalom-elmélet sémái közé. Ezt végül úgy igyekeztek megoldani, hogy a polgári forradalomként értelmezett nagy francia forradalom fejlődési logikáját vetítették rá az amerikai forradalomra. Eszerint, az utóbbi egy „korai polgári forradalom" volt, amelyben – a jakobinus diktatúra franciaországi megbuktatásához hasonlóan – a mérsékelt burzsoázia reakciós fordulata vezetett a kapitalista rend konszolidálódásához. Ezt a reakciós fordulatot a marxista történészek az úgynevzett Shays felkelés leverésében, valamint az 1787-ben kidolgozott új szövetségi alkotmány elfogadásában látták megtestesülni. Lényegében ez a felfogás maradt az amerikai forradalom „hivatalos" értelmezése egészen a szocialista rendszer összeomlásáig. Ez azonban nem jelenti azt, hogy e negyven év alatt ne történtek volna bizonyos hagsúlyváltások az amerikai forradalom magyarországi értelmezésében. A Kádár renszer 1956 utáni konszolidálódásával, a Magyar Szocialista Munkáspárton belül jelentkező reform-törekvésekkel, a „békés egymásmellett élés" politikájának meghirdetésével, valamint a Magyarország és az Egyesült Államok közötti diplomáciai kapcsolatok rendeződésével összefüggésben, az amerikai forradalommal foglalkozó magyar historikusok számára is lehetővé vált, hogy az 1960-as évek végétől, valamelyest tágítsanak az amerikai forradalom marxista-leninista értelmezésének dogmatikus korlátain. Ez elsősorban a gyarmatok forradalom előtti életének és a függetlenségi háború történetének színesebb, „emberközelibb" bemutatásában, az amerikai események magyar résztvevőinek hangsúlyosabb méltatásában, s a forradalommal foglalkozó amerikai történetírás néhány olyan klasszikus mûvének magyarországi megjelenésében mutatkozhatott meg, amelyek felfogása rokonítható volt a forradalom marxista értékelésével.

I started my university studies in the fall of 1983, after a year of military service, which was compulsory for every male at that time. I had two majors: history and literary history. In the training of historians and history teachers the emphasis traditionally was laid on the history of Europe and Hungary in my country. The continents outside Europe were rarely mentioned, if at all, in connection for example with European colonization. And all of this was true mainly for the modern periods. Generally it was also true for the history of the United States. It was mainly mentioned in connection with the 20th century when it became one of the most important players in great power politics. The number of works concerning American history in Hungarian was extremely limited. The colonial era was practically unmentioned, and the American Revolution was only briefly touched. Naturally it was interpreted according to the official Marxist-Leninist ideology. This means that it was called an "early bourgeois revolution".

By the year of 1949 the Communist Party took over power in Hungary and from the beginning of the 1950s it was forbidden to publish evaluations of the American Revolution, which did not strictly follow the Marxist-Leninist interpretation of the great event. The problem of Marxist historians was that it was not easy to fit the American Revolution in the framework of the official Marxist-Leninist theory of revolution. Was it, like the French Revolution, a "bourgeois revolution" which destroyed feudalism and created the preconditions for capitalist development, or was it the "first anticolonialist uprising"? But there was no feudalism in North America in the European sense of the word, so there was no *ancien regime* [old regime] to bring down. And if it was fundamentally a movement for independence led by colonial bourgeoisie to make them free from the patronage of the British capitalists, what kind of role did the mass of working people play in it? Nevertheless, Marxist historians could find a solution to these dilemmas, mainly thanks to the Marxist interpretation of the French Revolution. According to this, the Jacobins represented the most progressive political movement, since they endeavored to destroy the structure of feudalism the most consistently. But the moderate bourgeoisie became terrified of the active political role of the working people and they brought down the Jacobin regime, and because of this reactionary turn they were able to consolidate capitalist rule. In the case of the American Revolution, Marxist historians considered the Shays rebellion in Massachusetts in 1786-1787 as the culmination of the revolutionary political activity of the masses, which terrified the moderate bourgeoisie. Their counter revolutionary reaction was to force the new federal constitution on the masses, with the help of which they could consolidate their rule.

This opinion was represented by a two-volume history of the United States written by Soviet authors in the late 1950s, published in Hungarian in 1964. According to it

> the Shays rebellion indicated the height of the democratic movement after the war. It showed to the ruling classes how dissatisfied the masses were with the results of the war, in which victory was secured by the heroic efforts and self-sacrifice of the latter. The war and the follow-up setback of the economy resulted in misery and pauperization of the farmers, artisans and the

> working class people on the one hand, and favored the economic strengthening of the bourgeoisie and the planter class on the other[1].

The Soviet authors described the federal constitution of 1787 as "a great step backward as compared to the *Declaration Independence* and several state constitutions especially those of Pennsylvania". The approach of Soviet Marxist historians to the American Revolution was essentially positive, since they considered it fundamentally a progressive event in the history of mankind, which after all established a pure capitalist economy and society in the United States, and in this sense, created the preconditions for the socialist revolution. This is the reason why they added, with respect to the federal constitution, that "in the context of the period, and especially after the adoption of the *Bill of Rights*, we could consider it a progressive document... America showed the world in those days how to wage a revolutionary war, as it was pointed out by Lenin, and here lies the real importance of the war for independence from the point of view of the progress of history"[2]. To sum up, the American Revolution had a great impact on the revolutionary events in France and on the wars for independence in Latin America, and in this way contributed to the great struggle against feudalism and the consolidation of a capitalist society and economy, led by the progressive bourgeoisie.

A long summary of American historiography was also attached to this history of the United States written by Soviet Marxist scholars. From the different schools of American historiography the approach of the progressive historians and especially of Charles A. Beard proved to be the closest to the Marxist interpretation. No wonder Soviet historians applauded Beard's approach and that of the other "economic historians". Nevertheless they also heavily criticized the interpretation of progressive scholars who "use such terms as class struggle, property, etc. in a wrong way, and their interpretation of these terms is not in coincidence with the correct, scientific Marxist definition of these concepts". According to the Soviet authors the progressive historians

> could call the attention to the economic conflicts which provided the economic basis of the struggle between the colonies and the mother country at the end of the 18th century, and they pointed out the restrictions which were imposed upon the colonies concerning the functioning of manufacture, commerce etc... But one should also take into account that according to the representatives of the economic school, the political behavior of the social classes had been determined not by class interests, but by the selfish and narrow-minded interests of individuals, which characteristics are the eternal features of human nature.

Not to mention the fact that Beard had given up his progressive ideas by the end of the Second World War[3].

This means that the Soviet authors applauded unequivocally the works only of those American historians who were the members of the Communist Party, or who openly declared themselves as Marxists. Although not a historian an example of such a person is William Z. Foster (1881-1961) who was the leader of the Communist Party of the United States of America in the 1920s and again after 1945, and who was the presidential candidate of the party in 1924, 1928, and 1932. Foster was a loyal supporter of the leadership of the Soviet Union during the 1950s and he died in Moscow. He wrote a history of the American communist party which was also published in Hungarian in 1953. According to the evaluation of the Soviet authors of the two volume history of the United States, in his work Foster "exposed the forms and methods of the exploitation of the masses. He pointed out that the state serves the interest of monopolies, and expounded the development of state monopolistic capitalism, analyzing the real characteristics of the economic crises"[4].

The Soviet historians also praised the works of Anna Rochester (1880-1966) who was also a member of the Communist Party of the United States of America from 1927 to the end of her life. As a consequence of the racial discrimination of the African Americans in contemporary Unites States, some prominent African American historians also joined the Communist Party. Such a figure was W.E.B. DuBois (1868-1963) who became a member of the communist party at the very end of his long life. He was one of the most influential African American intellectuals of his age, and in 1895 became the first African American to receive a Ph.D. from Harvard University. DuBois started to develop a Marxist interpretation of race relations in the 1930s and he was indicted as an agent of the Soviet Union in 1951. Although he was acquitted of the charge, the State Department denied him a passport until 1958. After such antecedents, he joined the communist party in 1961 and went to Ghana where he died two years later[5].

From the point of view of the historiography of the American Revolution the works of Herbert Aptheker (1915-2003) played an even more important role. Like many young intellectuals of his generation he joined the communist party at the end of the 1930s, in 1939. He served in the United States Army in the Second World War and reached the rank of major by 1945. However, Aptheker suffered from the effects of McCarthyism in the 1950s. Although he had a Ph.D. from Columbia University, he was unable to obtain a full-time appointment as a university lecturer in this period. Aptheker fought against Cold War anticommunism, testifying on behalf of Communist Party officials facing persecution in these years. Nevertheless, he was able to publish such pioneering works as the *American Negro Slave Revolts*, which was the first scholarly effort to summarize the history of the resistance of African Americans against slavery. He remained loyal to the communist movement even after Nikita Khrushcew's denunciation of Stalinism in 1956. In his *The Truth about Hungary* he publicly defended the Soviet Union's subsequent suppression of the Hungarian anti-communist uprising in the same year. And Aptheker also defended the intervention of the armies of the socialist countries in Czechoslovakia in 1968 in a pamphlet entitled *Czechoslovakia and Counterrevolution: Why the Socialist Countries Intervened?* As one of his critics pointed out "The historian who celebrated slave revolts in the Americas opposed freedom for the peoples of the Soviet Union and Eastern Europe". However, the Soviet authors applauded Aptheker's work, which "describes the struggle of the Negro slaves for their liberation", and "unmasked the reactionary feature of present day concepts of bourgeois historiography". Aptheker also authored a booklet entitled *The Negro in the American Revolution*, which was praised by the authors of the Soviet history of the United States, and which was one of the first efforts to explore the role that African Americans played in the American Revolution[6].

Textbooks for university students also reflected the official Marxist-Leninist interpretation, of course. The *World History, 1500-1789* of Tibor Wittman written in the 1960s is a good example. In this work Wittman, the excellent pioneer historian of Latin-America in Hungary, declared that at the beginning of the American Revolution the "revolutionary class alliance of revolutionary democrats (Jefferson, Samuel Adams, etc.), the liberal bourgeoisie (Franklin etc.), and the planters (Washington etc.) supported by the people, introduced terror against the English and the counter-revolutionary loyalist forces. This alliance was transitional, of course". The "liberal, profit seeking bourgeoisie and the planter class, who were afraid of the people" started to monopolize power in the second half of the revolutionary struggle. The people tried to defend "their lands and liberty" under the leadership of Captain Shays, and this uprising forced the "bourgeoisie and the planter class to realize the commonness of their class interests". And they came to the conclusion that "for the sake of the subordination of the people and the defence of the interests of the capitalists, a stronger state administration was needed". As a result, the new federal constitution of 1787 defended the "economic rights only of the businessmen, the speculators, and the slave holders". The evaluation of Wittman was also very similar to those of Soviet authors. In his view

> despite its anti-democratic features, the victory of the United States, its social and political structure had a great influence on the progressive forces of Europe, especially in France, and it supported the bourgeoisie in its struggle against feudal absolutism... It also made clear that social progress is not the exclusive monopoly of European capitalist nations. Besides its impact on world economy, here lies the historical importance of the event[7].

Wittman's textbook went through sixteen printings up to the late 1980s when it was still in use.

The approach of Géza Kis was similar to that of Wittman. In his textbook written for the students of teachers' training colleges, he stated that "political power was in the hands of the local merchant-planter oligarchy" in the British colonies in the late colonial era. According to him, the main cause behind the outbreak of the American Revolution was that after the peace treaty of Paris "the English bourgeoisie decided to drown its more and more dangerous rival, the American bourgeoisie". Under the inspiration of the bourgeoisie, the English parliament imposed economic restrictions upon the American colonies. But these restrictions had negative effects on all segments of colonial society, which united the different classes against the British. The most important result of this development was the outbreak of the armed conflict between the two parts and the declaration of American independence. Kis highly applauded the *Declaration of Independence*, which was "the first state paper in history which declared popular sovereignty the basis of state authority". In his judgement, American victory in the war for independence was "the victory of American bourgeoisie in the first place", which restricted the rights of the people especially in regard to the purchase of new Western lands. And in order to be able to control the emerging movements of the "landless masses, the rebellious slaves, and the Indians, defending their lands", the bourgeoisie decided to stabilize its power. The result was the federal constitution of

1787, which "strengthened the bourgeois democratic republic, which was historically a progressive development in an age when most of Europe was still under the rule of feudal absolutism"[8]. Kis's textbook was written in the 1980s and was still in use at the end of the decade.

These summaries clearly reflected the Marxist-Leninist interpretation of the American Revolution as did the more ambitious project of László Solti, who published a work about the historiography of the birth of the federal constitution of 1787. His aim clearly was to adapt the history of the American Revolution to the requirements of Marxist-Leninist revolutionary theory through the critical analyses of American historiography. As he stated in the preface, with his book he wished to investigate to what extent the process and the internal dynamics of the American Revolution had something in common with the dynamics of the other great bourgeois revolutions. And he came to the conclusion of course that there was a common dynamics in all bourgeois revolutions described by the founding theorists of Marxism-Leninism, and the American Revolution was not at all an exception. What were the main characteristics of this common dynamism? According to Solti the

> radical movements of the people without property and of the petit bourgeoisie played significant role in the American Revolution, although the intensity and the political results of these movements were not as spectacular as in the French Revolution... As a result of the one-sided economic policy of the ruling classes, the enormous tax burden, the extensive indebtedness, the confiscation of property, the imprisonment of the farmers etc., a clear decline in the economic position of small property owners was observable.

The masses responded with the Shays rebellion, which was followed by movements of the workers and the farmers in other states. "No wonder that according to the interests of the bourgeoisie and the large landowners, the rapid and urgent political consolidation became the number one aspiration of the ruling classes". This reactionary goal had been achieved by the ratification of the new federal constitution. In Solti's view a similar scenario could be observed in the French Revolution, since Jacobin rule was followed by the reactionary regime of the Thermidor Convent and Napoleon Bonaparte. The ruling classes in both countries did "what the historical and social conditions allowed to them to do, which was their actual historical task: to consolidate the rule of the bourgeoisie, endangered by the overflowing of revolutionary activity". This meant that the reactionary setback which was observable in both bourgeois revolutions was the result of the very nature and the internal logic of all bourgeois revolutions, including the American one. Solti did not deny that there were clear differences between the two events. The most important difference is that in France the bourgeoisie was forced to apply "sadistic and bloody methods" to restore capitalist order, while in the United States it was enough to use methods of constitutional lawmaking. But according to Solti the essential dynamics of the two revolutions were the very same[9].

Solti analyzed the works of the different schools of American historiography from this point of view. No wonder he preferred the economic interpretation of the progressive historians, especially that of Charles A. Beard, but he also praised the works of such scholars as John Franklin Jameson or Elisha P. Douglass. He noted that the works of the progressive historians are not perfect. Nevertheless, "they made a significant step towards the integration of the analysis of the American Revolution into the general framework of the investigation of all bourgeois revolutions, and called attention to the fact that the American Revolution is not excepted from some general tendencies of the internal dynamics of all bourgeois revolutions". Solti heavily criticized such schools of American historiography as the "consensus school" of the 1950s, or the representatives of the "republican synthesis" in the 1960s and 1970s. However, through his criticism of the American studies of the 1950s and 1960s, Hungarian audiences could at least obtain information about the work of such well-known Americans historians of the revolutionary era as Louis Hartz, Daniel Boorstin, Edmund S. Morgan, Carl N. Degler, Bernard Bailyn, Gordon S. Wood or Jack P. Greene[10].

There is no doubt that the Marxist-Leninist approach remained the official interpretation of the American Revolution in Hungary up to the collapse of the socialist regime at the end of the 1980s. Nevertheless, a gradual change within this interpretative framework was observable, mainly from the second half of the 1960s on. There were several factors behind this development: first, the appearance of a "real" image of the United States behind communist propaganda among Hungarians during the 1950s and 1960s, and second the changing policies of the Communist Party from the middle of the 1960s.

During the years of the Cold War the American republic became the leading power of the "free world", and as a result, it gradually reached the position of a positive example and the symbol of those values which were inaccessible for the Hungarians under communist rule. Due to the oppression of the people and the serious lack of information, Hungarians started to develop a fundamentally positive and highly idealized picture of the United States, which was in sharp contrast with the official communist propaganda of the 1950s according to which, Coca Cola for example was a dangerous drug through which bourgeois imperialists kept the American youth under control. The model of the American Revolution did not play a significant role during the anti-communist insurrection in 1956, since the rebels considered the Hungarian Revolution of 1848-49 as their prime example. The United States did not help the Hungarian freedom fighters and the defeat of the revolt was followed by disappointment with the United States. But by the end of the 1960s America became the embodiment of the free world for many of the Hungarians again, despite the official anti-American propaganda in connection with the Vietnam War and the civil rights movement. Communist propagandists argued that the crisis of American capitalism had come and underlined the anti-democratic nature of the American political system. But for many Hungarians under communist rule the protest against the Vietnam War and the civil rights movement were not the signs of the final crisis of American capitalism, but the expressions of a democratic society in which one can protest legally with the hope of success for his or her rights. And from the Hungarian perspective, the social and material welfare enjoyed by the "oppressed and exploited" average white Americans was almost unthinkable. Let us illustrate this paradoxical situation with the help of an interesting story. According to the Organization of the Communist Youth the organization held a demonstration in front of the building of the American Embassy in Budapest sometime at the end of the 1960s to protest against "American intervention in Vietnam". When the young people began to shout communist propaganda slogans, some American officials started to drop out of one of the embassy windows hundreds of pieces of chewing gum, which was not available in Hungarian shops at that time. And the mob of "aware" young communists started to pick up the packages of chewing gum from the pavement. No wonder the demonstration practically collapsed in a few minutes. It is highly probable that many of the participants of this "spontaneous demonstration of the people" really opposed the Vietnam War and the American intervention. But on the other hand, they were also eager to own at least some pieces of the material welfare which was inaccessible for them in a socialist country. Similarly, in Western Europe Coca-Cola and McDonald's became the symbols of American imperialism and political and military hegemony. But in Hungary they were considered to be small pieces of the free world. From this perspective, the arrival of Coca Cola in Hungary at the end of the 1960s and the opening of the first McDonald's fast food restaurant in Budapest in 1986 were very important events. Some Hungarian young people may have been disappointed that to find that Coca-Cola is not a serious drug, but it was very good for them to know that they had the opportunity to drink what Elvis Presley drank, for example. The same was true of American pop and rock music. Hungarian bands imitated them partly as an effort to establish an alternative culture to the official socialist entertainment industry.

Coca-Cola, blue jeans, some American literary products and movies became available by the second half of the 1960s in Hungary, which was a clear sign of the change of the policy of the Hungarian Socialist Workers' Party, as the communist party was renamed after 1956. The 1956 revolt was a great lesson for the communist leaders of Hungary too. They wanted to avoid a second uprising at almost any price and fundamentally this was also in the interest of the Soviet Union. János Kádár (1912-1989), who became the leader of the communist party as a result of the Soviet intervention in 1956, was imposed upon Hungary by the Soviets. The retribution after the defeat of the uprising was cruel and brutal and Kádár was considered by most ordinary Hungarians "the butcher of the nation" in the second half of the 1950s. But he also realized that the communist party had to change its policy in order to gain the support at least of some segments of Hungarian society. The communist party started to lay much greater emphasis on the standard of living of the people, and there was a real and significant improvement in this respect in the second half of the 1960s and in the 1970s. As a result of some economic reforms there was also an increase in the productivity of the economy, and Hungary became the food supplier of the other socialist countries. Many Hungarians accepted and supported this new policy because they compared it to the dogmatic Stalinism of the 1950s and also to the situation in some other socialist countries where shortage of food was still the part of everyday life. By the end of the 1960s Kádár had evolved to the position of the beneficial "uncle or father of the nation". A somewhat more liberal cultural policy was an integral part of this new line. It was allowed to publish works of American authors who criticized contemporary American society, as well as works that were indifferent from an ideological point of view. And this was also true for the products of the American film industry. In the eyes of many Hungarians this was a radical change, in sharp contrast with the almost complete ban of the 1950s. All these developments culminated in the restoration of the diplomatic relations on the ambassadorial level between the two nations in 1966, and the conclusion of an agreement on compensation for American property nationalized in Hungary after World War II in 1973. The Holy Crown of Saint Stephen, the symbol of Hungarian sovereignty had been captured by the American troops as war booty at the end of World War II, but the Carter administration decided to restore it to Hungary in 1978. One year later an Institute of Hungarian Studies was established at Indiana University (Bloomington), which was sponsored partly by the Hungarian government[11].

All these changes had been also observed by the few historians who still had an interest in the history of the American republic. As a side-effect of this new policy they were permitted to put greater emphasis on the drama of the American colonists' experiences and the sensational campaigns of the War for Independence, provided the studies remained within a more broadly interpreted Marxist framework. The three thin volumes by Ervin Szuhay-Havas were the results of this new policy. The title of his first book for example was the *Heroic Age of America* and it was about the history of the mainland British colonies in North America, but he also included a brief survey of the American Revolution in his work. Szuhay-Havas followed the Marxist-Leninist interpretation, but in a more sophisticated manner. In his opinion the American Revolution was a war for independence, a colonial revolt, and a social revolution at the same time. It was a war for independence which led to the founding of an independent new state. But it was undoubtedly the first "successful colonial revolt of a small nation", which set an example to such modern political developments as the movement of the "non-aligned nations" of the Third World. "But, was it also a revolution? Yes, of course. The Founding Fathers, the members of the Continental Congress inflamed the torch of the revolution in the New World, and they could rise to power by the help of an effusive popular movement. But after victory they were ready to restrain the movement of the tens and thousands of armed ordinary people". The leaders of the young American republic reacted with violence to the claims of the participants of the Shays rebellion. It is clear that for Szuhay-Havas the Shays rebellion represented the embodiment of the revolutionary nature of the event. "It was a struggle for independence, a colonial war, and a revolution, the result of which was not a popular government". This means that the dynamics of the American Revolution were similar to that of the French Revolution according to Szuhay-Havas. The only difference was that in America the popular movement was not strong enough to come to power, and the "bourgeoisie of the 'Thermidor Directory' was able to keep the power firmly in its hands throughout the revolution". Accordingly, quoting the evaluation of Karl Marx, Szuhay-Havas declared the federal constitution a "typical bourgeois-patrician" document[12].

Szuhay-Havas' book was written for a wider audience. Consequently it was full of interesting details concerning the daily life of the colonist, or the relations between the white settlers and the Native Americans. It is curious to note that in spite of its clear commitment to Marxism, the book also included many elements in common with the interpretation of the American historians of the 1950s. The members of the highly anti-communist consensus school argued that the historical development of the United States was exceptional. Paradoxically, this interpretation in many respects was in agreement with the Marxist approach in the sense that Marxist scholars also emphasized some differences between American and European history in order to be able to explain the special features of their "early bourgeois revolution". Szuhay-Havas also published a small volume about the American Civil War and in 1976 for the bicentenary of American independence a short book about the history of the American Revolution[13].

As compared to the other Marxist scholars mentioned above, in this book Szuhay-Havas emphasized the complexity of the American Revolution. He wanted to explain to his readers, for example, such problems as why some rich bourgeois decided to support independence and why some others remained loyal to the British Crown. He called the attention of the Hungarian public for the first time to the fact that the American Revolution was also a civil war. However, his final conclusion was pretty much the same as in his earlier book: The reactionary bourgeoisie decided to strengthen the federal government after the destruction of the Shays rebellion, and they imposed the new federal constitution on the people. For Szuhay-Havas the American Revolution represented the "third level in the history of bourgeois revolutions, after the rebellion of the Netherlands, and the English Revolution. This was the first in which religious issues did not play significant role... The classics of Marxism-Leninism were fully aware of the fact that the American Revolution was an early bourgeois revolution". But, quoting Lenin he also added that it was a progressive event of human history, since "this was one of the rare really revolutionary wars in the history of mankind"[14]. The volumes of Ervin Szuhay-Havas clearly had become outdated. Not only did they reflect official Marxist ideology but the author was rarely aware of the important changes that occurred in the historical interpretation of the colonial era and the revolution in the 1960s and 1970s. Of course this was not simply the author's fault.

When I was in my first and second year at the beginning of the 1980s my English was still quite poor so I could not read books in English. At that time of course, I was not aware of the deficiencies of Szuhay-Havas's books. I read them and as a consequence of the features mentioned above they attracted me strongly. From them, it was clear that the birth of the United States was a heroic human experiment and we cannot understand great power of the 20th century without knowledge of its historical roots. It became also evident for me that the story is much more complicated than its official Marxist version.

When I was in my third year we had a guest professor named. Mihály Mózes. He was history teacher in the best high school in my town. He had a PhD and he also held classes at the university. He had relatives in Australia and he became interested in the history of the territories outside Europe, mainly Australia and the United States. He announced an introductory course in 19th century U.S. history, which was the first class of this kind at my University in Hungarian. There were great difficulties because of the lack of literature. This is why the publication of a collection of fundamental texts of American history in Hungarian was such an important development in 1981. The editor, Aladár Urbán, professor of history at the University of Budapest, published for the first time in the Hungarian language such important documents of the American Revolution as the *Declaration of the Causes and Necessity of Taking up Arms*, or *The Treaty of Alliance with France* and many others[15].

The relatively relaxed policy of the Communist Party continued into the 1980s and two classic works of early American historiography were published in Hungarian. The first was the first volume of Henry Adams' *The History of the United States during the Administration of Jefferson and Madison* (published in 1986), and the second was Charles A. Beard's *An Economic Interpretation of the Constitution of the United States* (published in 1988). As mentioned before, Beard's approach was relatively close to the official Marxist-Leninist interpretation of the American Revolution and was fundamentally applauded by Marxist historians. Nevertheless, it was also clear that his evaluation of the ratification of the federal constitution was not totally identical with that of the Marxist scholars. Consequently, the publication of Beard's original text was a very important development from the point of view of the emergence of a more sophisticated picture of the American Revolution in Hungary. Not to mention that the introduction, written by Forrest McDonald, one of the greatest living experts of the topic, had also been translated. Aladár Urbán also attached an afterword, and with the help of these two explanatory writings, Hungarian readers received very good information about the historiographical debates on Beard's work. The Hungarian historical journal *Világtörténet* [World History], dedicated to the history of the world outside Hungary, also published a special issue for the bicentennial of the federal constitution in 1987, which included a study by Forrest McDonald and Aladár Urbán about the ratification of the constitution and the *Bill of Rights*[16].

The collapse of the socialist regime at the end of the 1980s reopened the way for the publication of non-Marxist interpretations of the American Revolution. In addition, the American Revolution came to be seen as representing a moderate change of regime in contrast with the violence of the French and the Russian Revolutions. In Hungary the reformist wing of the communist party as well as the opposition strove for a peaceful constitutional transformation. Consequently, the example of the birth of the United States – and especially the processes through which its constitution had been made – was compelling. Hungarians had to face the same problem the American Founding fathers had confronted two centuries earlier: how to establish a functioning democracy? The Declaration of Independence, the Federal Constitution of 1787 and various other documents had already been translated into Hungarian, and these were now joined by several essential texts of early American political thought including the Articles of Confederation and the Federalist Papers, as well as key writings by leading figures of the American Revolution such as Thomas Jefferson, John Adams, James Madison and Alexander Hamilton[17].

Three general histories of the United States were published in four years during the first half of the 1990s. It is very interesting on the other hand that two of these works represented the strongly anti-Marxist American consensus historiography of the 1950s, and only one of them could be regarded as a contemporary approach. The publication of the two former books was probably an effort on the part of the Hungarian editors to counterbalance the ruling Marxist interpretation of the former decades. Not to mention the fact that both of them had been originally written for a wider audience, and Hungarian publishers might have thought that the publication of such works could be attractive for the Hungarian public after the collapse of the socialist regime[18].

In 1994 Aladár Urbán published the first detailed account of the political history of the American Revolution written by a Hungarian historian. As a political history the book was accurate, and filled a definite need. But the social, economic and intellectual history of the American Revolution was hardly mentioned by the author. And as a Marxist historian, Urbán's approach in this book was not fundamentally different from the official opinion of the former decades. He annexed a brief chapter about the historiography of the revolution to his book. No wonder he applauded the approach of the progressive historians whose interpretation was closest to his own. Urbán concluded that "a significant part of the American historical profession shares the opinion that the revolution was a *bourgeois revolution*, with all the political, social and economic consequences of this fact"[19].

Nevertheless, the collapse of the socialist regime made possible the pluralistic interpretation of the American Revolution and the latest university textbooks also reflect this change. The author of one of these textbooks, Péter Hahner, who also published a short, popular biography of George Washington at the end of the 1980s, clearly wanted to distance himself from the Marxist interpretation of the socialist era. He intended to avoid even describing the event as a revolution, since he mentioned that "it is called by the Americans a revolution, although there were no radical inventions, social upheaval, terror or dictatorship". He argue for the distinctiveness of the American events in contrast to the French and the Russian Revolutions. In his eyes the "remarkable political changes", such as the establishment of the new federal government, represented the real magnitude of the American events. But he also added that there were "significant social consequences of the political transformation as well", for example the abolition of primogeniture and the introduction of "republican simplicity" in the manners of the people. Hahner concluded that the "American War for Independence was a political revolution with some social consequences, which resulted the further strengthening of the democratic tendencies of the political and social system, inherited from England"[20].

There is no doubt that the collapse of the socialist regime has created vastly improved conditions for the study of the American Revolution in Hungary. More and more sources and databases are available on the net. More and more Eastern and Central European students can speak English and more and more of them will be able to do research in the United States and complete their dissertations there. Hungarian scholars of the American Revolution have much better opportunities to participate in international research networks and projects. On the other hand, financial sources are still limited, and fifteen years after the collapse of the communist regime the enthusiasm of the early 1990s has faded; most history students consider the American Revolution as an important but not especially relevant event. The younger generation have grown up in, and thus do not find remarkable, a democratic and pluralist society and culture.

Notes

1 *Az Egyesült Államok története*, I. kötet, Budapest 1964, p. 80.

2 *Ibid.*, pp. 89-90.

3 *Az Egyesült Államok története* cit., II. kötet, pp. 390, 393.

4 W.Z. Foster, *Az Egyesült Államok Kommunista pártjának története*, Budapest 1953; *Az Egyesült Államok története* cit., II. kötet, p. 399.

5 *Az Egyesült Államok története* cit., II. kötet, pp. 399-400.

6 H. Aptheker, *American Negro Slave Revolts*, New York 1943; S. Armeny, *Letter to the editor*, "Journal of American History", 87, 2000 December, p. 1176; *Az Egyesült Államok története* cit, II. kötet, pp. 404-405; H. Aptheker, *The Negro in the American Revolution*, New York 1940. This booklet was only 47 pages long and was surpassed by Benjamin Quarles' book with the same title (Chapel Hill 1961) pp. 231.

7 T. Wittman, *Egyetemes történet, 1500-1789*, Budapest 1989, pp. 162-167.

8 G. Kis, *Egyetemes történet, 1640-1789*, Budapest 1987, pp. 70-78.

9 L. Solti, *1787. Az amerikai történetírás évszázados vitájának újabb állomásai*, Budapest 1985, pp. 7-9.

10 Solti, *Az amerikai történetírás* cit., pp. 21, 31.

11 On the policy of the communist party in this period see: L. Kontler, *Millennium in Central Europe. A History of Hungary*, Budapest 1999, pp. 430-468.

12 E. Szuhay-Havas, *Amerika hőskora*, Budapest 1969, pp. 320-21, p. 324.

13 On American historiography in the 1950s see for example J. Higham, *The Cult of the 'American Consensus': Homogenizing Our History*, "Commentary", February 1959; C. Lévai, *American historiography in the 1950s: the case of Daniel J. Boorstin*, Proceedings of the 2003 Biennial Conference of the Hungarian Association of American Studies, Budapest 2005, pp. 183-189.

14 E. Szuhay Havas, *Tizenhárom csillag*, Budapest 1976, p. 265.

15 A. Urbán (ed.), *Dokumentumok az Egyesült Államok történetéhez 1774-1918*, Budapest 1981.

16 H. Adams, *Thomas Jefferson első elnöksége, 1801-1805*, Budapest 1986; Ch.A. Beard, *Az Egyesült Államok alkotmányának gazdasági értelmezése*, Budapest 1988; A. Urbán, *Az Egyesült Államok alkotmányának életbe léptetése és első kiegészítései (1789-1791)*, "Világtörténet", 1, 1988, pp. 20-26; F. McDonald, *Mi az Egyesült Államok népe...*, "Világtörténet", 1, 1988, pp. 3-20.

17 Cs. Lévai (ed.), *Új rend egy új világban. Dokumentumok az amerikai politikai gondolkodás korai történetéhez*, Debrecen 1997; P. Bődy - A. Urbán (eds.), *Szöveggyűjtemény az Amerikai Egyesült Államok történetéhez 1620-1980*, Budapest-Pécs 2001; A. Hamilton - J. Madison - J. Jay, *A föderalista. Értekezések az amerikai alkotmányról*, Budapest 1998.

18 D. Boorstin, *Az amerikaiak: a gyarmatosítás kora*, Budapest 1991; C.N. Degler, *Az élő múlt. Milyen erők formálták Amerika mai képét?* Budapest 1993; Ch. Sellers - H. May - N.R. McMillen, *Az Egyesült Államok története*, Budapest 1995. On the Hungarian editions of Boorstin's and Degler's books see Cs. Lévai, *Az amerikaiak és a történetírás*, "BUKSZ-Budapesti Könyvszemle", 1, 1993, pp. 434-443.

19 A. Urbán, *Köztársaság az Újvilágban. Az Egyesült Államok születése, 1763-1789*, Budapest 1994, p. 323. On this book see C. Lévai's review in "BOOKS-Budapest Review of Books", 1, 1995, pp. 40-42.

[20] P. Hahner, *A régi rend alkonya. Egyetemes történet 1648-1815*, Budapest 2006, pp. 435-437; P. Hahner, *Így élt Washington*, Budapest 1991.

Bibliography

Az Egyesült Államok története, I-II. kötet, Budapest 1964.

Boorstin D., *Az amerikaiak: a gyarmatosítás kora*, Budapest 1991.

Bődy P. - Urbán A. (eds.), *Szöveggyűjtemény az Amerikai Egyesült Államok történetéhez 1620-1980*, Budapest-Pécs 2001.

Degler C.N., *Az élő múlt. Milyen erők formálták Amerika mai képét?* Budapest 1993.

Hahner P., *Így élt Washington*, Budapest 1991

Id., *A régi rend alkonya. Egyetemes történet 1648-1815*, Budapest 2006, pp. 435-437.

Kis G., *Egyetemes történet, 1640-1789*, Budapest 1987.

Kontler L., *Millennium in Central Europe. A History of Hungary*, Budapest 1999.

Lévai C., *Az amerikaiak és a történetírás*, "BUKSZ-Budapesti Könyvszemle", 1/1993, pp. 434-443.

Id. (ed.), *Új rend egy új világban. Dokumentumok az amerikai politikai gondolkodás korai történetéhez*, Debrecen 1997.

Id., *American historiography in the 1950s: the case of Daniel J. Boorstin*, in *Proceedings of the 2003 Biennial Conference of the Hungarian Association of American Studies*, Budapest 2005.

Sellers Ch. - May H. - McMillen N.R., *Az Egyesült Államok története*, Budapest 1995.

Solti L., *1787. Az amerikai történetírás évszázados vitájának újabb állomásai*, Budapest, 1985.

Szuhay Havas E., *Amerika hőskora*, Budapest 1969.

Id., *Tizenhárom csillag*, Budapest 1976.

Urbán A. (ed.), *Dokumentumok az Egyesült Államok történetéhez 1774-1918*, Budapest, 1981.

Id., *Köztársaság az Újvilágban. Az Egyesült Államok születése, 1763-1789*, Budapest 1994.

Wittman T., *Egyetemes történet, 1500-1789*, Budapest 1989.

Source

Mi az tehát amit a polgári történetírás nem ért, mi viszont világosan látunk? Nem érti sokszor a tudós burzsoá sem, hogyan állhatott az ingékony tömeg élére annyi száz, annyi ezer dúsgazdag John Hancock, annyi száz, annyi ezer dzsentri neveltetésû George Washington. Megfordítva, még kevésbé értik, miért bukkannak elénk a pellengérre állított amerikai toryk között boltosok, cipészek, kovácsok, molnárok, sőt szolgák és bérmunkások. Pedig a magyarázat kézenfekvő. Az amerikai polgári forradalom folyamatában, az első tisztán "világi" forradalom folyamatában azért szerepelnek nagy számban gazdagok, mert a saját törvényhozásaikra büszke, a brit kereskedelmi törvényeket és vámintézkedéseket sérelmezô uralkodó osztályok, saját érdekeik védelmében, összefognak egyetlen szövetségesükkel, a néptömeggel. Önmaguk nem vívhatnák meg a harcot a siker reményében egy világbirodalom ellen. Közöttük és a kizsákmányolt tömegek között természet szabta osztályharc feszül.

What bourgeois historiography could not understand, and what is clear for us? Even the scholarly bourgeois cannot understand how could it happen that so many extremely rich people like John Hancock, and so many educated gentry like Gorge Washington, led the unsteady mob. It is even more obscure for them why there were so many shopkeepers, shoemakers, forgers, millers and even servants and wage workers among the disdained American Tories. In turn the explanation is clear and simple. There were so many rich people in leading roles in the process of American *bourgeois* revolution, in the course of the first "secular" revolution, because the ruling classes, so proud of their legislations, and which so vehemently opposed the commercial and tariff regulations of the British, in order to protect their own interests, joined forces with the masses. There was no hope to defeat a world power alone. But there was also a natural class struggle between them and the exploited masses.

From: E. Szuhay-Havas, *A tizenhárom csillag*, Budapest 1976, pp. 237-38.

All Quiet For Forty Years: the Hungarian Participation in the American Civil War. A Historiographical Essay

István Kornél Vida
University of Debrecen

A tanulmány írásakor arra vállalkoztam, hogy az amerikai polgárháború magyar részvételével foglalkozó, tudományos igényű munkákat vegyem nagyítóüveg alá. Noha a magyar-amerikai történelmi kapcsolatok egyik legnagyobb érdeklődésre számot tartó fejezetéről van szó, mindössze három ilyen könyvet találhatunk. Pivány Jenő, Vasváry Ödön és Ács Tivadar könyvei feltétlenül hiányt pótlóak voltak korukban, azonban helyenként elégtelen módszertani megközelítésük, a referenciák teljes hiánya, s az a tény, hogy a szerzők egyike sem igyekezett elhelyezni a magyarok polgárháborús részvételét a konfliktusban szerepelt vállalt külföldiek között, mind arra figyelmeztetik a témával foglalkozó történészt, hogy szükség van egy modern, az objektív értékelést mindig szem előtt tartó szintézisre, amely a modern polgárháborús amerikai kutatások eredményeit is hasznosítja. Természetesen ezt a témát sem lehet kontextusából kiemelni, ezért írásom első felében a magyar-amerikai kapcsolatok szintézis-törekvéseivel foglalkozom, majd pedig a Kossuth-emigráció történeti feldolgozásai kerülnek előtérbe. A magyarok polgárháborús szereplésével kapcsolatban az olvasó betekintést nyerhet az utóbbi egy-két évtized törekvéseire, amelyek elsősorban az eddig fel nem tárt források publikálására koncentrálnak, s a dolgozat utolsó részében pedig egyfajta iránymutatást kívánok nyújtani ahhoz, hogy milyen irányú kutatások szükségesek a téma alapos és "mítoszcsinálás-mentes" feldolgozásához, s mindezzel talán elérhető, hogy megtörjön Ács Tivadar 1964-ben megjelent műve óta tapasztalható "negyven esztendős csend", amelyre cikkem címében is utaltam.

It is not at all an exaggeration to say that Americans are obsessed with the history of their Civil War (1861-1865). So far more than 50,000 books have been published on probably all possible aspects of the conflict one can imagine and the number is still constantly growing. We could enumerate quite a few possible reasons for this immense popularity and interest (this was the bloodiest fratricidal war in American history; at its end the institution of slavery was done away with; the conflict brought around the "real" United States of America, exempt from sectional divisions; many consider this the first modern war, etc.), but it remains a fact that the heroes of the Civil War are very much alive in American memory. However, among the numerous Civil War-related issues, there seem to be some which have been neglected by several generations of historians. One of these is the involvement of foreign-born soldiers in the conflict. The appearance of Ella Lonn's trail-blazing *Foreigners in the Confederacy* (1940), which was followed more than a decade later by her *Foreigners in the Union Army and Navy* (1951)[1], indicated a shift of emphasis in modern Civil War studies: historians started to show more sensitivity to the social and ethnic background of the soldiers, they seemed to be more interested in the foot soldiers than in the commanding generals, etc. Although there have been some other books published studying the involvement of the foreign-born in the war between the states, Lonn's books are still the definitive works on the subject[2]. Of course, almost every ethnic group has its own historian who studied its presence in the United States. The problem with these works in general is that they are too biased and they attach too much importance to the specific ethnic group they scrutinize and to which they themselves belong. Therefore, one has to be very cautious when reading these books, as the overwhelming majority of these works are pure mythmaking devices in the hands of ethnic groups, the overall aim of which is to create cohesion within the group and justify its presence in America. These groups are often competing against each other and, unfortunately, most of the time it is historical accuracy which falls victim to these kinds of rivalry. Therefore, it is of utmost importance, for those who study the history of various ethnic groups in the United States, to be dedicated to giving an impartial account of this episode of historical links and contacts between our homeland and the United States. This necessitates a constant development in the historiography on the topic and that is why I have assigned this as the primary goal of my dissertation, now in progress. Below, I wish to survey the historiography of the so-called Kossuth emigration in general and the Hungarians' participation in the American Civil War in particular.

But before getting down to this, it is worth mentioning that very few have attempted to write about those who have studied the Hungarian-American past. In her article on Károly Rácz Rónay, one of the often-neglected students of the subject, Mária Kórász devoted a couple of lines and footnote references to the historiography of the presence of Hungarians in America. Nevertheless, the definitive work to turn to for historiographical information in this field is Béla Várdy's *Magyarok az Újvilágban* [Hungarians in the New World] (2000)[3], which contains an extensive bibliography of virtually all accessible archival and published works dealing with Hungarian-American historical relations. Várdy considered this subject crucial enough to devote an entire subchapter of his thick volume to it. And, more or less, that is about it. Unfortunately, so far no other historian has attempted to write about those who studied the past of the Hungarian-American community.

Attempts to synthesize the history of Hungarian Americans

There is no shortage of works, however, offering a comprehensive study of the history of people of Hungarian origin in America. The first of these works was an article by Sándor Márki, professor of history from Kolozsvár, entitled *America and the Hungarians* (1893)[4], which not only is of excellent scholarly quality, but also definitely served as a basis for further investigations for subsequent generations of researchers. Eugene (Jenő) Pivány (1873-1946), the ardent and prolific student of the topic undoubtedly did a lot of research and discovered numerous documents revealing various pieces of information concerning the life of Hungarian immigrants in the United States. However, he did not compose a synthesis of Hungarian-American history, yet some aspects of his research were summarized in a number of articles. He published a volume under the title *Hungarian-American Historical Connections* (1927) which followed the Hungarian version of the book published the year before[5]. In this work he concentrated on the history of Hungarian-Americans up to the time of the Civil War. The intended second volume was never completed. Pivány did not use references in any of his works and, unfortunately, the overwhelming majority of his collections was lost during the Second World War, so many of his claims are almost impossible to validate. Still, he undeniably had a great impact on later generations of historians. Géza Kende (1879-1933), journalist, editor of the Cleveland *Szabadság* daily, contributed to this field of study with the first synthesis of the history of the Hungarian presence in America. He published a two-volume work entitled *Magyarok Amerikában. Az amerikai magyarság története* [Hungarians in America. The History of Hungarian-Americans] (1927)[6], the third volume of which was never completed. *Magyarok Amerikában* is a colourful collection of anecdotes, yet it is riddled with numerous errors. Still, we must agree with Professor Várdy who writes that this is "almost an indispensable book, which is worthy of a new edition containing the so-far unpublished third volume"[7]. Let us remark here that Kende did not include references in his work either.

One of the most prolific Hungarian-American historians was Edmund (Ödön) Vasváry (1888-1977) who not only was an excellent researcher, but also authored a vast number of articles about the Hungarians in the United States. Nevertheless, just like many of his forerunners, he did not attempt to organize his material into a single volume. The vast amount of material he put together during many decades of active life constituted the basis of the collection which is named after him and is in the possession of the Somogyi Library in Szeged, Hungary. This library published a posthumous book entitled *Magyar Amerika* [Hungarian America](1988)[8] which is practically a collection of articles by Vasváry, although they cover only a tiny fragment of his life's work.

The first synthesis in English about this subject was written by Emil Lengyel (1895-1985). His *Americans from Hungary* (1948)[9] was partly based on the works of the above-mentioned historians and was, unfortunately, not free of many of their factual errors. However, the second half of the book (discussing the period from 1914) was based on Lengyel's own research, and this makes it an excellent contribution to the study of Hungarian-American historical links and contacts.

The following decades saw a great number of historians researching various related topics, although no further syntheses were written in the period. Julianna Puskás published her *Kivándorló magyarok az Egyesült Államokban, 1880-1940* (1982), the somewhat abridged version of which was published in English as well: *From Hungary to the United States, 1880-1914* (1982)[10]. As the title suggests, Puskás concentrated on the so-called New Immigration and treated the Ante-bellum waves of Hungarian emigration to the United States as if they had never existed, which is definitely the gravest shortcoming of her work. However, the hefty volume is based on extensive research and it definitely targets the academic audience, and for that reason it is not as well known as some of the popular books of dubious scholarly quality. In 2000 Professor Puskás published an excellent synthesis in which she made use of the results of her more recent research: *Ties that Bind, Ties that Divide: 100 Years of Hungarian Experience in the United States*[11].

At the same time, there were attempts to create a synthesis in America as well. Steven Béla Várdy published his *The Hungarian Americans* (1985)[12], which more than one and a half decades later was followed by another, the already-mentioned *Magyarok az Újvilágban* (2000). Várdy is undoubtedly the most prolific historian studying the past of the Hungarian-Americans, he authored or co-authored sixteen books and some 450 articles, essays and reviews. *Magyarok az Újvilágban* is a readable book intended for the amateur reader as well as for professional historians, however, when writing the first half of his book, especially the chapters dealing with the Old Immigration and the Civil War, he borrowed extensively from the available secondary literature and often did so without questioning it. For this reason he inevitably keeps some recurrent mistakes alive. Nonetheless, Professor Várdy's book is excellent and exhaustive, and being so it is one of its kind in the literature examining the presence of Hungarians in the United States. One can only hope that he will be proven wrong when he writes that "after the retirement of the present generation of scholars there is not going to be another Hungarian American generation that can continue this work"[13].

The Kossuth Emigration

Those eager to get reliable information about the first sizeable wave of Hungarian emigration to the United States are not at all kindly treated by the historians. There is only a single major comprehensive work on this subject: Lajos Lukács's *A magyar politikai emigráció, 1849-1867* [The Hungarian Political Emigration, 1849-1867] (1984)[14], which is by no means an exhaustive work. Of course, much information can be acquired from the above-mentioned general studies of the Hungarian-American past, yet sometimes they do not go beyond scratching the surface. Therefore, one has no other option but to get down to reading the more specific works on the topic.

What can be realized right away is that the majority of the books about this initial period of mass emigration are publications of primary sources: diaries, memoirs, correspondence between emigrants and those who stayed behind in Hungary, etc. This is to be appreciated, as many documents have been made accessible to a wide range of readers. However, the evaluation of these sources requires some preliminary knowledge of the subject, which is often not provided in the works; furthermore, many of the editors of these volumes did not bother to include correct references, which makes it almost impossible to track down their sources. Another problem with these books, and this is always a problem when dealing with historical links between two countries, is that one half of the sources is available in Hungary and the other in the United States. Some of them were written in Hungarian, some in English, and some even in German. Therefore, reading knowledge of at least two languages is a prerequisite here, as, unfortunately, only some of these documents have been translated into English and Hungarian.

Unfortunately, a full analysis of this group of works would go way beyond the scope of this essay. Therefore, what I propose here is to give a brief outline of the most important and most useful monographs.

The two-volume *A Kossuth emigráció Angliában és Amerikában, 1851-52* [The Kossuth Emigration in England and America, 1851-52] (1940-1944)[15] is an essential work, although, as is apparent from the title, it concentrates only on the first two years of this wave of immigrants to the United States and ignores the rest of the 1850s. Fortunately, there are many other works covering this period. The name of Tivadar Ács has to be mentioned in this context, as he published and edited a number of accounts of first-hand immigrant experience: *Kossuth papja: Ács Gedeon* [Kossuth's Priest: Gedeon Ács](1940); New-Buda (1941); *Akik elvándoroltak* [Those who Transmigrated](1942); *Magyarok idegenben* [Hungarians Far From Home](1946); *Magyar úttörők az Újvilágban, László Károly naplófeljegyzései, 1850-1867* [Hungarian Trailblazers in the New World: The Diaries of Károly László, 1850-1867] (1942); *A száműzöttek. Fiala János emlékiratai* [The Castaway: The memoirs of János Fiala] (1943)[16]. Similarly intriguing insight into the everyday life of Hungarian Americans is offered by the volumes entitled *Mészáros Lázár külföldi levelei*[The letters of Lázár Mészáros written abroad] (Ed.Viktor Szokoly) (1867); Perczel Miklós's *Naplóm az emigrációból* [My Diary from the Emigration](1977); and Kinizsi István's recently-published *A Sánta Huszár naplója* [The Diary of the Lame Hussar](1999)[17]. All these books offer bits and pieces of information, yet it is indeed a hard work to systematize them – no wonder that so far no historian has attempted to do this immensely challenging, and at the same time crucial, work.

Writing about the Participation of the Hungarians in the American Civil War

Considering the fact that the Kossuth emigration has been somewhat ignored by historians, it may sound surprising that one – albeit important – episode of this period has excited the interest of Hungarian as well as Hungarian-American historians, so much so that three volumes have been written on this topic alone! Notwithstanding, if one takes a closer look at these works, it will become apparent that these three books are actually not three, but just one or two!

Jenő Pivány's *Hungarians in the American Civil War,* which was published as early as in 1913[18], is a pioneering work indeed. The problem with it was, however, that it is riddled with factual errors and – especially in the light of modern Civil War studies and research – one cannot escape noticing that Pivány, who was a journalist after all, lacked the interest (and probably the ability) to place the Hungarians within the wider framework of foreign participation in the American Civil War. Like the chroniclers of other ethnic groups, he exaggerated the number of Hungarians participating in the conflict and he applauded their extraordinary heroism. (Interestingly, his estimation of the total number of people of Hungarian origin living in the United States around the time of the outbreak of the Civil War was fairly moderate, or approximately 4,000. Nevertheless, he wrote that about 800 of them got involved in the conflict, which would mean that one out of five Hungarians took up arms in the Civil War. No other ethnic group in the United States was even close to this high representation in the war effort.) In spite of all these shortcomings of his book, Pivány did an excellent job as a pioneering researcher, and he showed the way for the next generations of historians.

Edmund Vasváry devoted his only book-length work to this subject matter: he published his bilingual *Lincoln's Hungarians Heroes* in 1939[19]. His work is definitely the one to consult if someone wishes to get a preliminary picture of the Hungarians' involvement in the Civil War. He managed to revise and implement the earlier work by Pivány and he placed the topic in its correct historical context. Vasváry broke away from the 'traditions' of his predecessors, including an extensive list of references and brief biographical sketches in his work. Of course, all this does not mean that *Lincoln's Hungarian Heroes* is without mistakes and misconceptions, because it is indeed also riddled with errors, many minor and some major ones. I personally believe that he did not choose wisely when he chose the title of the book, because it suggests that Hungarians fought only in the Union Army, which was not the case – as is acknowledged by the author as well. Similarly to Pivány, he exaggerated both the number of Hungarians living in the United States at the time of the Civil War and of those who took up arms in the conflict. In 1963-64 the William Penn Fraternal Association published a series of articles by Vasváry under the title *Lincoln and the Hungarians*[20], which, however, did not represent a brand new approach to the topic, although some new information can be acquired from them.

The third book on this subject is the only one published only in Hungarian. Tivadar Ács finished his *Magyarok az észak-amerikai polgárháborúban 1861-65* [Hungarians in the North American Civil War] in 1964[21] and this is still the most recent book on the subject. Ács thought that the estimations of his precursors had to be revised and, according to him, no fewer than 5,000 Hungarians fought in the Civil War. Of course, on the basis of modern Civil War research and the census data of 1860 and 1870, we can conclude that in all likelihood the grand total of the Hungarians living in the United States at the time of the Civil War was considerably lower than 5,000, not to mention the number of those who actually participated in the fights. Ács made use of the fact that the first two books on this subject had been relatively unknown in Hungary and his aim was to celebrate the "Hungarian heroes", whose names "should be sacred and their bravery and honour with which they shed their blood in defence of freedom outside their homeland must be forever remembered"[22]. Some parts of *Magyarok az amerikai polgárháborúban* is pure mythmaking and, apart from the many factual errors, this is probably its greatest shortcoming. Ács's knowledge of the Civil War was clearly superficial and he obviously failed to put the Hungarian participation in the war in its correct context.

Modern Research on the Hungarians' Involvement in the Civil War

The title of this chapter begins with the phrase "All quiet for forty years", which is supposed to indicate that not a single book has been published on this topic since 1964. No wonder that Martin Öfele, in his book entitled *German-Speaking Officers in the U.S. Colored Troops, 1863-1867* (2004)[23] concludes that "the participation of Hungarians in the American Civil War has so far received only scarce attention in historical literature". He himself used Vasváry's outdated book as a reference.

This does, however, not mean that there has not been any research carried out in this field of study in the last couple of decades. A Canadian-Hungarian, Stephen Beszedits, is definitely the most ardent and prolific contemporary student of the Hungarians' involvement in the American Civil War. Although he is not a historian by profession, he does not commit the same mistakes as Pivány, Vasváry or Ács: he has researched the topic extensively, his arguments are judiciously constructed, and he avoids mythmaking and jumping to unfounded assumptions. Primarily, he has focused on the lives of some Hungaraians (Charles Semsey, Julius H. Stahel, Frederick Knefler and Rudolf Tauszky), and he summarized his findings in shorter articles, which are accessible on the Internet. His only book is the publication of the prison diary of Emeric Szabad, a Hungarian prisoner of war during the Civil War: *The Libby Prison Diary by Colonel Emeric Szabad* (1999)[24]. He has managed to accumulate a huge amount of material on the topic and one can just hope that he will summarize all his findings in a longer work in the not-so-distant future. As for the present author, I started to examine this topic while I was still an undergraduate student and I gave an overview of the results of my research in a paper titled *Doing Away with Myths: A New Look at the Participation of the Hungarians in the American Civil War* (2001)[25], which won the national first prize at the Hungarian Students' Conference in the same year. As a postgraduate student, I have continued my studies and the ultimate goal of my dissertation is to provide the first objective analysis of this intriguing subject.

The Course to Follow

The question may arise whether new research can provide additional information on this subject. It is true that the majority of the primary sources used by the present author are similar to those used for the already published books. One can rely on memoirs, diaries and travelogues, but, unfortunately, most of these works concentrate on the 1850s; therefore, hardly any first-hand information can be gained from them about the Civil War. An analysis of these memoirs was published as early as 1917 by Géza Kacziány[26], who gives an overview of the memoranda which can be connected to the emigration as well. Politicians, soldiers and travellers are discussed and Kacziány's work is really useful, although the fact that it is out-dated can be disturbing. Moreover, the reader has to be highly critical concerning the author's judgements, too.

As we have seen, a number of memoirs have been published in Hungarian, but in spite of the fact that the author of many of them did fight in the Civil War, they contain no reliable information on the war itself. The works by János Fiala, István Kinizsy and others, all belong to this group. Other authors reflect on the war and very briefly on their participation in it (see for example Miklós Perczel). There are several works published only in English, but they belong to a trend which was very typical for the post-Civil-War period when the authors' basic aim was self-justification. The best example of this group is Col. Estván's *War Pictures from the South*[27], which earlier had been considered a serious and reliable work. As a matter of fact, Estván was a Munchausen-like figure, whose recollections are full of distortions, and therefore his work can hardly be used without reservations[28].

It is heartening that there seems to be a need among Hungarian-Americans as well to search for unpublished documents in connection with their history and that their range of interest also covers the Civil War, which has been ignored until recently. The latest manifestation of these efforts is *The Libby Prison Diary*. Stephen Beszedits, who is "a chemical engineer by vocation" and "a historian only by avocation", has taken great efforts in locating so-far unknown material, and he is in touch with a few descendants of Hungarian Civil War participants, who own a number of invaluable primary sources. Just to mention one of them, Janet Kozlay is dedicated to publishing the documents of Eugene Kozlay (1826-1883), of the 54th New York Volunteer Infantry Regiment, and we look forward to reading it.

The primary documents which can be found in military archives are as useful from our perspective as the above-mentioned sources, and since the research in these archieves and their accessibility has gone through remarkable development during the past few decades in the United States they can reveal new details on the Hungarian soldiers as well. We are fortunate that many of these documents can be researched via the Internet, which makes it possible to investigate Civil War battle reports, regiment muster-rolls, individual war records, etc., from afar. Earlier it would have taken several months to get hold of these pieces of information, whereas it is just a matter of minutes now.

The most difficult task for the historian is to identify Hungarian soldiers in the records of the War Department, despite the fact that many of these records are now available on the Internet too. If the place of birth of a certain soldier is not mentioned in the rosters, we can only start out from the appearance of his name, which can often be misleading. Many foreign names bear a close resemblance to Hungarian ones; therefore the form of the name by itself cannot be decisive. Historians have to find sources in which the names suspected to be Hungarian had already appeared and this can put an end to uncertainty.

It must be mentioned that not only the primary sources, but the secondary ones as well are much more accessible for us now than they were a few decades ago. Although – as has been already pointed out – not a single comprehensive work has been published in Hungarian on this subject since 1964, plenty of works dealing with the Kossuth-emigration, the Koszta affair and other episodes of Hungarian-American relations have appeared in recent years. But it is the research done on the Civil War in the United States which is staggering, as manifested both in archival documents and published material. Moreover, the present and possibly the future generations of historians are much luckier than those who worked in the decades during the socialist regime, as there are more opportunities to travel and do research overseas. Hopefully, this will convince many young scholars that there is a point in studying the historical links and contacts between Hungary and the United States of America.

Notes

1 E. Lonn, *Foreigners in the Confederacy*, Chapel Hill 1940; E. Lonn, *Foreigners in the Union Army and Navy*, Baton Rouge 1951.

2 For one of the recent works on this subject-matter, see D. Mahin, *Blessed Place of Freedom: Europeans in Civil War America,* Washington, DC 2002.

3 B. Várdy, *Magyarok az Újvilágban*, Budapest 2000.

4 S. Márki, *Amerika s a magyarság*, in "Földrajzi Közlemények", 2, 1893, pp. 49-94.

5 J. Pivány, *Magyar-amerikai történeti kapcsolatok*, Budapest 1926; J. Pivány, *Hungarian-American Historical Connections*, Budapest 1927.

6 G. Kende, *Magyarok Amerikában. Az amerikai magyarság története*, 2 vols., Cleveland 1927.

7 Várdy, *Magyarok az Újvilágban* cit., p. 589.

8 Ö. Vasváry, *Magyar Amerika*, Szeged 1988.

9 E. Lengyel, *Americans from Hungary*, Philadelphia 1948.

10 J. Puskás, *Kivándorló magyarok az Egyesült Államokban 1880-1940*, Budapest 1982; J. Puskás, *From Hungary to the United States, 1880-1914*, Budapest 1982.

11 J. Puskás, *Ties that Bind, Ties that Divide*, New York 2000.

12 B. Várdy, *The Hungarian Americans*, Boston 1985.

13 Várdy, *Magyarok az Újvilágban* cit., p. 594.

14 L. Lukács, *Magyar politikai emigráció, 1849-1867*, Budapest 1984.

15 D. Jánossy (ed.), *A Kossuth-emigráció Angliában és Amerikában, 1851-52*, 2 vols., Budapest 1940-1944.

16 T. Ács, *Kossuth papja: Ács Gedeon*, Budapest 1940; T. Ács, *New-Buda*, Budapest 1941; T. Ács, *Akik elvándoroltak*, Budapest 1942; T. Ács, *Magyarok idegenben*, Budapest 1946; T. Ács, *Magyar úttörők az Újvilágban, László Károly naplófeljegyzései, 1850-1867*, Budapest, 1942; T. Ács, *A száműzöttek. Fiala János emlékiratai*, Budapest 1943.

17 V. Szokoly, *Mészáros Lázár külföldi levelei*, Pest 1867; M. Perczel, *Naplóm az emigrációból*, 2 vols., Budapest 1977-1979; I. Kinizsi, *A "Sánta Huszár" naplója*, Marosvásárhely 1999.

18 J. Pivány, *Hungarians in the Civil War*, Cleveland 1913.

19 Ö. Vasváry, *Lincoln's Hungarian Heroes*, Washington, DC 1939.

20 Ö. Vasváry, *Lincoln and the Hungarians,* Pittsburgh 1963-64.

21 T. Ács, *Magyarok az észak-amerikai polgárháborúban 1861-65*, Budapest 1964.

22 Ács, *Magyarok* cit., p. 124.

23 M. Öfele, *German-Speaking Officers in the U.S. Colored Troops, 1863-1867*, Tallahassee 2004.

24 S. Beszedits, *The Libby Prison Diary by Colonel Emeric Szabad*, Toronto 1999.

25 I.K. Vida, *Doing Away With Myths: A New Look at the Hungarians' Participation in the American Civil War*, Szeged 2001.

26 G. Kacziány, *A magyar mémoire-irodalom 1848-tól 1914-ig*, Budapest 1917.

27 B. Estván, *War Pictures from the South*, New York 1864.

28 Several authors have come to the same conclusion. See M. Coulter, *Travels in the Confederate States*, Oklahoma 1948, pp. 90-91.

Bibliography

Ács T., *Magyar úttörők az Újvilágban – László Károly 1850-67 naplófeljegyzései*, Budapest 1942.

Id., *A száműzöttek. Fiala János emlékiratai*, Budapest 1943.

Id., *Magyarok az észak-amerikai polgárháborúban 1861-65*, Budapest 1964.

Áldor I., *Vázlatok a magyar emigráció életéből*, Pest 1870.

Beszedits, S. (ed.), *The Libby Prison Diary by Colonel Emeric Szabad*, Toronto 1999.

Estván B., *War Pictures from the South*, New York 1864.

Jánossy D. (ed.), *A Kossuth-emigráció Angliában és Amerikában, 1851-52, 2 volumes*, Budapest 1940-1944.

Kacziány G., *A magyar mémoire-irodalom 1848-tól 1914-ig*, Budapest 1917.

Kende G., *Magyarok Amerikában. Az amerikai magyarság története*, 2 volumes, Cleveland 1927.

Lengyel E., *Americans from Hungary*, Philadelphia 1948.

Lonn E., *Foreigners in the Confederacy*, Chapel Hill 1940.

Id., *Foreigners in the Union Army and Navy*, Baton Rouge 1951.

Lukács L., *A magyar politikai emigráció 1849-1867*, Budapest 1984.

Márki S., *Amerika s a magyarság*, "Földrajzi Közlemények", 1893, 2, pp. 49-94.

Pivány J., *Hungarians in the Civil War*, Cleveland 1913.

Id., *Hungarian-American Historical Connections*, Budapest 1927.

Pivány J., *Magyar-amerikai történelmi kapcsolatok. A Columbus előtti időktől az amerikai polgárháború befejezéséig*, Budapest 1926.

Puskás J., *Kivándorló magyarok az Egyesült Államokban 1880-1940*, Budapest 1982.

Id., *From Hungary to the United States, 1880-1914*, Budapest 1982.

Id., *Ties that Bind, Ties that Divide*, New York 2000.

Várdy B., *The Hungarian-Americans*, Boston 1985.

Id., *Magyarok az Újvilágban*, Budapest 2000.

Vasváry Ö., *Lincoln's Hungarian Heroes. The Participation of Hungarians in the American Civil War*, Washington, DC 1939.

Id., *Lincoln's Hungarian Heroes*, Washington, DC 1939.

Id., *Lincoln and the Hungarians*, Pittsburgh 1963-64.

Id., *Magyar Amerika*, Szeged 1988.

Vida I.K., *Doing Away with Myths: A New Look at the Hungarians'* Participation in the American Civil War, "Hungarian National Students' Conference Paper", Szeged 2001.

Irish Historical Writing on Latin America, and on Irish Links with Latin America

Mary N. Harris
National University of Ireland, Galway

Cé gur beag staraí Éireannach atá ina shaineolaí ar stair Mheiriceá Laidinigh, nó ar stair na nGael i Meiriceá Laidineach, tá réimse leathan daoine tar éis tabhairt faoi stair an cheantair sin a scríobh; ina measc siúd faighimid scoláirí i ndisciplíní éagsúla, saighdiúirí, iriseoirí, sagairt, agus Éireannaigh a thug turas ar an áit. Thairis sin, tá scoláirí iasachta tar éis altanna ar Mheiriceá Laidineach a sholáthar do leabhair aistí agus irisleabhair a cuireadh i gcló in Éirinn. Tá na scríbhneoirí seo go léir tar éis cur le díospóireachtaí in Éirinn faoi Mheiriceá Laidineach.

Baineann scríbhinní Éireannacha faoi Mheiriceá Laidineach, don chuid is mó, le hábhair a mhúsclaíonn suim an phobail in Éirinn, Chuir Caitlicigh na hÉireann suim mhór sa ghearleanúint a rinneadh ar Chaitlicigh i Mheicsiceo sna 1920í agus sa Chogadh cathardha a tharla in El Salvador sna 1980í: bhí tionscnamh ag Trócaire ann, bhí misinéirí ó Éirinn ag obair ann agus dúnmharaíodh bean óg Mheiriceánach de shliocht Éireannach. Spreag na géirchéimeanna sin daoine chun cúlra na ngéirchéimeanna a iniúchadh.

Baineann roinnt mhaith taighde leis na Gaeil i Meiriceá Laidineach. Tá éachtaí na nGael a ghlac páirt i gcogaí na saoirse i dtús na 1800í agus in imeachtaí míleata eile á ríomh le fada, agus cuireanna staraithe áitiúla agus ginealeolaithe suim sna réimsí sin freisin. Tá scoláirí eile tar éis cúl a thabhairt le stair na ngníomhartha gaisce agus díriú ar shaol na nGael a chuaigh thar tír amach, go háirithe iad siúd a thug aghaidh ar an Airgintín. Tuigtear anois na castachtaí a bhaineann le cur síos a dheanamh an an bpobal sin agus an cineál féiniúlachta a bhí acu. Is mór an cúnamh do na scoláirí sin an dul chun cinn mór atá ar siúl i léann an diaspora tré chéile, agus an t-eolas atá le fail ar shuíomhanna idirlín ar nós Irish Migration Studies in Latin America, suíomh Chumann Éireannach Léann Mheiriceá Laidinigh agus irishdiaspora.net. Cé go bhfuil teora i gcónaí leis an méid taighde atá ar siúl sna réimsí seo, is cinnte go bhfuil na cúinsí taighde níos fearr ná riamh maidir le cursaí cumarsáide agus acmhainní ar an idirlíon.

Irish historical writing on Latin America focuses primarily on Irish links with Latin America and on issues of common concern. The pattern of Irish relations with Latin America, described by Edmundo Murray as "heterogeneous, fragmentary and erratic"[1] is reflected in the variety of writings on the topic, highlighting the exploits of Irish individuals who won acclaim in Latin America and the varied experiences of Irish settlers in there. Colonialism and Catholicism emerge as the key issues of common interest. In the early decades of Irish independence, Irish Catholics, who frequently harked back to the injustices faced by their forefathers under British Protestant rule, took a keen interest in problems facing the Catholic Church in Latin America; in later decades Irish missionary presence in Latin America maintained Irish interest in that region. Irish attitudes towards Spanish colonization, however, were complicated by the historic friendship between Irish nationalists and Spain.

In seeking out Irish historians of Latin America it soon becomes apparent that the categories of 'historian' and 'Irish' are problematic. Writers on the history of Latin America include not only academic historians, but also scholars in the fields of geography and Hispanic studies, as well as journalists, genealogists, priests, travellers to Latin America and participants in Latin American political struggles. These are not watertight categories; a number of important writers have had chequered careers, journalists have become academics, academics have contributed to newspapers, literary scholars have become historians, and collections of essays are often multidisciplinary. Nor is the category 'Irish' entirely clear cut; many of the writers were born and raised in Ireland but some are Irish emigrants, second generation Irish or foreign scholars who come to work or study in Ireland. In some cases the distinction is not clear. Furthermore, Irish journals and collections of essays seeking to explain the background to issues contemporary relevance in Latin America frequently invite contributions from experts outside Ireland. All of these have contributed to Irish discussions of Latin American history.

This chapter takes a broad definition of Irish historiography*:* it focuses on works of a historical nature written or published by people in Ireland or with a strong Irish connection in the 20th and 21st centuries. It is organised thematically, looking at the issues of exploration and colonization, Irish contributions to political and military campaigns, the Catholic Church in Latin America, international relations and the Irish diaspora in Latin America. Finally, it considers the questions raised by these studies for certain aspects of Irish historiography and some possible future lines of investigation.

Exploration and Colonization

Tales of Saint Brendan having sailed from Ireland to Mexico in the 6th century must remain in the realm of mythology. The themes of exploration and colonization from the late 15th century, however, have received Irish scholarly attention. While Nicholas Canny and D.B. Quinn have focussed on English expansion in North America, they have also touched on issues relating to the Spanish Empire. Canny's interest in explorers' accounts of the new world is reflected in his *Remembering Columbus*[2]. Published on the 500th anniversary of Columbus's first voyage, this examines Columbus' perception of the world, its size and possible routes. D.B. Quinn has compared English, French and Spanish colonial ambitions and approaches. Quinn's documentary history of North America to 1612 includes material relating to areas under Spanish control there[3]. He also examined the visualization of the new world, looking at expectations, interpretations and accounts of Christopher Columbus and Amerigo Vespucci[4]. Clare Carroll has compared the accounts of Amerindians by Bartolomé de Las Casas and Jean de Léry with Philip O'Sullivan Beare's account (1621) of the depredations of the English in Ireland, as part of her argument for the relevance of postcolonial theory to Ireland[5].

Quinn discusses early Irish links with Latin America in *Ireland and America: Their Early Associations, 1500-1640*[6] noting the fate of John Martin, a Cork man who was executed by the Inquisition in Mexico in 1575. A more detailed account of Martin's fate by P.E. Hair appears in "Irish Historical Studies"[7]. Another casualty of the Inquisition was William Lamport of Wexford. After a colourful military career in the Spanish army and a scandalous love affair, Lamport found his way to Mexico. He was accused of plotting against the state for seeking land reforms, the abolition of slavery and independence from Spain, and was arrested in 1642. He escaped but was ultimately sentenced to execution in 1659. Lamport's life is the subject of an article in "History Ireland" by Fabio Troncarelli, who drew on Inquistion records, and a detailed biography by Gerard Ronan[8].

Irish settlement in 17th-century Latin America is the subject of a number of articles by Aubrey Gwynn S.J. His *Documents relating to the Irish in the West Indies*[9] includes Spanish and English archival material and relating to Irish proposals to settle on the Amazon. In a separate article, Gwynn examined the progress of Irish tobacco planters in Amazon basin[10], an issue addressed in Quinn's *Ireland and America.* Gwynn has also examined Irish missionary activity in 17th-century Latin America, looking, in particular at Fr Thomas Field, an Irish Jesuit whose work in Paraguay prefigured that of the Jesuit reductions a few years later, and is the main source for Peadar Kirby's useful survey of Jesuit activities in Mexico and South America[11].

Irish Involvement in Military and Political Campaigns

Significant Irish involvement in Latin American military campaigns is not surprising, given the longstanding Irish tradition of serving in foreign armies. Following political upheavals in 17th-century Ireland, many Irishmen left to serve in the Catholic armies of Europe, in particular in the Spanish Army. By the early 19th century, the British Army attracted large numbers of Irish recruits. Many others who left poverty, pressure on land and famine in 19th-century Ireland joined armies in North America. Some of these went on to participate in military struggles in Latin America; others were recruited in Ireland to fight in Latin American campaigns. Some achieved considerable acclaim: maritime and military historian John de Courcy Ireland has based an article on Irish soldiers and seamen who had Latin American naval vessels named after them[12]. "The Irish Sword", journal of the Military History Society of Ireland, has provided the main forum for Irish and international historians writing on Irish military achievements, and, to a lesser extent Irish failures in Latin American conflicts, but local history publications have also highlighted the exploits of local men who won fame overseas.

In 1768 the Regimiento de Ultonia, one of three regiments making up the Irish Brigade in Spain, arrived in Mexico to protect Mexico in the invent of any British attack. W. S.

Murphy describes their experiences and their difficult relationship with the local population[13]. By the early 19th century, however, most Irish soldiers in Latin America were fighting against Spanish authority. Peter Pyne's *The Invasions of Buenos Aires, 1806-1807: The Irish Dimension*[14] highlights the involvement of Irish soldiers in assaults that contributed to the collapse of Spanish rule a few years later. In a further study Pyne examines in detail the activities of James Florence Burke, an Irish soldier who began his military career in the French army, switched allegiance to Britain and engaged in espionage in Latin America in the same period[15].

Among those involved in Latin America struggles was Admiral William Brown, from Foxford, County Mayo, celebrated in both Ireland and Argentina as the father of the Argentine navy. Having worked as a seaman and a soldier, Brown arrived in Buenos Aires in 1810, the year in which Creoles in the Viceroyalty of Río de la Plata declared independence from Spain. Following the capture of two of his boats by the Spaniards in 1813, he came to sympathise with the patriot cause, was appointed commander of the patriot navy and helped to consolidate independence. Brown's exploits are the subject of a biography by John de Courcy Ireland[16]. He was honoured in a commemorative issue of "The Irish Sword" in 1957, the centenary of death; this included a contribution from John de Courcy Ireland[17], a list of unpublished documents relating to Brown in Madrid[18] and condensed translations of papers delivered in Argentina to mark his centenary. A subsequent note by Ireland includes a long article from the *Wexford Herald* relating Brown's exploits as a privateer off South America's Pacific coast and in the Caribbean[19]. Further accounts of Brown's exploits appear in Mayo local history publications. Tom Walsh's two-part article on Brown in the journal of the Westport Historical Society draws heavily on "Irish Sword" material but is more accessible and contextualises Brown's exploits well[20]. Brown also features among the famous Mayo men in Bernard O'Hara's *Mayo*[21].

Irish involvement in Simón Bolívar's campaigns to liberate much of South America from Spanish rule has also aroused much Irish interest, not least because Daniel O'Connell, Ireland's leading nationalist figure in the first half of the 19th century, admired Bolívar. His son, Morgan, enlisted in an Irish Legion at the age of 15 to fight for Bolívar, but ultimately saw no action, as Eric Lambert and F. Glenn Thompson have briefly recounted[22]. Lambert's three-volume study of British and Irish volunteers in Bolivar's campaigns was published in Spanish in Caracas[23]. Lambert has also provided a detailed survey for "The Irish Sword" of Irish military involvement in South America in the years 1818-30, considering the soldiers' motivations their military activities and their ultimate fate[24]. Furthermore, Lambert has penned a detailed survey of the career of Daniel O'Leary, a Cork man who enlisted in the Red Hussars of Venezuela in 1817 and served as aide-de-camp to Simón Bolívar[25].

Apart from his military exploits, O'Leary was the author of the most substantial Irish contribution to the history of Latin America: a work entitled *Memorias del General Daniel Florencio O'Leary publicados por su hijo Simón B. O'Leary, por orden del Gobierno de Venezuela.* This consists of twenty-nine volumes of documents, including many kept by Bolívar himself, and two volumes of O'Leary's own memoirs together with an appendix. These writings were edited by O'Leary's son, Simón Bolívar O'Leary, and published in Caracas in 1879-88 by order of the Venezuelan Government. In 1959, J.G. Healy, professor of Spanish at University College, Cork, marked the appearance of Manuel Pérez Vila's award winning biography *Vida de Daniel Florencio O'Leary, Primer Edecán del Libertador*, with an article O'Leary's role in South America in the "Journal of the Cork Historical and Archaeological Society"[26]. The same journal carries a short article by Laurence Geary on Corkman Francis Burdett O'Connor, whose memoirs were also published posthumously in Bolivia in 1895. O'Connor's turbulent youth, his involvement in Bolívar's campaigns and his political career in Bolivia after independence are discussed by Eric Lambert[27]. A less well-know figure from the same period was a former member of the British navy, Thomas Charles Wright, from Drogheda, Co. Louth, whose involvement in Bolívar's campaigns and subsequent role in founding the Ecuadorian navy are recounted by John de Courcy Ireland[28].

Two figures frequently mentioned but not in any detail in Ireland are Ambrose O'Higgins, an Irishman who served as viceroy of Peru from 1796-1801 and his son Bernardo O'Higgins, who fought against Spain and became independent Chile's first head of state. Perhaps the uncertainty regarding Ambrosio's origins has left him without Irish local interest, though this uncertainty has been addressed by Brian De Breffny[29].

Writings on Irishmen who fought in Spanish America tend emphasise their achievements. The experience of Irishmen who were recruited to serve in newly independent Brazil in 1826, however, was disillusion. These are also recounted in Irish journals, though not always by Irish authors. In an article in "The Irish Sword" Frederic von Allendorfer relates the experiences of 2,400 Irish would-be soldiers and their families who arrived in Brazil only to find appalling living conditions, poor pay and hostility from the local black population who eventually joined in mutiny with a German corps. Those who could be found were rounded up and returned to Ireland[30].

The tragic fate of the San Patricios has captured the imagination of subsequent generations. The San Patricios, an Irish battalion who fought for Mexico during the US war with Mexico in 1846-8, were led by John Riley, a deserter from the American army who formed a company from other deserters and Catholic foreigners living in Mexico. Having withstood major assaults they were captured, court-martialled, tortured and hanged in 1847. "The Irish Sword" published an article by Richard Blaine McCornack of Dartmouth College, New Hampshire, on the San Patricios' engagement with the American army, drawing on evidence presented at the subsequent courts martial to provide a nuanced examination of the San Patricios' political allegiances[31]. The "Sword" also reprinted extracts from "Life Magazine" (New York) detailing the execution of some of the San Patricios[32]. One hundred and fifty years later they were commemorated in both Ireland and Mexico. "History Ireland" has published a short article by Michael Hogan, Irish-American author of a detailed study of the San Patricios. Hogan has examined the motivation of the soldiers, noting the high level of anti-Catholicism in America and the American army at the time[33]. The *Irish Migration Studies in Latin*

America website has also posted short articles on the San Patricios by Jaime Fogarty and Michael Connaughton[34].

Nationalist Humanitarians in the Colonial Service

Richard Robert Madden (1798-1886), best known in Ireland for his nationalist sympathies and his writings on Irish history, worked in the British colonial service in the Caribbean. His writings on the Caribbean include a translation of the life and poems of a recently liberated Cuban slave, Juan Franciso Manzano. Madden, Manzano and the Cuban Slave narrative are the subject of a recent study by Irish scholar Fionnghuala Sweeney, currently based at the Institute of Latin American Studies in the University of Liverpool. Her research focuses on Cuba in the context of the black Atlantic and examines the literary interaction and exchange between Cuba and other Atlantic sites, including Ireland[35].

Writings by and about Roger Casement, another humanitarian and nationalist, exemplify the impact of political and ideological concerns on Irish studies of Latin America. Casement (1864-1916) is best remembered in Ireland as a martyr for the nationalist cause, convicted of treason for seeking German assistance for a rebellion in Ireland and executed by the British government. At an earlier stage, however, Casement had believed in the benefits of extending British rule[36]. He served as British consul in Africa and in Brazil from 1906-1913 and was knighted for his services in exposing the ill-treatment of workers in the Congo and Putumayo[37] basins. In addition to Casement's official reports, his copious personal papers provide invaluable accounts of the ill-treatment of indigenous workers and immigrant workers from Barbados; they also highlight the attitudes of officials of the Peruvian Amazon Company who flogged and mutilated workers, locked them in stocks and sometimes killed them. However, the study of Casement's role and findings in the Putumayo region has been eclipsed by debates surrounding the authenticity or otherwise of the so-called "Black Diaries". Two of these cover Casement's time in South America; they include many observations on the physique of young men and boys, of their sexuality, his longing for them and his sexual experiences with them[38]. The diaries, in the possession of the British government, were shown to a number of influential figures shortly before Casement's execution. Little was known about them until the publication in 1936 of *The Forged Casement Diaries* by W.J. Maloney, a British Army Officer who had come to sympathise with radical Irish nationalism[39]. The ensuing debate continues to this day; some scholars consider the diaries authentic, others suspect that they were a British forgery, concocted with view to discrediting Casement and discouraging appeals for a reprieve of his death sentence remain. The diaries did not enter the public domain until limited access was permitted in 1959, and an edition of them was published in Paris[40]. Unlimited access was permitted in 1994 and was followed by further conferences and publications on the debate[41].

Meanwhile, in 1930, prolific Irish writer Denis Gwynn had published *The Life and Death of Roger Casement* drawing extensively on Casement's official report for his account of the Putumayo. Brian Inglis's later and more wide-ranging *Roger Casement* explores the complexity of Casement's character[42]. His treatment of the Putumayo draws on incorporates extracts from the "Black Diaries" as well as drawing on Casement's private and published observations on the Putumayo. Casement's analysis of the Putumayo came to light again with the publication in 1993 of *The Amazon Journal of Roger Casement,* edited by Angus Mitchell. Born in Kenya and educated in Britain, Mitchell is now working in the University of Limerick and is a frequent contributor to Irish debates on Casement[43]. Mitchell along with Roger Sawyer, had been commissioned by London publisher Pimlico to edit the 'Black Diaries" but withdrew when he became convinced that they were forgeries. The *Amazon Journal,* published in Dublin, draws on different papers and includes Casement's reflections on the historic roots of the problems of South America[44], and his concern that United States influence and commercial interests were providing immunity to the exploiters of indigenous people[45]. It also provides much ethnographic information.

Casement's ethnographic interests, which extended to taking body measurements of Putumayo Indians, have been examined by Séamas Ó Síocháin. Casement believed that European civilization, Christianity and commerce would enable Indians to progress to a higher level[46]. Furthermore, as, Ó Síocháin notes, Casement condemned Spanish and Portuguese colonisation: 'The curse of this continent has been its Latinization' and, more graphically, '400 years of Spaniards at its sources, 300 years of Portuguese at its mouth ... first hell, then, a desert'[47].

The study of Casement's ideology received a further boost with the Royal Irish Academy's organisation of a symposium on 'Casement in Irish and World History' in 2000. *Taoiseach* [prime minister] Bertie Ahern had proposed such a seminar to examine the Black Diaries controversy, but the 2000 symposium, as well as presenting valuable evidence in relation to the diaries, also addressed a wider range of issues, and its proceedings were subsequently published[48]. A number of papers related Casement's thinking on the Putumayo and the Congo to his views on Ireland. In *Roger Casement's Vision of Freedom,* Séamas Ó Síocháin the common threads of interest in landholding and sympathy for the underdog running though Casement's observations on Ireland, the Congo and the Putumayo. Margaret O'Callaghan's *"With the Eyes of Another Race, a People Once Hunted Themselves": Casement, Colonialism and a Remembered Past* notes the recurring theme of nationalism in Casement's writings. O'Callaghan cites Casement's comment 'Ireland is the British peon, the great peon of the British empire'[49]. Nevertheless, as Andrew Porter points out in *Sir Roger Casement and the International Humanitarian Movement,* Casement 'did not emerge as an obviously systematic thinker'; his achievement and his mode of operating were of a different kind[50].

The Mexican Crisis

Early 20th-century Irish Catholics showed a keen interest in the wider Catholic world. Religious publications and the "Irish Independent", Ireland's best-selling daily newspaper, devoted much space to church-state relations. With a strong sense of the injustices their forefathers had suffered under British rule, Irish Catholics were quick to identify with Catholics suffering persecution and discrimination elsewhere. Not surprisingly, the difficulties facing the Catholic Church in Mexico in the 1920s generated much interest in Ireland. The restrictions imposed on the Catholic Church in Mexico under the 1917 constitution and by President Calles in the 1920s met with strong Catholic opposition, culminating in the 'Cristero Rebellion', so called as the rebels claimed to fight in defence of Cristo Rey, Christ the King. As news of these events broke, writers and editors of religious journals such as the "Catholic Bulletin", "The Irish Monthly" and "Studies" sought to provide explanations and historical background to the events in question. Over the next two decades articles appeared in the religious conflict in Mexico. Comparisons with the Irish past were drawn: Lambert McKenna S.J. argued, 'The Catholic Church in Mexico is undergoing an ordeal as savage as the early Roman Persecutions or the Irish Penal Laws'[51].

One of the recurring themes of these articles is the rejection of the 'black legend', the view that the Spanish conquest was particularly cruel and bloodthirsty. In an article entitled 'Martyred Mexico' the author, "An Irish Exile", criticised "the English propaganda against Spain which has passed for history in almost every English-speaking country for the past 300 or 400 years". Rejecting the romantic image of the Aztecs, he defended Spain's role in Mexican history: 'Mexico before the coming of the Spaniards was a land of blood and terror, a land of which human sacrifice was the predominant trait,' and that 'the conquerors strained every nerve to bring peace, happiness and Christian culture to the new nation which they had added to the Spanish dominions'[52]. The benefits of Christianity for indigenous people are also noted by Lambert McKenna, a leading Irish Jesuit intellectual, who saw the Catholic Church as the main civilizing influence in Mexico[53].

Many of these articles drew on pro-Catholic American publications, in particular *Blood-Drenched Altars* by Francis Kelley, bishop of Oklahoma and Tulsa, who is noted in a number of Irish articles and is discussed by P.E. Magennis, an ardent Irish nationalist and Carmelite priest. *No God Next Door* by Michael Kenny S.J. of Spring Hill College, Alabama, was another popular source. Kenny also contributed an article on the causes and consequences of the Mexican Crisis, highlighting United States influence on Mexico's government, and Masonic influence on both the American and Mexican governments[54]. A further commentator on American influence was Irish war correspondent, Captain Francis McCullagh, author of *Red Mexico* (1928) and many other works. McCullagh, who previously visited and written on Russia[55], drew strong parallels with Soviet Russia and was highly critical of American support for Mexican revolutionary leaders. McCullagh also contributed articles to "Studies" on American press coverage of Mexico and on Calles[56]. Such writings chimed with Irish concerns about Bolshevism and Freemasonry in this period.

The Catholic Truth Society of Ireland also entered the debate, publishing a pamphlet, *Mexico* (1930) by C.M. Davis. This provides a well-informed account of the historic relationship between Spaniards, Creoles and indigenous in Mexico, followed by an account of government treatment of the Catholic Church after independence.

Irish interest in Mexico declined as the conflict between church and state in Mexico abated. Since the early 2000s, however, Matthew Butler, an English scholar now lecturing in Latin American studies at the Queen's University of Belfast, has published a number of scholarly articles on the Cristero rebellion. His *Popular Piety and Political Identity in Mexico's Cristero Rebellion Michoacán, 1927-29*[57] examines local responses to the conflict, drawing on a range of ecclesiastical and state archives as well as oral testimony.

Irish Missionaries in Latin America

Few Irish missionaries worked in Latin America before the mid-20th century, and many of those Irish religious who did work there aimed to serve the Irish community. Peadar Kirby[58] has surveyed the history of Irish missionary efforts from the mid-20th century to the early 1990s. Kirby notes the role of lay missionaries working through the Legion of Mary in the 1950s, and the growing involvement of Irish missionary orders in the area following Pope John XXIII's appeal for more missionary priests for Latin America. Kirby also comments on the challenges facing Cork priests who served in Peru: in 1965 the Diocese of Cork and Ross undertook pastoral responsibility for a shanty town on the edge of the city of Trujillo in northern Peru[59]. The establishment of Trócaire, the Catholic Church's development agency in Ireland, in 1973 further promoted interest in Latin America; it set up projects in the region. Trócaire committed 20% of its funding to raising awareness in Ireland[60] and commissioned various studies, including Peadar Kirby's *Ireland and Latin America: Links and Lessons*, published in 1992 in the context of the 500th anniversary of Columbus's arrival in the Americas. This is the only survey of its kind. It grew out of his report for a project entitled "Programme on Political Relations and Co-operation Europe-Latin America" examining the role of non-governmental organisations in various European countries involved in development work in Latin America[61]. *Ireland and Latin America* provides a survey of Latin American history, commenting on the legacy of colonisation, the missed opportunities following independence and more recent challenges, as well as an exploration of Irish and Latin American links from the 16th to the 20th centuries. Kirby, who had spent seven months travelling in Latin America in 1979 and had published on religious issues there, later went on to become Director of the Centre for International Studies at Dublin City University and to focus on more contemporary issues of the impact of globalisation on Latin America.

Crisis in Central America

The Central American crisis of the early 1980s aroused much interest in Ireland. In El Salvador left-wing guerrillas, the armed forces and right wing death squads were engaged in civil war. The murder of Archbishop Oscar Romero in 1980 aroused much interest; Dermot Keogh covered the funeral mass, which came under attack, for RTÉ, the national television station. The following year Keogh, by now a lecturer in the History Department of University College, Cork, published *Romero: El Salvador's Martyr*[62]. Irish interest in El Salvador increased when it emerged that one of four American missionaries were raped and murdered in El Salvador in December 1980 was Jean Donovan, an Irish American who had studied at University College, Cork, in the 1970s, and had addressed a youth mass in Cork during a visit a few months before her murder. In 1984 a Jean Donovan Memorial Committee involving friends of Jean Donovan, Dermot Keogh and others, was established in Cork and organised a number of memorial conferences, addressed by Irish and international academics, journalists, politicians, diplomats and church figures. In 1985 the proceedings of the first of these conferences, *Central America: Human Rights and U.S. Foreign Policy* appeared edited by Dermot Keogh[63]. This included Keogh's own study of the United States and the 1979 coup in El Salvador. A further collection of conference proceedings, *Witness to the Truth: Church and Dictatorship in Latin America* appeared in 1989[64]. In 1990 Keogh edited *Church and Politics in Latin America*[65]a collection of articles by Irish and other writers, including a foreword by the novelist Graham Greene, and a number of essays by Rodolfo Cardenal, Jesuit historian in El Salvador. Irish contributors included Patrick Rice, who had worked as a priest and human rights organiser in Latin America, and had 'disappeared' in Argentina in 1976 and Conor Cruise O'Brien, former diplomat, politician and historian. Keogh went on to publish a number of articles on El Salvador's recent history, as well as a study of the 1932 Peasant Revolt in that country[66].

During the 1980s and 1990s a number of research students at University College, Cork further explored Central American themes. David Ryan's doctoral thesis examined diplomatic relations between the United States and the Sandinista government in Nicaragua during the Reagan presidency within the broader context of U.S. policy in the region during the Cold War, and highlighted the tension between diplomatic and covert approaches towards Nicaragua[67]. This led to the publication of Ryan's *US-Sandinista Diplomatic Relations: Voice of Intolerance* (London 1995). At MA level Julia Crowley examined the historiography of the Catholic Church in Latin America, focussing in particular on Guatemala, Nicaragua and El Salvador and drawing on her field work in Central America[68]. Denis Dineen looked at the Carter administration's policies regarding the Nicaraguan Revolution of 1979[69]. Earlier Central American themes were explored by Josephine Vaughan, who analysed British-Nicaraguan diplomatic relations 1926-34, Marita Foster, who looked at US perceptions of and policies towards El Salvador in the 1930s and 1940s[70] and Treasa Landers, who investigated El Salvador's Peasant uprising in 1932[71].

Among the Jean Donovan conference contributors was Gary MacEoin, an Irish-born writer who, for reasons he never discovered, was been forced to leave a Redemptorist seminary just weeks before his ordination was due. MacEoin went on to become a prolific religious affairs journalist, travelling extensively in Latin America. His *Memoirs and Memories*[72] among other works, provides many insights into Latin American conditions and their underlying causes, the role of the Catholic Church in Latin America and the impact of the United States on them.

Much Irish debate at this time was critical of the United States' support for El Salvador's military and its attempts to undermine the revolutionary government in Nicaragua through assisting its opponents. Hostility towards Ronald Reagan's foreign policy in Central America was evident when the president visited Ireland in 1984. For some in Ireland the prestige of having links with such a powerful president and appreciation for his family values did not outweigh the impact of his foreign policy. There was a mixed reception to the National University of Ireland's decision to grant Reagan an honorary doctorate of laws. Protests were held when he arrived in Galway to receive his degree and the local bishop, Eamon Casey, who was also chairman of Trócaire, stayed away from the event.

International Relations

In addition to the research on Central America mentioned above, a number of dissertations on international relations have been written, mainly on British and US foreign policy. Cuba, in particular the Cuban missile crisis, has proven the most popular topic, but no particular Irish approach to Cuba emerges. Louise Kingston, John O'Shea and John Farrell have examined U.S. foreign policy towards Cuba[73]. Patrick Horgan has examined Irish-Cuban relations 1959-62[74] and Caroline Buckley the Soviet perspective[75]. Tomás Ó Murchú has looked at the survival of the communist regimes in Cuba, Vietnam and North Korea[76] and John O'Neill at changing directions in Cuba[77]. Alexander Gray, whose dissertation at the University of Limerick examined the involvement of NGOs in Cuba[78] is currently pursuing this theme at doctoral level at the University of Deusto, Bilbao. Fiona Carr's study of US foreign policy in relation to Columbia, considers questions relating to drugs and human rights[79].

A number of MA students at University College, Cork, have examined British relations with Latin American countries. Marina Hayes has investigated Anglo-Chilean relations[80], Geraldine Barry, Anglo-Cuban relation[81] and Ann Cronin, Britain and Venezuela[82]. Gertrude Cotter's dissertation on Britain's relationship with Perón's Argentina, 1946-55, is a very substantial work, drawing on a wide range of primary sources[83] It considers the evolution of British policy against a background of Britain's longstanding economic relations with Argentina, and studies Britain's responses to economic, political and social change under Peron.

Most of these topic allow students to rely heavily on English language sources. It is regrettable, however, that few Irish students have sufficient Spanish to allow them investigate the Latin American perspective in any detail.

The Irish Diaspora in Latin America

An estimated eight million Irish men, women and children left Ireland between 1800 and 1921, and emigration remained a recurring feature of Irish life for much of the 20th century. Irish diaspora studies, investigating Irish immigrant communities as well as noting the exploits of exceptional individuals, has developed considerably in the past twenty years, and while this has concentrated on Irish immigrants in popular Anglophone destinations, it has also impacted on the study of Irish immigrants and their descendants in Latin America, particularly Argentina, the most popular Latin American destination. This interest in the Latin American Irish was not unprecedented: Thomas Murray's *The Story of the Irish in Argentina* was published in New York in 1919 but remains the only published book on this topic. Murray wrote with a decidedly Catholic nationalist slant, and was scathing in his criticism of prominent newspaper owner Michael Mulhall for his identification with English settlers. In 1949 John Murray's article, *The Irish and Others in Argentina*[84] also examined the sense of identity of the Irish Community. Since then, a number of important theses have been written articles published and informative websites set up. The growing interest in Irish family history has further promoted this field; family history journals such as "Familia" and "Irish Roots" have provided platforms for short essays on the Irish in Latin America[85].

Patrick McKenna has pioneered academic research in this area: his MA dissertation[86] examined the context of Irish emigration, the profile of Irish emigrants, and their organisation and social conditions in Argentina. McKenna has published some of his findings in contributions to the Irish World Wide: History, Heritage and Identity series and to Andy Bielenberg (ed.) *The Irish Diaspora*[87] McKenna profiles of successive waves of Irish emigrants: those involved the exploration of South America in the 16th century, Irish landowners and merchants in and around Buenos Aires in the 18th century, skilled tradesmen who found work in the beef industry in the late 18th century; Irish soldiers and sailors in the British service settled in Argentina in the early 19th. McKenna argues that the patriotism of those Irish who fought against the Spaniards in the war of independence "contributed greatly to the acceptability of the Irish as immigrants throughout the 19th century"[88]. McKenna examines rural life on the Pampas of Argentina, noting the opportunities for Irish immigrants. McKenna notes the central role of the Catholic Church, in particular the role of Fr Anthony Fahy, a Dominican priest from County Galway, who helped newly arrived Irish immigrants to find accommodation, employment and social opportunities. The combined activities of Fahy and Westmeath man Thomas Armstrong, who formed a stock exchange and a bank in Argentina, helped to promote a rather self-contained Irish community. Recruitment of Irish priests and nuns to teach the Irish in Argentina contributed to this development, and Daniel Murphy, in his study of Irish emigrant and missionary education, attributes the progress of the Irish in Argentina to this education[89].

The question of Irish immigrant identity has been taken up by other writers. A heightened sense of Irish nationalism is discussed in Edward Walsh's article on a broadsheet produced by the Irish Catholic Association of Argentina, probably in 1918, in relation to the annual St Patrick's Day pilgrimage to the shrine of the virgin of Luján. This document called for prayers for peace, as the Pope had recently urged, for consolation for those afflicted by war, inspiration for negotiations leading to a universal just peace that would establish an Irish republic, return Gibraltar to Spain, the Malvinas to Argentina, and bring liberty for all the people oppressed and exploited by the British Empire[90].

Irish local history and family history publications have also contributed to studies of Irish settlers in Argentina. Pat Nally, secretary of the Longford-Westmeath Argentina society, has written on this topic, focussing in particular on migrants from Westmeath and Wexford[91]. He also notes the reflection of Irish political divisions between moderate and radical nationalists in Irish newspapers in Argentina. Helen Meehan's study of 'The McManus brothers – Patrick: 1864-1929. Seamas: 1868-1960' also addresses nationalist issues[92]. Seamas McManus was a well known Irish writer involved in various nationalist organisations. His brother Patrick emigrated first to America and then to Argentina, but maintained contact with those involved in cultural activities at home and established a branch of the Gaelic League, an organisation aiming to promote the Irish language, in Buenos Aires as well as producing a publication known as the *Fianna* for the Irish community in Argentina.

Nationalist issues also feature in Michael Kennedy's study of Irish diplomats in Latin America during the war of independence. In 1919 members of the radical nationalist Sinn Féin party who had been elected to the British parliament set up an alternative assembly, known as Dáil Éireann, in Dublin and declared independence. The Dáil appointed envoys to various countries with view to raising funds and promoting recognition of the Irish republic. Michael Kennedy discusses such efforts by Frank Egan, who operated a mining company in Chile and whose in-laws were related to the Chilean president by marriage, and Eamon Bulfin, born in Argentina but educated in Ireland and deported to Argentina following his involvement in the 1916 Easter Rising[93]. Kennedy notes that Argentina's close economic ties with Britain and divisions within the Irish Argentine community itself created difficulties for those seeking to promote the cause of the Irish republic.

Tensions of a different sort surface in Tim Pat Coogan's treatment of Latin America in *Wherever Green is Worn: the Story of the Irish Diaspora*[94]. Coogan surveys Irish involvement in Latin America up to the 20th century and writes in more detail on Irish Argentine reactions to the 'Dirty War' in Argentina, drawing on interviews he conducted there. He notes that liberals recalled the 'disappearances' of political suspects with horror, and conservatives recalled the activities of 'guerillas'. This tension was reflected in interpretations of the killings of three priests and two seminarians belonging to the Pallotine Order were gunned down, apparently by the navy, in 1976; Irish members of the Order were deeply affected by the event. Coogan goes on to discuss the torture of Pat Rice, a Cork missionary priest serving in Argentina in this period. Another victim of this era was Irish Argentine Rodolfo Walsh, investigative journalist and critic of the regime, and subject of Michael McCaughan's *True Crimes: the life and times of a radical intellectual*, London 2002. In this study McCaughan, a journalist who writes for the "Irish Times" and the "Guardian", reprints some of Walsh's own writings.

The study of Irish communities in Latin America has benefited considerably from the work of Brian McGinn, Born in New York of Irish parents, McGinn spent some of his childhood in Ireland, an experience shared by many others and one that highlights the complexity of defining "Irishness". McGinn produced a lengthy annotated bibliography on the Irish in Latin America for irishdiaspora.net, the website of the Irish Diaspora Research Unit at the University of Bradford[95], and contributed numerous articles on the Irish in Latin America to genealogical and other publications. Reacting against the assertion of American writer William B. Read[96] that the 'Irish contributed little to the South American way of life, except a pattern of Puritanical ... thrift and industry" and that the Argentine-Irish were "money-grubbing bourgeoisie", McGinn surveyed Irish efforts in the fields of engineering, medicine, naval and military affairs, and journalism[97] A further article on newspaper proprietors Michael and Edward Mulhalls highlights both the potential and the divisions within the 19th-century Irish community[98].

McGinn has highlighted some of the problems confronting investigators of Irish migrants and their descendants[99]. Argentines tended to refer to all English-speaking foreigners as English. Language difficulties arise and the Hispanicization of Irish names causes confusion: Lynch became *Lince*, Martin *Martínez*. Personal histories have been fabricated and misinformation has gone unchallenged. Francis Burdett O'Connor, who fought with Bolívar, is a case in point: although he was descended from a Protestant landlord family named Conner, O'Connor, in Bolivia, claimed descent from the last high king of Ireland. In the preface to O'Connor's memoirs, published in 1895, his grandson repeated this claim and asserted that his ancestors had been martyrs to the Catholic faith. McGinn asks, "Who in Tarija, Bolivia was going to contradict him?"

The formation of the Irish Argentine Society in 2003, renamed the Society for Irish Latin American Studies [SILAS] in 2005 has proven a significant development in Irish Latin American studies. By early 2006 the Society had over 70 members from ten countries. The Society's website "Irish Migration Studies in Latin America", is intended, according to its editor, Edmundo Murray, as a resource for historians, literary scholars, anthropologists and geographers of Irish and British migration to Latin America[100]. It provides databases relating to emigration, short articles on the Irish in Latin America, and short biographies of Irish men and women in Argentina. Its reprints from other sources include a useful and often cited lecture by David Barnwell on 19th-century emigration to Argentina[101]. Murray himself has provided most of the short biographies on the websites, but other contributors include Máirtín Ó Catháin of the University of Ulster on Irish-Argentine anarchist Dr John O'Dwyer Creaghe (1841-1920) and Claire Healy of the National University of Ireland, Galway, on Daniel Florence O'Leary. The Society also provides grants of up to €1,000 to support research on the Irish in Latin America. Recipients for the academic year 2004-5 included Irish doctoral students scholars Helen Kelly (Trinity College, Dublin) working on an analysis of the Irish community in Argentina from the 1830s to the turn of the century and Claire

Healy (National University of Ireland, Galway), studying migration to Buenos Aires, 1776-1890, including an analysis of the interaction between Argentina, Afro-Argentine and Irish-Argentine peoples at local level.

Edmundo Murray notes that most writings on the Irish in Argentina have focussed on the positive contribution of Irish migrants to Argentina, overlooking migrants who were not Catholic nationalists and those whose contribution was negative. He sees SILAS as 'an open invitation to articulate alternative discourses about the history of the Irish in Argentina'[102]. In a study of Irish Argentine writings, he discusses the peculiar position of Irish Argentines in relation to postcolonial discourse, colonised in Ireland but colonisers in Argentina, noting that they wrote with an English view of the natives'[103]. Nevertheless, he points out that this was not the case for William Bulfin, father of nationalist Eamon Bulfin mentioned above; Bulfin's characters "share common ground of colonised against the English and the native bourgeoisie"[104].

Other Areas of Research

The decades leading up to the struggles for independence in Latin America were a period of intellectual ferment, particularly evident in the periodicals of that period. Fiona Clarke, currently a postdoctoral fellow at St Patrick's College, Drumcondra, Dublin, has worked on the literary-scientific periodical press in 18th-century Mexico, and has published on the *Gazeta de Literatura de México*, 1788-95[105]. She has given numerous papers on issues of identity in late 18th-century Mexico. Joe Cleary, in an article arguing for the location of Ireland within a postcolonial framework, drew parallels between Latin American Creoles' sense of nationalism in this period and the position of Irish Protestants in Ireland[106].

Belfast born H.Montgomery has published a detailed history of Maxmilian and Carlota of Mexico, drawing on archival work in Mexico and the U.S.[107]. Maxmilian, a member of the Habsburg family, was installed as Emperor of Mexico in 1864, but failed to win support and was executed in 1867. Hyde was a prolific writer whose chequered career included working as a lawyer, civil servant, member of parliament, British intelligence.

Peter Pyne, formerly of the University of Ulster, has published a number of articles on the nature of Ecuadorian politics in the 1960s. He has examined the nature of presidential powers in Ecuador, taking the presidency of José María Velasco Ibarra, 1960-1, as a case study[108]. Pyne notes the personalised nature of political power, high expectations of the presidency and virtual impossibility of meeting with the expectations of his loyal followers. He considers the conflict between the president and the legislature and assesses Velasco's contribution to his own downfall. Pyne's doctoral dissertation subsequently examined *Ecuador's Junta Militar, 1963-6*, examining military reformism in that period[109].

More contemporary Latin American topics have been pursued by students on the MA in Equality Studies programme at University College, Dublin, and in Limerick,

Rory Finegan completed a study on the important subject of insurrection in Chiapas, Mexico[110].

Conclusions

Weighty Irish academic studies of Latin American history are very few indeed. Irish interest in Latin American topics outstrips Irish expertise, and there is a recurring tendency on the part of editors to rely for the most part on international authors. Lack of fluency in Spanish has seriously limited the fields of research in relation to Latin America, and other areas; many of the MA dissertations listed above dealt with either U.S. or British foreign policy in relation to Latin America, drawing primarily on English language sources. Writing on the Irish in Latin America is undoubtedly on the increase, though most articles on this theme are rather short and vary in quality. Nevertheless, the growing recognition of Irish communities in Latin America is evident in the inclusion in Brian Lalor (ed.) *Encylopaedia of Ireland* (2003) of entries on the Irish in Brazil and Mexico, by Brian McGinn, and an entry on the Irish in Argentina, by Patrick McKenna.

Irish Latin American studies is a dynamic field. Research in this area is very much a co-operative, interdisciplinary venture, involving scholars on both sides of the Atlantic; much interaction takes place in a virtual space rather than a physical location, Irish or otherwise. The great facilitator is undoubtedly Edmundo Murray, born in Argentina, of Irish descent, and currently running the Society of Irish Latin American Studies and its website from his base in Geneva. The website's assistant editor is Irish scholar Clarie Healy. Murray has challenged the tradition of 'contributionist' studies; Irish publications tended to emphasise heroic Irish exploits of which the heroes' birthplaces in Ireland back in Ireland could be proud, Murray calls for a recognition of the diversity of Irish Latin American experiences. Thus the biographical notes on *Irish Migration Studies* website include not only military heroes but also Eliza Lynch (1835-86), first lady in Paraguay, though she never actually married Solano López, and Camila O'Gorman (1828-48), executed by firing squad along with a priest with whom she had an affair. Murray also includes biographies of female educationalists and benefactors, a welcome addition to a field focussing very much on men.

Irish and Irish Argentine writings combined offer a new perspective on Irish diaspora studies: Irish communities in white settler countries found themselves economically disadvantaged and on the defensive in predominantly Protestant surroundings. The Irish in 19th-century Argentina, however, were in a Catholic environment and their knowledge of English proved an advantage in a country that had close economic ties with Britain.

The history of the Irish in Latin America presents challenges for scholars who might wish to locate Ireland within the discourse of colonialism. Irish men at various points have participated in colonial administration, have fought with the Spaniards and fought against them, and at other points lauded the Spaniards for bringing Christianity and civilization to Mexico. Catholicism, rather than postcolonialism proved the strong point of Irish identification with Latin America: culturally, the Irish were European. Murray notes that 19th-century Irish immigrants in Argentina "behaved as English colonisers in a remote location of the Anglosphere"[111]. Not surprisingly, Irish migration to Argentina extended to Irish settlement in the Falklands/Malvinas, the subject of articles by Dermot Keogh and Edward Walsh[112]. The possibility of exploring the Irish in South America in a broader Anglophone context is also indicated by the work of Oxford historians Oliver Marshall on English-speaking communities in Latin America[113] and Leslie Bethell, whose *Brazil by British and Irish Authors*[114] provides much useful information on Irish writings.

Finally, the international dimension of Irish Latin American Studies is also promoted by increasing scholarly mobility. Irish scholars can now apply for travel bursaries for research in Latin America and international scholars in the field have come to Ireland. During the academic year 2005-6, for example, Van Gosse, from Franklin and Marshall College, Lancaster, Pennsylvania, was visiting scholar in the History Department, Cork. Gosse, author of various works on American foreign policy, among other themes, is currently working on the theme "Complicating the Cold War Narrative: Ronald Reagan's 1984 visit to Ireland". Félix Flores Varona, a Cuban expert on the life and works of 19th-century Cuban nationalist José Martí, spent a semester in the National University of Ireland, Galway, working on Martí's Irish interests. His presentations led to the discovery of new areas of common ground. It is to be hoped that Irish historians of Latin America will continue to benefit from close international links and discover new lines of investigation.

Notes

I would like to thank James Amelang, Matthew Butler, Fiona Clark, Van Gosse, Claire Healy, Dermot Keogh and Oliver Marshal for points of information for this article.

1 E. Murray, *Ireland and Latin America*, forthcoming in J. Byrne - P. Coleman - J. King (eds.), *Ireland and the Americas: Culture, Politics and History*, Santa Barbara CA, 2006. Available at http://www.irishargentine.org/murrayintro2.htm.

2 N. Canny, *Remembering Columbus 1492-1992*, "Journal of the Galway Archaeological and Historical Society", 44, 1992, pp. 1-10.

3 D.B. Quinn, *New American World: A Documentary History of North America to 1612*, vol. 5: *The Extension of Settlement in Florida, Virginia, and the Spanish Southwest*, New York 1979.

4 D.B. Quinn, *Explorers and Colonies. America 1500-1625*, London-Ronceverte 1990. See especially chapter 5: *New Geographical Horizons: Literature* and chapter 8: *Colonies in the beginning: Examples from North America.*

5 C. Carroll - P. King, *Barbarous Slaves and Civil Cannibals: Translating Civility in Early Modern Ireland*, in C. Carroll - P- King (eds.) *Ireland and Postcolonial Theory*, Notre Dame, Indiana 2003, pp. 63-80.

6 D.B. Quinn, *Ireland and America: Their Early Associations, 1500-1640*, Liverpool 1991, pp. 11-16

7 P. Hair, *An Irishman before the Mexican Inquisition, 1574-5*, "Irish Historical Studies", 17, 1971, pp. 97-319.

[8] F. Troncarelli, *The Man Behind the Mask of Zorro: William Lamport of Wexford*, "History Ireland", Autumn 2001, pp. 22-25 and G. Ronan, *The Irish Zorro: The Extraordinary Adventures of William Lamport (1615-1659)* Dublin 2004.

[9] A. Gwynn, *Documents Relating to the Irish in the West Indies* "Analecta Hibernica", 4, 1932, pp. 139-286.

[10] A. Gwynn, *An Irish Settlement on the Amazon*, "Proceedings of the Royal Irish Academy", 41 C, 1932, pp. 1-54.

[11] A. Gwynn, *The First Irish Priests in the New World*, "Studies", 21:82, 1932, pp. 213-228 and A. Gwynn, *Father Thomas Field, S.J*, Dublin 1924; P. Kirby, *Ireland and Latin America: Links and Lessons*, Dublin 1992, pp. 81-3.

[12] J. de Courcy Ireland, *Irish Soldiers and Seamen in Latin America*, "The Irish Sword", 1:4, 1949-53, pp. 296-302.

[13] W.S. Murphy, *An Irish Regiment in Mexico 1768-1771*, "The Irish Sword", 2:8, 1956, pp. 257-263.

[14] P, Pyne, *The Invasions of Buenos Aires, 1806-1807: The Irish Dimension*, Liverpool 1996.

[15] These, include P. Pyne, *A Soldier under two flags: Lieutenant-Colonel James Florence Burke: Officer, Adventurer and Spy*, "Études Irlandaises", 23:1, 1998, pp. 121-38.

[16] J. de Courcy Ireland, *The admiral from Mayo: a life of Almirante William Brown of Foxford, father of the Argentine navy*, Dublin 1995.

[17] J. de Courcy Ireland, *Admiral Brown at Martin García and Montevideo, 1814*, "The Irish Sword", 3:10, 1957, pp. 20-24.

[18] M. Walsh, *Unpublished Admiral Brown Documents in Madrid*, "The Irish Sword", 3:10, 1957, pp. 17-19.

[19] J. de Courcy Ireland, *Admiral William Brown*, "The Irish Sword", 6:23, 1964-4, pp. 119-121.

[20] T. Walsh, *Admiral Brown of Argentina* Part I, "Cathair na Mart: Journal of the Westport Historical Society", 10:1, 1990, pp. 47-58 and Part II, in the same journal, 11:1, 1991, pp. 105-117.

[21] B. O'Hara, *Mayo*, Galway 1982, pp. 258-9.

[22] E. Lambert - F.G. Thompson, *Captain Morgan O'Connell of the Hussar Guards and the Irish Legion*, "The Irish Sword", 13:53, 1979, pp. 281-2

[23] E. Lambert, *Voluntarios Británicos e Irlandeses en la Gesta Bolivariana*, Caracas 1981-93.

[24] Id., *Irish Soldiers in South America, 1818-30*, "Studies", 58:232, 1969, pp. 376-95.

[25] Id., *General O'Leary and South America*, "The Irish Sword", 11:43, 1973, pp. 57-74.

[26] J.G. Healy, *Daniel Florence O'Leary*, "Journal of the Cork Historical and Archaeological Society", 64, 1989, pp. 28-34.

[27] L. Geary, *Fraternally Yours: Roderic and Francis Burdett O'Connor*, "Journal of the Cork Historical and Archaeological Society", 95:254, 1990, pp. 120-123 and E. Lambert, *General Francis Burdett O'Connor*, "The Irish Sword", 13:51, 1977, pp. 128-33.

[28] J. de Courcy Ireland, *Thomas Charles Wright: Soldier of Bolivar; Founder of the Ecuadorian Navy*, "The Irish Sword", 6:25, 1964, pp. 271-275, and Ireland, *Irish Soldiers and Seamen* cit., pp. 296-303.

[29] B. de Breffny, *Ambrose O'Higgins: An Enquiry into his Irish Origins*, "The Irish Ancestor", 2:2, 1970, pp. 81-89.

[30] F. von Allendorfer, *An Irish Regiment in Brazil, 1826-1828*, "The Irish Sword", 3:10, 1957, pp. 28-31.

[31] R.B. McCornack, *The San Patricio Deserters in the Mexican War, 1847*, "The Irish Sword", 3:13, 1957-8, pp. 246-55.

[32] J.L.G., *The Battalion of St Patrick in the Mexican War, 1846-47*, "The Irish Sword", 3:10, 1957, pp. 65-7.

33 M. Hogan, *The Irish Soldiers of Mexico*, "History Ireland", 5:4, 1997, pp. 38-43.

34 J. Fogarty, *The San Patricio Battalion: The Irish Soldiers of Mexico* originally published, "Voices of Mexico", April-June, 2000, in http:www.irishargentine.org/sanpatriciosB.htm, and M.G. Connaughton, *Beneath an Emerald Green Flag The Story of Irish Soldiers, in Mexico*, in http://www.irishargentine.org/sanpatriciosA.htm

35 F. Sweeney, *Atlantic Counterculture and the Networked Text: Juan Francisco Manzano, R.R. Madden and the Cuban Slave*, "Narrative, in Forum for Modern Language Studies", 40:4, 2004, pp. 401-14.

36 S. Ó Síocháin, *Roger Casement's Vision of Freedom*, in M. Daly (ed.) *Roger Casement in Irish and World History*, Dublin 2005, pp. 1-10.

37 A tributary of the Amazon.

38 R. Sawyer, *Roger Casement's Diaries*, London 1997

39 W.J. McCormack, *Roger Casement in Death or the haunting of the Free State*, Dublin 2002, p. 30

40 P. Singleton-Gates - M. Girodias, *The Black Diaries: an account of Roger Casement's life and times with a collection of his diaries and public writings*, Paris 1959.

41 The most comprehensive account of this debate is McCormack, *Roger Casement* cit. McCormack organised a number of conferences on this issue.

42 B. Inglis, *Roger Casement*, London 2002.

43 See, for example, A. Mitchell, *Casement's Black Diaries: closed books reopened*, "History Ireland", 5:3, 1997, pp. 36-41 and Id., *The Casement Black Diaries Debate: the story so far*, "History Ireland", 9:2, 2001, pp. 42-4.

44 A. Mitchel (ed.) *The Amazon Journal of Roger Casement*, Dublin 1993, pp. 500 ff.

45 Mitchel, *Amazon Journal* cit. p. 499

46 S. Ó Síocháin, *Roger Casement, Ethnography and the Putumayo*, "Éire-Ireland", 39:2: 33, 1994, pp. 29-41.

47 Id., *Roger Casement* cit. p. 37.

48 Daly (ed.) *Roger Casement* cit.

49 'Peon' is a Latin American term for agricultural labourer, frequently victim of exploitation

50 A. Porter, *Sir Roger Casement and the International Humanitarian Movement*, in Daly (ed.) *Roger Casement* cit., 25 pp. 11-25.

51 L. McKenna, *The Mexican Imbroglio*, 17, 1928, p. 621

52 "An Irish Exile", *Martyred Mexico,* "Catholic Bulletin", 24:9, 1935, p. 714. See also P. Magennis, "*Blood Drenched Altars*", "Catholic Bulletin", 24:10, 1935, pp. 816-19.

53 McKenna, *Mexican Imbroglio* cit., 623

54 M. Kenny, *The Mexican Crisis: its causes and consequences*, "Studies", 14, 1926, pp. 23-42.

55 F. McCullagh, *Prisoner of the Reds* New York 1922.

56 Id., *Who is Calles?*, "Studies", March 1928, pp. 1-17 and *Mexico and the Press*, "Studies", 18, 1929, pp. 225-239.

57 M. Butler, *Popular Piety and Political Identity in Mexico's Cristero Rebellion Michoacán, 1927-29*, Oxford 2004. See also M. Butler, *The "Liberal" Cristero: Ladislao Molina and the Cristero Rebellion in Michoacán, 1927-9*, "Journal of Latin American Studies", 31:3, 1999, pp. 645-71.

58 P. Kirby, *Ireland and Latin America: Links and Lessons*, Dublin 1992.

59 http://www.corkandross.org/jsp/history/historyoverview.jsp.

60 Trócaire, *On the Journey towards a just world Trócaire 1973-1998*, Dublin 1998, p. 4.

61 Kirby, *Ireland and Latin America* cit., p. 9.

[62] D. Keogh, *Romero: El Salvador's Martyr*, Dublin 1981.

[63] Id., *Central America: Human Rights and US. Foreign Policy*, Cork 1985.

[64] Id., *Witness to the Truth: Church and Dictatorship in Latin America*, Cork-Dublin 1989.

[65] Id., *Church and Politics in Latin America*, Basingstoke 1990.

[66] Id., *El Salvador: Tragedia En El Cafetal*, "Historia", 16, Año VI, No. 59, 1981, pp.11-22; Id., *Peasant Revolt in El Salvador, 1932*, "Cranebag", 6:2, 1982, pp. 7-14; Id., *El Salvador and the United States*, "Millennium: Journal of, international Studies", 13.2, 1984, pp. 153-183.

[67] D. Ryan, *An examination of Diplomatic Relations between the United States and Nicaragua during the Reagan Presidency*, PhD, University College, Cork 1992.

[68] J. Crowley, *The Catholic Church: an Analysis of historiography and recent trends in the Latin American Church 1945-1982*, MA thesis, University College, Cork 1987.

[69] D. Dineen, *The Carter Administration's Policy Toward the Nicaraguan Revolution*, MA, University College, Cork 1995

[70] M. Foster, *The United States and El Salvador: An Analysis of United States Legation reporting, 1930-1944* MA, University College, Cork 1988.

[71] T. Landers, *The Politics of Agrarian Revolution: El Salvador's peasant Uprising of 1932* MA, University College, Cork 1985.

[72] G. MacEoin, *Memoirs and Memories* Mystic, Connecticut 1986. See also G. MacEoin, *No Peaceful Way: Chile's Struggle for Dignity*, New York 1974.

[73] J. O'Shea, *U.S. foreign policy towards Cuba: domestic and international pressures*, University of Limerick, 1998; J. Farrell, *The United States and the Cuba crisis,* MA, New University of Ulster 1970; L. Kingston, *Castro, Kennedy and Khrushchev – the Cuba Triangle,* University of Limerick 1997.

[74] P. Horgan, *Irish-Cuban relations 1959-62: From the Rise of Castro to the Cuban Missile Crisis*, MA, University College, Cork 2002.

[75] C. Buckley, *The Caribbean Crisis of 1962: The Soviet Perspective* MA, University College, Cork 1995.

[76] T. Ó Murchú, *The survival of the Communist regimes in Cuba, Vietnam and North Korea after the fall of the Soviet Union*, University of Limerick 2004.

[77] J. O'Neill, *From Castro's Cuba: from Marxism to market socialism*, University of Limerick 1997.

[78] A. Gray, *Deconstructing civil society in a revolutionary socialist state: the genesis of NGO participation in contemporary Cuba*, University of Limerick 2002.

[79] F. Carr, *The Complexities of U.S. Foreign policy in Columbia: conflict, drugs and human rights*, University of Limerick 1998.

[80] M. Hayes, *Anglo-Chilean Relations: 1932-1958: a survey of British Diplomatic attitudes towards the second Ibañez regime*, MA, University College, Cork 1991.

[81] G. Barry, *Batista to Castro: Anglo-Cuban Relations in Transition 1958-1959*, MA, University College, Cork 1993.

[82] A. Cronin, *Britain and Venezuela 1945-1958: A Study in Diplomacy* MA, University College, Cork, 1991.

[83] N.G. Cotter, *Britain and Peron's Argentina: 1946-55*, M.A. University College, Cork 1980.

[84] J. Murray, *The Irish and Others in Argentina*, "Studies", 38, 1949, pp. 377-88.

[85] See, for example, B. McGinn, *The Irish in Brazil*, "Irish Roots", 2, 1997, pp. 24-5; P. Nally, *Los irlandeses en la Argentina*, "Familia", 2:8, 1992, pp. 69-77.

[86] P. McKenna, *Nineteenth century Irish Emigration to, and Settlement in, Argentina*, MA, National University of Ireland, Maynooth 1994.

87 P. McKenna, *Irish Migration to Argentina*, in P. O'Sullivan (ed.) *Patterns of Migration*. Vol. 1 of *the Irish World Wide: History, Heritage and Identity series*, Leicester 1992, pp. 63-83, and P. McKenna, *Irish Emigration to Argentina: A different Model*, in A. Bielenberg (ed.) *The Irish Diaspora*, Harlow 2000, pp. 195-212.

88 McKenna, *Irish Emigration*, p. 199

89 D. Murphy, *A History of Irish Emigrant and Missionary Education* Dublin 2000, p. 516.

90 E. Walsh, *An Irish Catholic Association Pilgrimage to Luján, Province of Buenos Aires*, "Collectanea Hibernica", 42, 2000, pp. 243-4

91 Nally, *Los irlandeses en la Argentina* cit., pp. 69-77.

92 H. Meehan, *The McManus brothers – Patrick: 1864-1929. Seamas: 1868-1960*, "Donegal Annual", 46, 1994, pp. 5-18

93 M.l Kennedy, *Mr Blythe, I Think, Hears from him Occasionally': The Experiences of Irish Diplomats in Latin America, 1919-23*, in M. Kennedy - J.M. Skelly (eds.), *Irish Foreign Policy, 1919-66,* Dublin 2000, pp. 44-60.

94 T.P. Coogan, *Wherever Green is Worn: the Story of the Irish Diaspora,* London 2000, ch. 9.

95 B. McGinn, *The Irish, in South America - An Annotated Bibliography*, in http://www.irishdiaspora.net.

96 W. Ready, *The Irish and South America*, "Éire-Ireland", 1:1, 1966, pp. 50-63.

97 B. McGinn, *The South American Irish*, in C. Ryan (ed.), *Aspects of Irish Genealogy 3*, Dublin 1999, pp. 25-55.

98 Id., *An Irishman's Diary: the Mulhalls*, in http://www.illyria.com/irish/mcginn_mulhalls.html.

99 Id., *South American Irish* cit., pp. 27-33.

100 *Welcome to 'Irish Migration in Latin America'. The Web Site of the Society for Irish Latin American Studies*, in http://www.irishargentine.org/about.htm.

101 *Nineteenth-century Irish Emigration to Argentina*, originally delivered to Columbia Irish Studies Seminar. <http://www.irishargentine.org/biblioarg.htm>

102 E. Murray, *Researching the Irish in Argentina: An Argentine History or a History of the Irish Argentines*? in http://irishargentine.org/researching.htm.

103 Id., *How the Irish Became Gauchos Ingleses: Diasporic Models in Irish-Argentine Literature*, p. 61, <http://www.irishargentine.org/ia_last.htm>.

104 Id., *How the Irish became Gauchos Ingleses*, cit. p. 62

105 F. Clark, *The Gazeta de Literature de México (1788-1795): the formation of a literary-scientific periodical in late-viceregal Mexico*, "Dieciocho: Hispanic Enlightenment", 28:1, 2005, pp. 7-32.

106 J. Cleary, *'Misplaced Ideas'? Colonialism, Location, and Dislocation in Irish Studies*, in Carroll - King (eds.), *Ireland and Postcolonial Theory* cit., pp. 16-45.

107 H. Montgomery Hyde, *Mexican Empire: the History of Maxmilian and Carlota of Mexico*, London 1946.

108 P. Pyne, *Presidential Caesarism in Latin America, Myth or Reality?: A Case Study of José María Velasco Ibarra, 1960-1*, "Comparative Politics", 9:2, 1977, pp. 281-304; Id., *The Role of Congress in the Ecuadorian Political System and Its Contribution to the Overthrow of President Velasco Ibarra in 1961*, Glasgow 1973.

109 Id., *Ecuador's Junta Militar, 1963-1966: a case study of military reformism,* D.Phil, University of Ulster, 1990.

110 R. Finegan, *Insurrection in Chiapas: Revolution in Mexico*, University of Limerick 2002.

111 E. Murray, *How the Irish Became Gauchos Ingleses Diasporic models in Irish-Argentine Literature*, p. 61, http://www.irishargentine.org/ia_last.htm.

[112] See D. Keogh, *Argentina and the Falklands (Malvinas) – the Irish Connection*, in A. Hennessy - J. King (eds.) *The Land that England Lost: Argentina and Britain, a Special Relationship*, London 1992, pp. 123-41, and E. Walsh, *Documents and Correspondence concerning anf from James Foran, Irish priest and chaplain in the Falkland Islands 1876-86*, "Collectanea Hibernica", 46-47, 2004-5, pp. 241-274.

[113] O. Marshall, *The English-Language Press in Latin America: an Annotated Bibliography*, London 1995; Id., *English-speaking communities in Latin America since Independence*, Houndsmills 2000 and Id., *English, Irish and Irish-American Pioneer Settlers in Nineteenth-Century Brazil*, Oxford 2005.

[114] L. Bethell, *Brazil by British and Irish Authors*, Oxford, 2003.

Bibliography

Journals

"Irish Roots"

"The Irish Sword"

"Studies"

Books and Articles

Casement R., *The Amazon Journal of Roger Casement*, edited by Mitchell A., Dublin 1993.

Coogan T., *Wherever Green is Worn: The Story of the Irish Diaspora*, London 2000.

Daly M.E. (ed.), *Roger Casement in Irish and World History*, Dublin 2005.

Keogh D., *Central America: Human Rights and US. Foreign Policy*, Cork 1985.

Id., *Church and Politics in Latin America*, Basingstoke 1990.

Ireland J., *The Admiral from Mayo: a life of Almirante William Brown of Foxford, father of the Argentine Navy*, Dublin 1995.

McGinn B., *The South American Irish*, in Ryan C. (ed.), *Aspects of Irish Genealogy 3*, Dublin 1999, pp. 25-53.

McKenna P., *Irish Emigration to Argentina: A Different Model*, in Bielenberg A. (ed.), *The Irish Diaspora*, Harlow 2000, pp. 195-212.

Id., *Irish migration to Argentina*, in O'Sullivan P. (ed.), *Patterns of Migration*. Vol. 1 of *The Irish World Wide: History, Heritage and Identity series*, Leicester 1992, pp. 63-83.

O'Leary D., *Bolívar and the War of Independence*, Austin 1970.

Websites

Irish Migration Studies in Latin America, website of the Society for Irish Latin American Studies: http://www.irishargentine.org.

Irishdiaspora.net the Irish Diaspora Studies scholarly network, website of the Irish Diaspora Research Unit at the University of Bradford: http://www.irishdiaspora.net

Source

Martyred Mexico

Irish people at home are, no doubt, well aware that the Church is undergoing persecution in Mexico, but probably not one of them has any real conception of the actual horrors of that persecution. Neither the Christians of the period of Nero and Caligula, nor the Irish Catholics of the Penal times, were victims of a more savage or diabolical tyranny than that which is now crushing the Mexican people. A Catholic nation is suffering martyrdom while the rest of he world nods approvingly or else is strangely silent.

In order to understand the present situation in Mexico it is necessary to go back to the time of the Spanish conquest which began in 1519 A.D. In dealing with this period, one has first of all to disabuse his mind of the false English propaganda against Spain which has passed for history in almost every English-speaking country for the past 300 or 400 years. From the time of Queen Elizabeth onwards, Spain was the enemy of the "progressive" Protestant world. Long before the theory of Nordic superiority was broached as a "scientific truth" the official histories of England taught that the Catholic nations of Europe were superstitious, lazy and ignorant. This kind of "history" was taken over by the United States, and has had its influence even upon American Catholics.

From: "An Irish Exile", *Martyred Mexico,* "Catholic Bulletin", 24:9, 1935, pp. 714-22.

Portuguese Baroque Art in Colonial Brazil: the Heritage of 18th-Century *Azulejos*

Maria Alexandra Trindade Gago da Câmara
Open University of Portugal, Lisbon

Utilizado com carácter monumental desde o século XVI, como em nenhum outro país da Europa, o Azulejo é um elemento central da cultura artística em Portugal, rica e vasta memória patrimonial do nosso país, assumindo – com especial incidência especificamente no século XVIII – um sentido mais alargado do que o revestimento simples da arquitectura, modelador e regularizador, sendo hoje entendido como expressão artística maior, transmissor de ideias através das imagens.

Este ímpar conjunto de características e a sua intensiva produção tiveram também especial relevo no Brasil, onde particularmente na zona da Baía se conhecem deslumbrantes e magníficos exemplos. É pois desse fantástico e importante património, do seu estudo e da sua inventariação que propomos tratar neste sucinto artigo.

Introduction

In Portugal the *azulejo* was widely used. Its complex adaptation to various spaces and diverse ends exceeds the purely decorative role initially conceived for it. Its relief and colour and the natural shine of glazed ceramic plates, resulting from irregular exposure to heat or deficient firing conditions, added to this medium a specific plasticity that distinguishes the *azulejo* from other materials. Furthermore, the dematerialization of surfaces and the animation of architectural spaces to create fictional, illusory environments made the *azulejo* a fundamental element of scenographic creation, especially within the baroque space.

The most significant art product of Portuguese culture, the *azulejo* indicates in each period the social, mental and artistic evolution of Portugal, as well as the country's major transformations, often assuming more of a spatial, architectural character than a merely decorative one. Its permanent and widespread use has elevated its status to that of national icon[1].

The 18th century was no doubt the period in which the *azulejo* played a major role, becoming at this time a key feature of Portugal's physiognomy. It emerged as a luminous presence, a view held unanimously among Portuguese and foreign art historians. A privileged medium for painting on many dignified occasions and a cornerstone of the Portuguese collective imagination, the *azulejo* possessed an important functional value throughout the 18th century, and is today recognized as a multifunctional artistic medium.

The true essence of the *azulejo* resides in its intimate relation with architecture. The *azulejo* stands out for its architectural application, the spatial configuration it promotes and the adequacy of the decorative and iconographic programs of the buildings for which it was conceived. This mutual dependency – architecture/the *azulejo* and the *azulejo*/architecture – was capable of integrating the formal and semantic transformations experienced by the *azulejo*, particularly during the 18th century.

In the period in question, the art of the *azulejo* was an active force in the architectural context and an essential component of the Portuguese version of Total Art[2], in its relationship of interdependency not only with architecture but also with painting, sculpture and other decorative arts.

Relative to the expansion of the Portuguese art of the *azulejo* and the unifying role it played in Lisbon, we may speak of a genuine diaspora of the *azulejo*. During the Ancien Regime, Lisbon played a fundamental role as the center of *azulejo* production and made a decisive contribution to spreading this art throughout continental Portugal, as well as to its island and colonial territories. The volume and dynamic nature of Lisbon's exportation of the *azulejo* to these regions not only impacted upon the adoption of the *azulejo* elsewhere but also played a considerable role in renewing other regional arts.

This impact was primarily felt during the 18th century, as has been mentioned, the period of the widest *azulejo* production, its aesthetic values, erudite expression, formal language, scenographic effect and decorative motifs serving as the main unifying force behind the art of remote regions, on different continents, due to the influence of its decorative elements on these regions.

Such is the notable – but not unique – case of Brazil, which will be considered here. The journey of the *azulejo* throughout this Portuguese-speaking space had a significant impact on this vast art. Mass levels of production led to some of the most complex and spectacular examples of architectural integration, yielding some of the most important and captivating baroque collections of this period.

Let us now turn to this Portuguese art as it was assimilated in Brazil, particularly between the 1730s and 1790s, a broad chronological span starting with the so-called "Great Joanina Production" and extending to the Mariano period; a span during which a diversity of thematic motifs, decorative vocabularies and scenes became blended together.

Methods and approaches

Both Portuguese and Brazilian art historians have shown an interest in this aspect of the Portuguese cultural heritage, many significant contributions having emerged from a range of different editorial projects over the past sixty years.

One of the earliest of these contributions is Reinaldo dos Santos's *A Arte luso-brasileira do século XVIII*, published in 1948, which offers a broad view of the art of the *azulejo* in open dialogue with other artistic domains, such as architecture, painting, sculpture and wood-working, and which, for the first time, calls attention to the genuine "transfusion" of Portuguese baroque art into the principal centres of religious and civil Brazilian life during the 17th and 18th centuries[3].

In the 1950s, João Pereira Dias published an important article on the pages of the "Revista Belas Artes" in which he offers the first analysis of the 18th century *azulejos* adorning the Cloister of the Third Order of Saint Francis of Bahia (in the city of Salvador), an interest he further developed in a paper delivered at the IV International Colloquium for Luso-Brazilian Studies held in that city in 1959.

One of the first essays in which the *azulejo* was the main object of study was the article by Joaquim de Sousa Leão which appeared in the "The Burlington Magazine" in 1944 under the title *Portuguese Tiles in Brazilian Architecture*. In 1945 Carlos Ott published an article in the "Revista do Serviço do Património Histórico e Artístico Nacional" (no. 7) on *The* Azulejos *of the Monastery of Saint Francis of Bahia*, in which he gives particular emphasis to the sources of inspiration that provided the basis for painting the *azulejos*.

Still in the 1950s and 60s, many attempts were made to recover and define a cycle of Portuguese baroque *azulejos* in Brazil. Among these are the first great overview provided by Mário Barata in *Azulejos no Brasil* (1955), in which, covering the period between the 17th and 18th centuries and drawing on archival sources, Barata develops a coherence description of the function of *azulejos* in Brazilian architecture, taking into account both models and sources of inspiration, as well as reflecting on the authorship of certain ceramic panels. In 1953 José de Valladares published a study – *Azulejos da Reitoria* – of the ceramic tiles adorning the University of Bahia building, which had been transferred from the old Aguiar manor house, also known as Bom Gosto.

The great pioneering work in this area involved the gathering and inventory of all the centers of *azulejos* existing on Brazilian soil, a task carried out by Santos Simões in the 1960s[4]: the monographical *Corpus da Azulejaria Portuguesa* resulted in the publication of five separate volumes, one of which exclusively devoted to the *Azulejaria Portuguesa no Brasil: 1580-1822* (1965). The aim of the series was to provide a panoramic vision of this art across the Atlantic.

The policy of inventorying and classifying the architectural heritage[5], specifically in the case of Bahia (between the 16th and 19th centuries), allowed gathering more complete knowledge on certain group of *azulejos*.

The 1980s and 90s saw an increase in the number of publications on the subject. Notable contributions include those made by Pedro Moacir Maia (1990) and Ponce de Leon (1998), and two sequential works, *Azulejos na cultura luso-brasileira* (ed. Dora Alcântara, 1997) e *Azulejos-Portugal e Brasil* ("Revista Oceanos", 1998/1999). The published

Proceedings of the Luso-Brazilian Conference of Art History, held every two years, has constituted a forum for the exchange of information among specialists from the two countries whose research has most focused on this matter. Finally, two recent works have appeared on the subject. The broader one, which includes contributions of various authors, the Portuguese art historian José Meco among them, is entitled *Les Metamorphoses de L'Azur. L'art d'azulejo dans le monde latin* and was published in 2002 by Ars Latina; the other work is a specific study of the *azulejo* panels of the Cloister of the Third Order of Saint Francis of Bahia, undertaken during restoration process carried out by the Ricard Espírito Santo Silva Foundation in 2002.

It was specifically on the coast of Brazil (more concretely in the area of Bahia) that the baroque *azulejo* revealed levels of artistic excellence. Bahia possesses the largest and most noteworthy concentration of *azulejos*, an immense collection which, despite significant efforts, still remains an open field of study.

The detailed description of the legacy of 18th century Portuguese *azulejos* across the Atlantic remains to be done, hampered by difficulties which include not just the loss of certain sets due to demolition, theft and transfers but also piece-meal restoration work, which raises the considerable problem of identifying the most sophisticated, effective (and urgently necessary) methods for carrying out a complete study.

Nonetheless, there is some work of recording, analysis and even diagnosis which has slowly emerged from a range of different research projects and which is important to take into account.

The systematic use of *azulejos* in murals in both religious and secular spaces along the Brazilian coast varies in accordance with the uses and aims of the space in question. An analysis of the geography of the *azulejo* allows us to identify areas that received the *azulejo* from the continent and thus to discover the intentions that governed its usage at any given time.

A geography of the heritage of 18th-century *azulejos* and the cross-checking of information and documentation relative to each specific space allow us to identify architectural and decorative rhythms, the interests and tastes of the commissioner of the work, the "transplanting" of ornamental and figurative models and matrixes from one country to the other, and the dialectic between the desire for monumentality and wealth in the service of God and the spirit of restraint underlying certain religious orders (as in the Saint Francis monastery in Bahia).

From this perspective on the geography of the baroque *azulejo*, we can immediately distinguish two main groupings: the religious space, composed of cloisters, sacristies, church interiors, stairways, libraries and reception halls, and the secular space, including palaces and manor houses,[6] both places where the secular motifs of the *azulejo* are blended with religious figures.

Let us review several specific examples:

Among the diverse larger collections of *azulejos* belonging to the "Great Joanina Production" period in the north-eastern Brazil, one of the main ones is the substantial collection at the Saint Francis monastery in Salvador, the most noteworthy *azulejo* nucleus in the Portuguese-speaking world.

Of its vast spoils the thirty-seven *azulejo* panels placed on the bottom floor of the monastery stand out. Dated between 1746 and 1748; these panels came from Bartolomeu Antunes' workshop and were based on the *Teatro Moral de la Vida Humana y de toda la Philosofia de los Antigos e Modernos* (Fig. 1)[7]. In this baroque environment, the *azulejos* bring together a certain tradition of monumental architecture with the possibility of a medium incorporating both a formal language and a "modern" narrative.

The placement of symbolic *azulejos* in these cloisters is related to the circulatory and use-oriented nature of these architectural structures: on one hand, penitence; on the other, the pedagogical confrontation with the vision of the Holy Spirit.

Still within the same religious space, on the landing of the stairway – the space between the main chapel, the sacristy and the cloister – on the first floor of the monastery, six

Fig. 1
Convent of San Francisco in Salvador da Baía, workshop of Bartolomeu Antunes.

Fig. 2
Convent of San Francisco, first floor, allegorical figures.

arches open onto the galleries, which depict three great iconographic themes: the senses, the months of the year and the four parts of the world (Fig. 2)[8]. Significant here is the expression of a systematic relationship between allegorical figuration and the baroque valorisation of the image. The allegories thus direct us towards a specific knowledge of the world, nature and man himself.

In the upper cloister of the monastery one finds five invitational figures[9], which though not the primary decorative features of the space, contribute to its courtly dimension. The figures represent halberdiers, appearing in fabricated military garb (plumed helmets, chest plates, leather-fringed skirts and Roman sandals), thus reinforcing their eminently decorative value and symbolizing an involvement in the etiquette of courtly life.

Still within this same type of architectural space, the Venerable Third Order of the Saint Francis Congregation of Bahia is one of the most noteworthy of Portuguese artistic efforts on Brazilian soil. The *azulejos* are spread throughout the entry hall, the atrium, the cloister, the side corridors of the church, the stairway, the consistory and assembly hall, the gallery of the nave and other compartments. These were the result of different commissions and not all can be found in their original locations, some having been moved for restoration work.

The most striking *azulejos* of the building belong to the great baroque decorative campaign of the second quarter of the 18th century, among which are the linings of the cloister and the consistory (Figs. 3-4), which recently benefited from conservation and restoration work[10]. The historical value of these works is unquestionable[11], as they represent the Portuguese capital prior to its partial destruction by the 1755 earthquake.

The cloister presents this unusual narrative horizontal pannel depicting the royal arrival at Lisbon of the Prince and Princess D. José e D. Mariana Vitória in 1729, along with their respective nuptial procession leading up to the See Cathedral. The framing of these scenes is simple, with straight-lined bases and entablature, centring on panels bordered by figures of young children and interwoven with spiralling baroque compositions. The supposed images of Lisbon that provide the background for the procession are entirely invented, there being not a single building or space reproduced faithfully enough for identification. Its main interest is scenographic, and lies in its framing of the royal arrival. The panels stand out for their picturesque representations and for their suggestive images of the procession and the triumphal arches. The immense procession was condensed by the painter of the *azulejos*, and of the twenty-six actual arches only the most important were reproduced. Through the raised arches, almost all bearing inscriptions,

Figs. 3-4
Panels of the *Consistory Room.*

a few carriages pass, observed in the foreground by a series of identifiable social types: members of the church and of the nobility, commoners, children and beggars.

The *azulejos* belonging to the consistory are organized into ten ceramic paintings surrounding this magnificent room, conveying the contrasts and irregularity of the city, with its dense and varied buildings. The panels reveal buildings whose details are severely distorted, which raises the difficult questions of the scale being used and of the model or source of inspiration.

Both sets of *azulejos* perform their function with complete effectiveness: to reproduce and thus perpetuate the idea of the capital as an urban centre with a representative function, while translating the affirmative rhetoric of the Portuguese colonial empire.

Halfway through the 18th century, between 1750 and 1760, new ornamental styles were introduced, including an increased decorative use of shell patterns. The rococo style thus began to spread, a style in which blue and white tones predominated, offering greater compositional density and drawing out the transparency and depth of the figurative walls.

A good example of an ornamental surface with rococo motifs can be found in the sacristy of the Boa Viagem church (Fig. 5) and in that of the Saint Anthony of Cairú monastery. In the latter case, the theatricality of the baroque is visible in the *washroom* – in the curtain surrounding the *spring*, and, on the remaining walls, in the magnificent framings of the doors, windows and chest of drawers, reflecting a conceptual elegance brought about by the fluid shell patterns characteristic of the French Regency style.

Fig. 5
Sacristy of the *Boa Viagem* church.

Fig. 6
Sacristy of the Monastery of Saint Anthony of Cairú.

Among the secular *azulejos* of this general context, though somewhat later, the Conde dos Arcos manor house (Figs. 7-8) offers one of the most impressive collections of Portuguese neoclassicism in Brazil. This manor house maintains four distinct nuclei of *azulejos*, each full of loose ribbons and branches, with delicate floral patterns in rich alternations of colour. One may find medallions filled with manganese purple landscapes flanked with dolphins, coastal landscapes and seascapes in blue, bunches of feathers and other motifs centred on a peacock with its tail spread open and the small head of a girl with a hat.

The other secular collection is to be found today at the administration building of the University of Bahia, having been transferred from the Bom Gosto manor house. These panels are monochromatic, with blue forms against a white background, and the scenes represented are expertly designed. Iconographically, the themes depicted range from mythological scenes to scenes of idealized daily life and *chinoiseries*. The placing of these *azulejos* in their new setting obeyed strict criteria, their grouping having been dictated by type and theme (Figs. 9-10)[12].

In closing we might state that, as it was used in Portugal and overseas, the 18th-century art of the *azulejo* represents genuine contribution to the universal history of art.

Figs. 7-8
The *Conde dos Arcos* manor house.

Perspectives

As we have seen, the heritage of the *azulejo*, transported to Brazil by the Portuguese, constitutes a "spatialized" cultural product, given its architectural fixity and its essentially practical, aesthetic and symbolic functioning within the building that houses it, often actively structuring the space in question and charging it with meanings and significance.

Nevertheless, the great diffusion and dispersion of the Portuguese *azulejo* throughout this period has complicated an exhaustive inquiry into this subject, as well as the subsequent work of comparative analysis. The baroque *azulejo* in Portuguese – speaking environments – specifically that of Brazil – has yet to be adequately characterised, embracing (as we have seen in the examples cited) a multitude of styles and tastes, and having been drawn into large production cycles which still require precise definition.

Figs. 9-10
Administration building of the University of Bahia.

A great portion of these *azulejos* is anonymous, providing no information about who produced or commissioned them.

We are well aware of the many paths available today for the study of this heritage in Brazil. We need to define new methods and work perspectives[13], to think of new forms of aesthetic agency, as we search for an understanding and common pattern between this art and other art objects, drawing on historical information, artistic analysis and iconographic readings.

We must discover how to establish specific lines of action, to define a common method, checking criteria for the identification of the pieces existing in private and public collections, registering and preserving *azulejos in situ*, cultivating an effective restoration policy and putting together an inventory of the 18th-century *azulejo* heritage. This requires starting with complete or partial inquiries and articulating them with well-conducted multidisciplinary projects[14], oriented to ensure the convergence of the knowledge they produce. This means constructing an integrated system through which it will be possible to assess the degree of preservation of particular examples of the *azulejo* heritage, to determine the methods used in previous interventions and to provide a continuous reading of the evolution of this same heritage.

A continuous and up-to-date inventory of this important heritage will supply material for reflection in disciplinary areas as diverse as art history, the history of culture and mentalities, sociology, anthropology, museum science, conservation and restoration, and the preservation of urban heritage.

We believe that an exhaustive inventory of the *azulejo* heritage in Brazil, accompanied by particular studies and development projects, with careful attention to current conditions and states of conservation, may soon offer a field of study for future generations of art historians and scholars from other fields.

In sum, within the context of colonial art in Brazil in this period, we can now recognize that the art of the *azulejo* offers us a dynamic approach to a decorative tradition that remains very much alive.

Notes

1 "[T]he *azulejo* is "naturalized" Portuguese in its decorative thematics of polychromatic patterning and in its scale as applied to walls, with such bold uses as the decoration of entire walls, a singular instance in the conception of Western ornamentation" (J.M. Santos Simões, *A Azulejaria em Portugal no século XVIII*, Lisbon 1979, p. 3).

2 On this matter see L. Moura Sobral, *Bel Composto: a obra de arte total do primeiro barroco português*, in *Struggle for Synthesis. A obra de arte total nos séculos XVII e XVIII*, Braga, vol. I, p. 303 ff..

3 Among the foreign scholars who have devoted attention to the Brazilian side of issues in the history and criticism of Luso-Brazilian architecture, particularly to the question of the art of the *azulejo*, are Germain Bazin (*Architecture Religeuse Baroque au Brésil* [São Paulo 1949]) and Robert Smith (*Robert Smith [1912-1975]. A Investigação na História de Arte* [F.C.G. Serviço de Belas Artes, Lisbon 2000]).

4 In 1960 the Calouste Gulbenkian Foundation (F.C.G.) created the Group for the Study of the Art of the

Azulejo, directed by J.M. Santos Simões, whose objective was to gather information on the *azulejo* in Portugal, carrying out a systematic survey of the most representative and most aesthetically valuable *azulejo* nuclei in Portugal. By 1968 the full territory of continental Portugal, the adjacent islands and Brazil had been covered. See M.A.T. Gago da Câmara, *O estudo da azulejaria barroca em Portugal: história, análise e evolução*, in *II Congresso Internacional de História de Arte. Portugal: encruzilhadas de culturas, das Artes e das Sensibilidades*, Associação Portuguesa dos Historiadores de Arte, Porto 2001, pp. 163-72.

5 Cf. *Inventário da Protecção do Acervo Cultural*, vol. I – Monumentos do Município de Salvador, Bahia 1974.

6 These constructions of Portuguese design are called "sobrados", and are currently being studied as important elements of Portuguese heritage in their own right.

7 On this matter see the important article by A. Nobre Pais, *O Theatro Moral de la Vida Humana no Convento de São Francisco da Baia*, "Revista Oceanos, Azulejos", 36/37, 1998-1999, pp. 100-12.

8 See P. Moacir Maia, *Os cinco sentidos, os trabalhos dos meses e as quatro partes do mundo em paineis de azulejos no Convento de S. Francisco em Salvador.*, Bahia 1990.

9 These are figures done on a human scale which appear in strategic areas and spaces. They first became an object of study in the pioneering work by L. Arruda, *Azulejaria Barroca Portuguesa – Figuras de Convit*, Lisbon 1993.

10 See *Festa Barroca a Azul e Branco. Os azulejos do Claustro da ordem Terceira de São Francisco, São Salvador da Baía*, Lisbon 2002.

11 See M.A.T. Gago da Câmara, *Lisboa Reencontrada: registos iconográficos na azulejaria Setecentista*, "O Imaginário da Cidade, Revista Discursos: Língua, Cultura e Sociedade", 3rd series, 5, 2002, pp. 167-79.

12 See J. Valadares, *Azulejos da Reitoria*, Salvador 1953.

13 See M.A.T. Gago da Câmara, *Azulejaria Barroca em Portugal: história, análise e evolução*," in *Actas II Congresso Internacional de História de Arte. Portugal, encruzilhadas de culturas. Das Artes e das Sensibilidades*, pp. 163-72.

14 There is currently a Ph.D. project underway on the devotional figurative panels at the Igreja de Nossa Senhora da Pena in Rio de Janeiro. The project is being carried out by the architect Maria das Graças Ferreira and, focusing on the conservation of Portuguese *azulejos* in Brazil, involves a more general effort of theoretical grounding, as well as an exhaustive photographic and iconographic inquiry.

Bibliography

Actas dos Colóquios Luso-Brasileiro de História da Arte, Ouro Preto 1992; Belo Horizonte 1993-1996; Bahia 1997.

Alcântara D., *Azulejos na colecção Castro Maya*, in *Azulejos na Cultura Luso-Brasileira*, Rio de Janeiro 1997.

Id., *Azulejos Portugueses em São Luís do Maranhão*, Rio de Janeiro 1980.

Azulejos de Portugal. Séculos XVII e XVIII, Rota de África (Catalogue), New Delhi- Goa 1993.

Arte do Azulejo em Portugal, Cultura Portuguesa, in Centro Virtual Camões, Lisbon 2000: www.instituto-camoes.pt/cvc/azulejos/index.html

Azulejos Portugal - Brasil., "Revista Oceanos", 36/37, 1998/1999.

Barata M., *Azulejos no Brasil, Séculos XVII, XVIII e XIX*, Rio de Janeiro 1955.

Costa Tribe T., *Metáfora e Saber: um programa didáctico azulejar do século XVIII*, "Callipole. Vila Viçosa", 1, 1993, pp. 59-77.

de Léon Ponce F., *História da Arte Luso-Brasileira. Guia Bibliográfico*, Recife 1998.

de Souza Leão J., *Decorative art: the azulejo*, in Livermore H.V. (ed.), *Portugal and Brazil; an Introduction*, Oxford 1953, pp. 385-394.

Dias P., *História da Arte Portuguesa no Mundo (1414-1822)*, 2 vols., Lisbon 1998-99.

Inventário da Protecção do Acervo Cultural, vol. I, Bahia 1975.

Festa Barroca a Azul e Branco. Os Azulejos do Claustro da ordem Terceira de São Francisco, São Salvador Baía, Lisbon 2002.

Gago da Câmara M.A.T., *Espaço e Quotidiano na Azulejaria Portuguesa do Século XVIII: a cerâmica rococó na região de Lisboa*, in *IV Colóquio Luso-Brasileiro de História de Arte*, Salvador da Bahia 1997, pp. 303-329.

Id., *O estudo da azulejaria barroca em Portugal: história, análise e evolução*, in *II Congresso Internacional de História da Arte. Portugal: encruzilhadas de culturas, das Artes e das Sensibilidades*, Associação Portuguesa do Historiadores de Arte, Almediana, Porto 2001, pp. 163-172.

Id., *Lisboa Reencontrada: registos iconográficos na azulejaria Setecentista*, in "O Imaginário da Cidade, Revista Discursos, Língua, Cultura e Sociedade", III Série, 5, 2003, pp. 167-179.

Id., *"Arte de Bem Viver": a encenação do quotidiano na azulejaria portuguesa da segunda metade de Setecentos*, FGC, FCT, Lisbon 2005.

Gomes Machado J.A. (coord.), *A Arte no Espaço Atlântico do Império Português*, III Colóquio Luso-Brasileiro de História da Arte, Universidade de Évora, 1997.

Les Metamorphoses de L'Azur. L'art d'azulejo dans le monde latin, France 2002.

Meco J., *Azulejaria Portugues*, Lisbon 1985

Moacir Maia P. ,*Os cinco sentidos, os trabalhos dos meses e as quatro partes do mundo em painéis de azulejos no Convento de S. Francisco em Salvador*, Bahia 1990.

Ott C., *Os Azulejos do convento de São Francisco da Baía*, "Revista Património Histórico, artístico nacional", 7, 1943, pp. 7-34.

Pereira Dias J., *Os azulejos do claustro da Ordem Terceira de São Francisco*, "Revista de Belas Artes", II, 7, 1975, pp. 31-44.

Santos Reinaldo dos, *A Arte Luso-brasileira do século XVIII*, "Revista de Belas Artes", 2nd series, Lisbon 1948, pp. 3-17.

Santos Simões J.M., *Azulejaria portuguesa no Brasil (1580-1822)*, Lisbon 1965.

Id., *A Azulejaria em Portugal no século XVIII*, Lisbon 1979.

Sousa Lopes V. (coord.), *Estudos de Azulejaria*, Lisbon 2001.

Valadares J., *Azulejos da Reitoria*, Salvador 1953.

Id., *Estudos de Arte Brasileira:* Publicações de 1943-1958.

Biographies

Anna Agnarsdóttir

Anna Agnarsdóttir was born in Reykjavik and educated at Sussex University, the University of Iceland and the London School of Economics and Political Science. She is now Professor of History at the University of Iceland. Her research interests are European and Icelandic history from 1500-1830, including international relations between Iceland and the world, and the history of trade and exploration. She has written many articles both in Icelandic and foreign journals and edited several books, including *Voyages and Explorations in the North Atlantic from the Middle Ages to the XVII Century* (Reykjavík 2000). She is now completing *The Letters and Journals of Sir Joseph Banks: Iceland and the North Atlantic 1772-1820* for the Hakluyt Society, London.

Ana Paula Menino Avelar

Ana Paula Menino Avelar was born in Lisbon and studied at the University of Lisbon. She is now Auxiliary Professor in the Universidade Aberta (Open University), Portugal. Her current research interests are Modern History, Cultural Studies, Interdisciplinary Studies, History and the Arts, and her publications include *Fernão Lopes de Castanheda, historiador dos portugueses na Índia ou cronista do governo de Nuno da Cunha?* (Lisbon 1997), *Visions of the Orient, ways of feeling in 16th-century Portugal* (Lisbon 2002), *Ars Historica* (Lisbon 2003). She is member of the Portuguese Academy of History, the Portuguese Maritime Academy, and the Portuguese Geographical Society.

Attila Bárány

Attila Bárány was born in Cegled, Hungary. He was educated at the University of Debrecen and the Central European University, Budapest, and has been a research fellow at the Hungarian Academy of Arts and Sciences. He now teaches at the University of Debrecen and his research interests are Anglo-Hungarian, Anglo-Imperial/German relations in the Middle Ages, medieval Hungarian diplomacy, and military history. Recent publications include *Zsigmond király 1416-os angliai kísérete* [The entourage of King Sigismund in England in 1416], "AETAS", 19, 2004, *Angol lovagok a nikápolyi csatában* [English knights at the battle of Nicopolis], "Hadtörténelmi Közlemények", 118, 2005 and *Anglo-Luxemburg Relations during the reign of Emperor Sigismund*, in Michel Pauly and Philipp von Zabern (eds), *Sigismundus Rex et Imperator, Art et Culture a l'Époque de Sigismond de Luxembourg 1387-1437* (Luxembourg-Mainz 2006).

Geert Castryck

Geert Castryck was born in Belgium in 1974 and studied at Ghent University. He is currently a research and teaching assistant in African History at Ghent, lecturing on Islam in Africa, Islam in the modern World-System, and the theory and methods of African and colonial history writing. He is completing a dissertation on the Muslim communities of colonial Bujumbura (Burundi), 1897-1962. His current research interests are minorities and exclusion in the local and global contexts of state formation in colonial and postcolonial East- and Central-Africa. He has published on the historiography on Belgian colonialism, the historiography of Ethiopian Jewry, the social meanings of ethnicity in Burundi, and language under Belgian colonial rule.

Vinita Damodaran

Vinita Damodaran is a historian of modern India. Her work ranges from the social and political history of Bihar to the environmental history of South Asia. Her publications include *Broken Promises, Indian Nationalism and the Congress Party in Bihar* (1992), *Nature and the Orient, Essays on the Environmental History of South and South- East Asia* (1998) and *Post Colonial India, History Politics and Culture (2000).* She is particularly interested in questions of identity and resistance and is completing a manuscript on landscape and indigeneity in Chotanagpur. She directs the Centre for World Environmental History at the University of Sussex.

Gábor Demeter

Gábor Demeter was born in Debrecen, Hungary, in 1980, and educated at the University of Debrecen. He is now assistant lecturer in Physical Geography and Geoinformatics at Debrecen and is completing a doctoral dissertation on the diplomacy of the Balkan Wars in 1912-1913. His other research interests are economic history, historical geography, and the question of ethnicity and nationality in the historical Hungary. His publications include *Bolgár kísérletek az elszigetelődés elkerülésére a második Balkán-háború előestéjén* [Bulgarian attempts to avoid isolation on the eve of the Second Balkan War], "Történeti Tanulmányok", XIII, 2005, and he has co-edited (with V. Árvay and E. Bodnár) a study of the Balkans and the Eastern Question in the Policy of the Great Powers (2005).

Maria Alexandra Trindade Gago da Câmara

Maria Alexandra Trindade Gago da Câmara was born in Lisbon and educated at the New University of Lisbon and the Open University of Portugal, Lisbon, where she now teaches Portuguese art history. Her research field is the 18th century, particularly the relationship between the ceramic tile art of *azulejaria* and Portuguese culture. At present she is director of the project entitled *A National Inventory of the Heritage of Eighteenth-Century Azulejos: The Constitution of Iconographic Repertories*, financed by the Science and Technology Foundation (FCT).

Mary N. Harris

Mary N. Harris was born in Cork, Ireland, in 1958. She studied at University College, Cork, and Cambridge University and now teaches the history of modern Ireland and colonial Spanish America at the National University of Ireland, Galway. Her current research interests are the political, cultural and religious history of modern Ireland, particularly Northern Ireland, and Irish links with Latin America. Recent publications include *The Catholic Church from Parnell to Partition* in B. Bradshaw - D. Keogh (eds.) *Christianity in Ireland: Revisiting the Story,* Dublin, 2002, pp. 205-219 and *Religious Divisions, Discrimination and the struggle for Dominance in Northern Ireland*, in *Racial Discrimination and Ethnicity in European History*, Pisa 2003, pp. 205-234. She is a contributor to the forthcoming *History of the Irish Book*, vol. V (Oxford University Press, 2007).

Matjaž Klemenčič

Matjaž Klemenčič was born in Ljubljana, Slovenia, in 1955 and studied at the University of Ljubljana, Slovenia. He is professor of history at the University of Maribor and teaches also at the University of Ljubljana and the University of Primorska/Università del Litorale in Koper/Capodistria. His research interests are the history of U.S. immigration, ethnic diversity and the dissolution of Yugoslavia, and Slovenes in neighbouring countries. Recent publications include (with Mitja Zagar), *The Former Yugoslavia's Diverse Peoples: A Reference Source Book* (Santa Barbara, Ca. 2004). His study of the Slovenes of Carinthia after World War II, co-authored with Vladimir Klemenčič , is to be published in 2006 as is his *The International Community and the FRY / Belligerents* in *The Scholar's Initiative: Confronting the Yugoslav Controversies* (Purdue University).

Danijel Grafenauer

Danijel Grafenauer was born in Maribor, Slovenia, in 1976, and is currently a doctoral student at the Department of History, University of Maribor, working on Dr. Julij Felaher LL.M. and Carinthian Slovene clubs in Slovenia in the 20th century, Felaher's contacts with politicians overseas and Slovene overseas communities. His broader research interests are the Carinthian Slovenes in the 19th and 20th centuries, and minority protection in Slovenia and EU. He has published a study of Angela Piskernik (1886-1967), the first Slovenian botanist and environmentalist, and a short biographical study of three Slovenian priests associated with the Academy of Slovenian seminarians in Klagenfurt/Celovec.

Csaba Lévai

Csaba Lévai was born in Debrecen in 1964. He was educated at the University of Debrecen and the Loránd Eötvös University of Budapest, and has been a Fulbright scholar at the University of Virginia. He teaches 18th- and 19th-century history at the University of Debrecen. His research interests are the history of the British colonies in North America, the history of the American Revolution, the political philosophy of the American founding fathers, especially Thomas Jefferson, and the comparative study of the Habsburg and the British Empires in the 18th century. His publications include an edition and translation of *Új rend egy új világban* [New Order in a New World], a collection of writings by the American Founding Fathers in Hungarian (Debrecen 1997); *Tolerance and Intolerance in History* (edited with Vasile Vese, Pisa 2003) and *The Republicanism Debate. A Historiographical Discussion of the Intellectual Background of the American Revolution* (Budapest 2003). He is now working on a book on the history of slavery in British North America.

Donal McCracken

Professor Donal McCracken was born and educated in Ireland. He is dean of the Faculty of Humanities, Development and Social Sciences and senior professor of History at the University of KwaZulu-Natal, South Africa. His research is in the fields of Ireland and South Africa, and in environmental history and his many publications include *Gardens of Empire:Botanical Institutions of the Victorian Empire* (London 1997), *MacBride's Brigade: Irish commandos in the Anglo-Boer war* (Dublin 1999), and *Forgotten Protest: Ireland and the Anglo-Boer war* (Belfast 2003).

Emilio Sáenz-Francés San Baldomero

Emilio Sáenz-Francés San Baldomero was born in Logroño-La Rioja, Spain, in 1979. He has studied history at Deusto University and journalism in the University of the Basque Country. He is currently a doctoral student at Deusto, but has spent a year during his doctoral studies at the University of Edinburgh. His interests include Spanish foreign policy and Soviet history, and his doctoral dissertation is on Spanish Foreign Policy during the Second World War. He has published *The Secret Memoirs of Ambassador von Moltke, a Preliminary Study* in *Letras de Deusto*, 2006

Guy Vanthemsche

Guy Vanthemsche was born in Ghent, Belgium, in 1958, and grew up near of Brussels. He studied at the Free University (Vrije Universiteit Brussel). He obtained his Ph.D. at this institution in 1987 with a study on the history of Belgian unemployment insurance. He has published several books on the history of the welfare state, the banking system, and commercial aviation in Belgium. His current research interest is the history of the Belgian colonial system and his *Belgique et Congo: empreintes d'un empire colonial (des années 1880 aux années 1980)* is to be published in 2006.

István Kornél Vida

István Kornél Vida was born in Debrecen in 1977. He is currently a doctoral student at the University of Debrecen where he teaches American culture and institutions, and the social influence of American sports. His interests include American military history from colonial times to the second world war, the American Civil War and the presidency and the mythical figure of Abraham Lincoln, as well as historical links and contacts between Hungary and the United States. His doctoral research investigates the first wave of Hungarian emigration to the United States in the 1850's and the Hungarian participation in the American Civil War. He has published articles on the relationship between the political and the military leaders of the Union, and various aspects of Hungarian emigration to the United States in the mid-19th century in general and the Hungarians' involvement in the American Civil War in particular.

Victor Zakharov

Victor Zakharov was born in 1951 and was educated at Moscow State (Lomonosov) University. He finished his university studies in 1979, and completed his doctoral dissertation in Russian History in 1983. He received his Habilitation in 2001. Since 1985 he has been teaching at Moscow Regional State University. He was appointed a full professor and head of the Department of Medieval and Modern Russian History in 2002.

Under the aegis of CLIOHRES.net

www.cliohres.net

Printed in May 2006
by Industrie Grafiche Pacini Editore S.p.A.
on behalf of Edizioni PLUS - Pisa University Press